WITHDRAWN

*Pierrots
on the Stage
of Desire*

Robert Storey

PIERROTS ON THE STAGE OF DESIRE

Nineteenth-Century French Literary Artists and the Comic Pantomime

Princeton University Press

Copyright © 1985 by Princeton University Press

Published by Princeton University Press, 41 William Street,
Princeton, New Jersey 08540
In the United Kingdom: Princeton University Press, Guildford, Surrey

All Rights Reserved

Library of Congress Cataloging in Publication Data will be
found on the last printed page of this book

ISBN 0-691-06628-0

Publication of this book has been aided by the
Andrew W. Mellon Foundation of Princeton University Press

This book has been composed in Linotron Galliard
Clothbound editions of Princeton University Press books
are printed on acid-free paper, and binding materials are
chosen for strength and durability

Printed in the United States of America by Princeton University Press
Princeton, New Jersey

Designed by Laury A. Egan

For my father and mother

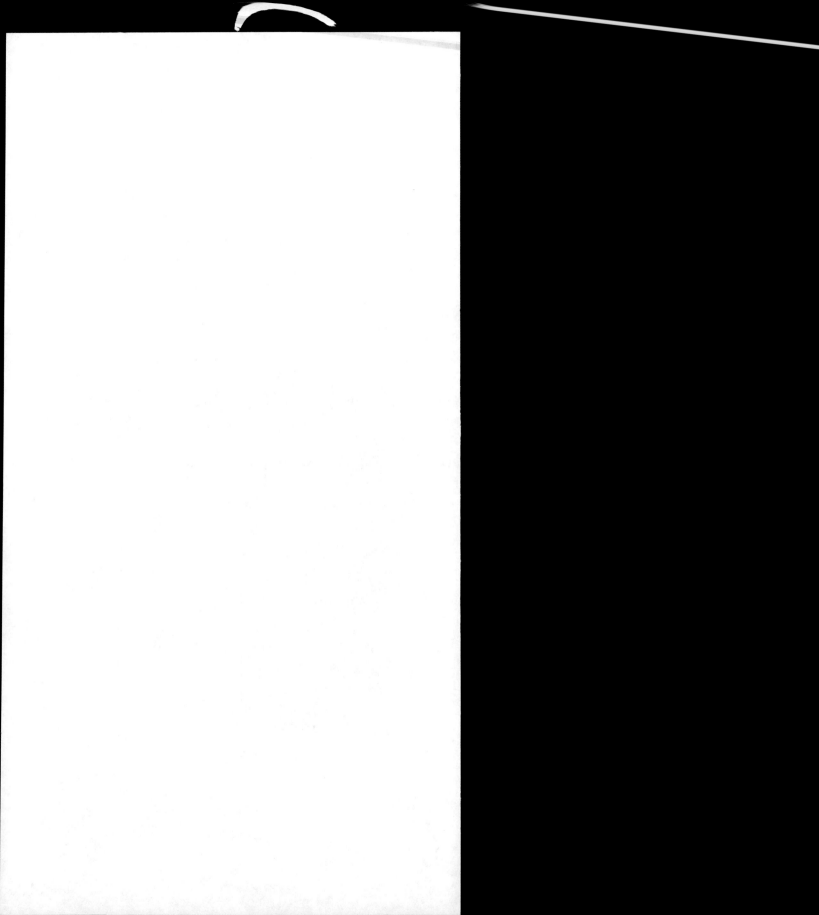

Contents

vii

Illustrations

Frontispiece: Jules Chéret: *La Pantomime*, panel reproduced in Ernest Maindron, *Les Affiches illustrées (1886-1895)* (Paris: Boudet, 1896).

1. Jean-Louis Barrault as J.-G. Deburau Paying Court to the Moon: still from Marcel Carné, *Les Enfants du Paradis* (1945). Museum of Modern Art/Film Stills Archive.

2. Charles Patémont: The Théâtre des Funambules in 1862: engraving in the Bibliothèque Nationale.

3. Auguste Bouquet: *Le Repas de Pierrot*: J.-G. Deburau as Pierrot-Gourmand: engraving in the Harvard Theatre Collection.

4. Eustache Lorsay: Four Caricatures of J.-G. Deburau in *Satan, ou le Pacte infernal*: from *Le Musée Philipon, album de tout le monde* (c. 1842).

5. Cham: Caricature of J.-G. Deburau in *Pierrot en Afrique*: from *Le Musée Philipon, album de tout le monde* (c. 1842).

6. Eustache Lorsay: Caricature of J.-G. Deburau in the Apotheosis of a *Féerie*: from *Le Musée Philipon, album de tout le monde* (c. 1842).

7. Hutchisson: Madame Saqui at Vauxhall (1820): engraving in the Bibliothèque Nationale.

8. F. Robineau and G. Levilly: *Galerie Paul Legrand* (1858): Legrand in His Most Memorable Roles at the Funambules and Folies-Nouvelles: engraving in the Billy Rose Theatre Collection of the New York Public Library at Lincoln Center, Astor, Lenox and Tilden Foundations.

9. Louis Morin: Polichinelle in an Encounter with Death: from Champfleury, *Les bons contes font les bons amis* (Paris: Truchy, n.d.).

10. Adrien Tournachon: Charles Deburau (*c.* 1858): photograph in the Bibliothèque Nationale.

11. Anon.: A Late *Féerie* at the Funambules: *affiche* in the Bibliothèque de l'Opéra. Photo: Bibliothèque Nationale.

12. Jules Chéret: Paul Legrand at the Tertulia (1871): poster reproduced in Ernest Maindron, *Les Affiches illustrées: Ouvrage orné de 20 chromolithographies par Jules Chéret* (Paris: Launette, 1886). Arts, Prints and Photographs Division, the New York Public Library, Astor, Lenox and Tilden Foundations.

13. Charles Baudelaire: La Fanfarlo: pencil-drawing in Jacques Crépet, ed., *Dessins de Baudelaire* (Paris: Gallimard, 1927).

14. Nadar: "So the Harlequinade Is Your Chosen Form . . ./Don't Stay Astraddle This Hobbyhorse, Gautier;/and Just To Give the Good Public a Momentary Laugh/Don't Make Poetry Cry This Way!": Caricature of Gautier as Pierrot, After the Production at the Vaudeville of *Pierrot posthume*: from *Le Charivari*, October 20, 1847. Photo: Bibliothèque Nationale.

15. Anon.: The Hanlon-Lees in the Scene with the Flask from *Le Voyage en Suisse* (1878): poster in the Billy Rose Theatre Collection of the New York Public Library at Lincoln Center, Astor, Lenox and Tilden Foundations.

16. Georges Rochegrosse: Pierrot Abandoned by the Fairy Urgèle: frontispiece to Théodore de Banville, *Le Baiser* (Paris: Charpentier, 1888).

17. Adolphe Willette: "Oh! Banville, Don't Abandon Your Pierrots, Your Pierrot 'Uncustomarily Pale' ": from *Le Pierrot*, March 20, 1891. Photo: Bibliothèque Nationale.

18. Anon.: The Hanlon-Lees in the Drunken Scene from *Le Voyage en Suisse* (1878): poster in the Billy Rose Theatre Collection of the New York Public Library at Lincoln Center, Astor, Lenox and Tilden Foundations.

19. Anon.: The Hanlon-Lees in *Superba* (1890): poster in the Billy Rose Theatre Collection of the New York Public Library at Lincoln Center, Astor, Lenox and Tilden Foundations.

20. Jules Chéret: *Pierrot sceptique*: title-page for J.-K. Huysmans and Léon Hennique, *Pierrot sceptique* (Paris: Rouveyre, 1881).

21. Adolphe Willette: *Deux Pages d'Amour* (I): Pantomime in Pictures: from *Le Chat Noir*, January 17, 1885.

22. Adolphe Willette: *Deux Pages d'Amour* (II): Pantomime in Pictures: from *Le Chat Noir*, January 17, 1885.

23. H. Lanos: *Pierrot assassin de sa femme*: from *L'Illustration*, March 26, 1887. Photo: Library of Congress.

24. Adolphe Willette: *Pierrot assassin de sa femme* (*c.* 1888): from Adolphe Brisson, *Nos Humoristes* (Paris: Société d'Edition Artistique, 1900).

25. Adolphe Willette: *Pierrot assassin de sa femme*: from *Le Pierrot*, December 7, 1888. Photo: Bibliothèque Nationale.

26. Atelier Nadar: Sarah Bernhardt in the *Pierrot assassin* of Jean Richepin (*c.* 1883): photograph in the Bibliothèque Nationale.

27. Anon.: Raoul de Najac as Pierrot: frontispiece to Raoul de Najac, *Souvenirs d'un mime* (Paris: Emile-Paul, 1909).

28. J.-M. Le Natur: A Rehearsal at the Cercle Funambulesque: from Félix Larcher and Paul Hugounet, *Les Soirées Funambulesques* (Paris: Kolb, [1890-93]).

29. Adolphe Willette: *L'Enfant prodigue* (1890): poster reproduced in Ernest Maindron, *Les Affiches illustrées (1886-1895)* (Paris: Boudet, 1896).

30. Jules Chéret: *Le Miroir* (1892): poster reproduced in Ernest Maindron, *Les Affiches illustrées (1886-1895)* (Paris: Boudet, 1896).

31. Happichy: Séverin in *Chand d'habits!* (1896): poster in the Billy Rose Theatre Collection of the New York Public Library at Lincoln Center, Astor, Lenox and Tilden Foundations.

Preface

"He had never wanted to set foot in the Théâtre-Français, or in the Opéra," wrote one Cécile L. of Charles Nodier, whom she seems to have known in his later years. "On the other hand, he didn't budge from the lobby of the Variétés, and he was the friend of all the Pierrots and of all the Jocrisses."[1] The same could be said, at least in a figurative sense, of a great number of the major poets and novelists of nineteenth-century France. Faced with the prospect, in 1846, of reviewing a revival of Voltaire's *Adélaïde du Guesclin, "cette lamentable tragédie en vers peu rimés,"* Gautier concluded that the task was beyond his strength, and so directed his steps "to the other side of the city, into a dirty little theatrical hole-in-the-wall made illustrious by a celebrated clown just recently deceased."[2] When, in his *Souvenirs,* Théodore de Banville described the theater of his ideal, it was precisely that *bouge* of Gautier's admiration, home of the celebrated Pierrot.[3] And even after the demise of both this clown and his stage, the artists of Paris habitually directed themselves to the little theaters of the Boulevard, to take their pleasures, like Nodier, among all the Pierrots and Jocrisses.

[1] In *L'Evénement,* January 9, 1849; cited in Jean Richer, *Autour de l'*Histoire du Roi de Bohême: *Charles Nodier "dériseur sensé," suivi de* La Plus Petite des pantoufles *de Charles Nodier* (Paris: Archives des Lettres Modernes, 1962), p. 20.

[2] Review of *La Gageure* at the Théâtre des Funambules: *La Presse,* August 31, 1846.

[3] Théodore de Banville, *L'Ame de Paris: Nouveaux Souvenirs* (Paris: Charpentier-Fasquelle, 1890), pp. 20-37. That Pierrot, Jean-Gaspard (known as "Baptiste") Deburau, is the subject of my first chapter.

xiii

Preface

Jean Starobinski has suggested some of the reasons for their delight in (and identification with) the ubiquitous *saltimbanque*: the worlds of the pantomime, the circus, the *fête foraine* were domains in which "vital spontaneity, illusion, simple feats of skill or clumsiness mingled their seductions for the spectator tired of the monotony of the tasks of serious life." Before spectacles that seemed destined "to be fixed in a pictorial or poetic transcription," the artist felt a "nostalgic connivance with the microcosm of the *parade* and of the elemental *féerie*." Starobinski's *Portrait de l'artiste en saltimbanque* is a remarkable analysis of this connivance, suggesting why the *saltimbanque* exercised an enchantment over so many painters and writers of the last century, and why its appeal survives. But it seems to me that his most provocative remarks go undeveloped. For the modern artist, he observes, in words that apply to Flaubert as well as to Rouault, the images of the circus, of the music-hall, of the popular stage, "will appear like the reflections of a lost world; they will live in a space of recollection; they will bear the mark of a passion for a return. These will be creatures of regressive desire [. . .]."[4] So, I shall argue, were the Pierrots of Nodier's affections. The popular theater stirred passions that were utterly alien to the Opéra, passions which the spectator himself was often unconscious of having. The pantomime, the melodrama, the circus *entrée* were all spectacles expressive of fantasy and wish, of a most potently infantile kind.

In the following pages, I shall try to show how one of these genres, the pantomime, elicited the regressive desire of those writers who most admired it—and how the pantomime itself was gradually destroyed by the ardor of their admiration. This book has a double theme. The framing chapters offer a history of the pantomime *funambulesque*, from its early nineteenth-century apogee, when it trafficked in wishful puerility, to its demise as a literary divertissement at the end of *la Belle Epoque*. The central series of essays suggests how the energy of which the pantomime was depleted served to animate the art of its admirers, to excite the elemental conflicts to which that art owes much

---

[4] Geneva: Editions d'Art Albert Skira, 1970, pp. 8, 9, 25.

of its dynamic life. The "stage" of my title, in other words, is more than *"l'espace"* of Marceau's epigraph: it is psychic as well as scenic. It takes its imagery from the *commedia dell'arte*, for both the ballet-pantomime and the pantomime *dramatique* lie outside my ken: among the writers, only Gautier, that poet of catholic curiosity, took any serious interest in either. I have restricted my study to the Parisian scene, since in Marseille, where the pantomime survived after mid-century while it all but died in the capital, the art of Rouffe and the young Séverin inspired no literary response. For the most part, my argument is directed to students of French fiction and poetry, although the historian of theater will find here, I think, much that is new about the pantomime. My research has tended to discredit, in fact, so much received opinion about the genre that I have spelled out many disagreements at length in my notes for the first two chapters.[5] At the same time, I have tried to assume no special knowledge on the reader's part about this all but irrecoverable entertainment—save a vague familiarity with the old Boulevard district, or an acquaintance with Carné's magical evocation of it in *Les Enfants du Paradis*. One omission may seem troubling: Jules Laforgue obviously has a

[5] Louisa E. Jones's *Sad Clowns and Pale Pierrots: Literature and the Popular Comic Arts in 19th-Century France* (Lexington, Ky.: French Forum, Publishers, 1984) appeared after this book had gone to press, and I regret that I cannot offer specific responses to her discussion in the chapters that follow. Jones's study, like this one, stands, as she remarks, "at the crossroads between history and legend" (p. 9): her account of Pierrot's "legend"—especially as elaborated by Champfleury, George Sand, and Gérard de Nerval—is stimulating indeed, but her historical perspective, unfortunately, has a short vanishing point. She has failed to consult much of the primary material on pantomime, most importantly the scenarios in manuscript, and relies for most of her reconstruction upon late-nineteenth-century accounts and script-compilations, using them sometimes with an expert eye, sometimes with too fond a weakness for their anecdotes (and errors), often with an indifference to such crucial matters as dating scenarios and so determining when (as well as by and before whom) they were first performed. Her discussion of *fin-de-siècle* pantomime, notably of the Cercle Funambulesque and of its associates like Najac, seems to me particularly unfortunate, marred by a tendency to see Decadent excesses everywhere and by a selectivity of illustration that simply misrepresents the facts. But for those readers concerned less with the pantomime than with the "literary legend" to which it gave rise, Jones's book corroborates, corrects, and complements my own in extremely interesting ways.

Preface

place among the writers enthralled by Pierrot. But since I devoted a full chapter to his *vers pierrotiques* in my earlier study of the figure, I have not thought it necessary to work over that same ground again.

As the language of these last two paragraphs implies, my perspective is psychoanalytic. I hope to justify its relevance to the study of the pantomime in the course of my opening chapter, but if it needs a general defense—hardly possible to make with any persuasiveness within the short space of a preface—I can offer no more eloquent an apology than that of Harold Bloom:

> [. . .] Freud has usurped the role of the mind of our age, so that more than forty years after his death we have no common vocabulary for discussing the works of the spirit except what he gave us. Philosophers, hard or soft, speak only to other philosophers; theologians mutter only to theologians; our literary culture speaks to us in the language of Freud, even when the writer, like Nabokov or Borges, is violently anti-Freudian. Karl Kraus, being Freud's contemporary, said that psychoanalysis itself was the disease of which it purported to be the cure. We come after, and we must say that psychoanalysis itself is the culture of which it purports to be the description. If psychoanalysis and our literary culture no longer can be distinguished, then criticism is Freudian whether it wants to be or not.[6]

It was the nineteenth century, of course, that bequeathed us the voice of our culture: and if Freud now speaks to our spirit, it is because that century loosened his tongue.

Freud's work itself I have found an ever-provocative inspiration, but my sources are not confined to the classical texts of the master and his disciples. I have also drawn upon the Chicago school of "self" psychology, particularly the work of Heinz Kohut; upon Sartrean existential psychoanalysis, which, as Lacan has remarked, owes more than a passing debt to Freud; upon the studies of recent French exegetes, such as those of Jean Laplanche; and upon the

[6] *The Breaking of the Vessels* (Chicago: University of Chicago Press, 1982), p. 63.

phenomenology of the Geneva School, of Starobinski,
Poulet, and Richard. Lacan has of course influenced my
thinking, though not in many ways he would have ap-
proved: with Laplanche I reject what the "Seminar on 'The
Purloined Letter' " seems to argue—the "absolute primacy
of the 'signifier.' "[7] Murray Schwartz has given succinct definition to my own position: "[. . .] even though psychoanalysis is predominantly a verbal psychology, its proper scope
cannot be reduced to questions of language. Given its origins
in the undifferentiated matrix of the mother-child interplay,
linguistic representation always keeps its relation to bodily
experience, especially to the basic sensations of infancy:
fullness, emptiness, release, manipulation and so on."[8] It
may be necessary, too, to stress what I perceive to be the
elusively *dynamic* properties of the psyche described by Freud.
Leo Bersani, in many ways an extremely perceptive critic,
merely caricatures that psyche when he refers to its obsessional themes as "the writer's preferred version of his own
intelligibility."[9] What Bersani calls "obsessive modes of
contact with the world"—the observation should be self-
evident—are never adopted by "preference," although de-
fensive manipulation of those modes may be. And yet such
manipulation, at least for the writers discussed in this book,
settles rarely into a "version" of "intelligibility": the con-
flicting impulses of the psyche ultimately subvert all stabi-
lizing self-conceptions. Bersani's language is that of a
Freudian who is embarrassed by the determinism of Freud;
like the early Sartre, he enunciates a radical freedom, a freedom in which desire may be severed from the objects of its
infantile past. In this he affects to follow Derrida, but I
think the latter has slipped his grasp. For Derrida the writer
seems to exist *dans le pli*, within the fold of paradox, bound
up in the freedom of his own textuality. But these are points
that we must pursue at a later stage of our discussion.

[7] Jean Laplanche, *Life and Death in Psychoanalysis*, tr. Jeffrey Mehlman
(Baltimore: The Johns Hopkins University Press, 1976), p. 147*n*.

[8] "Critic, Define Thyself," *Psychoanalysis and the Question of the Text:
Selected Papers from the English Institute, 1976-77*, ed. Geoffrey H. Hart-
man (Baltimore: The Johns Hopkins University Press, 1978), p. 3.

[9] *The Death of Stéphane Mallarmé* (Cambridge: Cambridge University
Press, 1982), p. 19.

Preface

I have tried to write in English—which means more than to say that I have translated the passages in French. Towards the end of *Beyond the Pleasure Principle*, Freud expresses regret at "being obliged to operate with the scientific terms, that is to say with the figurative language, peculiar to psychology (or, more precisely, to depth psychology)."[10] The fact that I am working with a figurative language has inspired me to *hardiesses*: I have tried to use that language with as much elasticity and suggestiveness as its "scientific" precision would permit. I have avoided the jargon of Freud's English translators, except where it seems unavoidable. And the merciless caveat of that apostate Frederick Crews has always been before my inner eye:

> A critic who wants to avail himself of psychoanalysis would be well advised not only to seek out the most defensible and unmechanistic concepts within the system but also to think unsparingly about what is provincial and intolerant in that system. If he understands that Freudian reasoning ascribes key significance to its favorite themes, and that its supple rules of interpretation make the discovery of those themes a foregone conclusion; if he sees that the method tends to dichotomize between manifest and latent content even when the border between them is undiscernible; if he knows that psychoanalysis can say nothing substantial about considerations that fall outside an economics of desire and defense; and if he admits that it has a natural penchant for debunking—for sniffing out erotic and aggressive fantasies in the "purest" works and for mocking all pretensions to freedom from conflict—the critic may be able to borrow the clinical outlook without losing his intellectual independence and sense of proportion.[11]

My own success in having done so is for the reader to judge.

[10] *The Standard Edition of the Complete Psychological Works of Sigmund Freud*, gen. ed. James Strachey, XVIII (London: Hogarth Press and the Institute of Psycho-Analysis, 1955), 60. This edition will be cited throughout as *SE*, with appropriate volume and page numbers.

[11] "Reductionism and Its Discontents," *Critical Inquiry*, I (March 1975), 556-57.

Preface

My debts. They run wide and deep. Generous fellow-
ships from the John Simon Guggenheim Memorial Foundation for 1980-1981 and from Temple University for the
summer of 1980 enabled me to carry out my research in
France; a grant from the American Council of Learned So-
cieties (under a program funded by the National Endow-
ment for the Humanities) and a Study Leave from Temple
University in 1982-1983 freed me from teaching respon-
sibilities to write the book; a recent Grant-in-Aid from
Temple University has empowered me to illustrate it. I am
extraordinarily fortunate in having been blessed with such
benefactors, and my gratitude is, accordingly, immense. I
only regret that I cannot name the anonymous agents of
that benefaction along with the colleagues I wish to thank
here: Geoffrey Harpham, who followed Pierrot's pantomimic exploits with an intelligence enviably livelier than
they; Naomi Ritter and Anya Peterson Royce, *savantes* of
the pantomime and popular theater whose encouragement
and good sense never flagged; Robert Martin Adams, David
Allen, Joel Conarroe, Peter Conn, David DeLaura, Wallace
Fowlie, Bettina Knapp, and A. H. Scouten, who labored
selflessly on behalf of my vision; Gerald Weales, who, happily, was amused by it; and Alan Wilde, Sheldon Brivic,
and the other auditors of the Journal Club, who listened,
and seemed to approve.

My research would not have been possible without the
kind assistance of the staffs of several libraries and reposi-
tories—of the Archives Nationales, the Bibliothèque Nationale, and the Bibliothèque de l'Arsenal in Paris; and of the
New York Public Libraries, the Boston Public Library, the
Pusey Library of Harvard University, the Firestone Library
of Princeton University, the Conwell Library of Temple
University, and the Library of Congress in the United States.
For their tirelessness I am extremely grateful. Three persons, finally, merit a special word here: Madame Alla
Troubetzkoy, whose wit, great charm, and graciousness
sustained my spirit during a gray Parisian autumn; Monsieur Jacques Suffel, eminent *flaubertiste*, who admitted me
to the treasures of the Bibliothèque Spoelberch de Lovenjoul with a cordiality I shall always remember; and my wife,

Preface

Chom, who unerringly asked the right question whenever my progress faltered: "When is it going to be finished?"

Versions of Chapters I, V, and VIII of this book have appeared in *Theatre Survey, French Forum,* and *Nineteenth-Century French Studies.* I wish to express my appreciation to their editors for allowing them to be reprinted. The sources of my illustrations are credited in the List of Illustrations: for permission to reproduce I extend my gratitude here. The artists of the tailpieces are Jules Chéret (Chapter VIII), William Faulkner (VII and X), Tony Johannot (II), Eustache Lorsay (I), Odilon Redon (XI), and Adolphe Willette (III, IV, V, and VI). Permission to reproduce the two line drawings from Faulkner's *The Marionettes,* ed. Noel Polk (Charlottesville: University Press of Virginia, 1977), has been generously granted by the Trustees of the University Press of Virginia.

Abbreviations

General:

AN   Archives Nationales de France, Paris.

sc.   scene, Fr. *tableau.*

SE   Freud, Sigmund. *The Standard Edition of the Complete Psychological Works of Sigmund Freud,* gen. ed. James Strachey. 24 vols. London: Hogarth Press and the Institute of Psycho-Analysis, 1953-1974.

Chapter II:

MU   *Le Moniteur Universel.*

P   *La Presse.*

Chapter III:

C   Nodier, Charles. *Contes, avec des textes et des documents inédits,* ed. Pierre-Georges Castex. Paris: Garnier Frères, 1961.

CI   ———. *Correspondance inédite de Charles Nodier, 1796-1844,* ed. A. Estignard. Geneva: Slatkine Reprints, 1973.

F   Baudelaire, Charles. *La Fanfarlo,* ed. Claude Pichois. Monaco: Editions du Rocher, 1957.

H   Nodier, Charles. *Histoire du Roi de Bohême et de ses sept châteaux.* Paris: Editions d'Aujourd'hui, 1977.

JI   Baudelaire, Charles. *Journaux intimes: Fusées, Mon Coeur mis à nu, Carnet,* ed. Jacques Crépet and Georges Blin. Paris: Corti, 1949.

N   Nodier, Charles. *Nouvelles, suivies des fantaisies du dériseur sensé.* Nouv. éd. Paris: Charpentier, 1911.

Abbreviations

OC:B   Baudelaire, Charles. *Oeuvres complètes*, ed. Claude Pichois. 2 vols. Paris: Gallimard (Bibliothèque de la Pléiade), 1975-1976.

OC:N   Nodier, Charles. *Oeuvres complètes*. 12 vols. Brussels: Meline, Cans et Compagnie, 1832-1840.

Chapter IV:

MU   *Le Moniteur Universel.*

OC   Gautier, Théophile. *Oeuvres complètes*. 33 vols. Paris: Charpentier, 1877-1894.

P   *La Presse.*

PC   Gautier, Théophile. *Poésies complètes de Théophile Gautier*, ed. René Jasinski. Nouv. éd. 3 vols. Paris: Nizet, 1970.

Chapter V:

AP   Banville, Théodore de. *L'Ame de Paris: Nouveaux Souvenirs*. Paris: Charpentier, 1890.

B   ————. *Le Baiser*. Paris: Charpentier-Fasquelle, 1901.

C   ————. *Comédies*. Paris: Charpentier, 1902.

CF   ————. *Contes féeriques*. Paris: Charpentier, 1882.

DF   ————. *Dans la Fournaise*. Paris: Charpentier, 1892.

LC   ————. *Lettres chimériques*. Paris: Charpentier, 1885.

LM   ————. *La Lanterne magique*. Paris: Charpentier, 1883.

MR   ————. *Marcelle Rabe*. Paris: Charpentier, 1891.

S   ————. *Mes Souvenirs*. Paris: Charpentier, 1883.

SC   ————. *Sonnailles et Clochettes*. Paris: Charpentier, 1890.

I, II, III   ————. *Poésies complètes*. 3 vols. Paris: Charpentier, 1883-1888.

Chapter VI:

B&P   Flaubert, Gustave. *Bouvard et Pécuchet*, ed. Alberto Cento. Naples: Istituto Universitario Orientale, and Paris: Nizet, 1964.

C:C ——. *Correspondance*. Vols. XII-XVI (separately numbered I-V) of the *Oeuvres complètes* (see below).

C:P ——. *Correspondance*, ed. Jean Bruneau. 2 vols. Paris: Gallimard (Bibliothèque de la Pléiade), 1973-1980.

J Goncourt, Edmond and Jules de. *Journal: Mémoires de la vie littéraire*, ed. Robert Ricatte. 4 vols. Paris: Fasquelle-Flammarion, 1959.

OC Flaubert, Gustave. *Oeuvres complètes*. 16 vols. Paris: Club de l'Honnête Homme, *c.* 1971-1975.

Chapter VII:

FZ Goncourt, Edmond de. *Les Frères Zemganno*. Ed. déf. Paris: Flammarion-Fasquelle, [1924].

J —— and Jules de. *Journal: Mémoires de la vie littéraire*, ed. Robert Ricatte. 4 vols. Paris: Fasquelle-Flammarion, 1959.

MS ——. *Manette Salomon*. Ed. déf. Paris: Flammarion-Fasquelle, [1925].

Chapter VIII:

OC Huysmans, J.-K. *Oeuvres complètes de J.-K. Huysmans*. 18 vols. Paris: Crès et Cie, 1928-1934.

Chapter IX:

OEP Verlaine, Paul. *Oeuvres en prose complètes*, ed. Jacques Borel. Paris: Gallimard (Bibliothèque de la Pléiade), 1972.

OPC ——. *Oeuvres poétiques complètes*, ed. Y.-G. Le Dantec, rev., completed, and presented by Jacques Borel. Paris: Gallimard (Bibliothèque de la Pléiade), [1977].

Chapter X:

C Mallarmé, Stéphane. *Correspondance, 1862-1871*, ed. Henri Mondor and Jean-Pierre Richard. Paris: Gallimard, 1959.

D Derrida, Jacques. *Dissemination*, tr. Barbara Johnson. Chicago: University of Chicago Press, 1981.

Abbreviations

L   Schérer, Jacques, ed. *Le "Livre" de Mallarmé: Pre-mières Recherches sur des documents inédits.* Paris: Gallimard, 1957.

OC   Mallarmé, Stéphane. *Oeuvres complètes de Stéphane Mallarmé,* ed. Henri Mondor and G. Jean-Aubry. Paris: Gallimard (Bibliothèque de la Pléiade), 1945.

*Pierrots
on the Stage
of Desire*

La pantomime classique, romantique, féerique, acroba-
tique, avec ses feux de Bengale, place l'homme au centre
de l'action, le lie par l'Amour, mais aussi par le geste, au
coeur de l'espace [. . .].
MARCEL MARCEAU, "Préface" to Marian Hannah Winter,
Le Théâtre du Merveilleux (1962)

Mais le génie n'est que l'enfance retrouvée à volonté,
l'enfance douée maintenant, pour s'exprimer, d'organes virils
et de l'esprit analytique qui lui permet d'ordonner la somme
de matériaux involontairement amassée.
CHARLES BAUDELAIRE, "Le Peintre de la vie moderne"
(1863)

I

Deburau

Et chose curieuse, un beau jour ces poètes, ces littérateurs, ces peintres, ont tenu, en chair et en os, ce Pierrot de la légende entre leurs mains; ils l'ont touché, ont pu lui parler, l'ont vu placer son grime; belle occasion cependant qui s'offrait aux Janin, Théophile Gautier, Champfleury et tant d'autres, de descendre un peu de l'éther et de lui demander à brûle-pourpoint: Mais qui es-tu donc et d'où viens-tu?

CHARLES HACKS, *Le Geste* (1892)

" 'Now, I don't want to take anything away from the French resistance,' " protests a character in a recent novel.

> "[. . .] Its brave raids and acts of sabotage undermined the Germans and helped bring about their downfall. But in many ways Marcel Carné's movie, his *Children of Paradise*, was more important than the armed resistance. The resisters might have saved the skin of Paris, Carné kept alive its soul."[1]

It is a fatuous remark, the kind we expect from the determinedly fatuous hero, but its praise of Carné suggests with embarrassing accuracy the seductiveness of *Les Enfants du Paradis*. A Paris of romantically roiling passions, of pure Pierrots and gay Robert Macaires, of the Boulevard du Crime, whose little theaters stand as metaphors for the brash vitality of *le peuple*—it is a spectacle that few of us can resist. All our dreams of the City of Light (save those of shabby accordionists strolling beneath balloon-bedecked

[1] Tom Robbins, *Still Life with Woodpecker* (New York: Bantam Books, Inc., 1980), p. 259.

Eiffel Towers) are contained in its opening shot, alive with the turbulent crowds of the old quartier du Temple.

And if its spirit is seductive, its portrait of Baptiste, the Pierrot (and hero) of the film, is—for all but a handful of theater historians—definitive. In resurrecting the great mime "Baptiste" Deburau, Carné's script-writer, Prévert, had only to turn to history to recover a figure indistinguishable from legend. For, despite the softening of outline effected by Sacha Guitry's earlier *Deburau* (1918) and especially by the vicissitudes of Pierrot himself after the mime's death in the mid-nineteenth century, the figure that Deburau presented in 1943 was essentially the creation of his first apologist, Jules Janin: a Pierrot of the People, "by turns gay, sad, sickly, robust, cudgeling, cudgeled—a musician, a poet, a simpleton, always poor, like the common people."[2] It was in vain that the mime raised protests with George Sand ("[. . .] the Deburau of M. Janin is not me. He has not understood me").[3] The Deburau that survived, and whom Jean-Louis Barrault elegantly incarnates in Carné's film, is a symbol, however emasculated, of the mythical spirit of *le peuple*. And it is as such a symbol that many historians, including his most recent biographer, regard Jean-Gaspard Deburau today.[4]

It is not hard to understand how the myth was created or how it quickly gained currency. To lunge, with the Romantics, at the moribund figure of the Comédie-Française, Janin, then a budding prince of critics, needed a ready and

[2] Jules Janin, *Deburau, histoire du Théâtre à Quatre Sous pour faire suite à l'histoire du Théâtre-Français* (1832; rpt. in 1 vol., Paris: Librairie des Bibliophiles, 1881), p. 75.

[3] In George Sand, *Histoire de ma vie*, in *Oeuvres autobiographiques*, ed. Georges Lubin (Paris: Gallimard [Bibliothèque de la Pléiade], 1971), II, 136.

[4] "[. . .] Deburau's Pierrot embodied the common people, with all their virtues and vices": Jaroslav Švehla, "Jean Gaspard Deburau: The Immortal Pierrot," tr. Paul Wilson, *Mime Journal*, No. 5 (1977), 24. (This long article is a translated condensation of Švehla's book-length study *Deburau, nesmrtelny Pierot* [Prague: Melantrich, 1976].) Of course the writers who have embraced the myth most ardently are those who, like Carné, have tried to turn the legend of the mime's life to the purposes of art: see especially the novel by František Kožík, *Největsí z Pierotu* (1939; tr. Dora Round, *The Great Debureau* [New York and Toronto: Farrar & Rinehart, Inc., 1940]).

sharp-edged foil. He found one on the Boulevard, in the popular Théâtre des Funambules.

> The Theater, such as we understood it in the seventeenth century, is dead among us. [. . .]
> There is no longer any Théâtre-Français; there is only the Funambules; there is no longer any literary, learned, brilliant pit of spectators, the Pit of the Café Procope; instead, there is the Pit of the Funambules, animated, energetic, a pit in shirtsleeves, fond of crude wine and barley-sugar. [. . .]
> [. . .] Since comedy is in its Decadence, let us write the History of the Art such as it is, squalid, filthy, beggarly, drunken, exciting a squalid, filthy, beggarly, and drunken Pit; since Deburau has become the King of this world, let us celebrate Deburau the King of this world.[5]

His "single goal," as he explains in the "Préface" to his *Deburau* (1832), is to "summarize the History of the Dramatic Art considered under its ignoble aspect, the only new aspect under which it can still be regarded."[6] But from there it is an easy step to eulogizing Deburau, not as King, but as presiding genius of the place. If Molière's misanthrope was the conscience of *le Parterre savant*, Deburau's creations are the conscience of *le peuple*: "he is the people's actor, the people's friend, a windbag, a glutton, a loafer, a rascal, a poker-face, a revolutionary, like the people."[7] And to give him sufficient popular presence, Janin surrounds the events of his life with the fabulous air of folk tale. The clumsiest of three sons, all of a poor Bohemian father, Jean-Gaspard is ridiculed and reviled when, as itinerant *saltimbanques*, they take to the dusty roads ("for his brothers, the admiration of the crowd by day, and by night the bit of bacon, the steaming cabbage [. . .]; for him, the contemptuous smile, the dry bread, the melted snow [. . .]").[8] He is turned into a humble Paillasse, "not a sober and poised Paillasse, as we see him today, but a laughing, flushed, gamboling, leaping Paillasse—a vulgar Paillasse, a clown of

[5] Janin, *Deburau*, pp. 5-9.
[6] Ibid., p. 5.
[7] Ibid., p. 69.
[8] Ibid., pp. 22-23.

the public square."[9] But the hero's face soon glimmers through the greasepaint. In Constantinople, playing a (probably apocryphal) scene before an invisibly curtained harem, Jean-Gaspard mounts, all a-tremble, the wavering Perilous Ladder; at the top, he spies, over the gauzy curtain, a circle of semi-nude odalisques. "This was precisely the first happy event," writes Janin, "that made Deburau believe that he was perhaps a man of the same nature as his brothers and sisters."[10]

An awakening to identity that is privileged in its point of vantage yet universal in its sexual power—that is, moreover, triumphant yet precarious, heroic yet grotesque—its appeal to the Romantic readers of the mercurial rebel of the *Débats* could have been nothing but irresistible. For Théophile Gautier and Théodore de Banville, George Sand and Charles Baudelaire, Deburau the *saltimbanque* entered a Romantic mythology in which clown, artist, and common man found common cause. Paillasse, proletariat, poet: they were facile but inevitable identifications, identifications that account for the casual interest of most literary historians in the Théâtre des Funambules. But to rest on the surface of the myth is to do a disservice both to Deburau's fascinating art, unique in the history of the theater, and to the artists who took delight in it. To see that art clearly we must discard the myth. And we should do so with little regret: as always, the facts are more interesting.

The first is that the Boulevard had lost all of its romantic turbulence at the time of Deburau's emergence from obscurity. "The legend of the perpetual fair that reign[ed] on the Boulevard du Temple," writes Tristan Rémy, the mime's chief biographer, "with its shouts of joy, its careless ambiance, the blissful crowd before the acrobats' carpet, the merrymaking of festivals and carnival-time, the masterfully painted descriptions, the brilliantly colored frescoes—all of this exist[ed] only in the imagination of historians at the end of the nineteenth century who talk[ed] about the beginning of that century as today one recalls 1900 and *la Belle Epoque*."[11] By 1830, when Deburau had at last caught

[9] Ibid., p. 23.
[10] Ibid., pp. 32-33.
[11] *Jean-Gaspard Deburau* (Paris: L'Arche, 1954), p. 68.

the eye of the Romantics and when the Boulevard had reached what Georges Cain calls its "apogee,"[12] the *parades* and spectacles of an earlier epoch had completely disappeared. The *boulevardier* Nicolas Brazier, whose *Chroniques des petits théâtres de Paris* (1837) most imaginatively preserves the flavor of that epoch, recalls that he was "a child . . . a quite young child"[13] when the Boulevard was most alive; now at fifty-four, only a year from his death, he describes it regretfully as "a boulevard like any other."

> [. . .] And soon [he adds] it will no longer be anything but a Parisian street. Although it boasts six theaters, it is sad and deserted; only towards seven o'clock in the evening does one begin to hear a little noise, to see a little movement [. . .].[14]

The theaters, including the Funambules, survived the general debility only by attracting a diverse clientele. There can be little doubt that Deburau's earliest—and most loyal— public was that idealized by Gautier, Banville, and Janin: the *enfants du Paradis*, the laborers, loafers, and *titis* who seemed to give to the house an air "artistically *canaille*."[15] The first journalist to call attention to the theater (probably Charles Nodier) made note of its unbuttoned insouciance, its unsavory smells, adding that such "little annoyances are driving you away from a theater that you would be delighted to come back to, if you once had the courage to cross its threshold, and if you could forget that it is not yet *fashionable*."[16] In the early 1830s, largely owing to Janin's audacious *Deburau*, the theater indeed came into fashion, enjoying a vogue that, although momentary, brought a kind of respectability in its wake. The subsequent slow shift in its repertoire, in favor of vaudevilles and *pièces dialoguées*,

---

[12] *Anciens Théâtres de Paris: Le Boulevard du Temple, les théâtres du Boulevard* (Paris: Charpentier-Fasquelle, 1906), p. 41.

[13] *Chroniques des petits théâtres de Paris*, ed. Georges d'Heylli (1837; Paris: Rouveyre et Blond, 1883), I, 306.

[14] Ibid., I, 317.

[15] Hippolyte Hostein, "Causeries d'un ancien directeur": undated article appearing in unidentified newspaper on occasion of publication of Champfleury's novel *La Petite Rose* (1877): in Ro 11521 ("Rec. fac. d'art. de presse, textes de pièces, arguments, progr., doc. icon. concernant le théâtre des Funambules"), f. 5, Bibliothèque de l'Arsenal, Paris.

[16] "Deburau," *La Pandore*, No. 1884 (July 19, 1828), 2.

reflects the managers' attempts in the 'thirties and 'forties to please a "better" public, sometimes in defiance of their licensed privileges. The novelist Champfleury, inventing a performance at the theater in 1843, peoples the orchestra with "the honest bourgeois of the quarter, the merchants of the Temple, families accompanied by their children"; his public includes, moreover, "wealthy 'socialites' from among the bourgeoisie" as well as "elegant spectators who came seeking in this little theater a kind of entertainment akin to that of the *Descente de la Courtille*."[17] Happily less gifted with imagination than either Banville or Gautier, he remembers what the latter often forgot: that Deburau played to the *loges* as well as to the *parterre*.

Unusually intimate with the theater—he saw almost all of his own pantomimes produced there[18]—Champfleury may be trusted for the details of its interior and for those of a typical *soirée*. The stage was deep, accommodating "the celebrated and invariable décor of the apotheosis," the climactic scene of the *pantomime-féerie*, painted in fresco on the back wall.[19] During a pantomimic performance, the stagehands worked behind the scenery of the various *tableaux*, "which succeeded one another like the slides of a magic lantern."[20] The wings were small; there was no space for a greenroom. Banville adds that the stage was equipped with three traps, with "neither more nor less than that of the

[17] *La Petite Rose* (Paris: Dentu, 1877), pp. 5-6, 60, 59. The *Descente de la Courtille* was a popular parade of maskers through the quartier du Temple in the nineteenth century which began at dawn on Ash Wednesday at the cabarets of Belleville.

[18] *Pierrot, valet de la Mort* (1846), *Pierrot pendu* (1847), *Pierrot marquis* (1847), *Madame Polichinelle, ou les Souffrances d'une âme en peine* (1848), *La Reine des Carottes* (1848: in collaboration with Albert Monnier), *Les Trois Filles à Cassandre* (1849), and *La Cruche cassée* (1849) were all produced at the Funambules after Deburau's death. *Les Deux Pierrots* (1851) was produced at the Galeries des Associations des Peintres et des Musiciens, *Pierrot millionnaire* (1857: a slightly revised version of *Pierrot marquis*) at the Folies-Nouvelles, and *La Pantomime de l'avocat* (1865) at the Fantaisies-Parisiennes. Champfleury's *pièces funambulesques* published in *Les bons contes font les bons amis* (Paris: Truchy, n.d.) were apparently never produced, at least in their original forms: at the end of the century a version of *Polichinelle et la Mort*, revised by Eudel and Mangin, was produced at the Cercle Funambulesque.

[19] Champfleury, *La Petite Rose*, p. 270.
[20] Ibid., p. 271.

Opéra, an arrangement that permitted the changes of scene, the transformations, the perpetual variety of a vision ceaselessly metamorphosed for the pleasure of the eyes and to the heart's content."[21] The spectacle that gave flesh to this vision was the main attraction of an evening's entertainment, usually the final item on the program. Preceding it— in the days of the theater's prosperity—might have been a *comédie régence*, followed by a vaudeville, both received with impatience by the Paradise. The fall of the curtain was the signal for silence among the seven hundred and seventy-six spectators: there reigned then in the house "a peculiar silence, comparable to the contemplation of Breton peasants attending the performance of a mystery-play."

The awaiting of this solemnity provoked the final noisy questions among the spectators, while the program-seller announced, for the modest price of one sou, the explanatory sheet containing the details [of the pantomime]. The vendor of oranges and apple-sugar strode up and down the aisles between the benches for one last time, profiting from the fact that the public had not yet settled down by offering his refreshments. The biography of "Monsieur Deburau" was hawked in every corner of the house for the devotees who wished to add the portrait and the life of the mime to the booklet of the play in vogue.[22]

When the curtain rose, it was upon one of a great number of pantomimes in an extremely varied repertoire.[23] In

---

[21] Théodore de Banville, *Mes Souvenirs* (Paris: Charpentier, 1883), p. 216.

[22] Champfleury, *La Petite Rose*, pp. 56-57.

[23] Much of that repertoire may be reconstructed from two sets of reliable sources. The first, which includes fifty-two pantomimes in manuscript first produced at the Funambules from 1835 to 1846, comprises documents F[18] 1083-1089 ("Censure dramatique: Manuscrits de pièces [. . .] représentées à Paris et dans la banlieue: Théâtre des Funambules, 1835-1846") in the Archives Nationales de France (hereafter: AN), Paris. The second, including pantomimes from the early years of Deburau's career (1819-1834), consists of eight texts in various forms: four as manuscripts submitted to the censor for later revivals (*Le Songe d'or, ou Arlequin et l'avare* [1828], *Pierrot mitron* [1831], *Le Page de la Marquise* [1832], *Les Epreuves* [1833]), one as a scenario (less its prologue) included in Janin's *Deburau* (*Ma Mère l'Oie* [1830]), one as a published pamphlet (*Le Boeuf enragé* [1827]), and two as full texts reproduced in Louis Péricaud's *Le*

several pieces of that repertoire, Deburau seems to have had no role at all—in *Un Secret* (1838), for example, a "pantomime with dialogue in three scenes, intermingled with song and dance," or in *M. de Boissec et Mlle de Boisflotté* (1841), in which the mime Paul Legrand performed, or in *Les Deux Pendus, ou Lequel des deux, pantomime en un acte* (1845). But by far the larger class of pantomimes was that in which Baptiste appeared—often as a comic character-type sharing vague points of resemblance with his various Pierrots. He was probably the student-sailor Blanchotin in *Jack l'orang-outang* (1836), for example, and the farmhand Cruchon in *Le Tonnelier et le somnambule* (late 1838 or early 1839), and the goatherd Mazarillo in *Fra-Diavolo, ou les Brigands de la Calabre* (1844). He was certainly the Jocrisse-like *comique* of *Hurluberlu* (1842) and the engagingly naïve recruit Pichonnot of *Les Jolis Soldats* (1843). When, after Deburau's death, Gautier expressed his surprise and disappointment at seeing his successor dressed "half as a comic-opera Colin, half as a Tyrolean hunter," he was betraying ignorance of much of Baptiste's own repertoire.[24]

Gautier was expressing a viewpoint that too many chroniclers of the Funambules have favored: that its pantomime is reducible to a single formula and Deburau to a single role.[25] The haphazard acceptance of scripts at the theater

---

Théâtre des Funambules (Paris: Sapin, 1897): *Poulailler, ou Prenez garde à vous!* (1827) and *Pérette, ou les Deux Braconniers* (1829). Péricaud also publishes the texts of *Le Boeuf enragé, Le Songe d'or,* and *Pierrot en Afrique* (1842). Unfortunately, however, his dates of first production, at least for the post-1834 pantomimes, cannot be trusted: except in a few instances, they are identical with those on which the manuscripts were registered at the Ministère de l'Intérieur for the censor's authorization, a process that took at least several days, sometimes weeks.

[24] Review of *La Gageure* (with Paul Legrand as Pierrot) at the Funambules: *La Presse*, August 31, 1846. In an undated letter to Gautier, obviously written in response to this review, the director-proprietor of the theater, Charles-Louis Billion, objected that "you have been under the impression that Debureau [sic] had never abandoned Pierrot's traditional costume save on two occasions. That is an error, for we have some thirty-odd plays performed by Debureau in different costumes, and Paul has simply continued the practice [. . .]" (MS C491, f. 529, Bibliothèque Spoelberch de Lovenjoul, Chantilly).

[25] Švehla is one of the few critics to credit Deburau with having created a number of different characters, but that is because he—misguidedly, I think—sees in the mime a frustrated dramatic actor who "was limited by the naive scenarios, which often did little more than group together and

as well as the variety of sources that inspired their *anonymes* ensured that its productions were always rather generously diverse. Adaptations of older pieces, imitations of newer ones, burlesques of other offerings on the Boulevard du Temple—all found an audience at the Funambules. *Jack*

---

repeat traditional, threadbare, primitive and in many cases absurd situations and mimic gags (*cascades*), insulting to even a slightly refined taste," and who, in turn, "longed to represent a better character" than Pierrot ("Immortal Pierrot," pp. 22-23, 32). Péricaud simply equates all of Deburau's type-characters with Pierrot—e.g., "Blanchotin [. . .] is the Pierrot of this pantomime" or "Here Pierrot is called Cruchon" (*Théâtre des Funambules*, pp. 168, 201). He also frequently implies that the pantomimes are all alike: "The more the titles change, the more it's the same thing" (ibid., p. 227). Similarly, in her study "Jean-Gaspard Deburau and the Pantomime at the Théâtre des Funambules" (*ETJ*, XXVII [October 1975]), Adriane Despot claims that the apparent variety among Deburau's pantomimes "is misleading, for [. . .] most of the pantomimes are essentially the same; they share the atmosphere of light, small-scale, nonsensical adventures enlivened with comic dances, ridiculous battles, and confrontations placed in a domestic or otherwise commonplace setting" (p. 366). Despot was familiar, however, only with the scenarios in Péricaud and in the collection published by Emile Goby: *Pantomimes de Gaspard et Ch. Deburau* (Paris: Dentu, 1889). The Goby collection, put together from what Deburau's son, Charles, had been able to recall of the pantomimes and reproducing (as Champfleury observes in his "Préface") only "a repertoire easy to perform in the course of many peregrinations through the provinces" (p. xi), is doubly unreliable: it omits the spectacular *pantomime-féerie*, the most numerous and most admired of Deburau's productions, and it represents the pantomime of Baptiste much less accurately than that of Charles himself. Comparison of the censor's copy of *Pierrot mitron* with the Goby version, for example, reveals significant differences in both the conduct of the plot and the character of Pierrot; Goby's scenario for *Le Billet de mille francs* (1826) does not agree either with Auguste Bouquet's portrait of Deburau in that pantomime or with a remark by Gautier about a detail of its plot (in a review of Champfleury's *Pantomime de l'avocat* at the Fantaisies-Parisiennes: *Le Moniteur Universel*, December 4, 1865). Even Rémy, who has apparently consulted the censor's manuscripts of the pantomimes, is led by his conviction of their uniformity to make erroneous remarks about both them and the mime himself. Noting that Pierrot usually triumphs in the *pantomimes-pierrotades* of the late 'thirties, he asserts, against clear evidence to the contrary, that he does so in the *arlequinades* as well: "The apotheosis, whether there is an Arlequin or not in the piece, is reserved now to Jean-Gaspard." He is then forced to conclude that when Pierrot does not triumph, the role has been relegated to the understudy, Legrand: "Arlequin Triumphant is not a fitting dénouement for a *chef d'emploi*" (*Jean-Gaspard Deburau*, 166, 184). As my subsequent discussion will suggest, Rémy is confusing the exigencies of professional vanity with the stable conventions of genre.

l'orang-outang, for example, frankly advertised its source in
its title. As a *singerie dramatique* on the model of *Jocko, ou
le Singe du Brésil* (1825), first produced with immense success at the Porte-Saint-Martin, it doubtless solicited the favor of the public by a shameless admission of resemblance.
Roberta, chef de brigands, a pantomime of 1838, was in fact
a burlesque of an adaptation of a translation. Here a travesty of Lamartelière's high-minded hero[26] appeared with a
change of sex, having been born of the banditti in Schiller's
Räuber. But the variety suggested by such pillaging should
not drive us, like Rémy, to declare that Deburau himself
"was a personality, a character identical to himself."[27] For
Deburau created both discrete type-characters and consistently distinct roles. Although the roles were all called Pierrot, the sobriquet was not simply (as Rémy would have it)
"a skeleton-key name, a convenient appellation, a character
devoid of its original substance."[28] He by no means presented the same face in every pantomime, but neither was
he a mere Proteus *enfariné*. Within the rich welter of the
scripts that survive, we can easily identify four pantomimic
subgenres, and, in those, four types of Pierrot.

We should note before doing so that Pierrot was, of
course, older than Baptiste. But the role that the mime in-
herited from his predecessors at the theater showed only
the rudiments of his own mature creations.[29] As much a
simple Gilles as a Pierrot—indeed, the early scripts employ
the two types interchangeably[30]—the character was for-

[26] Of *Robert, chef de brigands* (1792). A translation of its distant source,
Die Räuber, by Friedel and Bonneville (under the inexact title of *Les Voleurs*) had appeared in 1785.
[27] *Jean-Gaspard Deburau*, pp. 211-12.
[28] Ibid., pp. 131-32.
[29] His innovations are suggested by his changes in the costume. For the
close-fitting woolen suit of tradition he substituted an ample cotton blouse
and trousers, their sleeves and legs very wide; he removed the frilled col-
larette and covered the white skullcap with a piece of black velvet. These
changes were apparently intended to set off the comic lankiness of his
own figure as well as to free his expressive face of shadow and frame its
mobile pallor.
[30] In the manuscript that survives for *Le Petit Poucet, ou Arlequin écuyer
de l'ogre des montagnes*, Pierrot's name in fact changes to Gilles midway
through the pantomime: uncoded MS in the Collection Rondel ("Rec.
des pantomimes jouées au Théâtre des Funambules et copiées par Henry
Lecomte"), Bibliothèque de l'Arsenal.

merly the invariable embodiment of laziness, sexlessness, and gluttony. He was usually attached to Arlequin, as valet, cousin, or friend, but his loyalty was often weaker than his cowardice. Typical in all these respects is the Pierrot of *Saphir l'enchanteur, pantomime en 3 parties* (1817). The companion of the Swiss archer Arlequin, who is in love with the lovely Claudine, Pierrot is content with a full belly and, insouciant, "makes fun of the lovers."[31] When the wicked enchanter, Saphir, carries Claudine off to his realm (*"Whatever pleases you is permitted you,"* proclaim the corrupt cupids of his gardens),[32] Arlequin rescues her on the silver cloud of Love. But all is nearly lost when the enchanter meets the fool in the forest and Pierrot fearfully stammers out the heroes' counterplots. Before Love's final intervention, both the *amoureux* and old Simon, feeble father of Claudine, all but fall pathetic victim to the mage. At times, as in *Arlequin sorcier, ou la Fête du Seigneur (c.* 1817), Pierrot enjoys a comic access of courage and brings off a triumphant dénouement. In this piece he foils several robbers who are burgling his master's farm, and so secures, in naïve fashion, Arlequin's happiness—the hand of the farmer's daughter, Julienne.[33] But his ingenuousness rarely engenders selfless heroism. As a simple sluggard in *Le Génie rose et le génie bleu, ou les Vieilles Femmes rajeunies* (1817), he abuses his companion, Arlequin, and misuses the magic powers granted him by the titular Blue Genie. Because he shows "only the signs of an unjust and wicked heart" (in the severe judgment of *le génie rose*),[34] he is clapped in a cage and buried by four demons in the earth.

More significant than the character of Pierrot in these pieces is the diversity of the pantomimic forms. We encounter here exotic melodrama (*La Pauvre Mère, ou Arle-*

---

[31] Uncoded MS in the Collection Rondel ("Rec. des pantomimes jouées au Théâtre des Funambules et copiées par Henry Lecomte"), p. 4, Bibliothèque de l'Arsenal.

[32] Ibid., p. 16.

[33] At least we must assume that the events take their usual course: before Arlequin is united with Julienne (who at first bears the name of Colombine), the manuscript breaks off: uncoded MS in the Collection Rondel ("Rec. des pantomimes jouées au Théâtre des Funambules et copiées par Henry Lecomte"), Bibliothèque de l'Arsenal.

[34] D., *Le Génie rose et le génie bleu, ou les Vieilles Femmes rajeunies* (Paris: Morisset, 1817), p. 33.

quin bon fils), tearful domestic comedy (*Arlequin séducteur, ou le Chien victime de sa fidélité*), and every geographical variation on the *féerie*: in *Le Petit Poucet, ou Arlequin écuyer de l'ogre des montagnes*, for example, the action unfolds in fairyland; in *Le Génie protecteur, ou la Vengeance d'Arlequin*, in the gothic landscape of the melo; in *L'Amour forgeron, ou les Deux Arlequins rivaux*, in the green shade of the village.[35] Not all of the forms survived: the mute *comédie larmoyante* was edged out by the melodrama and by certain of the *pièces villageoises*. But of greater importance is the fact that, for those that retained the public favor, Deburau evolved subtly different Pierrots. The evolution of both the pantomime and Pierrot himself is impossible to trace, since so few scripts from the mime's apprentice years exist.[36] It is obvious, however, that, by the late 1820s, three crucial developments had occurred: the pantomime had become less acrobatic in execution and less serious in tone;[37] Pier-

[35] All of these pantomimes survive in manuscript as part of the previously cited *recueil* in the Collection Rondel ("Rec. des pantomimes jouées au Théâtre des Funambules et copiées par Henry Lecomte"), Bibliothèque de l'Arsenal. Only *L'Amour forgeron, ou les Deux Arlequins rivaux* bears a date (1818), but both the centrality of their Arlequins and the comparative seriousness of tone in the others indicate that they were produced at the theater roughly during the years 1816-1823; the character of Pierrot (or of Gilles) is, moreover, consistent with that in the pantomimes known to belong to this period.

[36] On grounds that now seem to me suspect, Rémy argues that Deburau's début in Pierrot's role did not take place until about 1825. Švehla, who accepts Péricaud's earlier date (1819), makes a sensible case: "[. . .] Deburau's first appearance as Pierrot merely hinted at the rudimentary outlines of the new phenomenon he was to become. What stood out from the very beginning were his singular facial features and certain details in gesture and mimicry which differed happily from his predecessor's and from all other contemporary Pierrots. But it would be a long time yet before the Pierrot who began a new era in pantomime evolved, totally transformed, from his costume down to the most subtle features of his character" ("Immortal Pierrot," pp. 10-11). For the period 1819-1826 information is especially meager about his pantomime: Péricaud provides what little we know of these years (*Théâtre des Funambules*, pp. 20-59).

[37] The *Almanach des Spectacles [. . .] pour l'an 1823* (Paris: Barba, 1823) offers a spectator's view of the early pantomime at the Funambules: "We [. . .] noticed that the pieces there were of a more serious kind than at [the Spectacle Acrobate]; although they employ no words, they are usually types of melodrama, in which ingenuous and candid Innocence is persecuted by Crime, which dares all, and by dissembling Treachery and

rot had succeeded Arlequin as the pantomime's principal *vedette*;[38] and Deburau was experimenting with various interpretations before his audience—interpretations that would eventually define and be defined by four broad pantomimic forms. Champfleury classified three of those forms, all outgrowths of the earlier *arlequinades*, in his *Souvenirs des Funambules*. The first is the *pantomime-mélodrame*, more and more commonly in dialogue, though Pierrot is always mute. The second he calls the *pantomime-réaliste*: "the action adheres to the reproduction of scenes from everyday life."[39] The third is the *pantomime-féerie*, whose genii and fairies have replaced *l'Amour* of the initial, more primitive scenarios. We may add a fourth, rather minor, type: the *pantomime-villageoise*, in which Pierrot is the protagonist, and sometimes victim, of a little *drame rustique*.

In the latter, Pierrot is the lover—of Lisette (*Les Cosaques, ou la Ferme incendiée* [1840]), Finetta (*Pierre-le-Rouge, ou les Faux-Monnayeurs* [1843]), or Babette (*Les Deux Mousquetaires* [1845]). He is honest, but poor, and so rarely favored by his girlfriend's thick-skinned *père*. Yet when the ingénue is abducted by Cossacks or (more improbably) by two musketeers, Pierrot's snatching her from the maw of military perdition always softens the old man's heart. Fusing the melo and the farce, these playlets present the hero as a naïve *paysan* whose courage gets the better of his meekness.[40] The opening scenes are almost always purely comic:

Perfidy. There are, moreover, dances, battles, maneuvers, and conflagrations. The only essential difference between these pieces and others regarded by their authors as greatly superior is that the lover can not take part in the action—and attend to the affairs of his heart—without first having made several leaps and cut a few capers" (p. 245).

[38] Titles of pantomimes alluding to *commedia dell'arte* characters suggest the succession: *Arlequin médecin* (1819), *Arlequin dogue* (1819), *Le Père barbare, ou Arlequin au tombeau* (1820), *Arlequin statue* (1820), *Pierrot somnambule* (1823), *La Forêt de Bondy, ou Pierrot chef de voleurs* (1824), *La Bouteille d'encre, ou le Petit Blanc* (1824). When, very late in the mime's career, Arlequin was still enjoying his traditional conquest of the ingénue in the *pantomime-arlequinade-féerie*, Pierrot was the center of attention for the public.

[39] Champfleury, *Souvenirs des Funambules* (Paris: Lévy Frères, 1859), p. 86.

[40] It was undoubtedly the *pantomime-villageoise* (and not the *pantomime-mélodrame*) that Banville was recalling when, in his *Souvenirs*, he described

Pierrot faints in fear as his cap is shot off in a clumsy duel with a soldier (*Les Cosaques*); he hides under a table, silently stuffing his gut, while the villains paw over Babette (*Les Deux Mousquetaires*). The dénouements are milked for pathetic effects, such as Pierrot's rescue from a firing-squad at the end of *Pierre-le-Rouge*, or for thrilling scenic spectacle, as in this final *tableau* of *Les Cosaques*:

> The Cossacks set fire to the farmhouse; all the millers and Russians reenter: battle royale. Pierrot spears a Cossack with a pitchfork and hurls him into the flames; all the Cossacks are vanquished. Group *tableau*.[41]

Two pantomimes, *Les Dupes, ou les Deux Georgettes* (1836) and *Les Noces de Pierrot* (1845), stand at the formal limits of the genre. The former is exclusively farce, its Pierrot a duped suitor among a host of other dupes; the latter is straight melodrama, in which Pierrot's unjustly persecuted (and prosecuted) brother is delivered from his *condamnation à mort*.

These pieces differ from the *pantomime-mélodrame* in a number of important ways. Invariably they are set in a farm or a village; their hero is always Pierrot. But Pierrot is technically a subaltern in the *pantomime-mélodrame*: in the consecrated formula of Pixérécourt, he is the "comic" or *niais*. He usually turns up as a soldier—among the French troops in *Pierrot en Afrique* (1842), among the English in other plays (*Le Mandarin Chi-han-li, ou les Chinois de paravent* [1842], *Pierrot chez les Mohicans* [late 1843 or early 1844]). In *Le Corsaire algérien, ou l'Héroïne de Malte* (1845), he is made head of a regiment of women hastily formed, by the Duke of Malta, to combat "the savage corsair Nouradin."[42] But the Pierrot of the most interesting melo is that of *La Pagode enchantée* (1845). Not a soldier, here, but a "*fou*," in the court of the mandarin Babouki, he enjoys the protection of a mysterious voice from the Shadow of the Crypts ("*Babouki, never strike the idiot—or misfortune for you will*

Pierrot as "a peasant by turns timid and brave who, aided by a fighting woman habitually played by Madame Lefebvre, slaughtered all the brigands in a combat with broadswords set to the rhythm of the music" (p. 223).

[41] AN document F^{18} 1085, MS 3035, p. 6.

[42] AN document F^{18} 1088, MS 7032, sc. 1 (unpaginated).

follow!").[43] After Pierrot saves the young hero-prince—a prisoner in one of the melo's ubiquitous *cachots*—the voice hollowly informs the assembly of his traitress's unhappy fate: "*she is going to be buried alive in this tomb unless she consents to marry the madman, restored to reason by the release of Prince Kamouiski.*"[44] The settings of these pieces, as their titles suggest, are all in the exotic *lointain*: Africa, America, Malta, China. But their dramatic resolutions never violate the Boulevard proprieties. It is the French officer, Léon, and not the dark-skinned Mahomet, who weds Zelmire in this pantomimic *Afrique*; the English never fail to overcome the wily heathen, either Mohican or inscrutable Chinee. And since these events occur, not at the Porte-Saint-Martin, but at Deburau's Funambules, Pierrot is, though still a subaltern, always rather more than a simple *niais*. He is what Gautier calls—somewhat later, and with rare but witty contempt—a "*Providence enfarinée.*"[45]

Both the nature of his role and the artlessness of the playlets may be suggested by the plot of *Le Corsaire algérien*. When the eponymous corsair captures the stronghold of the Duke, Pierrot "conceives the idea of gaining entrance to the fortress by means of the ladders that have been left standing against the walls."[46] He rescues the Duke and the *jeune premier* by overpowering a careless guard; he next turns his attention to the captive "*jeunes filles,*" making use of a somewhat cryptic ruse. Surrounded by corsairs, he

> presses a button [*un ressort*] . . . immediately two of the corsairs disappear under the floorboards. Their comrades, furious, raise their sabers against Pierrot, who presses another button. A soldier emerges from an alcove and fights one of the corsairs; the other runs off [. . .].[47]

The last scene discovers Nouradin, the *chef des corsaires*, in the obligatory "mountainous region": he has carried off the ingénue, Palmyre. He hurls her into the sea (from which

---

[43] AN document F¹⁸ 1088, MS 6974, sc. 1 (unpaginated).

[44] Ibid., sc. 6.

[45] Review of *Pierrot et les Bohémiens* at the Funambules: *La Presse*, July 26, 1847.

[46] AN document F¹⁸ 1088, MS 7032, sc. 2 (unpaginated).

[47] Ibid., sc. 4.

she is promptly recovered by young Dumois, her intended); then he fires upon the Duchess, who falls into her husband's arms. To redress these wild atrocities, Dumois finally "rushes upon Nouradin and finishes him off."[48] And the curtain falls upon a somber but elevating *tableau*.

The ingenuousness of the hero in the *pièces villageoises* has been replaced, in all these pantos, by a more ambiguous naïveté. No simple rustic, Pierrot is a schemer of some pluck and resourcefulness; he is, at times (as in *La Pagode enchantée*), a kind of Wise and Holy Fool. Unfortunately, most of the business in the scripts is rather sketchy; it is impossible to know exactly how the character was played. The *cascades* that Deburau improvised are, of course, never indicated: there remain to us only the censor's scripts, submitted for approval before production. But Pierrot's playful malice as both soldier and *fou* suggests that he had more than the dubious assurance of the peasant; if nothing else, he had more knowledge of the world. The role was a comparatively late creation in Deburau's career: the melo flowered in belated glory only towards the end of the 1840s, when Charles Charton, the *régisseur* and Léandre of the theater, began penning his wonderfully foolish *drames*.[49] The pantomimes for which Deburau was best known—and celebrated—were in fact those of the remaining types: the *pantomime-réaliste* and the *pantomime-féerie*.

Although Champfleury asserts that, in the former, Deburau "abandoned the costume of Pierrot,"[50] there are a fair number of pieces in which Pierrot appears that fit comfortably within the class. *Pierrot et ses créanciers* (1836), *En v'là des bamboches* (1838), *Le Marrrchand d'habits!* (1842): all present Pierrot in rather commonplace settings (shops, salons, public streets) and among recognizably "realistic"

[48] Ibid., sc. 7.

[49] *Les Naufrageurs de la Bretagne* (1849: in collaboration with Ambroise), *Les Bandits écossais* (1849), *Le Juif de Satan* (1849), *Sébastiano le bandit* (1850), *Les Pêcheurs napolitains* (1851), *Arcadius, ou Pierrot chez les Indiens* (1852), *Les Circassiens* (1854), *Les Prisonniers de la Tchernaïa* (1855), *Le Soldat Belle Rose* (1857), *La Moresque* (1858), *Le Crocodile de Java* (1862), *Pierrot et les bandits espagnols* (after 1850). Péricaud ascribes the authorship of *Le Mandarin Chi-han-li, ou les Chinois de paravent* to Charton (*Théâtre des Funambules*, p. 258).

[50] *Souvenirs des Funambules*, p. 86.

companions. We may, in fact, widen the limits of the genre to include superficially unlikely pieces, several with more exotic locales—*Les Recruteurs écossais* (1839), for example, in which the action unfolds in "Scotland," or *L'Ile des Marmitons* (1844), which follows the exploits of Pierrot and company on the island of Queen Stewpot. Even when his company surpasses the ordinary and includes Arlequin, Léandre, and Colombine, we can sense, in, say, *Pierrot et l'aveugle* (1841), lines linking still other pieces to the class. For what these playlets have in common is not any great fidelity to "reality" (or close ties with the emergent *réalistes*), but an absence of the villains of the melo and the supernatural agents of the *féerie*. They also share, more significantly, the same conception of Pierrot.

It is this Pierrot that a critic of *La Pandore* called, in 1828, a "naïve and clownish Satan."[51] For the malice that seems merely incidental to his character in the *pantomime-mélodrame* here emerges with almost brutal force. Always of the most unpretentious profession—he is a case-maker and packer in *Pierrot et ses créanciers*, a grocer's assistant in *En v'là des bamboches*, a common valet in *Le Marrrchand d'habits!*—Pierrot, nevertheless, gains a kind of reckless control over the whole social world of these pantos, manipulating the fortunes, persons, and wives of the other characters for his own egoarchical ends. Libidinous and unscrupulous, often spiteful and cruel, he is redeemed only by his criminal innocence. When Françoise, a servant-neighbor, pledges to sell her few jewels to deliver him from the fists of his creditors, he thanks her profusely while filling his pockets with fruit from her shopping basket (*Pierrot et ses créanciers*). Imprisoned for accepting the pay but not the service of a recruit, he offers to play a game of blind-man's buff with his guard; and as the old man is groping gleefully toward a grim superior officer, Pierrot is out whooping with his companions in crime (*Les Recruteurs écossais*). He kills a peddler so that he may court a duchess in garments stolen from his pack (*Le Marrrchand d'habits!*); he shrewdly attaches himself to a blind beggar only to pilfer his food and alms (*Pierrot et l'aveugle*). And he usually man-

---

[51] "Deburau," p. 2: the critic was probably Charles Nodier.

ages a final slip from Justice. At the end of *Pierrot et ses créanciers*, his neighbor, Galichon, must himself pay Pierrot's creditors—or go to jail for lusting after his wife. It is innkeeper Williams, not his pale rival in love, who ends up in a coal-sack, belabored by peasants, at the curtain of *Les Recruteurs écossais*. But in two skits Pierrot is not nearly so lucky. At the end of *Le Marrrchand d'habits!* (a special case, as we shall see), he is run through by the sword with which he had stabbed his victim; and the Arlequin of *Pierrot et l'aveugle* finally takes lawlessness into his own able hands. First charming his pursuers into motionlessness, he "takes up a hammer and long skewers."

> He fastens Cassandre to the closet door with a skewer that goes through his hand.
> Léandre stays fixed to the ground by a skewer that goes through his calf.
> Pierrot is nailed to the wall by a long skewer that enters his mouth and comes out at the back of his head.[52]

With a wave of his bat, Arlequin restores their mobility, setting them struggling against their restraints. Then, free at last of their persecution, he leads Colombine into the liberty of the wings.

Although neither fairies nor demons intervene in *Pierrot et l'aveugle*, it is clear that, with this scene, we stand at a pantomimic threshold—that which divides pure farce from fantasy, the *pantomime-réaliste* from the *pantomime-féerie*. "The largest and grandest" of the "various schools of pantomime,"[53] the *pantomime-féerie* subsumes at least three important subtypes within its own capacious class. In what we may call the *pantomime-pierrotade-féerie*, Pierrot is the only *commedia dell'arte* character (with the sometime exception of Cassandre). As a hero or hero's companion, he ventures into the fantastic realm of faerie—sometimes in flight with his master's beloved (*Le Diable boiteux* [late 1836 or early 1837]), sometimes in pursuit of his own (*Pierrot et Croquemitaine, ou les Ogres et les moutards* [1840], *Biribi*

[52] AN document F[18] 1086, MS 3924, p. 9.
[53] Champfleury, *Souvenirs des Funambules*, p. 84.

[1841]), sometimes in quest of adventure or fortunes (*Pierrot errant* [1838]). At times, as in *La Sorcière, ou le Démon protecteur* (1838), a sorceress merely gives him the means (here a giant turkey) by which to traverse a familiarly quotidian world. But whether we are in the land of dandies or demons, the supernatural everywhere reigns. It often makes its appearance in the opening scene—as a "little monster, with a yellow-and-black face," or as a fairy masquerading as a peddler in distress, testing Pierrot's "Courage and [. . .] good Heart," or as a sorceress before "a large cabalistic book"[54]—and usually within suitably gothic settings: in *Le Diable boiteux* the curtain rises on an astrologer's laboratory, in *Biribi* on a chamber in hell, in *La Sorcière* on "a wild landscape bristling with frightful crags."[55] The fairies and magicians grant boons, help redress the wrongs of enchantment and circumstance, offer loquacious companionship and advice.[56] The intrigues are too various for a single formula. A rapid succession of farcical scenes, of often dizzyingly baroque incongruity, the *pantomime-pierrotade-féerie* seems on first encounter best described by a censor's note: "This pantomime [. . .] eludes analysis."[57] Filled with bizarre transformations of characters, unexpected shifts of locale, magic talismans, warring sorcerors, Amazons, ogres,

[54] These quotations are taken, respectively, from *Le Diable boiteux* (AN document F[18] 1083, MS 797, p. 5), *Pierrot errant* (AN document F[18] 1084, MS 1987, p. 11), and *La Sorcière, ou le Démon protecteur* (AN document F[18] 1084, MS 1957, sc. 1 [unpaginated]). The first, describing Asmodée, the crippled devil of the title, paraphrases Lesage's portrait in his own *Diable boiteux*, the source for the pantomime.
[55] AN document F[18] 1084, MS 1957, sc. 1 (unpaginated).
[56] Their roles are always in dialogue; but it is not true, as Banville (and others) observed, that while "the divinities spoke in lyric verse, [. . .] the human beings did not utter a sound [. . .]" (*Ame de Paris*, p. 36). Often Pierrot is the only mute character in the *pantomime-pierrotade-féerie*—and even his silence was not absolute. As Gautier pointed out in a review of Fernand Desnoyers's *Le Bras noir* at the Folies-Nouvelles (*Le Moniteur Universel*, February 11, 1856), "Deburau [sic] permitted himself a little inarticulate cry, a bizarre clucking, in extreme situations [. . .]."
[57] AN document F[21] 984 ("Procès-verbaux de la censure à Paris: Classement par théâtres: Théâtre des Funambules"), MS 1485. The remark is in reference to the plot of *La Chatte amoureuse* (1838), a *pantomime-arlequinade-féerie dans le genre anglais*, but it is equally applicable to the *pantomime-pierrotade-féerie*.

and Russians disguised as bears, it is marvelously (and un-
cannily) prodigious in its sheer exuberance of plot.

Equally prodigious are the two other types: the *pantomime-arlequinade-féerie* and its variant, the *pantomime-arlequinade-féerie dans le genre anglais*. In the first, it is Arlequin
who is always the lover—of Colombine (*Pierrot partout*
[1839], probably by Charles Charton) or of Célesta (*Les
Trois Bossus* [1842]). Cassandre, the ingénue's father, intends her for Léandre or Pierrot; but a dispute over her
hand ends in Arlequin's carrying her off, through landscapes both fabulous and banal. A good fairy promotes Arlequin's interests—though in *Pierrot partout* (until the penultimate scene) she favors the suit of Pierrot. *De rigueur*,
however, is Arlequin's union with his beloved in the last
pyrotechnical *tableau*: at the Temple of Hymen he receives
Cassandre's dry blessing, and the comic benediction of
Pierrot. When the *pantomime-arlequinade-féerie* is cast "*dans
le genre anglais*," these events are preceded by a prologue,
the equivalent of the "opening" of Grimaldian pantomime
and, like the latter, in dialogue and song.[58] The English
opening often dramatized the amorous dilemmas of characters already familiar to its audience—characters from
nursery rhymes, folk and fairy tales, well-known novels,
events of the day. The French prologue, on the other hand,
usually presents original characters in sometimes ingenious,
sometimes very simple, intrigues. The simplest, such as we
find in *Souffre-douleur* (1840) or *L'Amour et la Folie, ou le
Grelot mystificateur* (1840), features two suitors contending
for the same young lady, the daughter of a miserly old man.
When the richer (and more foolish) is chosen over the sentimentally more deserving, a fairy takes up the latter's cause:
he is changed to an Arlequin covered in brilliant spangles[59]

[58] In the pantomime that follows the prologue, all of the characters—
save the supernatural agents—perform in silent mime. (Deburau's role, in
both the prologue and the pantomime, was of course always mute.) The
first pantomime to be preceded by the prologue in verse with couplets
and choruses (probably by Eugène Grangé) was Charles Charton's *Les
Epreuves* (1833). On the English "opening," see David Mayer III, *Harlequin in His Element: The English Pantomime, 1806-1836* (Cambridge: Harvard University Press, 1969), pp. 23-24.

[59] According to Péricaud, it was the elder of the two Laurent brothers,
an English Harlequin responsible for introducing the *pantomime-arlequi-*

and armed with a magic bat. Sometimes other transformations ensure that the chase that follows is animated by characters from the *commedia dell'arte*—Colombine as the daughter, Cassandre as the father (abetted by his servingman, Pierrot), and Léandre as the foppish *prétendu*. Often the prologue is more inventive. In, for example, *Le Cheveu du Diable*, the prologue of *Les Epreuves* (1833), Christophe (the future Léandre) reveals that he has been endowed with a magic hair. Tignaço, an enchanter and *accoucheur* of his mother, had (in gratitude for the pleasures of his midwifery) called up a hair on her infant's skull to render him "invulnerable." He is now Isabelle's suitor, but she ("How Christophe bores me, and how very stupid he seems!")[60] has eyes for Lindor-Arlequin. At last a fairy appears: "For a modern Samson, be thou Delilah," she sings to Isabelle.[61] And at the end of the pantomimic turbulence that ensues, *le cheveu du Diable* is plucked.

In all of these spectacles, images from dream, myth, and the *Cabinet des fées* are jumbled indiscriminately into a remarkable whole. It was this obscure prodigality—"this confusion of things and ideas, in the midst of [a] waking dream"[62]—that delighted the Romantics of Deburau's public, for whom the *féerie* was his supreme (sometimes only) creation, the *pantomime classique*. Banville rhapsodized, characteristically, over the productions of Charles Charton, who "possessed the divine ignorance, which is the beginning of genius: little versed in exegetical studies, he jumbled together all the Gods of every race, all the sylphs, all the fairies, all the genii, thereby anticipating the supreme conclusions of modern Science."[63] The Science to which Banville—rather precociously—alludes will find articulation in Claude Lévi-Strauss, who detects in the universal binary oppositions of myth what Gautier saw casually in the *féerie*:

nade-féerie dans le genre anglais to the Funambules's public in the 1820s, who "had the idea [borrowed from his fellow-countryman, James Byrne] of sprinkling spangles over Arlequin's costume" (*Théâtre des Funambules*, p. 146).

[60] AN document F[18] 1083, MS 112, p. 12.
[61] Ibid., p. 18.
[62] Janin, *Deburau*, pp. 80-81.
[63] *Ame de Paris*, p. 36.

an "innocently Manichean"[64] world, whose forces move towards the mediations of comedy. In the *pantomime-féerie*, the oppositions are naïvely elemental: against the powers of malevolent darkness are pitted benevolent powers of light. The latter are almost always female, agents of water, air, and azure, such as the fairy Diamantine of *Pierrot partout*, whom we first encounter as a dove, or the princess Léa of *Pierrot errant*, "daughter of the Grand-Priest Zoroaster, and devoted to the cult of the Sun."[65] The former, on the other hand, are male: they are magicians of infernal resources (the enchanter Pillardoc in *Le Diable boiteux*) or genii brandishing brands of fire (the Génie du Mal in *Pierrot errant*) or wickedly insatiable ogres (Croquemitaine in *Pierrot et Croquemitaine*) or libertines of Satanic powers (the title-character of *Biribi*)—or even, as in *Satan Ermite* (1841), His Satanic Majesty himself.

The fundamentally sexual nature of the agents' struggle is suggested, not only by their allegiances with the suitors, but by the visible symbols of their authority—the talismans they give to their wards. Arlequin's bat needs no exegesis (or reminder of the comic uses to which it was probably put),[66] but the significance of the other talismans is usually

---

[64] Review of a revival of *Les Pilules du Diable* (1839) by Anicet Bourgeois, Ferdinand Laloue, and C.-P. Laurent at the Théâtre du Cirque: *Le Moniteur Universel*, April 9-10, 1855.

[65] AN document F[18] 1084, MS 1987, p. 11.

[66] Of Deburau's pantomime in general, George Sand wrote that "the poem is buffoonish, the role cavalier, and the situations scabrous" ("Deburau," *Le Constitutionnel*, February 8, 1846); several months later, after Deburau's death, Paul de Saint-Victor made the same observation: "Indeed, in plenty of places, the poem of his roles was free, scabrous, almost obscene" ("Mort d'un artiste et de son art," identified—by hand—as from *La Semaine*, July 1846: Ro 11577 ["Rec. fac. d'art. de presse sur Jean-Gaspard Deburau (1796-1846). 1829-1950"], f. 21, Bibliothèque de l'Arsenal). Of course, very little that is suggestive of mature sexual innuendo may be glimpsed through the censor's copies of the pantomimes. The vigilance of the censor's readers may be inferred by the changes that were demanded in the dialogue of *Le Mandarin Chi-han-li, ou les Chinois de paravent*. Pierrot has just filched some of the mandarin's chocolate, a theft that has elicited an exasperated threat from his host: "I'm going to cut off his head!" The next line, spoken by one of the women in the "seraglio," is struck out, and an "Oh! no" substituted in its place: "Oh! don't cut anything off of him [*Oh! ne lui coupez rien*]." Similarly, after the woman remarks that Pierrot "is so amusing," the mandarin's response is partially

no less clear. In *Les Epreuves*, the powers of Christophe's *cheveu du Diable* are combatted with those of a hat from the *fée*: "It is a large felt with great horns;/It is the Saint's diadem in the pictures [*qu'on voit sur le tableau*]."[67] A sanction of Lindor-Arlequin's sexual aggressiveness, it equates his quest with that of the saint. So, too, Pierrot's talismans may be symbols of his (sentimentally sublimated) sex: in *Pierrot errant*, for example, he is awarded a long feather from his guardian fairy's wing. But they usually mock his prowess in an obliquely obscene way, as in *L'Amour et la Folie*, when a bell hangs suspended, with comic importunity, from the end of his bony nose.

Like the circus (another enthusiasm of Gautier, Banville, Baudelaire), the *pantomime-féerie* offered frankly infantile fantasy to the habitués of the Funambules. The authority on nineteenth-century English pantomime, David Mayer III, has described its early structure as that of a rescue fantasy, in which an "asexual mother" (the fairy-protectress) confers a magical manhood on her child. She "twice intervenes" in the action, "as fantasy-mothers are wont":

> It is she who gives Harlequin his penis-equivalent, his magic bat or sword, the potent instrument with which to make his own way, to secure Columbine, to ward off and to frustrate his enemies. And it is this same benevolent agent who again intervenes in the closing moments of the pantomime, restoring to Harlequin the sword his enemies have wrested from him. It is she who permanently unites the lovers.[68]

Not all of his remarks are strictly applicable to the *pantomime-arlequinade-féerie dans le genre anglais*. The form of the latter always tended to be looser than that of the English entertainment. The loss and recovery of Harlequin's bat occur, almost invariably in the English panto, in the

censored (i.e., the phrase here in italics is struck out): "Hush, now, he's so amusing! You don't need him to be amused: *find your fun by yourselves* [*amusez-vous toutes seules*]" (AN document F[18] 1087, MS 4523, sc. 2 [unpaginated]).

[67] AN document F[18] 1083, MS 112, p. 25.

[68] "The Sexuality of Pantomime," *Theatre Quarterly*, IV (February-April 1974), 59.

penultimate, so-called "dark scene," set in a grotto or dense wood. These events sometimes find rough equivalents at the end of the French pantomime—in, for example, *Les Trois Bossus, Bamboches & taloches* (1844), and *Les Sorcières de Macbeth* (1845). But just as often Arlequin's talisman is stolen in a comparatively early scene—in the fifth (of the eleven scenes) of *La Chatte amoureuse* (1838), in the fifth (of the nine scenes) of *Pierrot partout*, and in the eighth (of the twelve scenes) of *Souffre-douleur*. Sometimes Arlequin retrieves it himself; sometimes it is not stolen at all. But the variations seem insignificant in the face of the inevitable dénouements. The triumph of the fairy over the fiery demons reveals clearly what Mayer suggests: an attempt by the hero both to master and to evade sexuality by recourse to regressive romance. For the Temple of Hymen, where the pantomime climaxes, in a fantasy of purling cascades, evokes never so much the passionate lover's bed as his mother's watery womb.

Of course in all the other types of panto—in the *pantomime-villageoise, -mélodrame*, and *-réaliste*—may be detected the sort of "deep" structures that Mayer is describing here. The melodrama enacts a rescue of another kind, in which what the unconscious perceives as a fallen woman (the prostitute-mother of an oedipal fantasy) is "restored" to virtue by a doting suitor(-son). That her fall is involuntary and virtual—the villain never has his wicked way—ensures that her restoration is always complete, even as the conventions of the genre hold it in titillating suspension. In the dramatically less coherent *pantomime-réaliste*, the id-energies of Pierrot are unleashed on a hard-edged and intractable world—on its agents of pleasure and pain, its figures of authority and constraint. But in none of these pantomimes do such structures assume more importance than the apparent dramatic values: in other words, both the melo and the farce are apprehended primarily by an audience in formal, not psychological, terms, raising (and then answering) such questions as: Who will dispatch the villain? What, within the bounds of farcical probability, will Pierrot try to bring off next? In its dreamlike structural incoherence, the *pantomime-féerie* makes a different sort of appeal: logic of plot has little importance; what immediately seizes the public (now a reader, alas!) are its images of desire and brute mayhem, all in an explicitly regressive key.

A scene from *Pierrot et Croquemitaine, ou les Ogres et les moutards* best illustrates the general regressiveness of the *pantomime-féerie*. Pierrot and Cassandre, both prisoners of the malevolent agents, are starving on an empty plain. Croquemitaine, *le roi des Ogres* (the "bogyman," to an American child), asks if Pierrot wants to see his *femme*:

> There she is, over there!—He points to the back of the stage; Pierrot looks and catches sight of a headless woman on a pedestal, bearing this inscription: "Here is a good woman." Pierrot laughs—but hunger is dogging both him and Cassandre. All of a sudden a shallow basket filled with provisions appears on the woman's shoulders; they seize it and eat. The woman disappears. Croquemitaine comes out of the hovel with Clorinde [Pierrot's beloved]. Pierrot has eaten so much that his belly, which has become enormous, no longer permits him to walk.
>
> The hovel changes to a house with the sign "Laying-in Doctor." Croqueciboule [Croquemitaine's assistant] appears as a doctor. He opens Pierrot's belly, from which he draws out three or four little pierrots and the fairy Cocotte herself. Croqueciboule runs off.[69]

We detect easily under these apparent absurdities the associations of the infantile mind. Deprived of her chattering and snapping mouth (the better to eat you with, my dear), a "good woman" merely supplies the oral gratifications by which belly-babies are conceived. The scene does not elaborate this primitive fantasy, nor does it screen it in any way. Throughout the wordless pantomime of all the *féeries*, we are encountering, as it were, improvisations of the primary process, a random succession of wishes and fears of the most nakedly regressive kind.

Each of the principal *commedia* characters—I refer only, of course, to the males—seems to incarnate an infantile sexual phase: Pierrot, that of gluttonous orality; Cassandre, of miserly anality; Arlequin, of emergent genitality. But all are

[69] AN document F^{18} 1085, MS 3357, p. 25.

shaken by the lusts and anxieties that indiscriminately crowd the pantomime. The wishes are very simple, if frequently obscene. In *Le Songe d'or, ou Arlequin et l'avare* (1828), probably by Charles Nodier, Pierrot demands milk in a chamberpot for a kind of gustatory *frisson*. Again, in *La Sorcière*, when a blind man asks Pierrot for his oboe, the latter, not one to hoard his pleasures, brightly passes him the clyster-pipe of a syringe. ("The blind man brings it up to his mouth and indicates that he finds it has a peculiar taste.")[70] And Pierrot is eager for still higher sexual *délices*. He is affianced to Inézia in *Le Diable boiteux* as a mere *époux de convenance*: her real lover (the hero of Lesage's novella) cannot possess her, by order of Satan, until a husband has abandoned her hand. Pierrot, "in his rapture, tries to kiss the hand of his future bride, but Cléophas, displeased, calls him to order by a kick in the rear."[71]

As in this last piece of business, the characters are often brought up short in the gratifications of their comic desires. Shortly after his kick in the pants, for example, we find Pierrot in his nuptial suite: he imperiously has his master removed, then tries to carry Inézia off. But *le diable boiteux*, Don Cléophas's protector, sends a monkey into his arms. The monkey is repulsed, but a second assault on Inézia's chamber drives her bed magically up to the ceiling; a third makes the furniture dance. When Pierrot and Cassandre sit down to a meal during the chase of *Le Songe d'or*, their table is transformed, by a genie's wand, into a (presumably unwelcome) *chaise percée*. When they stop for some wine in *Le Boeuf enragé* (1827), "the shop changes into a pharmacy":

> The wine becomes a drug: they contract stomach-aches. They are advised to take *pills of fizz-powder*. Cassandre swallows his pill easily enough, but they need a ham-

---

[70] AN document F[18] 1084, MS 1957, sc. 2 (unpaginated). Pierrot's own peculiar tastes persist even after Deburau's death. In Champfleury's *Pierrot pendu* (1847), while Pierrot and Polichinelle are having a meal, Arlequin slips an enormous rat into Pierrot's plate. Pierrot at first tries to interest Polichinelle in the morsel; then, "in the end, Pierrot eats it and declares it to be a very good dish" (AN document F[18] 1089, MS 7585, p. 6).

[71] AN document F[18] 1083, MS 797, p. 30.

mer to get Boissec's pill down his throat; as for Pierrot, it is only with the aid of a pavior's rammer that they succeed in driving it into his mouth. All of a sudden the pills take effect: a terrible explosion is heard, and a volley of sparks shoots out of the seat of the pants of the ailing trio.[72]

But one character's frustrations are often another's delight. Pierrot's is in aggressive cruelty: he is expert in humiliations, in bizarre mutilations, in acts of castrating terror. In *Les Epreuves* he cuts off Arlequin's head (three times), shoots him, then saws him in two. He fires a candle into the eye of a sapper (*Les Epreuves*), a carrot into the chest of a cannoneer (*Souffre-douleur*). He ties old men's wigs together and sets them alight (*Les Epreuves*), gives a blind man bill-sticker's paste to drink (*La Sorcière*), steals the crutches from the bed of a sick man (*Le Songe d'or*), humiliates a dandified hunchback (*La Sorcière*); once, in swatting at a coy butterfly, he murders a sleeping child (*La Sorcière*). Of course, he, too, is often a victim. For the terrors are everywhere: monsters biting off heads (*Les Epreuves*), crocodiles swallowing arms (*L'Amour et la Folie*), skeletons requesting a dance (*Les Trois Godiches* [1842]), nightmares looking for love (*Le Diable boiteux*).

It is this mad oscillation between desire and frustration, wish and anxiety, perpetration and punishment, that constitutes the heart of the *pantomime-féerie*. A scene from *Ma Mère l'Oie, ou Arlequin et l'oeuf d'or* (1830), a pantomime that Gautier called a masterpiece,[73] offers one of the most concentrated illustrations of its flux. Arlequin and Colombine, fleeing from their pursuers, take refuge in a peasant's cottage: Pierrot tries to follow them inside. He is at first refused admittance; then, when he persists in reaching for the knocker, the cottage swells to enormous size, its hammer evading his grasp. The door opens and a giant of a woman asks Pierrot his business. Pierrot "steps back, in great astonishment,"[74] but then gathers up the courage to

<hr>

[72] Laurent père, *Le Boeuf enragé, pantomime-arlequinade en 12 tableaux, dans le genre anglais* (Paris: Dechaume, n.d.), pp. 3-4.
[73] "Shakspeare aux Funambules," *Revue de Paris*, New Series, Year 1842, IX (September 4), 60.
[74] In Janin, *Deburau*, p. 138.

inquire after the lovers. She professes not to know them, the door closes behind her, and the house shrinks to its former size. When he decides to knock again, the cottage assumes tiny doll-house proportions, and a little woman, dressed like the first, comes out to turn him away. This time, when she reenters, Pierrot sticks his hand through a window, burgling some furniture, a flute, and a sheet of music. He plays "comically" a tune with the orchestra. Suddenly his instrument changes to a grill and his sheet-music to a mutton chop. The house resumes its former size. Arlequin and Colombine emerge from it; Pierrot calls to his companions, and they all three set after the fugitives.

A succession of naïvely theatrical "*trucs*," the scene seems the most opaque nonsense until we regard it from a child's perspective, the child being, here, Pierrot. It then seems to dramatize a redress of frustration—of the child's frustration before unreachable objects, before impenetrable mysteries in his mother's domain. The unreachable and impenetrable may be conquered by a wish, as they are when the cottage shrinks and its contents are rifled. But the masturbatory celebration that follows *comiquement* on this triumph soon turns ominously to anxiety in Pierrot's guilty hands. His music-making calls up a cutlet on the grill: in the punning language of dreams (and the pantomime), the fat is in the fire.

That Deburau had an intuitive grasp of the meaning of these oscillations is suggested by his style of interpreting Pierrot. In enumerating the "intellectual qualities necessary for a Pierrot such [. . .] as Debureau [sic] once realized," Gautier described the character as an oxymoronic embodiment of oppositions:

> imperturbable sang-froid, artful foolishness and foolish finesse, brazen and naïve gluttony, blustering cowardice, skeptical credulity, scornful servility, preoccupied insouciance, indolent activity, and all those surprising contrasts that must be expressed by a wink of the eye, by a puckering of the mouth, by a knitting of the brow, by a fleeting gesture.[75]

[75] Review of *La Gageure: La Presse*, August 31, 1846. Gautier's remarks

Pierrot has, on the one hand, the stupidity, the ingenuousness, the timidity, the gullibility, the submissiveness, and the idleness of the child whose ego stands, abject, before the superior world of reality and authority. He has, on the other hand, the poise, the audacity, the bluster, the superciliousness, the preoccupation, and the industry of that same child when—by means of wish, fantasy, or the burlesque role-playing of the tyro—he masters and subdues the world. It was through a style of acting that evoked both stupid inanition and calculated control that Deburau was able to slip subtly from one of these roles to the other. Banville observed that his style was "made up of proportions, of tact, of measure, and often of abstention";[76] Champfleury added that it was "remarkable especially for its exquisite finesse and its extreme sobriety of gestures."[77] Both tact and naïveté, artlessness and control, are suggested by the caricaturist Eustache in a series of sketches of Baptiste's Pierrot that he made for the *Musée Philipon*.[78] A Pierrot standing helplessly before an armed Arlequin, who is goading him into a duel, or stupidly before a vendor's tray, which he has clumsily let fall to the ground—this *niais* is succeeded by a Pierrot of calculation and *adresse*: the valet who, with only apparent inadvertence, sends a plate of sticking-plaster into a servant's face; the *serviteur* who, with an air of innocent obeisance, cuts off his master's coattails. It is a style that seems to unite the gestural elegance of Marceau with the ingenuous malice of Harpo Marx.

It had little in common with the style of his predecessors or with that of his counterpart in English pantomime. According to Louis Péricaud, the chronicler of the Funambules, Deburau's "placidity" formed "an enormous contrast

---

seem to have been based almost exclusively on his familiarity with the *pantomime-féerie*. Of Deburau's pantomimes mentioned repeatedly in his reviews, all but two, *Le Billet de mille francs* and *Pierrot en Afrique*, are of *le genre féerique*.

[76] *Ame de Paris*, p. 14.

[77] *Souvenirs et portraits de jeunesse* (1872; Geneva: Slatkine Reprints, 1970), p. 64.

[78] The drawings accompany a scenario, *Satan, ou le Pacte infernal*, apparently based on the pantomime *Satan Ermite* (1841); this number of the *Musée Philipon*, which also includes an illustrated parody (by Cham) of *Pierrot en Afrique* (1842), is undated: see plates 4 and 5.

with the exuberance, the superabundance of gestures, of leaps, that [. . .] his predecessors had employed."[79] Echoing the judgments of Banville, Champfleury, and Baudelaire, Gautier noted that "the English Pierrot differs considerably from our own," and went on to describe his character with customary *panache*:

> [. . .] he is a strapping athletic fellow, with prominent pectorals and knotty biceps, stuffed full of bloody roastbeef, glutted with whiskey and gin, stoked with ginger, cayenne pepper, and Indian spices. Two spots of blood mottle his powdered cheeks; red gashes lengthen his mouth to a maw and give him an air of cannibalistic voraciousness: you would think he was a man-eater who had just bitten into a morsel of human flesh. From his greedy ravenousness to the epicurism of the French Pierrot there is all the distance that separates the glutton from the gourmand. He is like the ostrich: he swallows the oyster and the shell, the wine and the bottle, the joint and the skewer: he would gladly eat the table, and would digest it with as little trouble. He has truculent and formidable accesses of gaiety, like an ogre in fine spirits; for every blow of the slapstick he receives, he sends back a punch that would kill a bull or a boxer. If he gives you a handshake, he dislocates your wrist and tears off your shoulder; his only natal air is fighting and mischief; he smashes the decorations, beats the supernumeraries half to death, and amuses himself in the action like a bull in a china shop.—The other characters—Harlequin, Hudibras, Colombine—provoke him only with a respectful terror.[80]

And yet the pantomime in which Clown gives expression to his ferocity seems much tamer than Deburau's productions. In, for example, *Harlequin and Mother Goose; or, The Golden Egg!* (1806), the source for *Ma Mère l'Oie*, there are the usual scuffles and blows; at one point Clown's leg is

[79] *Théâtre des Funambules*, p. 28.
[80] Review of the English pantomime *Harlequin et Hudibras* (with Richard Flexmore as Clown) at the Porte-Saint-Martin: *La Presse*, August 8, 1853.

even caught in the teeth of a trap. But nothing in the pantomime matches the nightmarish violence of its progeny at the Funambules, full of exploding bullets, decapitations, defenestrations, assassinations—violence that is in curious contrast with the imperturbable "placidity" of Baptiste. But neither the differences between the two types of pantomime nor the contrasts between Baptiste and his role were, I think, purely a matter of accident; nor were they, as Gautier implies, the results of "national character." Both may be best explained by the nature of pantomimic comedy and by its function with respect to its audience.

As I have been trying to show, the pantomime, like the circus, is regressive in its fantasy. But whereas the circus is "the child's theater, dramatizing the child's fantasies, conscious and unconscious, his daydreams, his games, his nightmares, his anxieties,"[81] the Funambules is—or was—a theater for adults, for whom *les épreuves* of early childhood are past. For a certain segment of the audience, the pantomime may indeed have played out current wishes and anxieties. George Sand implies as much when she describes Deburau as the "ideal" of "all these streetboys of the faubourg," who seem to have discerned in him a role with which to meet the world:

> They do not laugh very much: they examine, they study; they are conscious of the finesse, the grace, the elegance, the sobriety, and the precision of effect of all those gestures and of the smallest play of features on that face—so delicately outlined beneath its plaster mask that it could be taken for one of those charming grotesque cameos discovered at Herculaneum.
>
> [. . . Deburau is their] master of graces, [. . . their] professor of waggish good manners, [. . . their] model of off-hand insouciance, of unexpected perspicacity, and of sang-froid [. . .].[82]

But for those who were not sobered by the mime's sobriety, the pantomime served the ends of all comic art, or at

[81] Sidney Tarachow, "Circuses and Clowns," in *Psychoanalysis and the Social Sciences*, ed. Géza Róheim, III (New York: International Universities Press, Inc., 1951), 173.
[82] "Deburau" (*Constitutionnel*).

least of that "vulgar comedy" that Anthony Caputi calls *buffo*. Those ends, as Caputi argues (taking his cue from the psychologist Ernst Kris), are ultimately the pleasures of "mastery," the "feeling of temporary but triumphant security in a perilous world."[83] In the more technical language of the analyst, for whom the comic is "bound up with past [psychic] conflicts," comedy invites the ego to repeat its victories and in so doing "overcome half-assimilated fear."[84] The pantomime clearly reveled in such victories—while comically entertaining the primitive fantasies by which those victories were won.

The more outrageous the fantasies, the more dangerous were their consequences and, perforce, the more extreme their control. Pierrot could commit the most frightful atrocities because he was the epitome of "imperturbable calm";[85] Clown, on the other hand, an *enfant terrible* who threatened profoundly the stability of the world, was restricted in his license, exposing the ferocity of his demeanor at the expense of first-degree pantomimic crime. "Pleasure in mastery," as Kris points out, *"plays itself out in the present, and is experienced as such [by an audience]."*[86] The finesse of Pierrot was thus important for his public, his conspirators in his *délices à la de Sade*. Like the child, who courts the mastery of nightmare by assuming the determined grace of the clown,[87] the spectator of pantomime could indulge the wildest of infantile instincts because he was armed with Pierrot's control. He could, in fact, not only indulge but invite it, draw it forth from the unconscious and, delightedly, play with it, with something of the child's naïveté.[88]

[83] *Buffo: The Genius of Vulgar Comedy* (Detroit: Wayne State University Press, 1978), p. 196.

[84] Ernst Kris, "Ego Development and the Comic," *Psychoanalytic Explorations in Art* (New York: International Universities Press, Inc., 1952), p. 215.

[85] Critic (probably Charles Nodier) of "Deburau" (*Pandore*), p. 2.

[86] "Ego Development," p. 211.

[87] See Michel Soulé, "Oedipe au cirque: Devant le numéro de l'Auguste et du Clown Blanc," *Revue Française de Psychanalyse*, XLIV (January-February 1980), 99-125.

[88] Cf. the remarks by Annie Reich: "[. . .] in the comic sublimation the ego is really great and powerful. Deliberately it draws forth the otherwise repressed instinctual impulses from the unconscious and plays with them" ("The Structure of the Grotesque-Comic Sublimation," *Bulletin of the Menninger Clinic*, XIII [September 1949], 170).

As the buried metaphor in that last sentence implies, the pleasure was essentially masturbatory: it was the pleasure of the child vanquishing threat by a wish, decapitating his enemies before they castrated him, mastering the urges of sex through the grace of the girl who married dear old dad.

If Deburau made such pleasure possible, he also helped make it short-lived. His apparent predilection for the *pantomime-réaliste*[89] hastened the death of the *pantomime-féerie*. After his death, the latter was laid completely to rest, as Champfleury and others drove the fairies and demons forever from the silent stage. It was a banishment that meant the end of pantomime as a truly vital art. No longer an unmediated fantasy liberating instincts too deep for words, it became synonymous with mute farce—and in so doing became, theatrically, *de trop*. There is no reason, dramatic or otherwise, for farce to be silent; only the actor's genius for corporeal comedy explains why it in fact may be so. This, in turn, explains why the pantomime became simply an actor's medium, a curiosity of finesse and illusionist evocation, often a series of sketchy clichés. The *pantomime-féerie*, in all its naïve puerility, was the apotheosis of the art. And we may be grateful that its life was meteorically glorious at the Théâtre des Funambules.

[89] See Švehla, "Immortal Pierrot," pp. 26-32.

II

Paul Legrand, Champfleury,
and Pantomime after Deburau

Le regretté mime Farina, Séverin, le maître Georges Wague, Marcel Marceau, Jean-Louis Barrault et les chorégraphes restent, aujourd'hui, les derniers grands dépositaires de la tradition mimique. Sans doute le réalisme dont elle contenait le germe est-il responsable de sa disparition.

MARIAN HANNAH WINTER
Le Théâtre du Merveilleux (1962)

Deburau was, of course, not the only mime of the "Golden Age of the Boulevard."[1] There was the man-monkey Mazurier, the rage of Paris in *Jocko, ou le Singe du Brésil*; there was Emilie Bigottini of the Ambigu-Comique, "queen of the mimic art before Madame Quériau during the preromantic era";[2] there was, most famously, the rope-dancer Madame Saqui, who enthralled her public at the Spectacle Acrobate "on that rope, on that imperceptible wire," where— I am quoting Théodore de Banville—"she performed mimodramas all by herself in which she was all of the characters; in which she imitated—with what fidelity! with what poignant realism!—the fury of assailants, the horror of distraught mothers, the anguish of the dying, the acts of desperate heroism, the epic triumph of Victory hovering over

---

[1] I borrow this phrase from the title of Marvin Carlson's article "The Golden Age of the Boulevard," *The Drama Review*, XVIII (March 1974), 25-33.

[2] Marian Hannah Winter, *Le Théâtre du Merveilleux* (Paris: Perrin, 1962), p. 55.

scenes of carnage."[3] The great variety and fluidity of the
Boulevard genres, as well as the legal restrictions under which
the theaters often labored, encouraged every actor to be a
mime, a dancer, an acrobat. "In effect," observes Marian
Hannah Winter in her marvelous *Théâtre du Merveilleux*,
"actors and dancers of the Boulevard [were] often retained
in three capacities: as mime and dancer in the pantomimes
and mimodramas, as actor in the melodramas." And she
reminds us that it was "acrobatics, dance, and the stylized
art of mime" that formed the education of (among many
others) the legendary Frédérick Lemaître.[4]

But if this cross-breeding was to nourish the *drame romantique*, it was to debilitate ineluctably the *pantomime se-
lon Deburau*. At the great mime's death his white mantle
was passed on to a fugitive from the musical stage: Charles-
Dominique-Martin Legrand. Legrand, who took the name
of Paul Legrand, had made his début in 1839 at the Concert Bonne-Nouvelle, where his "unique ambition," according to an early biographer, "was, in this time of naïveté, to
play the Lovers of vaudeville [. . .]."[5] Later in the same year
he was engaged at the Funambules, where he appeared in
the vaudevilles as *le comique* and in the pantomimes as
Léandre. But Pierrot quickly became, as Rémy observes,
the "character that better suit[ed] his fancy,"[6] and, after a
short absence from the theater, Legrand contracted with
the managers of the Funambules to understudy Jean-Gaspard. He began appearing as Pierrot in 1845, probably re-
lieving Baptiste of the part in the numerous pantomimic
reprises, and in 1846, with Deburau's death, he stepped easily into all the new roles.

His Pierrot was very different from Jean-Gaspard's creations. At first assuming that Legrand was attempting to
imitate "his illustrious predecessor"—and failing to evoke

[3] "Théâtres," *Revue Fantaisiste* (October 1, 1861), III (Geneva: Slatkine
Reprints, 1971), 248.

[4] Page 55.

[5] J. M., *Biographie et portrait de M. Paul Legrand, premier mime des Folies-
Nouvelles et du Théâtre Déjazet* (Bordeaux: Péchade Fils Frères, 1861), p.
8.

[6] *Jean-Gaspard Deburau*, p. 168.

that *"thoroughly limber, loose* [ouvert], *and boneless"* Pierrot—Théophile Gautier counseled lessons in physical *adresse*, in "the difficult art [. . .] of delivering and receiving
the kick."[7] What the poet seemed to be seeking was the
spirit of barely repressed ferocity that had lurked beneath
Baptiste's suavely savage creations. He in fact expressed his
regret that Debureau had not been replaced by a Scandina-
vian named Lehmann, whom he had seen performing at
the Ambigu shortly before the mime's death:

> We are surprised, since Debureau [sic] was not im-
> mortal, alas! that M. Lehmann, the Scandinavian Pier-
> rot, was not engaged to replace him. M. Lehmann had
> realized a kind of titanic Pierrot of colossal propor-
> tions, violent, savage, rough, almost ferocious, such as
> one imagines he would have had to be in order to
> make merry with the formidable heroes of the Nibe-
> lungs or with the gods of Valhalla after their orgies of
> hydromel and barley-beer. (*P*, 8.31.46)

Legrand, he noted ruefully, did not have the physique for
pantomimic authority, "that unusually long musculature in
the legs and arms—natural in some [mimes], obtained in
others by dint of hard work—which allowed Mazurier and
Ravel to execute their astonishing leaps" (*P*, 8.31.46). Deburau's son Charles, a mime as boneless as his father, complained much later to one of his own *élèves* of Legrand's
unsuitability for the role: he was short and thick-set, with
small arms and a fat, round face; he lacked grace and elegance.[8]

There was more in these criticisms than the jealousy of a
rival, or the nostalgia of a reviewer for the *pantomime classique*; but they did no justice at all, as Gautier gradually
realized, to Legrand's genuine and original talents. Those
were the talents of a mute dramatic actor, of a vaudevillian
schooled in satire and sentiment, and in the coherent plots
of comedy. A little over a year after Gautier had recorded

[7] Review of *La Gageure: La Presse*, August 31, 1846. Gautier's reviews
in *La Presse* will be cited throughout this chapter as *P*, followed by the
appropriate date (month.day.year).

[8] Séverin, *L'Homme Blanc: Souvenirs d'un Pierrot*, introduction et notes
par Gustave Fréjaville (Paris: Plon, 1929), p. 70.

his rather severe first impressions of the mime, he saw Legrand perform in Champfleury's *Pierrot marquis* (1847), a piece outside "the old mold," unclouded by the "incessant storm of kicks, punches, and slaps," and concluded that only the *comédien* Bouffé could approach his finesse in certain scenes: "inasmuch as he is humble, piteous, melancholy, greedy, wheedling, stealthy, endearing, hypocritical in the first part of the piece, so is he arrogant, insolent, scornful—a regular Marquis de Moncade—in the second. What unprecedented truthfulness, what depth of observation [. . .]" (*P*, 10.18.47). This is a description, not of the bundle of infantile energies that was the old Pierrot of the *féerie*, nor even of the farcical type of Deburau's other creations, but of a character that undergoes a dramatically "realistic" transformation. The evocation of Bouffé is appropriate (it is not the last time Gautier made the comparison)— as appropriate as the names of those Realists and satirists that later came to his pen: "Paul Legrand, in this latest metamorphosis of Pierrot," he wrote of *Pierrot bureaucrate* (1856), "has revealed himself to be the equal of Henri Monnier and of Balzac in caricatural deftness and keenness of observation."[9] And if the mime lacked the agile suppleness of the Deburaux, *père* and *fils*, he had a mobility and expressiveness of face that invoked the most wide-ranging passions: "How many shades of feeling, how many ideas he summoned beneath this thick layer of flour that serves him as mask!" (*MU*, 11.2-3.57), Gautier exclaimed of his performance in *Les Brigands pour rire* (1857). And yet for Gautier, as for others, a reservation always remained: Legrand seemed an "excellent comedian who has condemned himself to mutism, one doesn't quite know why"; he "performs too much as an actor and not enough as a clown" (*MU*, 8.30.58).

But it was Gautier and the Romantics who had, quite inadvertently, made possible the new art of Legrand. For the literary world, the Funambules had been "discovered," around 1828, by that "pilot of Romanticism," Charles No-

[9] Review of Pol Mercier's *Pierrot employé* [sic] at the Folies-Nouvelles: *Le Moniteur Universel*, July 28, 1856. Gautier's reviews in *Le Moniteur Universel* will be cited throughout this chapter as *MU*, followed by the appropriate date (month.day.year).

dier, who eagerly introduced his *cénacle* to its mysteries: soon Balzac, Janin, Gautier, Nerval were marveling over *Ma Mère l'Oie*. And, not content to be spectators, a few wrote playlets themselves. Although its authorship was never acknowledged, *Le Songe d'or, ou Arlequin et l'avare* (1828) was apparently the work of Nodier, and Eugène Vermersch claimed that Méry, Balzac, and Frédéric Soulié each wrote a pantomime for the theater.[10] According to a letter to Gautier from the proprietor of the Funambules, the poet had promised, "at different periods," to supply a piece for its repertoire.[11] Gautier evidently never kept his promise[12]—

[10] "Les Funambules," *L'Eclipse*, dated (by hand) February 2, 1868: Ro 11532, f. 2, Bibliothèque de l'Arsenal.

[11] Letter from Charles-Louis Billion to Gautier, dated September 6, 1847: MS C491, f. 532, Bibliothèque Spoelberch de Lovenjoul, Chantilly.

[12] A copy of *Pierrot en Espagne* ([Paris]: Gallet, n.d.) at the Bibliothèque de l'Arsenal (Ro 11535[1]) bears the handwritten notation "by Théophile Gautier" on its titlepage. On the strength of this attribution as well as other evidence, Claude Book-Senninger argues in his *Théophile Gautier: Auteur dramatique* (Paris: Nizet, 1972), pp. 339-41, that Gautier was probably the author of this pantomime, which was produced at the Funambules in 1847. He admits that it is difficult to reconcile the date that Péricaud gives in his *Théâtre des Funambules* as the production date of the piece (August 4, 1847) with the date of the letter from the proprietor of the theater, cited above, requesting a pantomime from Gautier (September 6, 1847), but concludes that Péricaud is probably mistaken in his date of the première. Péricaud is indeed mistaken, but the truth of the issue does not favor Book-Senninger's argument. As usual, Péricaud has identified the date of the pantomime's reception for authorization at the Ministère de l'Intérieur as its date of production; but he has overlooked the very faint "2" that precedes the "4" in the date on the censor's manuscript, now in the Archives Nationales de France (AN document F[18] 1090, MS 8010). That the piece was registered for authorization on the twenty-fourth of August rather than produced on the fourth, however, does not alter the fact that the pantomime was received for production at the theater before Gautier was asked for a contribution. And still other pieces of evidence, overlooked by Book-Senninger, argue strongly against Gautier's authorship of the piece. First, the playlet is a type of *pantomime-mélodrame*, a mixed genre for which Gautier had the greatest contempt. In a review of *Pierrot et les Bohémiens*, a *pantomime-mélodrame* produced at the Funambules in July of 1847, Gautier attacked it as "a work whose tendencies are alarming. It is almost a melodrama—what are we saying: almost a tragedy!" (*P*, 7.26.47). Second, a version of *Pierrot en Espagne*, identified as the work of Deburau *père*, appears in Goby's *Pantomimes de Gaspard et Ch. Deburau* under a title that had originally headed—but was at some

but, in a sense, he went it one better. In the *Revue de Paris* of September 4, 1842, under the title "Shakspeare aux Funambules," he published a "review" of a pantomime he had ostensibly seen at the theater only a few evenings previous. A fantasy he thought worthy of "Shakspeare," rivaling the psychological penetration of *Macbeth*, this unnamed pantomime had followed the Faustian fortunes of its Pierrot from valet to fiancé of a duchess. The finery of an old-clothes man, treacherously murdered, had early won the vain duchess's respect—but the victim himself, a revenant Banquo, robs her at the altar of the criminal bridegroom: in a *danse infernale* the ghost skewers Pierrot on the sword with which the latter had put out the light. The pantomime is perhaps the best-known of the whole nineteenth-century repertory, having been performed in Carné's *Enfants du Paradis* by Barrault and later reworked (with Marceau as Arlequin) into Barrault's own pantomime *Baptiste* (1946). Tristan Rémy has argued, partly from evidence in Gautier's essay, that Deburau had originally nothing to do with the piece, his role having been appropriated by the more dramatic Pierrot, Legrand.[13] But however uncharacteristic of his repertoire, *Le Marrrchand d'habits!* was doubtless one of Baptiste's creations. A fact of far greater importance—up to now unconfirmed—is that it was born of Gautier's so-called review.

Champfleury described the actual sequence of events in an unremarked passage of his pamphlet *Pierrot, valet de la Mort*:

---

point cancelled from—the censor's manuscript, *Les Français en Espagne*. Third, the prose of the manuscript copy, which is much more detailed than the published résumé of the pantomime, could by no stretch of the imagination be attributed to Gautier. Although the handwriting may be assigned to a copyist, the author must be held responsible for the wretchedly graceless syntax: "*Labinette se trouve entouré par les espagnols, ce qui ne l'empêche pas d'envoyer un coup de balai au rentier, qui lâche Isabella, qui court se précipiter au devant de l'épée de Castellano qui allait frapper son époux* [Labinette finds himself surrounded by the Spaniards, a fact that does not hinder him from letting fly with his broom at the rentier, who releases Isabella, who runs to throw herself before the sword of Castellano, who was going to strike her husband]" (sc. 7 [unpaginated]). Théophile Gautier did not write *Pierrot en Espagne*.

[13] Rémy, *Jean-Gaspard Deburau*, pp. 174-76.

Théophile Gautier went more than once to the Funambules in the company of Shakespeare and Gérard
de Nerval. These impressions left a germ that developed one day under the form of a pantomime recounted in the *Revue de Paris*. [. . .]
One day [. . .] Gautier found himself an author of
the Funambules without knowing it: the regular librettist of the place had found the subject good (he
had a good nose), and he turned it into a pantomime
under the title of *Marchand d'habits*. The piece enjoyed
a great success [. . .].[14]

A number of details bear out the novelist's remarks. On the
censor's copy of *Marrrchand d'habits!*, which survives in the
Archives Nationales de France, it is noted by Cot d'Ordan,
the administrator of the theater, that the pantomime was
"received to be performed after authorization—this 17 October 1842."[15] The report of the censor's examiner is dated
October 18, 1842,[16] one day after the manuscript was received at the Ministère de l'Intérieur (according to a second
date on the titlepage) for authorization. These dates of course
indicate that the pantomime was neither submitted nor ap-
proved for production until a full month and a half after
the appearance of "Shakspeare aux Funambules." The manuscript itself is short and sketchy, but a comparison of it
with Gautier's detailed plot reveals clear borrowings of phrase
from the latter; where Gautier has bridged events with un-
playable narrative or introduced scenes requiring dialogue,
the scenarist—probably Cot d'Ordan himself[17]—has sub-

[14] *Pierrot, valet de la Mort* ([Paris]: n.p., [1846]), p. 6. I refer to this
passage in my *Pierrot: A Critical History of a Mask* (Princeton: Princeton
University Press, 1978), p. 108, but—relying upon the scholarship of
Péricaud and Rémy, who both assert that "Shakspeare aux Funambules"
is an actual review of a pantomime—conclude wrongly that Champfleury
has his facts confused.

[15] AN document F[18] 1087, MS 4426.

[16] AN document F[21] 984, MS 4426. Rémy quotes this report in his
Jean-Gaspard Deburau, p. 172, but he ignores both its date and the dates
on the manuscript itself.

[17] Cot d'Ordan had had earlier experience in "adapting" Gautier's work:
on August 18, 1841, his *Giselle, ou les Willis [sic], pièce en trois actes mêlée
de chants, tirée du ballet de l'Opéra* was received by the censor for authorization before production at the Funambules. Interested parties may consult the manuscript: AN document F[18] 1086, MS 3797.

stituted silent, stageworthy action. The playlet is still something of a hybrid: both its slapstick and its subtitle ("comic pantomime in 5 scenes")[18] suggest the *pantomime-réaliste* of Baptiste; and yet the death of its Pierrot (an unprecedented event on Deburau's stage) makes it utterly untypical of its class. It was probably the clumsiness of the experiment—the crude splicing of Pierrot's death onto a "plot" larded with Deburau's *cascades*—that was responsible for its short, seven-day run. Despite Champfleury's final observation, the pantomime was not a success.

But Gautier's essay was, and is, a success in every respect. Witty, elegant, affectionate, provocative, it confers a coherence upon the pantomime and a significance upon Pierrot that neither had previously known. Although the protagonist is clearly the *méchant* of Deburau's inspiration, with his naïveté, his cowardice, his gluttony, his malice, he is also a "symbol of the human heart still white and innocent, tormented by infinite aspirations towards the higher spheres."[19] The fortunes through which he struggles are eclectic in the extreme, with their echoes of Molière's Don Juan, of the business of popular *parades*, of the Romantics' *fatalisme*, and of what they perceived to be the tragicomedy of Shakespeare. But they are fortunes with a beginning, a middle, and an end—as well as, more importantly, an absolute allegorical integrity. The sword that catches Pierrot's covetous eye is "a striking emblem of the power of opportunity on already tempted and vacillating minds"; the ghost of the peddler relentlessly pursuing his murderer "symbol-

---

[18] And not, as Péricaud renders it, "pantomime in 4 scenes." The word "comic" indicates that its librettist regarded the piece as not very different—as, indeed, it is not—from the other pantomimic farces of Baptiste, with their random cruelty and mayhem. This fact helps answer one of Rémy's chief arguments against Deburau's having appeared in the piece: that his accidental murder of a man in 1836 would have prohibited the managers of the theater from asking him "to incarnate a character of an all-too personal truth" (*Jean-Gaspard Deburau*, p. 174). In the *pantomimes comiques*, murder was ubiquitous. Towards the end of *La Sorcière, ou le Démon protecteur*, for example, produced only two years after Deburau's real-life acquittal, Pierrot kills a baby sleeping in its crib, hides the body under a stack of linen, and slips a doll in its place (AN document F[18] 1084, MS 1957, sc. 5 [unpaginated]).

[19] "Shakspeare aux Funambules," p. 65.

43

izes remorse in the most dramatic and terrible fashion"; the party-ice that turns to fireworks in Pierrot's guilty hands "shows that, for the criminal, everything turns to poison, and that what refreshes the mouth of the innocent burns the palate of the wicked."[20] The exegesis unfolds with Gautier's usual seamless irony, fusing the mocking with the serious, the learned with the folk, the popular with the literary; and as it unfolds, it points the direction for a completely new kind of pantomime.

The shrewd manager-proprietor of the Funambules, Charles-Louis Billion, probably cared little for Gautier's literary myth-making, but he must have suspected there was money in whatever rekindled the interest of a high-toned public in his theater. On July 9, 1846, not yet a month after Deburau's death, appeared an unsigned note in the pages of *L'Echo*, a popular review of the arts:

> Deprived of the great comedian that made its fame, the Théâtre des Funambules is addressing an appeal to other elements of prosperity. Rejecting the scenarios that are without elegance, without interest, without poetry—scenarios by which it has been too long seduced—it has just asked from a number of known writers who are at the same time distinguished poets a *pantomime-féerie*, destined, it is said, to bring about a revolution.[21]

It is clear that, by his request for a *pantomime-féerie*, Billion was appealing to the widest possible interests—both to the *littérateurs* who had flocked to Nodier's *Songe d'or* and to the *titis* who had recognized the traditional *trucs* through its fantasy. But the concatenation of events I have been describing was, by 1846, rather hostile to pantomime in "the old mold." Gautier's "Shakspeare aux Funambules"— extremely influential among those "distinguished poets" alluded to above—prefigured a genre that was at least dramatically coherent in its action, at best "philosophical" in its content. It was a genre in which the gothic grotesquer-

---

[20] Ibid., pp. 65, 66.
[21] "Revue Dramatique," *L'Echo: Littérature, Beaux-Arts, Théâtres, Musique et Modes*, July 9, 1846.

ies of Baptiste's naïve scenarios were to acquire symbolic
profundity, and whose Pierrot was to be as pathetically sensitive as *méchant*. Such a genre needed only an actor of
Legrand's comedic talents to be realized successfully in the
theater. But it also needed an author. This it found in a
young man much obsessed with Romantic visions of Death,
with the fantastic art of Swift, Hoffmann, and *Ma Mère
l'Oie*, with the popular *imagerie d'Epinal* as well as the grotesque side of the emergent *réalisme*. The young man's name
was Jules-François-Félix Husson, known to literary history,
in which he enjoys (and merits) the reputation as one of
the most prosaic of Realists, as Fleury or Champfleury.

Early introduced to the stage by his father, who, "in his
capacity as secretary of the mayoralty, reveled in his great
and small *entrées* to the theater," Champfleury was fascinated by masks and costumes, felt transported by Molière
"into an ideal world of blows of the slapstick, as marvelous
for me as paradise."[22] The actors touring through his native
Laon seem to have left him with the strongest impressions,
especially the troupe that performed, "with all the pomp
that the masterpiece demanded," the horrific melo by Merle
and Beraud, *Le Monstre et le magicien* (1826), and the English company that, several years later, produced ("What magic
and what enchantment!") a number of pantomimes "in 'the
English style.' "[23] Even before he had entered the Funambules, the obsessions of his youth had been fixed; but it
was only in 1843, after he had come to Paris to see the
hero of Janin's *Deburau* perform, that he could formulate
those obsessions in specific terms. "Two things will have
amused me greatly in the life of my youth," he mused with
epitaphic reflexiveness in "Mon Testament": "the mutes of
undertakers and the mimes of the Funambules."[24] In Paris,
entering a circle of artists that included Henri Mürger, Pétrus Borel, and Baudelaire, Champfleury became a connoisseur of the macabre. "The motives peculiar to the ly-
canthrope, memories of the Morgue and of funeral

[22] Champfleury, *Souvenirs et portraits*, pp. 5, 31.

[23] Champfleury, "Charles Nodier: Auteur dramatique," *Le Livre: Revue
du Monde Littéraire*, 3rd Year (June 10, 1882), p. 173; Champfleury, *Souvenirs et portraits*, p. 63.

[24] *Souvenirs des Funambules*, p. 316.

ceremonials," he wrote in later years, "rubbed off momentarily on several young men, Baudelaire and myself first of all."[25] He devised his first pantomime in 1846 and sent it, apparently, to Gautier. Entitled *Arlequin dévoré par les papillons*, it doubtless condemned Arlequin to as unhappy a fate as Pierrot had suffered in *Marrrchand d'habits!*[26] But it was only with the writing of *Pierrot, valet de la Mort* several weeks later that Champfleury considered his work worthy of the Funambules—and of the program implicit in Gautier's *feuilleton*. For *Pierrot, valet de la Mort* was born of a "philosophical" idea, its plot an illustration of it. In several lines from a pamphlet by Wallon "of an illuminism worthy of Swedenborg," Champfleury discovered the dramatic spine of his fable: "The SPIRITUAL man will rid himself definitively of death: he will kill, will crush death in order to arrive at his superior destiny; then he will be delivered from the material and relative conditions that arrest his progress."[27]

Unlikely inspiration for an *arlequinade*, these imperatives are at best only travestied by the plot: Pierrot, mortally wounded by Arlequin during a contest for Colombine's hand, is revived by Death on condition that he send Arlequin and Polichinelle *en enfer*; he at first tries to honor his contract, but, stricken by conscience, he finally returns to virtue, and blesses the union of the lovers. Fired by the praise of Gérard de Nerval ("modern philosophy has formulated nothing clearer than this pantomime in seven scenes"),[28] Champfleury submitted a second pantomime to

[25] "Croquis Romantiques: Pétrus Borel," *Le Livre: Revue du Monde Littéraire*, 3rd Year (April 10, 1882), pp. 106-107. At the head of this article is a little sketch of Borel *en Pierrot*.

[26] No copies of the pantomime exist, but Champfleury mentions its title in his pamphlet *Pierrot, valet de la Mort*, and Gautier refers to it during the course of his review of *La Gageure* at the Funambules: "A grand *féerie* entitled *Arlequin dévoré par les papillons* has just been received [. . .]. The author is a young man of infinite wit who has prepared himself, by two years of serious study and preliminary sketches, for this important creation" (*P*, 8.31.46).

[27] *Pierrot, valet de la Mort*, p. 4.

[28] Review in *La Presse*: September 28, 1846. Although this review is signed by Gautier, Champfleury explains that the latter "was leaving for Spain on the day after the production of *Pierrot, valet de la Mort*, and he entrusted the review to Gérard de Nerval [. . .]" (*Souvenirs des Funambules*, p. 13).

the Funambules, which was produced in January of 1847, several months after *Pierrot, valet de la Mort*. Evidently, in his delight in finding a theater for his lucubrations, he wrote *Pierrot pendu* in little over a week—and his haste betrayed the obvious source of his inspiration for both pantomimic *essais*. For *Pierrot pendu* is merely *Marrrchand d'habits!* in which a maleficent Pierrot is hounded to hell by the voice of a man he has fleeced. Neither piece is wholly successful, especially in their original forms. The manuscripts that survive, bearing Billion's cuts and changes, reveal a theatrically naïve imagination. In *Pierrot, valet de la Mort*, Pierrot was to have descended to the "study" of Death in a coffin, accompanied by the coffins of two other corpses. Billion, protesting (with good reason) that the censor would disallow the scene, and that "it would be impossible for the machinist to lower three coffins with actors inside them [. . .] for fear of accident," substituted a single large box for the defuncts, accessible by a trap in the floor.[29] For the playwright's more self-indulgent *boutades*—human skulls, for example, for Death's stemware—he made discreet alterations, leaving the shape of the play intact. Even so, Nerval complained in his review in *La Presse* that "the last scenes bear the stamp of a certain haste":

> The peripeteiae are sudden; the interest is mismanaged. Pierrot hardly troubles about meeting the conditions imposed upon him by Death. His return to virtue is too abrupt and is completely unmotivated. (*P*, 9.28.46)

[29] Champfleury, *Souvenirs des Funambules*, p. 57. According to Champfleury's reconstruction of events leading to the production, it was only after Billion's objections had sent him to the censor's office, armed with a letter from Gautier in order to defend his *mise en scène*, that he began to encounter official opposition: originally, he implies, no changes in the manuscript of his play had been required by the censor, but his inquiry began to arouse suspicions. As the report on the manuscript indeed indicates, no changes had been demanded by the examiner—but this was so because Billion had already made several changes before the pantomime had been registered. In the first of the two censor's copies of *Pierrot, valet de la Mort* (AN document F[18] 1089, MS 7441), Billion's alterations appear directly on the manuscript in the form of black-inked cancellations; the second manuscript (AN document F[18] 1089, MS 7444) is a fair copy, incorporating the changes of the first.

The scenario of *Pierrot pendu* was less prone to such weaknesses, drawing structural strength from Gautier's "review." But the effect (as conceived originally by Champfleury) of having the victim appear after every scene, murmuring spectrally, "Pierrot, you shall hang!" would have been tedious in the extreme. Billion's cuts, eliminating his every other appearance, seem here, as elsewhere, judicious.

Champfleury's real difficulty as an *auteur funambulesque* is that he was drawn in two directions at once. On the one hand, he had a profoundly instinctive response to the savage and fantastic power of the old *pantomime-féerie*. In his *Souvenirs des Funambules* he admitted that "certain works of this school are remarkable," adding: "Often I began to doubt my theories, for I was jealous of the *Songe d'or*, and I would have gladly given all my realism in order to attain that strange ideal, which one so willingly attributes to Charles Nodier."[30] Almost all of his own pantomimes, despite their so-called "philosophy" and "realism," evince a naïve delight in the *cascade*, in the kicks, slaps, and blows that distinguish the *pantomime classique*. In several passages, he even attains to that subtle ferocity that Deburau could manage so well. Early in *Pierrot marquis* (1847), Pierrot assists a physician in cutting open Polichinelle's humps, where the hunchback has hoarded his treasure; then, not content with the spoils, Pierrot persuades the doctor to chop off the patient's limbs: "Despite Polichinelle's cries, they proceed with their dissection; [but] the first [leg] conceals no money—no more than the second."[31] At the opening of *Madame Polichinelle, ou les Souffrances d'une âme en peine* (1848), Polichinelle, exasperated by his incontinent child, "seizes a big cork that from now on will prevent the baby from doing his dirty business."[32] But neither Polichinelle's anal *bouchage* nor Pierrot's mercenary cruelty survived in either play: both passages were struck from the manuscripts. It was obviously not their inherent *grossièreté* that offended—much more vulgar business got through the scripts of the *féeries*[33]—but

---

[30] Pages 86, 87.

[31] AN document F[18] 1090, unnumbered MS, sc. 3 (unpaginated).

[32] AN document F[18] 1090, MS 8279, sc. 1 (unpaginated).

[33] At one point in Charles Charton's *L'Etoile de Pierrot*, a traditional *pantomime-féerie* produced at the Funambules in 1854, "the house at the

rather, and quite simply, their dramatic inappropriateness. In pantomimes where characters approach the "realistic" or "lifelike," whose behavior, in other words, seems motivated by more or less mature operations of reason and feeling— or at least by a quasi-satiric travesty of those operations— such business is more painful than comic. In short, the characters' motives here have overreached the infantile: greed is what Pierrot feels, not castrating power; annoyance drives Polichinelle to bung up his baby, not a furtive *nostalgie de la boue*. Because this is so, we feel (like the emending parties) that the scenes have crossed the line from the exhilarating to the offensive, and—putting aside for the moment our twentieth-century imperturbability—we are apt to be more shocked than amused.

That Champfleury was intent on establishing such motives is apparent from his criticisms of the *pantomime-féerie*, with its "disconnectedness," its "lack of logic," its "senseless mélange of traditional and mythological costumes."[34] Despite his respect for the regressive truth of its violence, Champfleury was led, as an aspiring *littérateur*, to "reform" the pantomime of its faults. Not a little professional vanity was responsible for this zeal. When he was first asked by Billion for a pantomimic *pièce à trucs*—for he was among those "poets" expected to "revolutionize" the genre—he naïvely admitted complete ignorance of the expression:

> At that point the director held up a mysterious box that contained movable little cardboard cut-outs, worked with strings.
> I realized with terror that these very complicated

---

rear [of the stage] changes into a chamberpot, forming a vessel with an enormous syringe for a mast and diapers for sails. —The garden is transformed into a rough sea on which the pursuers [of Arlequin and Colombine] are tossed about, to the laughter of the characters on stage. But Cassandre falls into the water and is caught and held by his legs" (AN document F^{18} 1091, unnumbered MS, sc. 9 [unpaginated]). The printed version of the piece reveals the identity of that "rough sea" (the censor's examiner would have guessed it immediately) when the pursuers' plight is rendered in a single poetical phrase: "they navigate over the Yellow Sea" (Charles [Charton], *L'Etoile de Pierrot, grande pantomime-arlequinade en douze tableaux, précédée de Le Ciel, le feu et l'eau, prologue en deux tableaux* [Paris: Dechaume, n.d.], p. 7).

[34] Champfleury, *Souvenirs des Funambules*, p. 87.

mechanisms required a convict's dexterity. I am not good at all with my hands; how could I ever put together any of those *trucs* representing rifles that change into ladders, wardrobes that change into chairs, all made out of cardboard?

I went home in gloomy spirits, having found the profession of the funambulesque author very troublesome, demanding as it did profound knowledge of the art of working in cardboard. [. . .] All the way back I kept saying to myself: "It is not possible for an author to take up such a profession. [. . .]"

From that point on, I vowed a ferocious hatred against the *truc*, and I adopted a system of employing the simplest combinations, of driving the supernatural characters from my plays, of adhering to reality, and of trying to realize for the mimic art what Diderot had done for the comedy—that is to say, bourgeoise pantomime.[35]

Although this program was not to be realized fully until the *Pantomime de l'avocat* (1865), it is announced aggressively, albeit obliquely, towards the end of *Pierrot pendu*. There Pierrot is being examined by a tribunal, who order him to empty his pockets. Among the objects that come spilling out on the table is Arlequin's once magically potent bat: "The president orders them to pass him the bat: he turns it over and over—and returns it contemptuously to Arlequin, as an object without value."[36] The *révolution réaliste* has been launched.

For Billion it must have seemed a mixed blessing. Champfleury had his fairly numerous detractors, especially among the unsophisticated *peuple*. When, in *Madame Polichinelle*, he went so far as to dispense with Polichinelle's costume, dressing him "symbolically" in black, the effect was so ill-received that the author fled the theater immediately after the performance, fearing he would be hissed. "There is no sense in mincing words," he confessed to Gautier soon after this failure: "the Funambules hardly believes in my work; each of my pieces brings about a notable change

[35] Ibid., p. 6.
[36] AN document F[18] 1089, MS 7585, p. 12.

in the receipts [. . .]."³⁷ The actors were for the most part impatient of his innovations, and the *régisseur* Charton, jealous of his own title as *auteur*, held his work "in supreme contempt."³⁸ But Billion's productions of Champfleury's experiments did have one much-desired effect: it drew back to the stalls those artists and writers who had once made the reputation of the theater. At the première of *Pierrot, valet de la Mort*, "it was a pit of kings," as one journalist observed: "Dispersed among the boxes, the galleries, the orchestra, were Théophile Gautier, Gérard de Nerval, Théodore de Banville, Henri Mürger, Baudelaire-Dufays, Privat d'Anglemont, Pierre Dupont, and the sculptor Préault—and Fiorentino, the only intelligent man among all the music critics of Paris." And the first performance of *Pierrot pendu* was also attended by "all the notables of art and criticism."³⁹

By June 14 of 1847, almost a year to the day of Deburau's death, Gautier could write in *La Presse* that

> Pierrot has become fashionable again, now that the humorist Champfleury has sprinkled his mask with one or two handfuls of that flour called wit—which is no less necessary for pantomimes in nineteen scenes than for comedies in five acts. It is now a question, among our young men of style, of who will write with the subtlest pen for this great actor [sic] who speaks not a word; for nothing succeeds in France like success.

Within this year, Champfleury's first two pieces had been quickly followed by *Pierrot récompensé*, *Pierrot pacha*, and *Pierrot marié*—all the work, not of the theater's usual *anonymes*, but of several young men anxious to catch the eye of that glittering *parterre de rois*. As Gautier's final remark

³⁷ "Lettres à Théophile Gautier sur la pantomime anglaise," *Messager des Théâtres et des Arts*, 1st Year, No. 17 (October 8, 1848). When the "letters" were reprinted in Champfleury's *Souvenirs des Funambules*, the words "the management [*la direction*]" were substituted for "the Funambules" in this passage (p. 167).

³⁸ Péricaud, *Théâtre des Funambules*, pp. 336-37, 339.

³⁹ Aug[uste] V[itu], "Pierrot valet de la Mort," *L'Echo: Littérature, Beaux-Arts, Théâtres, Musique et Modes*, September 27, 1846; Gautier, *La Presse*, January 25, 1847.

wryly implies, the motives of these aspirants were hardly as elevated as Champfleury's. Edouard Martin, the author of *Pierrot pacha*, lost no time in offering Gautier a *loge* for whenever "you are taken with the desire to come around these parts"; Jules Viard made a more direct appeal, begging the poet for a review of his *Pierrot marié*, one of those reviews "that you do so well and so lovingly."[40] Unfortunately, their ambitions were obviously greater than their feeling for the genre. Each of these pieces continues Champfleury's "reforms"—that is, carries the pantomime farther from the heady violence and dreamlike illogicality of the old *pantomime-féerie*—and, in their authors' eagerness to sprinkle Pierrot's face "with one or two handfuls of that flour called wit," each takes a more deplorable turn: toward the sentimental, the topical, and the satiric.[41]

Horebourg's *Pierrot récompensé* (March 1847) retains the basic structure of the *pantomime-arlequinade-féerie*, but it substitutes for the chase a feeble series of *lazzi* by which Arlequin answers his enemies. The most important convention of Deburau's comedy is completely overthrown: Pierrot is not the manservant of old Cassandre (who is known as Pandolfe here), but the faithful valet of Arlequin. It is he who fishes Arlequin's body from a river when the despairing bergamask attempts suicide; it is he, moreover, who frees the fairy from enchantment and to whom she consequently grants a wish. The wish—heretical in the extreme, at least as Deburau conceived the character—is that Arlequin and Colombine be united. ("Imbecile!" cries Gilles, Pandolfe's valet, "ask for some money or good wine!")[42]

---

[40] Letter from Martin to Gautier, dated April 23, 1847, and undated letter from Viard to Gautier: MSS C497, f. 93, and C500, f. 252, Bibliothèque Spoelberch de Lovenjoul.

[41] Deburau's pantomime was occasionally satiric, but his targets generally seem to have been broad and unspecific, as when, in the eleventh scene of *Le Boeuf enragé*, he dressed as a dandy of the Boulevard de Gand. Champfleury points up the great difference between the English and the French pantomime in this respect when, in one of his "Lettres à Théophile Gautier sur la pantomime anglaise," he describes the opening of the former as "a harsh satire that reminds one of the 'Reviews of the Year' in our French theaters" (*Messager des Théâtres et des Arts*, 1st Year, No. 17 [October 8, 1848]).

[42] AN document F[18] 1090, MS 7667, sc. 1 (unpaginated). Arlequin and Pierrot are the only mute characters in the piece.

And for the rest of the action, Pierrot, *bon enfant*, works diligently towards that end. *Pierrot pacha*, produced in April, about a month and a half after *Pierrot récompensé*, seems to take up where Horebourg's piece leaves off: "Arlequin and Colombine come to congratulate Pierrot on his good health. Peace now reigning among them, Pierrot obtains permission to give Colombine a kiss." Pierrot then goes for a walk, during which, "all his past misadventures coming back to mind, he conceives the project of committing suicide." But a fairy appears opportunely; she grants him a wish (*"la puissance"*): she decides she will make him a pasha. When he returns to prepare for his departure, there is a *brouillerie* with his free-thinking bootmaker: the man has been reading *Le Charivari*. (His tailor's tastes are much better: *L'Epoque* peeks out of his pocket.) There then follows a series of adventures, in and around an exotic island seraglio, all concluded by the fairy's admonition to Pierrot: "[. . .] renounce your ideas of grandeur and give a little thought, in memory, to your father Pierrot":

> ["]Amuse us as he once did, and whenever you feel sad, melancholy gnawing at your heart, look upon the picture that I am about to show you.["]
> [The scene changes, revealing Arlequin and Colombine.]
> Colombine goes to rejoin Arlequin.

In the final *tableau*, the theater "presents the apotheosis of all the roles of Pierrot."[43]

A Pierrot who is loyal to Arlequin, who is conversant with *Le Charivari* and *L'Epoque*, and whose guardian enjoins him to remember *père* Deburau—such could be the creation only of writers both self-conscious as wits and indifferent to the conventions of his roles. Champfleury provided the provocation for their audacities; and yet other factors were at work loosening up those conventions, establishing precedents for the transgression of Baptiste's traditions that would have rather far-reaching effects. In a review of *Une Vie de Polichinelle* (1847) by Charton and Ambroise, which was produced several days before *Pierrot*

---

[43] AN document F¹⁸ 1090, MS 7778, sc. 1, 2, 8, 9 (unpaginated).

récompensé, Gautier complained that "the authors [. . .] do not believe in the pantomime, a deplorable skepticism breaks through in several parts of their work; they are turning to the parody of the genre" (*P*, 3.1.47). The self-mocking style of the published scenario corroborates the poet's remarks: "The rheumy father, the intended bridegroom, and his respectable *maman* [we read in the opening scene] feel the need to eat—just as they ought to do every day in life and in the *pantomimes-arlequinades*."[44] And this self-consciousness carries over into the delineation of the characters themselves. Even before Deburau's death, Pierrot had been "poeticized" by an anonymous scenarist inspired by a tale of the Comtesse d'Aulnoy. At the end of his piece, *Les Trois Quenouilles* (1844), Arlequin, Léandre, and Pierrot are all trapped in the bowels of the earth; the fairy Ondinet then appears to release them and to deliver the following speech:

> "I have come to set you free [*vous arracher de ces lieux*] in order to unite you soon with those you love; however, I must tell you that my power is now useless on earth: it is on the moon that your happiness must be realized. Poor Pierrot [. . .] it is to you whom will be entrusted the leadership of the celestial voyage that we are about to take."[45]

To associate the Pierrot of pantomime with the moon-dreamer of *Au clair de la lune* was simply to misread Baptiste's unsentimental art. But such a "poetic" association

---

[44] Charles [Charton] and Ambroise, *Une Vie de Polichinelle, pantomime-arlequinade-féerie en onze tableaux* ([Paris]: Imprimerie de Bureau, n.d.), p. 2. Such self-mockery begins to be apparent in the pantomimes of the last years of Deburau's career, especially in scenarios by those authors who aspired for more than humble anonymity. In Varez's *La Naissance de Pierrot* (1843), the *jeune premier* of the prologue invites his Lisa to elope with him: "I have a friend, a good friend who has a friend who is friends with one of the friends of the steward of [the] great lord [Algésiras], and this friend has promised to take me under his wing and obtain for me a good position in the Duke's household. You can, of course, see that it's a sure thing [. . .]." Lisa's response has nothing of the Colombine about it: "Oh, what happiness: we'll be rich!" (AN document F[18] 1087, MS 4844, sc. 1 [unpaginated]).

[45] AN document F[18] 1088, MS 5850, sc. 7 (unpaginated). Péricaud attributes this piece to Charles Charton (*Théâtre des Funambules*, p. 400), but it bears little resemblance to Charton's other *féeries*.

was inevitable with the advent of Paul Legrand. It was made all the more inevitable by the introduction of a new character to the pantomime, a type whose familiar cruelty on the puppet-stage reduced Pierrot to the status of victim—by the introduction of Polichinelle. In 1842 Michel-Louis Vautier had been engaged at the Funambules as an Arlequin, dancer, and *amoureux*; but with his début as Polichinelle in *Pierrot et Polichinel [sic], ou les Quatre Rivaux* (1846), produced only weeks after Deburau's death, he instantly discovered his role. He soon became "so incarnated in Polichinelle's character," as Louis Péricaud observes, "that Polichinelle [was . . .] in all of the pieces, and there [was] no hesitation in coupling his name on the *affiches* with that of Pierrot."[46]

All of these factors clearly influenced the conception of Jules Viard's *Pierrot marié* (June 1847). That Viard's intention was in part to burlesque the genre is suggested by the full title of his piece: *Pierrot marié et Polichinelle célibataire, épopée-pantomime féerique et philosophique à très grand spectacle, en trois parties, parsemée de coups de pied, ornée de dix-neuf changements à vue, de danses nationales, de combats au sabre, à la hache et même au bâton.* A bridegroom more naïve than *méchant*—and more generously devoted than naïve—Pierrot suffers pangs of betrayal and cuckoldry in an intrigue that seems only nominally *féerique*. At the wedding, his coquettish Pierrette is seduced by the gay Polichinelle ("a little bit tipsy, his mustache curled up, his sword at his side, his pince-nez at his neck, his cigarette in his mouth, his eye, his conquering eye, agleam");[47] the children with whom she blesses her husband are, thereafter, humped on one side and *tout blancs* on the other. But even after she takes up with the hunchback, leaving a trail of infant half-breeds behind her, Pierrot remains doggedly loyal; and after finally venting his fury on Polichinelle, whom he flings beneath the paddles of a mill, he pardons, uxorious, her fall. A happy accident sorts out the breeds of their brood: in the shock of reunion, both drop all the babies, who split

[46] *Théâtre des Funambules*, p. 312.
[47] Jules Viard, *Pierrot marié et Polichinelle célibataire* (Paris: Gallet, 1847), p. 8.

down their unnatural seams; it is then an easy matter to match like halves to like, and to cement them with a little spit. At the curtain, the happy husband and wife are discovered cozily at an English tea, a uniform of the Garde Nationale on a hook near the table,[48] twenty little Pierrots round the board. An extremely clever piece, *Pierrot marié* later enjoyed enormous success, becoming a classic of Legrand's permanent repertoire. But as a pantomime *féerique* it is hardly "classical" in the funambulesque sense of the word. A fairy indeed makes two appearances—first, to exhort Polichinelle to restore Pierrette to Pierrot, and finally to unveil the bourgeois apotheosis—but these seem mere obligatory gestures: they have no effect on the plot. The play is actually a kind of fantastic mute comedy, its Pierrot fully domesticated to *la vie sentimentale.*

As Horebourg, Martin, and Viard were thus subverting the conventions, Champfleury was creating new ones to replace them. So the *réalisme* announced indirectly in *Pierrot pendu* was brought to the fore in *Pierrot marquis*, produced in October of 1847. Gautier declared that its première dated "a new era in the poetics of the Funambules":

Pierrot is in the service of a kind of Cassandre-miller [i.e., Polichinelle], the arms of whose mill turn limply throughout the action of the first act. In this extremely simple fact the observer detects the advent of rationalism. The ancient faith has disappeared, and M. Champfleury has assumed the role of Luther of the pantomime. [. . .]

[. . .] M. Champfleury gives to the allegorical whiteness of Pierrot a wholly physical cause: it is the flour from the mill that is sprinkled over the face of this pale and melancholy personage. One could not find a more plausible means of giving probability to this white phantom [. . .]: it is clear that the era of the Catholic art is closing for the pantomime and the era of the Protestant art beginning. Authority and tradition no longer exist; the doctrine of independent inquiry is about to bear its fruits. Goodbye to the naïve formu-

---

[48] This detail was cut before production (as was "*et Polichinelle célibataire*" from the title), the censor objecting to its implicit satire.

las, the byzantine barbarities, the impossible complex-
ions: analysis is opening its scalpel and is going to
begin its dissections. (*P*, 10.18.47)

Although Champfleury's intention was apparently not so
deliberate as these playful remarks suggest,[49] *Pierrot marquis*, like *Pierrot marié*, gestured only perfunctorily toward
the *féerie*; Champfleury's real interest was in sustaining a
plot based upon the changes in his titular type. A nephew
of the ailing Polichinelle, Pierrot steals into his uncle's
sickbed; he disguises his voice with a metallic quaver and
dictates a will favorable to himself alone. After his inherit-
ance, he reveals a character with new accesses of extravagance, of arrogance, of insolence, of hauteur; and with its
disappearance—in the burgling fists of Polichinelle *fils*—he
discovers new depths of despair. The fairy, apparently an
emissary of Jules Janin, defends him from utter madness:

> Pierrot, be happy! Wealth does not bring happiness!
> You are of the People: remain, Pierrot, of the People!
> The People are poor, but content with their humble
> lot. Throw these gentleman's clothes into the river;
> your simple and modest vestment is worth more than
> all these bespangled fripperies. Look to the fields, Pier-
> rot, and remember that one does not sleep peacefully
> beneath the gilded ceilings of palaces.

Straightway he "recovers his customary garb—and his joy."[50]
   As godfather of all these pantomimic innovations, Gautier could have been expected to receive them warmly. But
he was even more ambivalent than Champfleury about the
visitation of "rationalism" upon the Funambules. On the
one hand, he could deplore, as an *homme de lettres* himself,
"the lack of an aesthetic and philosophy" in *Une Vie de*

[49] When Champfleury revised the pantomime for the Folies-Nouvelles
as *Pierrot millionnaire* (1857), he "unprobabilized" Pierrot's pallor by making
him the apprentice of a blacksmith instead of a miller. In his *Souvenirs des
Funambules*, he expressed his surprise that Gautier had, at such an early
date, found traces of *réalisme* in the piece at all: "Up to that time the word
had been employed but very infrequently: no one was in the habit of using
it. Realism was not to appear until [the period] between 1848 and 1850
[. . .]" (p. 97).
[50] AN document F¹⁸ 1090, unnumbered MS, sc. 9 (unpaginated).

Polichinelle, citing as faults what in fact were the strengths of the old *pantomime classique*:

> Everything is sacrificed here to a multiplicity of events, to an aimless turbulence that dazzles and tires. [. . .] The characters seem to have quicksilver in their veins; they cannot stand still; they run and stamp around as if they were walking over a floor of red-hot iron. (*P*, 3.1.47)

In his review of *Pierrot marié*, his sympathies seem to hang in the balance, as he weighs the old against the new: "*Pierrot marié* contains a little less fairytale fantasy than do the pantomimes in which the white silhouette of our friend customarily flutters its long sleeves through a vagrant plot that seems to take place in the country of dreams; but, to make up for it, the comic and philosophical conception predominates" (*P*, 6.14.47). But when he takes up his pen to describe *Pierrot marquis*, he writes as a nostalgic *naïf*, obviously regretting the loss, now too clearly irrecoverable, of the old innocence of the genre:

> The absence of supernatural characters robs *Pierrot marquis* of that solemn and mysterious aspect, that "autosacramental" cast, from which results for the pantomimes of the Funambules a profound and inexplicable attraction, carrying the soul of the spectator, all unaware, back to the theurgic fictions of the first ages of the world [. . .].

"We prefer," he writes of the Pierrot-miller of Act I, "[his] mysterious and causeless pallor to this pallor thus [realistically] explained." And although he concedes that in Champfleury's piece "the study of the human heart, profound observation of character, and comic force take the place of the absent element of the marvelous," there seems a missing dimension: "The philosopher and the moralist have replaced the poet" (*P*, 10.18.47). There has passed away a glory from *le monde pierrotique*.

In early November of 1847, Deburau's son, Jean-Charles, made his début as Pierrot on the stage of the Funambules. Young (he was not yet nineteen), poised, and athletic, he seemed the very incarnation of his father's agility and *adresse*. When, somewhat later, his critics undertook to compare him with Legrand, he was consistently—and exclusively—praised for his technical finesse. Gautier seems to have expressed the general consensus when, in a review of *Le Duel de Pierrot* (1858), he noted that "the son recalls the father [. . .], but without servile imitation":

> The mask is the same in appearance, as it should be for a traditional character; yet a wholly original wit sends the grimaces wrinkling across it. Deburau is young, thin, elegant; his features are delicate and distinct, his eyes expressive—and his little mouth, which he knows how to distend to swallow the bigger morsels, has a kind of jeering disdain, an English "sneer," that is very piquant. A clown's agility animates this slender body, with its delicate limbs, on which the white blouse with its big buttons floats freely; he moves with ease, suppleness, and grace, marking without stressing the rhythm of the music [. . .]. (*MU*, 8.30.58)

His début came in *Les Trois Planètes, ou la Vie d'une rose, grande pantomime arlequinade féerie, dialoguée dans le genre anglais, en trois parties et douze changemens à vue, mêlée de danses, transformations et travestissemens.*[51] As its subtitle promises, it was a pantomime in the classical "old mold," with warring divinities, magic talismans, and a chase bristling with familiar riot. But if it seemed to announce a

---

[51] The published scenario of the pantomime (Paris: Gallet, 1847) bears on its titlepage the note that the piece was "presented for the first time [. . .] on the stage of the Funambules 6 October 1847," a date duly recorded by Péricaud. A letter from Billion, however, dated November 4, 1847, informs Gautier that the first presentation, "which should have taken place this evening, has been put off until tomorrow" (MS C491, f. 530, Bibliothèque Spoelberch de Lovenjoul). The scenarios were usually printed in advance of a première so that they could be sold to the public at the theater: the unusually long delay between the date announced on the pamphlet and that specified by Billion was probably owing to Deburau's having been called in as a last-minute replacement for Legrand, who had left suddenly for an engagement at the Adelphi in London. Before this much-touted première, Deburau had appeared as a pierrot in minor roles—as, for example, one of the white warriors assembled by Viard's titular hero to combat the troops of Polichinelle (Péricaud, *Théâtre des Funambules*, p. 313).

return to the days before Legrand, it aroused false expectations in its audience. The son had the grace and elegance and the obvious pantomimic skill, but he lacked the rough genius of his father. The merely respectful tributes of the critics of his art, the derivative complexion of his later repertoire, his rather vagabond career from stage to stage—all suggest no more than remarkable but unmemorable talent.[52] And without Baptiste's charismatic power, the *pantomime classique* could enjoy no renaissance.

Now, in fact, that the Funambules suffered an *embarras de mimique*, it seemed to lack all definition and direction. The "experiments" indeed continued, but in a rather haphazard way: the *statuaire* Père Jean wrote *Les Pérégrinations de Pierrot et Polichinelle*—"an essentially vagrant [. . .] tale," as Gautier described it (*P*, 1.3.48)—for Deburau in January of 1848; Nadar cast him, several months later, in *Pierrot Ministre*, in which Louis Philippe (as Robert Macaire) and Bertrand Guizot (as Pierrot) are expelled by Arlequin *le peuple*; late in this same year, Champfleury followed his ill-fated *Madame Polichinelle* with the more successful *Reine des Carottes*, a fantasy written with Albert Monnier, in which Pierrot-Deburau's carrot patch revolts against his vegetable tastes. Finally, the prolific Auguste Jouhaud (he wrote over eight hundred plays) tried, in two ambitious productions, to draw coherence out of all of this welter. In *Les Deux Pierrots* (1849), he put both Deburau and Legrand on the stage, giving the first a mask that was "*amusant*," the second one that was "*sympathique*."[53] And in *Les Trois Pierrots*

---

[52] In an article in *Le Figaro*, William Busnach notes that Legrand "is, as a mime, inferior to Deburau [sic] *fils*; but he shows more finesse in the play of his facial features" (2nd Year, No. 55 [April 1, 1855]). Gautier clarifies the comparison in terms not very favorable to Deburau when, in a review of *Les Deux Pierrots* at the Funambules, he writes: "Paul's art is more consummate, more extensive, more varied. Deburau has the sharper mask, the cleaner technique, the livelier leg" (*P*, 12.10.49). The son seems to have been more of an imitator than an innovator: as late as 1865, half of his repertoire at the Fantaisies-Parisiennes consisted of modified pieces from his father's repertory. On the many false starts in his career, see below, p. 63.

[53] A remark in Jouhaud's *Mes Petits Mémoires* (Paris: Tresse et Stock, 1888), p. 27, reveals this intention, hardly discernible in the published script of the piece ([Paris]: Dechaume, n.d.).

(1850), he conceived a pantomimic *Gesamtkunstwerk*: "It is a complete little play," he wrote as "*l'auteur*" in his preface, "with its situations, its peripeteiae; it has a coherent, well-developed plot . . . it is at one and the same time a mimed drama and a mimed vaudeville, forming a whole in which the interest dominates while gaiety is never excluded."[54] As for his three Pierrots—Deburau, Legrand, and Alexandre Guyon[55]—he took care that they "in no way resemble one another . . . the clever Pierrot [Deburau] has a completely different physiognomy from the naïve Pierrot [Guyon], and the loyal Pierrot [Legrand] is utterly unlike the two others"; his characters are "delineated in pantomime as if they had been sketched with the aid of the word: striking and distinct personalities!"[56] *Avec le secours de la parole*: the phrase expresses a melancholy ambition—and suggests to what extent the future belonged to Legrand.

It unfortunately did not belong to the Funambules. As early as 1847, Gautier had complained of the vaudeville's encroachment on its repertoire, and of the consequent effect on its public:

> These vaudevilles often degenerate into *opéras-comiques*, a sad state of affairs. The People, whose taste has, in the long run, been corrupted, regard the pantomime as a frivolous diversion, expressing their opinion of the home of Arlequin and Colombine by this somewhat unacademic phrase: "All that's just a lot of foolishness."

With no intuition that he would be castigating the pantomime very shortly for its "aimless turbulence," he continued:

> The crowd has lost the meaning of these lofty symbols, of these profound mysteries, which turn the poet and the philosopher into dreamers. Its mind is no longer

[54] I quote the censor's manuscript (AN document F^{18} 1091, unnumbered MS, p. 5), which is more detailed than the published pamphlet ([Paris]: Dechaume, n.d.).

[55] For the career of this mime, see Paul Hugounet, *Mimes et Pierrots: Notes et documents inédits pour servir à l'histoire de la pantomime* (Paris: Fischbacher, 1889), pp. 139-61.

[56] AN document F^{18} 1091, unnumbered MS, p. 5.

subtle enough to follow and comprehend this waking dream, this journey through things and events, this perpetual agitation, this aimless turbulence that paints life in such faithful hues. (*P*, 1.25.47)

And yet, by 1850, interest in the theater was waning, too, among the literati. Gautier's last review of a pantomime there was of Jouhaud's *Les Deux Pierrots*; in May of that year, 1849, *La Cruche cassée* was performed, Champfleury's feeble envoi to its stage. Then again, as in *l'époque deburalienne*, authorial hazard reigned. Henceforth, those librettists drawn from outside the theater would only parody the glories of its past—in Rimbert de Neuville's *Les Joujoux de Bric-à-Brac* (1852) or Maxime Delor's *La Mère Gigogne* (1859) or Emile Durandeau's *Les Quatre Intrigants, ou Suites funestes des amours occultes d'une princesse désordonnée, ou le Fâcheux Etat de la péninsule avant Christophe Colomb, et ses découvertes* (1860). For the most part, the staples of its repertoire in these, its declining years, were conceived by the inexhaustible Charles Charton, by Dautrevaux, its new director, by Vautier, its Polichinelle—or by the prolific Monsieur Anonyme.[57] And having neither the smack of literary

---

[57] Charton continued to contribute *pantomimes-féeries*—and occasionally a *pantomime-réaliste*—to the theater at least up to the mid-fifties: those not yet mentioned that are known to belong to his pen are *L'Oeuf rouge et l'oeuf blanc* (1846), *Pierrot le possédé, ou les Deux Génies* (1848), *Polichinelle Vampire* (1850: in collaboration with Vautier), *Pierrot maçon* (1851), *Les Mille et une Tribulations de Pierrot* (1851), *Pierrot sorcier* (1852), and—according to Péricaud—*Le Génie des eaux* (1855: a rewritten version of *Les Trois Quenouilles* [see note 45 above]). As Gautier complained in his review of *Une Vie de Polichinelle*, even the naïve Charton turned to the parody of the genre in his later pantomimes (cf. Péricaud, *Théâtre des Funambules*, p. 377). Dautrevaux, who, with Angrémy, succeeded Billion as director-proprietor of the theater in 1856, is known to have written a *Marius l'Africain* (1860) for its stage; in the closing years of the theater, Vautier satisfied its audience's taste for rather feeble ballets and *pantomimes-réalistes* with *Jocrisse, ou les Infortunes d'un coiffeur* (1857), *L'Homme des bois, ou Pierrot chez les Caffres* (1857), and *Le Retour de Pierrot* (1861). For a further discussion of its repertoire from 1850 to 1862, see Péricaud, *Théâtre des Funambules*, pp. 349-497; for pantomimes produced at the theater after its relocation from the Boulevard du Temple to the Boulevard de Strasbourg, see AN documents F[18] 1092-1093 and the two volumes of uncoded manuscripts in the Collection Rondel, Bibliothèque de l'Arsenal, entitled "Rec. fac. de pantomimes d'Hippolyte Demanet jouées aux Funambules."

revolution about them nor an interpreter of the stature of Baptiste, they all played to a diminishing house.

Legrand left the theater in 1853; Deburau, two years later. The latter was lured away by the singer Rosine Stoltz, who financed the restoration of the Délassements-Comiques on the understanding with Hiltbrunner, the director of the theater, that Charles would be immediately engaged. But neither as principal mime nor as *directeur de la scène* could Deburau turn the venture to profit, and in 1857, the year following his début, he took his repertoire to the provinces. Then, back in Paris in 1858, he opened the Spectacle Deburau at the Folies-Marigny; but this undertaking also proved a failure. He began another tour in 1859—through the provinces, through Egypt, where he performed for ten months, and finally to Bordeaux, for a two-year engagement at the Alcazar. In 1862 he interrupted these travels to sign on at the Funambules: there he appeared in *Le Rameau d'or* (1862) and *Les Mémoires de Pierrot* (1862), the last two pantomimes produced at the theater before its demolition under the picks of the Baron Haussmann. When he returned to Paris again in 1865, he found immediate employment at a newly established theater, the Fantaisies-Parisiennes. Champfleury, long eager to direct a *salle funambulesque*, was one of the co-administrators of the house, and for Deburau's début upon its stage he wrote his last pantomime, *La Pantomime de l'avocat*. But in March of 1866, not four months after the panto's première, Deburau was released from his engagement. "The less-than-tepid reception till then accorded the pantomime," as L.-Henry Lecomte remarks, "convinced the administration of the Fantaisies-Parisiennes to abandon the genre at about this time."[58]

The general fortunes of Parisian pantomime were in decline by the early 1860s. But this does not account for Deburau's failure to find, at the capital, an audience in the previous decade. The indifference of that public is probably best explained by a success in another quarter—that of Le-

---

[58] *Histoire des théâtres de Paris: Les Fantaisies-Parisiennes/L'Athénée/Le Théâtre Scribe/L'Athénée-Comique: 1865-1911* (Paris: Daragon, 1912), p. 18.

grand at the Folies-Nouvelles. When Legrand left the Funambules, he crossed to the Folies-Concertantes *en face*,
where Hervé, entrepreneur and *artiste lyrique*, produced
"*morceaux de chant de toute nature*" as well as little pantomimes.[59] In early February of 1854, the mime made his
début there in *La Fausse Douairière*, a piece he had written
with Charles Bridault. Other new pantomimes followed—
some by Legrand (either alone or in collaboration with Bridault or Charles Delaquis), some by more illustrious hands.
Then, after five months of "happy exploitation," the theater
closed for renovations. When it reopened, in October of
1854, it bore a new name, the Folies-Nouvelles, and was
administered by two new directors, Louis Huart and Marie-
Michel Altaroche. Their interests suggested a clear shape
for its repertoire. Huart, who had early been seized with
literary ambitions, was at twenty-one associated with the
Charivari; he was later the creator of the *Petites Physiologies*,
proto-Realist sketches of workers and tradesmen that had
a great vogue in the 1840s. A contributor to several other
publications—the *Cent et un Robert Macaire*, the *Muséum
Parisien*, the *Musée pour rire*, the *Galerie de la Presse*—he
made a speciality "of a type of humorous criticism," as Lecomte juridically describes it, "in which the facetious verve
precluded neither style nor good sense."[60] Altaroche, one
of the founders—and, soon after, the director—of the
Charivari, published political works and two volumes of
songs, and collaborated in the writing of plays. No unlettered Billion, each rode the lighter literary currents of the
day. And each had very sure instincts for the theater.

The renovations of the physical house itself were all con-
ducted with an eye for elegance: the decorator Renaud took
care to harmonize the crimsons, whites, and golds of the
salle; the painter Cambon put sprays of flowers at the angles of the cupolas, plump cupids overhead in the vines of
a gold trellis, and on the curtain little *amours à la* Lancret
or Watteau. The *littérateurs* who followed Legrand across

---

[59] L.-Henry Lecomte, *Histoire des théâtres de Paris: Les Folies-Nouvelles:
1854-1859, 1871-1872, 1880* (Paris: Daragon, 1909), p. 4. For much of
the detail of this paragraph, I am indebted to Lecomte's discussion on pp.
6-7.

[60] *Les Folies-Nouvelles*, p. 6.

the Boulevard were enchanted. For Gautier it was the perfect reproduction of a little theater at Naples or Venice, "this adorable little music-hall, where the orchestra is furnished with soft velvet armchairs, where the stage-boxes are barricaded behind the mystery of gilded grilles and silk screens, where convolvulus weeps through the trellis-work of the ceiling, like the bower of a garden in Cythera planted by Watteau [. . .]" (*P*, 12.19.54). For its opening, Banville composed a *pièce d'occasion*, *Les Folies-Nouvelles*, in which a Sprite, as the spirit of the theater, banished "pale Melancholy" from its boards. It was followed by *La Fine Fleur de l'Andalousie*, a "musical eccentricity" by Hervé, and by an unbridled farce by Emile Durandeau, *L'Hôtellerie de Gautier-Garguille*. Almost overnight the little theater became, in one journalist's words, "frightfully *à la mode*."[61]

Banville was soon only one of a number of notables in the arts to see their work come to life on its stage. Among those who would eventually contribute one or more pantomimes to its repertoire were the Comte de Noé, the humorist known as Cham (*Pierrot Quaker* [1855]); the sculptor of caricatural statuettes, Dantan *jeune* (*Pierrot indélicat* [1855], *Le Nouveau Robinson* [1858], *Pierrot épicier* [1859], all written in collaboration with Legrand); the cartoonist and photographer Nadar (*Pierrot boursier* [1856], written jointly with Charles Bridault); the poet Fernand Desnoyers (*Le Bras noir* [1856]); the *statuaire* J.-J. Perraud (*Gribouille* [1857]); the composer Charles Plantade (*Polichinelle notaire* [1857]); the painter Hippolyte Ballue (*Les Brigands pour rire* [1857]); and, finally, Champfleury (*Pierrot millionnaire* [1857], a revised version of his *Pierrot marquis*). And if the regular librettists of the theater were not so illustrious, their names at least suggested sure amusement—Durandeau, the self-styled "*simple poète*" (*Jean-Gilles* [1855], *Messire Barbe-Bleu* [1855]), Pol Mercier, versatile collaborator of the mime (*Biribi* [1855], *La Soeur de Pierrot* [1855], *Le Chevrier blanc* [1855], *Pierrot bureaucrate* [1856], *Les Deux Noces* [1856], *Les Carabins* [1856], *Pierrot qui rêve* [1858]), and Bridault and Delaquis, who wrote, with Legrand, a little over a dozen pantomimes between them.

[61] Taxile Delord, review of *La Soeur de Pierrot* at the Folies-Nouvelles: *Le Charivari*, April 10, 1855.

Despite the number of contributors to its repertory, the theater was quickly dominated by a single pantomimic mode: the *pantomime-réaliste*. No longer the episodic series of pranks and misfortunes enjoyed by Baptiste's malicious Pierrot, these playlets were usually slight, sometimes satiric, comedies in which Legrand oscillated between *bêtise* and tears. For Taxile Delord, reviewing *La Soeur de Pierrot* in *Le Charivari*, the revolutionary "Préface" to Hugo's *Cromwell* had at last caught up with the silent stage:

> The old pantomime no longer exists [. . .]; now we have a pantomime-Drouineau, a neo-Pierrotism, if such an expression is permissible. Pierrot is not content to rouse laughter: he also calls forth tears: the times demand it, we have become extremely sensitive, we want Pierrot to have an old mother, a sweet fiancée, a sister to rescue from the snares of a seducer. The egoistic, lazy, gluttonous, cowardly Pierrot of old offends the exquisite delicacy of the younger generations: they must have a Pierrot-Montyon. As men are never lacking to meet the new needs of a society, so Paul Legrand has appeared, and it is in him that the modern Pierrot has been incarnated. M. Pol-Mercier [sic] has just written a role for him that will mark a new date in the pantomimic literature. The great marriage of the sublime and the grotesque of which Romanticism dreamed has now been realized at the Folies-Nouvelles. [. . .] One oscillates by turns between sadness and joy; peals of laughter break from every breast; gentle tears moisten every barley-sugar stick.[62]

The range and intensity of Legrand's now mature art are suggested in a review by Gautier of *Pierrot Dandin* (1854), written by the mime and Bridault:

> [. . .] what absolutely must be seen is Paul Legrand in *Pierrot Dandin*. We doubt whether Tiercelin, who

---

[62] Ibid. Gustave Drouineau (1798-1878) was a novelist and dramatist, one of the founders of a "Neo-Christian" literature; Antoine-Jean-Baptiste-Robert Auget, Baron de Montyon (1733-1820), was a statesman, historian, scientist, and philanthropist; he founded, in 1780, a famous annual prize for the work of "greatest use to the temporal good of humanity."

played cobblers so well that it is said he could have been transferred to the shoemakers, was ever better at drawing on his hand-leather, at manipulating the knife and the awl, at squaring a sole, at nailing a bit of leather over a frame: one would truly think he has done nothing but this all his life. —But where he is superb is in the scene in which, returning home with a dress, a little shawl, and an apple turnover he has bought for his wife, he finds the conjugal nest deserted and, in place of the unfaithful spouse, a letter revealing that Madame Pierrot has left with the seducer Léandre. It must indeed be difficult to make people cry when one is wearing a little black skullcap, when one is sporting a face plastered with flour and a ridiculous costume. Well! Paul Legrand expresses his sadness in such a naïve, true, touching, and profoundly heartfelt manner that the puppet disappears, leaving only the man. In the stage-boxes, the giddiest madcaps forgot to run their tongues over their green barley-sugar sticks and smothered their sobs behind their lace handkerchiefs. (*MU*, 10.15.55)

At his new theater Legrand apparently exercised a control over the pantomime that Deburau had never known. It is suggested not only by his frequent collaboration on the writing of his playlets but also by his unitary conception of Pierrot. Baptiste was, obligingly, peasant, *niais*, or Satan: Legrand was always "Pierrot-Montyon," even when his librettists wished him to be otherwise. The censor's manuscript of *Pierrot bureaucrate* suggests that Mercier had conceived his title-character as an untypical Pierrot-*égoïste*:

> In the administrative bureau of a railroad, Pierrot is a very lazy, very inaccurate clerk.
> At the office he spends all his time in distracting his colleagues and playing a thousand little tricks on them.
> Sometimes he eats this one's lunch; sometimes he drinks that one's little carafe of wine.[63]

But Gautier's review in *Le Moniteur Universel* makes it clear that Legrand's realization of the role was quite different—and, in being different, characteristic of his art:

[63] AN document F[18] 1023, MS 3408, sc. 1 (unpaginated).

[. . .] the sight of this pantomime has filled our soul
with melancholy. What! Pierrot, from whom of old
one borrowed a pen—"to write a word"—and who
loaned it so willingly, having not the least bit of interest in it himself, has been reduced by the misery of the
times to making it run from morning to night over
musty old documents! [. . .] Pierrot! no longer daring
to wear his white blouse and his wide trousers! Pierrot
in a black suit! And what a black suit! threadbare, tight,
curled at the cuffs with age, its seams blackened with
ink: a perfect poem of respectable misery! —When he
sits down, what pitiful angles his knees make! How
pointed his elbows are! What a black gaze is in that
pale and flour-covered face! This is what has become
of the joyous Pierrot of the pantomime. Pierrot has a
profession; Pierrot is employed. He has been made to
realize that a century as serious as our own will not
suffer the idle! (*MU*, 7.28.56)

And when the piece joined the mime's permanent repertoire, part of which was published at the end of Legrand's
career, the Pierrot there, like this poem of respectable misery, had "a bored, exhausted, pitiful air."[64]
  In Gautier's final estimation, too much of the character
was lost on the stage of the Folies-Nouvelles:

[Legrand] mollifies; he calls forth tears and gives Pierrot—in order to have the pleasure of expressing them—
all kinds of good qualities that the rascal simply does
not have. With him, Pierrot has become a likable,
obliging, good-natured fellow, who administers the
obligatory kick to Cassandre (whom he would gladly
serve as Caleb) with reluctance. He still steals a little,
yes—but so honestly! By virtue of the verisimilitude
of his acting, [Legrand] turns the fantastic type into a
human character whose white face comes as a surprise.
He often even abandons the linen blouse and trousers,
retaining only the plaster mask, in order to represent
beings that are more real. (*MU*, 8.30.58)

[64] *Pantomimes de Paul Legrand*, comp. Félix and Eugène Larcher (Paris:
Librairie Théâtrale, 1887), p. 50.

Not only "in the playlets written for him has the traditional type of Pierrot not sufficiently been respected," but "there has been a certain dislike" at his theater "—wrongly, in our opinion—for the monotony of the classical pantomime, which admits, as characters, hardly any other than Cassandre, handsome Léandre, Arlequin, Colombine, Pierrot, and, with indulgence, Polichinelle [. . .]" (*MU*, 11.2-3.56). Only one *pantomime-arlequinade-féerie* was produced at the Folies-Nouvelles: entitled *Les Bamboches de Pierrot* (1857), its action was summarized in manuscript by hardly more than a dozen lines.[65] And such perfunctoriness was received as it deserved: "this pantomime," writes Lecomte, "merited—and obtained—no more than a mediocre reception."[66]

Legrand's audience was too superficially sophisticated for the marvelous puerilities of the *pantomime classique*. Among the mime's greatest successes were in fact parodies of serious drama, both on and off the Boulevard. In one of the best, *A Venise, ou Poignard, potence et mort-aux-rats* (1858), a parody by the mime and Bridault of the opera *Lucrezia Borgia*, Legrand played one Pierrotini ("of noble race, but very clumsy") opposite "Caliborgna" ("so named because of a halberd that had been stuck in her eye and forgotten") and "Gros-Bêta" ("villain, with no manners whatsoever").[67] When the fairies appeared at the Folies-Nouvelles, they did so only in travestied versions of Perrault—in *Le*

---

[65] After sketching out the initial situation—Cassandre insists that Colombine, who loves Arlequin, marry the rich Léandre—the scenario continues: "Pierrot, Cassandre's valet, allies himself with his master to make trouble for the two lovers, but Arlequin has as protectress an old sorceress who foils all of the wicked projects of the pursuers. Thence begins the comic business between the rivals. Arlequin writes to his Lady Fair. Pierrot seizes the letter and delivers it to Cassandre. *Lazzi* resulting from efforts to read the letter. Cassandre puts Pierrot on guard to prevent Colombine's being carried off. Pierrot steals a hunter's gun, shoots a rabbit: comic meal between Pierrot and Cassandre. The sorceress uses her power to put a spell on the three pursuers. Arlequin daubs them with blacking and makes them move like machines. Conclusion: Cassandre unites Arlequin and Colombine to put an end to his misfortunes": AN document F[18] 1024, unnumbered MS (unpaginated).

[66] *Les Folies-Nouvelles*, p. 93.

[67] AN document F[18] 1023, MS 4224 (entitled *Un Drame à Venise*), leaf descriptive of characters (unpaginated).

Petit Cendrillon (1857), for example, a tale of a white-faced Cinderfella, or in *Le Grand Poucet* (1858), the punning title of which suggests the seriousness of its faith in the *Cabinet des fées*. There is good reason to believe that many of Legrand's pantomimes were produced with a certain self-mocking irony. In Bridault's *Les Folies-Nouvelles peintes par elles-mêmes* (1858), which announced the theater's reopening after summer renovation of the *salle*, the concierge of the establishment, one Père Pétrin, invokes the pantomimic muse of its stage. It is she, he remarks, to whom the audience owes its entertainment, she who inspires its authors "in the simple goal of molding the mind and the heart." He cites as examples of such inspiration the maxims that conclude *Pierrot millionnaire* and *Le Petit Cendrillon*: "Money does not bring happiness!" and "Polished boots make good husbands!" The muse replies: "You're caustic, Père Pétrin!"[68] Arlequin, Pierrot, Léandre—none of the types seems to have escaped this causticity. In *L'Ex-Beau Léandre*, an *opérette-bouffe* registered for but apparently never produced at the theater, we see to what depths the librettists could fall. Here Léandre, traditionally the hero in the *opérette*, is old and fat, remorseful about his rakish past and determined that his godson, Flavio, should marry a girl with money. His audience is admonished in a final quatrain:

> *Il ne suffit pas de rire*
> *De morale il faut un bien*
> *Venez voir pour vous instruire*
> *La vieillesse d'Arlequin.*[69]

[It is not enough to laugh;/A useful moral is in order:/Come see for your instruction/The old age of Arlequin.]

Mercifully, the theater did not survive to record Arlequin's slow slide into senility. After it closed for the season in May of 1859, its direction was assumed by Eugène Déjazet, the son of the famous actress Virginie, and it reopened in September under the Déjazet name. Legrand,

[68] AN document F[18] 1024, unnumbered MS, p. 2.
[69] AN document F[18] 1023, MS 3687 (registered November 8, 1856), p. 29.

whose pantomimes had no place in its repertoire, left Paris, like his rival, to tour the provinces. In 1862 he sailed to Brazil, where he spent two years, then returned to the Théâtre Alcazar in Bordeaux; in 1870 he toured Egypt. His almost unbroken leave from the Parisian stage—he apparently made only sporadic appearances during the 1860s—closed a chapter on the pantomime. When he returned after the Siege, in 1871, for an eight-year engagement at the Tertulia, a *café-spectacle*, he seems to have been forgotten by his public, the pantomime itself suffering death-throes at the capital while struggling for rebirth in the south of France. And yet the last page of this chapter is, ironically, not Legrand's, but that of his rival, Deburau *fils*. It is the latter's role in Champfleury's last pantomime, *La Pantomime de l'avocat* (1865), that presents the most typical picture of the state of the genre in these years of its waning fortunes. A brief summary of the plot will highlight the strokes.

Pierrot is a clerk in the office of an attorney, the miserly and rapacious Cassandre. His "worn and tight black suit" is a matter of indifference to Colombine, the assistant, who loves him with a furtive ardor. When Cassandre leaves him to his customary luncheon of hard bread and thimble-sized cheese, she augments it with an elegant repast and, after a "scene of amorous gourmandizing between the two lovers," takes up her embroidery beside him. Arlequin appears: "He would like to beat his happy rival, but does not dare," and so steals into the adjoining room. Pierrot declares his intentions to Colombine, who answers, sensibly, that Cassandre would oppose their marriage. Inspired then by the idea of becoming a rich lawyer, like his master, Pierrot dons the black robes and strides manfully about the room. He plays out a scene with a client, his Colombine—who is driven to protest that indigent widows would endure too many liberties at his hands. Arlequin, in his astonishment, drops his sword and, after Pierrot's quickly finding him out, "emerges in shame from his hiding-place." During the scuffle that ensues, Cassandre reenters, and is very quickly drawn into the mêlée. Pierrot persuades Arlequin to side with him against the old man, thereby forcing him to submit to a mute tirade: "It is a veritable attorney-general's indictment that Pierrot delivers [. . .]." When he gathers himself up to pronounce his sentence, Cassandre begs Colombine's aid. In vain: Pierrot is her master. Cassandre asks mercy of his clerk, who grants it only on condition that he be given Colombine's hand. Suddenly Arlequin claims her, too, a claim that is annulled by a bottle of wine, "with which he consoles himself immediately." Cassandre gives his consent; he blesses the lovers; "little Bengal lights" throw their sparks across the stage.[70]

"*D'une trame légère*,"[71] Champfleury had said of this piece. *Légère* and enfeebled. One is tempted to protest, like Gautier, writing of an earlier pantomime of Legrand's, that "all this is full of enormous heresies" (*P*, 8.31.46). A Pierrot pathetically *amoureux*, a cowardly and gluttonous Arlequin, fastidious scenes of coquetry, and harmless skirmishes in a lawyer's office—how far we are from the gritty splendors of *Ma Mère l'Oie*. With *La Pantomime de l'avocat*, Champfleury's "revolution" reaches its crest—but the pantomime itself founders beneath it. Unlike the types in the *pantomime-féerie*, these characters have hardly a trace of the old psychic power behind them; they, rather, play out a farce in which each assumes a simple, sentimentalized role, all subordinate to a sublimated Pierrot. *Bon enfant*, he has adopted the mask in which he will die a stylized death on cheap ceramics. And now that the voluble fairies have been banished by the spirit of reason, and the dazzling apotheosis has been reduced to "little Bengal lights," the pantomime will retreat into a silence that is, in every sense of the word, complete.

Before it does so, however, it will inspire some rather provocative prose and verse. For even as the *littérateurs* were denaturing the form with a "realism" to which it was all too receptive, the greatest among them were appropriating its characters with an affection that was innocent of self-conscious reform. The result, for Arlequin, Pierrot, and Colombine ("and, with indulgence, Polichinelle"), was both

---

[70] All quotations in this paragraph are from Champfleury, *La Pantomime de l'avocat* (Paris: Librairie Centrale, 1866), pp. 3, 7, 8, 9, 10, 11.

[71] Ibid., p. 2.

invigorating and, in its own way, too, destructive. As public types of general outline, they were to be dissolved in the alembic of each writer's art. And yet as types appealing insidiously to the unbridled, the unconscious, they were in the transmutation to acquire renewed, if idiosyncratic, power. It was a power that revealed, of course, more about the alchemist than it did about Arlequin—revealed, more importantly, more about the dynamics of the former's work than about the *errements* of pantomime. A poem like "Pierrot gamin" says much, in its exploitation of certain potentialities in Pierrot's character, about its author, Paul Verlaine.

But let us begin at the beginning—with the writer who "discovered" the pantomime, that polymath Charles Nodier.

III

↶

In Pursuit of Colombine:
Charles Nodier and
Charles Baudelaire

*Cassandre représente la famille; Léandre, le bellâtre stu-
pide et cossu, qui agrée aux parens; Colombine, l'idéal,
la Béatrix, le rêve poursuivi [. . .].*

THÉOPHILE GAUTIER
La Presse, January 25, 1847

Nodier, if we can believe the expansively unreliable Dumas
père, "adored" three actors: Talma, Potier, and Deburau.
"When I became acquainted with Nodier," Dumas recalls
in his *Mémoires*, "Talma had been dead for three years; Potier had been retired for two; there remained to him then,
as an irresistible attraction, only Deburau [sic]."[1] The attraction, at least, is no invention. Indeed, so irresistible was
the mime's appeal that Nodier rented a *loge* for the year at
the Funambules after his daughter had persuaded him to
spend his first evening there;[2] he returned to assist at *Le
Boeuf enragé*—according to Dumas's insouciant hyper-
bole—"close to a hundred times." Nodier was the first to
have "deified the illustrious Pierrot";[3] after him came Janin,
Gautier, Banville, Champfleury. But his relations with the
theater and with the pantomime in general seem to have
been furtive and even short-lived. Although he was almost

[1] Alexandre Dumas, *Mes Mémoires*, V [CLXXXIII of the *Oeuvres complètes de Alexandre Dumas*] (Paris: Lévy, 1900), 122.
[2] [Marie] Mennessier-Nodier, *Charles Nodier: Episodes et souvenirs de sa
vie* (Paris: Didier & Cie, 1867), p. 309.
[3] Dumas, *Mémoires*, V, 122.

certainly the author of *Le Songe d'or, ou Arlequin et l'avare*, the pantomime produced at the Funambules in 1828, he apparently, as I have noted, never confessed his paternity; and it was Polichinelle, naturalized among the *fantoches* of Deburau's stage several years after Nodier's death, that most attracted him among the *commedia* masks.

His daughter tells us that three months after his first surge of enthusiasm—probably by late 1828—Nodier "was perhaps no longer as faithful" to the theater as his subscription promised he would be.[4] That single year seems to date both the beginning and the end of Nodier's ardent patronage of the Funambules, marking not only his discovery of the theater and its production of *Le Songe d'or* but also the publication of an article entitled "Deburau" in *La Pandore* (July 19, 1828), unsigned but commonly attributed to Nodier.[5] Polichinelle, that *zanni* to whom he would eventually be loyal, had prepared his reception of Pierrot: in 1828 Nodier was seeing through the press his *Histoire du Roi de Bohême*, a fantasy inspired by Sterne and Rabelais in which the scourge of the *commissaire* is apostrophized and extravagantly extolled. (Polichinelle would later be the subject of an 1831 essay and an object of analysis by "Dr. Néophobus," one of the writer's *dériseurs sensés*, in a late piece, "Les Marionnettes" [1843].) It was probably, at least in part, the broad polichinellesque streak of perversity that Nodier relished in Baptiste: a "*Satan naïf et bouffon*," the writer of "Deburau" characterized the mime's Pierrot.[6] And Deburau's comedy seems to have exercised, ultimately, less fascination than that of Polichinelle. For all of the intensity of Nodier's admiration, his interest in the so-called *pantomime classique* appears to have been an occasional, if obsessive, one. The brevity of that interest, I think, may be explained in some measure by the very reason for its intensity. In any case, neither may be accounted for—nor his undiminished affection for Polichinelle understood—without some consideration of Nodier's circumstances as a man and writer around 1828.

---

[4] Mennessier-Nodier, *Charles Nodier*, pp. 309-10.
[5] See Péricaud, *Théâtre des Funambules*, pp. 76-78, and Rémy, *Jean-Gaspard Deburau*, p. 82.
[6] *La Pandore*, p. 2.

He was passing through a severe psychological crisis, the "terrible moment" to which his daughter alludes in her *Souvenirs*.[7] His financial debts, losses, and obligations were a harrassment: "A generous host, an impenitent bibliophile," writes Pierre-Georges Castex, "Charles Nodier lived outside his means."[8] His health, weakened by nervous disorders since his youth, was becoming progressively worse. In a letter dated May 9, 1829, he apologized to his friend Charles Weiss for a silence of several months, explaining that

> I was even on the point of not writing you, for I felt my life slipping away. In the last analysis, it was only an immense fatigue that had come to a head. Three weeks on my back have cured me, if one is cured of life other than by death [. . .].[9]

The melancholy of that last clause finds repeated expression in the letters: "Outwardly, I am extremely happy," he writes to Weiss in January of 1829, "but I can neither put on such a face everywhere nor always keep up the pose," adding: "The ways of my spirit are accommodated badly to the world [. . .]" (*CI*, 218). He will later confess that "*la vie extérieure et communicative*" is "completely intolerable" to him (*CI*, 236). This darkening dissatisfaction with public life, the despairing admission in "Le Fou du Pirée" that "*rêver est tout le bonheur*,"[10] are both the result of a complicated history of disappointment and frustration dating from Nodier's earliest childhood. The Freudian familial drama—for Nodier a pathetic one—had a prominent place in it.

[7] Mennessier-Nodier, *Charles Nodier*, p. 313.

[8] "Notice" to "Le Cycle des Innocents," in Charles Nodier, *Contes, avec des textes et des documents inédits* (Paris: Garnier Frères, 1961), p. 153. This edition will be cited throughout this chapter as *C*, with appropriate page numbers.

[9] *Correspondance inédite de Charles Nodier, 1797-1844*, ed. A. Estignard (1876; Geneva: Slatkine Reprints, 1973), p. 220. The *Correspondance* will be cited throughout this chapter as *CI*, with appropriate page numbers.

[10] *Contes en prose et vers*, in *Oeuvres complètes*, XI (Brussels: Meline, Cans et Compagnie, 1837), 225. The *Oeuvres* will be cited throughout this chapter as *OC:N*, with appropriate volume and page numbers.

Shortly after his marriage to Désirée, Nodier wrote a revealing letter to Weiss:

> I think that the sight of you would do me good; despite the relief that the tenderness of my excellent Désirée brings to my ills, I'm lacking something that I can no longer find. My father has left a void that I hadn't expected. Can it be possible that I've lost a single day, a single moment of those I could have spent beside him? How dearly I'd pay for the instant when I left the paternal home with the greatest of haste, when I abandoned my father to go embrace my first mistress! I'd make quite another use of it. (*CI*, 42)

The real source of the void of which he complains, itself a void here, unnamed, unacknowledged, is, as Jules Vodoz has argued at length,[11] the mother whom he sought in Désirée and whom he is of course forbidden to enjoy. In relinquishing the father for the mistress, he chose, *à son insu*, the path to guilt, vague fear, and disillusionment. However consoling his reveries, his literary dreams are henceforth troubled: by fears of engulfment by the "Terrible Mother" in *Smarra*, by strategies to compromise sexuality itself in *Trilby* and *La Fée aux miettes*.[12] These are, admittedly, familiar arguments, invoked for their familiarity: they will help us appreciate Nodier's special position as husband and father—and as eulogist of the Polichinelle of his *Histoire du Roi de Bohême*—in 1828.

At least as early as March of that year, his daughter's

---

[11] *"La Fée aux Miettes": Essai sur le rôle du subconscient dans l'oeuvre de Charles Nodier* (Paris: Champion, 1925), pp. 58-59, 74, 111-12, 117.

[12] On *La Fée aux miettes*, see Vodoz's study, cited in the previous note; for a more recent psychoanalytic approach to all three works, see Laurence M. Porter, *The Literary Dream in French Romanticism: A Psychoanalytic Interpretation* (Detroit: Wayne State University Press, 1979), from whose chapter on *Smarra* I have borrowed Jung's phrase "the Terrible Mother." Both Vodoz and Porter, drawing upon the myth-making of analytic psychology, contend that the outcome of *La Fée aux miettes* suggests that Nodier—or Michel—finally mastered his obsessional anxieties. But I rather think that there he gave expression to a wish for sublimation that was never quite realized in his life: thus his rehearsing those obsessions in his last tale, *Franciscus Columna* (1844), and—as I shall argue—his attraction to the distempered Polichinelle.

inevitable betrothal was preying deeply on Nodier's mind. When he was obviously not trying to ignore it,[13] he was trying to wish it away. "Happily," he wrote to Jean de Bry, "her fancy is not turned towards marriage, and, content with the pure happiness that she enjoys among her two surest friends, she has desired up to this point nothing else."[14] In an earlier letter to Weiss, he seemed to dwell with a certain relief upon an apparent obstacle to his loss of Marie:

> As for Marie's marriage, I doubt that you'll be assist-
> ing just yet. She's extremely difficult, and the only man
> who would suit her convinced himself that he was too
> old, and while he took the time to think it over, his
> conclusion became somewhat true. On the other hand,
> she's happy, and that at least will be so much gained
> upon the hazards of life.[15]

Apparently no more difficult than any eighteen-year-old, Marie was engaged to be married to Jules Mennessier some time early in 1829. Long expecting the event, Nodier must nevertheless have felt devastated by this sacrifice of his only surviving child—a daughter for whom he felt an intensity of affection bordering subliminally, if inevitably, on the in-cestuous. "For him," Dumas wrote in his preface to *La Femme au collier de velours*, "*Thérèse Aubert, la Fée aux Miettes, Inès de la Sierra* [sic] had existed. They were his daughters, like Marie; they were Marie's sisters [. . .]."[16] And Marie herself, as Vodoz has observed, was her mother grown young.[17] A fantasmatic mother, to be sure: an object of

[13] On March 29, 1828, Weiss wrote to Nodier: "Madame Deis has just married off her daughter. When are you going to announce to me that you're thinking of marrying off your own? It's a question I put to you in all of my letters, and I can't guess what is hindering you from answering": *Lettres de Charles Weiss à Charles Nodier*, ed. Léonce Pingaud (Paris: Champion, 1889), pp. 46-47.

[14] Letter of May 12, 1828, cited in *C*, 154.

[15] In *CI*, 213, dated June 3, 1828. The letter apparently belongs to April or early May, however, since it elicited this clearsighted response from Weiss on May 30, 1828: "What you tell me about Marie doesn't satisfy me. It's precisely because she's happy now that it's necessary to attend to her future [. . .]": *Lettres de Charles Weiss à Charles Nodier*, p. 49.

[16] *Oeuvres complètes*, XCIV, 13-14.

[17] "*La Fée aux Miettes*," p. 119.

desire, both obscure and passionate; the source of "pure happiness" that Nodier had never known as a child. Marie, even more than Désirée, was for Nodier *le bibliophile* a phantasmal palimpsest, eliciting, by her confused (and unconscious) lines of force that half-cancelled and half-corrupted one another, the conflicts of an irresolute Oedipus.

In no other work by Nodier are those conflicts dramatized more tellingly than in the *Histoire du Roi de Bohême et de ses sept châteaux*. This may seem a curious remark about what appears to be a purely aleatory piece of *écriture*. In the most thoughtful essay about the novella to date, André Clavel's "Les Bandelettes de la momie," the *Histoire* is described as a "sarcophagus" enclosing an "absolute void," a *"déconstruction parodique"* of the "ideologies implicit in every literary act." Alinear, reflexive, patently apocryphal, it is Nodier's attempt at "an impossible book," relentlessly destroying itself by Sternean humor, by parody of Nodier's own Wertherism, by a Rabelaisian *jeu de mots* that results in a merciless "blocking of symbolization." And Clavel concludes that here the *parole* of Nodier, "to take up a phrase of Blanchot's, is *'une parole qui ne parle pas.'* "[18] Surely this is a contemporary's strongest impression of this bizarre and mysterious book. But it comes to be modified considerably when one presses into the vague circumstances of its birth. Clavel's description of its surface seems accurate enough: "*Un* texte [. . .], *banalement normé, truffé d'*inter-textes [. . .]";[19] that is, a series of interpolations of what seem to be fantastic and explosive digressions into the two sentimental "narratives" of the book, "Les Aveugles de Chamouny" and the very brief "Histoire du Chien de Brisquet." But if the imagination of Nodier is "engulfed" in the interstices of this "vast *arlequinade*,"[20] it relapses not into aphasia but into a *parole* that dare not speak its name.

Clavel is not alone in alluding to the *textes* of the *Histoire*—particularly the more important "Aveugles de Chamouny"—as parodies of Nodier's own narratives: every critic

[18] *Europe: Revue Littéraire Mensuelle*, 58th Year, Nos. 614-615 (June-July 1980), pp. 88, 84, 79, 83, 82.

[19] Ibid., p. 79.

[20] Ibid.

who discusses the book agrees.[21] But, as Jean Richer observes *malgré lui*, "it is apparent that the sentimental tendencies borrowed from Richardson and Sterne, from Rousseau, from *Werther*, remained strong in him."[22] All the evidence suggests, in fact, that Nodier was parodying neither himself nor his predecessors: "Les Aveugles de Chamouny," a tale spun upon one of Nodier's obsessive themes, is a tale told in earnest. Nodier himself had no compunction about lifting it from the novella to be reprinted—significantly, with "Polichinelle"—as a supplement to his *Oeuvres complètes*.[23] Removed from its context in the *Histoire*, it is neither more nor less parodic (and neither more nor less successful as art) than those later tales of doomed and visionary innocents, "Jean François les Bas-Bleus" (1832) and "Baptiste Montauban ou l'Idiot" (1833). It is clear, moreover, that the Sterne to whom "Les Aveugles"—indeed, the book as a whole—owes so much was, for Nodier, less a giddy deconstructionist than a rather disturbingly somber melancholic.[24] "Sterne's gaiety," he wrote in the *Miscellanées*, "is that of a somewhat morose old man who amuses himself in making his puppets dance." He added: "What dominates in Sterne is a bitter consciousness of the soul's disappointments, which is manifested by turns in laughter or tears, and beneath the development of which one always divines the poignant torments of some disguised anguish" (*OC*:N, V, 14).

That "*quelque angoisse déguisée*" is buried in "Les Aveugles de Chamouny"—Vodoz suspects it is so[25]—is attested

[21] See, for example, besides Castex (*C*, 465), Hilda Nelson, *Charles Nodier* (New York: Twayne Publishers, Inc., 1972), p. 113, and Jean Richer, *Autour de l'Histoire du Roi de Bohême*, p. 13.

[22] *Autour de l'Histoire du Roi de Bohême*, p. 14.

[23] In a letter to the Libraire Dumont, February 14, 1842, Nodier wrote: "I have verified that the *Aveugles* and the *Chien* would not make up an honest volume. It would be necessary to add to it two little pieces that had a fair amount of success in their day and which make up part of the *Livre des Cent-un*, *Le Bibliophile* and *Polichinelle*. It would all be called *Nouvelles et Mélanges*, and would form a natural supplement to the *Oeuvres complettes* [. . .]" (reprinted in Richer, *Autour de l'Histoire du Roi de Bohême*, p. 26).

[24] Rabelais's influence upon the book seems confined to the fantastic play of language: his influence upon the two *textes* is nil.

[25] "*La Fée aux Miettes*," p. 54.

by a letter to Weiss, superficially incommunicative, in which Nodier discusses his book. Its appearance, he implies, will coincide with his daughter's marriage; and as an expression of the depth of his loss in Marie and as a declaration of the book's importance, he both defends and deprecates its parturition:

> The failure of this poor book has been arranged between two newspapers [. . .], and if there's some means of turning up matter in it for a keen denunciation, I should have no doubts of my fate, which will no longer interest me in a month. My daughter is getting married February 9. That's the whole mystery. As for the book itself, I don't attach any importance to it. It amused me to write it, but it won't amuse anyone else. It's a work that doesn't harmonize with any mind of the present day and which is not of its time; I have resigned myself to its failure [*j'en ai fait mon deuil*]. (*CI*, 228)

Beneath the idiomatic sense of that final clause is an image that had special significance for Nodier. In a letter of March 3, 1844, Balzac remarked to Madame Hanska that Nodier had wanted to be buried in his daughter's wedding veil—a request the poet had, in fact, framed in "Changement de domicile" (1834).[26] *J'en ai fait mon deuil*: literally, "I have done my mourning for it" or—equally possible in the language of the unconscious—"I have made my mourning clothes of it": so he describes the *Histoire du Roi de Bohême*. The sympathetic identification with the dead that mourning clothes symbolize, Nodier's fantastic equation of his own death with Marie's marriage: both meet in that casual, dismissive line. What I am suggesting is that the writing of this book was an anticipatory act of mourning for Nodier, specifically for the loss of Marie. More profoundly, it was an act of *failed* mourning, an expression of melancholia, a confession of Nodier's inability to relinquish his daughter, and, with her, the conflicts of *son Oedipe*.

The *Histoire du Roi de Bohême* is composed with a dream logic; its motive force is sexual: thus the quest for a horse

[26] See Vodoz, "*La Fée aux Miettes*," p. 314.

to serve the narrator's imaginative flight, the witty para-
phrastic play with the Shandyan *pantoufle*, the invocation
of the "big, beautiful, energetic, and vigorous mare," Pa-
tricia.[27] But, however superficially exuberant, its sexuality
is, significantly, disturbed: the word *pantoufle* "harmonizes
sympathetically with all the melancholies of the soul" (*H*,
67), confesses the narrator; his judgment, personified in his
contentious companion Breloque, shies at mounting that
powerfully bucking mare (*"Eh! que je l'eusse bien montée si
je l'avois voulu!"* [*H*, 316]). His ambivalence is mirrored
structurally in the disruptions of the narrative *textes*, disruptions evoked obliquely by Nodier's description of "the
bizarre effects of the dazzling prism of dreams":

> Sleep, that blind tyrant of thought, amuses itself in
> outwitting our most familiar impressions and in baf-
> fling them, like a cunning charlatan, by opposed
> impressions. Hardly have its fingers set a harmonious
> and fantastic chord to vibrating than a coarse baccha-
> nalia or an obscene vaudeville has begun to embellish
> the majestic notes. Hardly has the movable decoration
> that obeys it offered to your eyes the venerable profes-
> sor's chair than it allows the grotesque trestle-stages of
> Mondor and of Gratelard to appear [. . .]. (*H*, 260)

This is the true relation between Nodier's *textes* and *inter-
textes*: it is a matter not of parody but of paradox. Nodier
privileges neither text over the other, neither the sublime
nor the ridiculous: each has its integrity, bears the stamp
of the dreamer's sincerity; the two are *"impressions opposées,"*
perspectives that at once declare their authority and cancel
each other out. Admittedly, these cancellations effect a "de-
construction" of the book—but it is not (in the terms of
Clavel's oxymoron) a *"déconstruction parodique."* Rather, it
is a strategy by which Nodier may give expression to both
the repressed and repressing forces of his psyche, by which
he may speak and repudiate his *parole*. Such is the equivocal
character of the language of dreams, according to Meredith
Anne Skura's recent revision of Freud's *Traumdeutung*:

[27] Charles Nodier, *Histoire du Roi de Bohême et de ses sept châteaux* (1830;
Paris: Editions d'Aujourd'hui, 1977), p. 314. This edition will be cited
throughout this chapter as *H*, with appropriate page numbers.

82

Freud claimed that dreams differ from waking life by discarding mature meaning and motives in their regression, but the source of the dream's unique quality is rather the way it makes us uncertain about meaning and motive, playing each one against a more primitive, regressed counterpart.

[. . .]

In other words, the dream draws not only on infantile consciousness but also on intellectual and sophisticated ways of seeing and thinking about things—on all the modes of consciousness which sort things out; which make judgments, diagrams, hierarchies, and anatomies; and which see things from all perspectives [. . .].[28]

A rigorous application of these ideas would take us deeply into the *Histoire du Roi de Bohême*; but they would also take us too far afield. My aim here is to look at only two sections of the book, "Les Aveugles de Chamouny" and the centrally disruptive series of chapters in which Polichinelle clamorously takes the stage. In comparing them I shall try to show, not that each deconstructs the other (as in a sense it obviously does), but rather that, beneath their superficial differences, each pursues a common constitutive project. In short, that "Les Aveugles de Chamouny" is not simply deconstructed (as *parole*) but that its subtext is *re*constructed (as *langue*) by an insurrectionary Polichinelle.

A story of lovers divided, like most of Nodier's *contes*, "Les Aveugles de Chamouny" is told in great part by its main character, Gervais, a blind villager of the Chamonix valley, to a narrator without a name. Gervais is grieving over a double loss—of his loyal dog, Puck (oddly the name of the narrator's spaniel), and, more devastatingly, his fiancée Eulalie. Having met and warmed to affection when Eulalie was brought, blind, to his village, they have been separated by her recovery of sight: slowly taking an interest in the new world outside their companionship, she has been persuaded by her father, Monsieur Robert, to travel—to winter in Geneva, then to summer in Milan. Gervais fears

[28] *The Literary Use of the Psychoanalytic Process* (New Haven: Yale University Press, 1981), pp. 137, 140.

that she will never return. The narrator, who has "also sorrows to distract, wounds to heal up" (*H*, 200), offers to find and speak with her in Italy. There, at a gathering of *le grand monde*, he is introduced by a casual acquaintance, a Monsieur Roberville (or Robertville: the name is indifferently rendered), to a woman who is revealed to be Eulalie. Suddenly, "a horrible germ of cruelty" (*H*, 309) begins to sprout in his breast: wanting her to suffer all that she has inflicted upon Gervais, he utters the name of her abandoned companion, and she falls in an ambiguous swoon to the floor. Returning to the Chamonix, he learns that Monsieur Roberville has preceded him and talked with Gervais, and that since their talk the blind boy has disappeared. In fear and dread, the narrator calls out his dog, left behind with Gervais, to find him. But Puck has strangely become blind as well and, in setting out on the trace, falls into "*le gouffre de l'Arveyron.*" Where Puck disappears nothing is visible to the narrator but a mantle of blue cloth, the customary garb of Gervais.

The tale seems a prodigious (albeit blind) unburdening of secrets. The protagonists are, first, clearly one: Gervais, Monsieur Robert, Monsieur Roberville, the narrator—all are obviously self-projections, split up, as Freud (and Nodier himself) would have observed, into several "part-egos."[29] Into the role of Eulalie's father Nodier has cast an idealized image of himself ("a kind of visionary, a man of bizarre ideas" [*H*, 307]);[30] but he is also Monsieur Roberville (Breloque notes the common root of the two characters' names), as well as, of course, Gervais. That Gervais and the narrator share a like-named companion—Puck, the genius of imaginative caprice—serves to strengthen the identification upon which Nodier insisted when the story was excised for the *Oeuvres*. In the later version, the narrator notes

[29] See Freud, "Creative Writers and Day-Dreaming" (1907), in *SE*, IX, 150. In "De quelques phénomènes du sommeil" (1831), Nodier remarked that sleep throws its "patient" into the middle of dreams "like an actor with a thousand faces and voices" (*OC:N*, V, 148).

[30] The description also recalls Nodier's image of his own father—an idealization that, as Vodoz and others have shown, hardly fits the biographical facts. It may be pertinent to note that Michel's father, in *La Fée aux miettes*, is known as the "late Robert" (*C*, 219).

that Gervais's *récit* "had left me with but a single impression, one that was moving and sad, but also vague and faint, like that of a dream, the memory of which is from time to time awakened by a conjunction of ideas that I can't account for" (*C*, 492-93). The sorrows that he himself suffers are, in short, inextricable from Gervais's own. And they seem anterior to the departure of Eulalie: they date from the awakening of Gervais's sex.

Early in his relationship with Eulalie, Gervais rejoices in their blindness, assuring her that "this dangerous fascination which the passions exert by the gaze will at least never claim a hold upon us" (*H*, 134). Their love is that of a father and daughter—or of a mother and her infant son: "It is not the magic of a woman's fleeting beauty that has captivated me in you," he tells Eulalie, "it is something that can neither be explained when it is felt nor forgotten when it has been experienced" (*H*, 134-35). To the narrator he exclaims that, in memory, "I see her again in my mind as more charming than my mother!" (*H*, 127). But after Monsieur Robert has consented to their union, Gervais's sleep is troubled by "a crowd of confused appearances": "I was almost sorry for having lost that past which had been without intoxication, but also without fears [. . .]," he tells the narrator, adding:

> It seemed to me that her father, in conferring a new privilege upon me, had imposed upon me a thousand privations. I feared to exercise the power of a word, the seductions of a caress. I felt much more securely that she was mine, and I felt much more dread of touching her. I would have feared to profane her in listening to her breathing, in lightly touching her dress, in catching one of her floating tresses in my mouth. (*H*, 139, 141-42)

Coincident with the excitement of Gervais's fears is Eulalie's recovery of sight, a fact that she reveals to her fiancé "as if she had confessed a fault to me, or recounted some misfortune" (*H*, 143). And Gervais, hoping to sustain the "delicious enchantment [*prestige*] in which we had passed our childhood," tries to convince himself that she will meet him henceforth with bandaged eyes, that she "has remained blind for me, my Eulalie! she won't see me! she'll love me forever! . . ." (*H*, 185).

Blindness is obviously more than physical infirmity here, and more than the innocence of naïveté: it is the darkness of willful repression. As Eulalie begins to take pleasure in her sighted world, she comes to resemble, to Gervais's chagrin, what Hugo called Nodier's daughter, Marie—*Notre-Dame de l'Arsenal*:[31]

> The château [. . .] had become, in effect, one of those hospitable manor-houses of another age, whose master never believed he was doing enough to enhance his guests' stay. Eulalie shone in this circle, a circle always new, always composed of rich strangers, of illustrious savants, of coquettish lady-travelers of sparkling wit; she shone among all the women, both by the charm of her speech, which is for us unfortunates the physiognomy of the soul, and by a thousand other attractions that I had not known in her. What an incredible mixture of pride and sorrow welled up in my breast, threatening to make it burst, when someone near me praised the fire of her glances, or when a young man, stupidly cruel, complimented us on the color of her hair! . . . (*H*, 193)

It is Nodier the father as well as Gervais the lover who is speaking here. Each is speaking out of the same despair, knowing that Eulalie-Marie will be lost. Once she leaves the château, the despair turns to hatred as the ambivalence that, as Freud notes, accompanies all acts of mourning finds expression in the narrator's cruelty. At the soirée in Milan, when he decides to confront her with Gervais's name, he seems inexplicably intent upon the brutal violence of his effect:

> I wanted this impression to be lacerating, and profound, and atrocious, and irresistible; I wanted it to strike her soul like a red-hot iron; I wanted it to penetrate the marrow of her bones like molten lead; I

[31] Albert Fournier, "Qui était Marie Nodier?" *Europe: Revue Littéraire Mensuelle*, 58th Year, Nos. 614-615 (June-July 1980), p. 130.

wanted it to envelope all her vital organs like the Centaur's destructive robe. (*H*, 309-10)

But Eulalie's punishment seems secondary to Gervais's (and the narrator's) own. Monsieur Roberville, Gervais's own dark familiar, compounds the latter's despondency with unendurable guilt: in the more technical language of the psychoanalyst—that of Freud, here, in "Mourning and Melancholia"—Gervais's suicide is the "satisfaction of trends of sadism and hate which relate to an object [that has been internalized so as not to be lost], and which have been turned round upon the subject's own self" (*SE*, XIV, 251). That the narrator survives as an emblem of Gervais's melancholiac suffering ("*Tout mon être, monsieur, c'est ma douleur*," Gervais tells him on first meeting [*H*, 131]) is suggested by the fate of his companion, Puck. First blinded then drowned, the dog seems a symbol of the narrator's sympathy—sympathy with the willful psychic blindness of the hero, and with the narcissistic destruction, both literal and metaphorical, of his life and imaginative vision.

It seems the most disturbing caprice to counterpoint such somber pathos with allusions to *le monde arlequinesque*. Why, one wonders, does the narrator enter the Chamonix valley "*à reculons*" by way of Arlequin's Bergamo (*H*, 45)? And why, from that valley to the Milan of Polichinelle, "*vous n'avez qu'une promenade*" (*H*, 350)? To discover Arlequin's relations with "Les Aveugles de Chamouny" we must exhume the pantomime—unknown, apparently, to *nodiéristes*—of *Le Songe d'or, ou Arlequin et l'avare*. But to answer the second question, we need turn only to the essay "Polichinelle." There we encounter a grotesque counterpart of the ego that dreams Gervais's dark tragedy. The puppet-booth in Milan, rendered *parallélogrammatiquement* in the narrator's pedantic "Dissertation," is, *parallèlement*, the psychic space of an insurrectionary Gervais. Like Gervais, Polichinelle is "deeply melancholic" (*OC:N*, X, 11); but he is insurrectionary because he embodies the hatred and cruelty that seem foreign to the blind hero of the *texte*. Whereas in "Les Aveugles" the ambivalences of melancholia are disarmed by the dreamwork of isolation—the cruelty is perpetrated by the narrator alone, while the burden of suffering is assumed by Gervais—these ambivalences converge in the bilious and implacable Polichinelle as through the lens of a burning glass.

Nodier seems frankly unaware of their doing so. What draws him to Polichinelle is his mystery:

> Polichinelle's secret, which has been sought for so long, consists in his hiding himself at the right moment behind a curtain that must be raised only by his *compère*, like the curtain of Isis; in his covering himself with a veil that opens only before his priests; and there is more of a connection than one might think between the companions of Isis [*les compères d'Isis*] and the grand-priest of Polichinelle. His power is in his mystery, like that of those talismans which lose all their virtue when their motto is betrayed. Accessible to man's senses like Apollonius of Tyana, like Saint-Simon, like Deburau, Polichinelle would have been perhaps only a philosopher, a *funambule*, or a prophet. (*OC*:N, X, 16)

But his mystery is not hard to divine. Gustave Kahn unveils it in his preface to "*le célèbre drame anonyme*" in which Polichinelle savagely vanquishes his foes: "[. . .] the secret of his triumphs is that he is strong, that he knows how to hit, that he decides immediately to strike out."

> The infant contains, in embryo, all the accesses of anger and all the blows of the fist; both education and fear disarm him, little by little; in Polichinelle he sees a spoiled child to whom nothing can offer resistance, and he acclaims Polichinelle as soldiers would applaud a Roland of tragedy or sages a Socrates of verse.

It is Polichinelle's "feeling of joy before the misfortune of others" that is "the secret of his formation, of his life, of his myth."[32]

But such a revelation would be painful to Nodier. For the suffering that he would inflict, as both mourner and melancholiac, is directed at the very object of his love. Consequently, his Polichinelle does not beat: in one of the familiar reversals of dreams, he is beaten: "What is certain—

---

[32] *Polichinelle (de Guignol)* (Paris: Sansot & Cie, 1906), pp. 39-40.

and what everyone can verify at this very moment on the Place du Châtelet, if these laudable studies still occupy a few good minds—is that Polichinelle, beaten by the sbirros, assassinated by the *bravi*, hanged by the executioner, and carried off by the devil, invariably reappears in his dramatic cage a quarter of an hour later, as lively, as robust, and as gallant as ever, dreaming only of clandestine love-affairs and of coarse pranks" (*OC*:N, X, 20-21). Grudgingly, Nodier admits, in "Les Marionnettes," that "I sometimes used to find him boorish, stupid, and brutal," but he explains these as the forgivable failings of a "young man": "Boorish, he seemed to me impudently sincere; stupid, he seemed to me naïve; brutal, his excesses appeared to me as a still unenlightened use of his strength."[33] Like *les aveugles de Chamouny*, Polichinelle is an unconscious and, hence, innocent victim of desire: "Polichinelle's history is, alas! the history of the entire human race, with all its blind beliefs, blind passions, blind follies, and blind joys" (*OC*:N, X, 29-30).

And yet, despite his blindness, Polichinelle is, curiously, a shrewd and merciless critic; he is a "*moraliste*" who shares with Arlequin, Gilles, and Pantalon a hatred for coarse pranks: "[. . .] under these clever and circumspect appearances, the primitive comedy [. . .] keenly censured coarse mores and rustic brutality, gluttony and laziness, guile and larceny, avarice and anger" (*N*, 395). In the polarities of the paradox reside the dynamics of the melancholiac conscience. Having internalized the target of his own cruelty, Nodier inflects the chastisements of Polichinelle: the latter thus seems both critic and victim, judge and criminal, the blind and restorer of sight. He becomes a metaphor for Nodier as an ego conflicted—by love of the object he cannot let go and hatred of the same object that would leave him.

But it is not, at least explicitly, as a wounded soul assaulting himself—a Sterne morosely twitching his *pantins*—that Polichinelle appears in the "Insurrection" of the *His-*

---

[33] Charles Nodier, *Nouvelles, suivies des fantaisies du dériseur sensé*, nouv. éd. (Paris: Charpentier, 1911), p. 430. This collection will be cited throughout this chapter as *N*, with appropriate page numbers.

toire. "O POLICHINELLE!!!" (*H*, 204), the narrator exclaims in an access of upper-case joy. The joy is a rhapsodic avowal of identification: it is an unsheathing of the sadism of which he declares Polichinelle innocent; and it announces a restorative recovery, in a single crude image, of a receptacle for the divisions of his mind. Through Polichinelle, moreover, Nodier enters a "*utopie régressive*," far beneath "*la vie extérieure et communicative*," the utopia that Jean Richer has said he seeks.[34] Confirmed in the narcissistic pleasures of his melancholy,[35] he can sink, heedless, into the inaccessibilities of the self. He thus becomes (as he imagines Polichinelle to be) an "inestimable Falstaff" (*H*, 204), "invulnerable," "insouciant and free" (*OC*:N, X, 21, 25). Ostensible victim of inexorable Law (as Polichinelle is the victim of the *commissaire*), he reigns in a drama of the eternal return. Revenge upon the never-to-be relinquished object is its ever-dynamic motif: the immortal ego, preserver and destroyer, is its always busy stage. "The comedy of *marionettes*," observes Dr. Néophobus, "was a reminder that one's private life must be walled up, as the wisest of philosophers has said [. . .]" (*N*, 394). In the puppet-booth of Polichinelle, Nodier found his own life reduced to its fundamental terms and walled up, secretly, as myth.

But it was only one scene from that life that he encountered at the Funambules. The dénouement of Deburau's pantomime was invariable, however ingeniously postponed: Cassandre relinquished Colombine to Arlequin. It was a lesson that Nodier was perhaps intent upon learning—and perhaps intent upon teaching himself: *Le Songe d'or, ou Arlequin et l'avare* seems an exercise in the self-mastery of mourning. A "*pantomime anglaise en 11 tableaux*," it offers but one wrinkle on the familiar formula: at rise, Cassandre is dreaming of a sack of gold that the genie Morphius is burying in his garden; after the chase, he not only loses his daughter to Arlequin but must share the treasure with Pierrot. That Nodier indeed wrote this

---

[34] *Autour de l'*Histoire du Roi de Bohême, p. 21.

[35] Freud notes in "Mourning and Melancholia" that the melancholiac's "object-choice has been effected on a narcissistic basis, so that the object-cathexis, when obstacles come in its way, can regress to narcissism" (*SE*, XIV, 249).

unremarkable pantomime was a belief shared by a number of his contemporaries, although none had the advantage of proof.[36] And his authorship is still a matter of conjecture. Apparently only one manuscript of the scenario survives— a copy submitted to the censor for approval of a *reprise* in early 1862. The prose is undistinguished;[37] but this should not be surprising, given the vicissitudes of a playscript recopied often (and carelessly) over the course of some thirty-five years.[38] In favor of Nodier's authorship is the recurrence of his obsessive motifs: the lucid truth of the "*féeries du sommeil*,"[39] the intoxication (in both the French and English senses of that word) of the meretricious glitter of gold. The latter is, of course, the motivic spine of "Le Songe d'or" (1832), one of the most accomplished of Nodier's tales. And pantomime and story may share more than title and theme: that naïve *kardouon*, "making the innumerable reflective scales of the wonderful tissue in which he is clothed sparkle under the fiery rays of the sun" (*C*, 349), seems a reptilian Arlequin.

To recognize Nodier himself in the *kardouon* helps explain his delight in the pantomime. For before Colombine changes hands from father to suitor, she is the portable

[36] Péricaud assembles the pertinent remarks of Gautier, Janin, and Champfleury in his *Théâtre des Funambules*, p. 80.

[37] The scenario of *Le Songe d'or* that Péricaud reproduces in his *Théâtre des Funambules* (pp. 80-87) is, in details of punctuation and turn of phrase, somewhat more elegant than that of the censor's version (AN document F^{18} 1092, MS 6130); but, despite Péricaud's avowal that he is publishing "*le plus complet*" of the manuscripts, I am skeptical of his being the more "authentic." As a comparison of the two versions reveals, the censor's copy is, in fact, more "complete." I suspect that Péricaud simply derived his scenario from the latter: in reproducing passages and whole scenarios elsewhere in his book he does not scruple to make small cuts and alterations in the censor's manuscripts, with no indication of his changes. The published scenario of the pantomime, *Le Songe d'or, pantomime fantastique, genre anglais, en 18 tableaux* (Bordeaux: Bord, 1864), is based upon Charles Deburau's adaptation and differs in important respects from the manuscript.

[38] A note by the censor's examiner (AN document F^{21} 984, unnum. MS) indicates that *Le Songe d'or* was resubmitted for approval many times after its première.

[39] "The fairy-plays of sleep [i.e., dreams]": the frequently quoted phrase appears in Nodier's 1832 "Préface" to *Smarra* (*C*, 39).

property of all—of the Cassandre in whom Nodier saw his ambiguous duty, the Pierrot through whose malice he could articulate his anger, and the Arlequin who shimmered with his desire. Spectator, if not author, Nodier could move from role to role in a kind of profligacy of identification. And he could revel safely in this *utopie régressive*. Here if a chair devoured people like a Terrible Mother, it vomited them up in the wings; if Cassandre bought a kiss from a girl of Colombine's years, Pierrot cunningly interposed his head. The fantastic oscillations of the *pantomime classique* matched the pulse of Nodier's psychic life: unlike Champfleury, Gautier, and others who followed him, he had no reason to alter its form. The very unremarkability of *Le Songe d'or* is an argument for its having come from his pen.

He would of course have wished to alter the ending, even as he was impressing upon himself its truth. That he could not fully accept it may explain his faithlessness to the Funambules. It was Polichinelle—a *pantin* largely of his own invention—in whom he found his lasting inspiration, that figure of splenetic melancholia whose "bitter experience of the perversity of the species [. . .] has deterred him from exposing himself to vulgar intercourse with society" (*OC*:N, X, 11). In his *cage dramatique*, "in the midst of this multitude which surges up at the sound of his voice, Polichinelle has cultivated the solitude of the sage; and he, whose heart, which has been extinguished by experience or misfortune, no longer sympathizes with anyone, remains estranged from the sympathies he excites everywhere [. . .]" (*OC*:N, X, 11). Nodier seems to have been rather happy sharing that cage, eating his heart with the same relish as Stephen Crane's masochist of the Thebaïd:

> I said, "Is it good, friend?"
> "It is bitter—bitter," he answered;
> "But I like it
> "Because it is bitter,
> "And because it is my heart."
> ("In the Desert," 1895)

If Nodier internalizes his object of desire in the course of his project to relinquish it, Baudelaire must fend it off in his novella *La Fanfarlo* (1847) even as he seeks its possession. Colombine caught is not the Colombine he would catch, the ever-to-be desired and never-to-be possessed. For, once caught, as she is by the fantastic Samuel Cramer, she "grows fatter every day":[40] no longer what Gautier calls "the dream pursued," she is incarnated in the all-too-lustrous flesh. Colombine off the stage, *sans rouge, sans jupe, sans allure d'actrice*, is, for Baudelaire-dandy, woman denuded of art. She is—in the famous phrase from *Mon coeur mis à nu*—"natural: that is to say, abominable."[41]

So Jean Starobinski contends.[42] But, as in Nodier's exercises upon the *scène funambulesque*, there is deeper drama here. Baudelaire, who was enamored of the pantomime, introduced it with special deliberateness into his *conte*. The actress upon whom he modeled la Fanfarlo, Marie Daubrun, was known for her roles in the melo and *vaudeville-comédie*, not in the pantomime.[43] The change—her translation from genre to genre—seems arbitrary, if not subtly misleading. If it is purely an aesthetic transformation that la Fanfarlo must undergo, then how much more appropriate to have made her a dancer *tout net*. Indeed Samuel invests her substance ("graceful" but "terrible") with poetry by virtue of her dance: "Dance is the poetry of arms and legs; it is matter, graceful and terrible, that has been animated, embellished by movement" (*F*, 82). But it is not for the dancer but for Colombine that he calls when they are alone in her rooms after the performance. And although the narrator declares that Samuel's love for the actress is "less an affair of the senses than of the reason" (*F*, 89), one suspects that the erotic fantasy in which Colombine must play a role has overmastered his respect for *le Beau*.

But "overmastered" is not quite the word here, for Sam-

---

[40] Charles Baudelaire, *La Fanfarlo*, ed. Claude Pichois (Monaco: Editions du Rocher, 1957), p. 93. This edition will be cited throughout this chapter as *F*, with appropriate page numbers.

[41] Charles Baudelaire, *Journaux intimes: Fusées, Mon Coeur mis à nu, Carnet*, ed. Jacques Crépet and Georges Blin (Paris: Corti, 1949), p. 53. This edition will be cited throughout this chapter as *JI*, with appropriate page numbers.

[42] *Portrait de l'artiste en saltimbanque*, pp. 60-65.

[43] See Claude Pichois, "Autour de 'la Fanfarlo': Baudelaire, Balzac et Marie Daubrun," *Mercure de France*, CCCXXVIII (December 1956), 607-14, 634-36.

uel *is* in possession of himself throughout their first night together. In a careful exposition of the irony in the tale, Nathaniel Wing argues precisely this point. Samuel, in Wing's Derridean perspective, enjoys the company of la Fanfarlo "not as the substance of presence, but as its sign." Having renounced "the Romantic search for sentimental unity parodied in the Mme de Cosmelly sequence," Samuel and the actress "act out a paradox: cultivating difference, the Poet and dancer sustain the illusion of unity."

> The quest of presence is successful only when recognized as an impossibility, and "unity" approached by the lucid cultivation of duality. The famous scene in which Samuel, about to possess the dancer, insists that she give herself to him not in "la splendeur radieuse et sacrée de sa nudité" [. . .] but in the costume she wore on stage as Colombine clearly represents more than a bizarre erotic fantasy. It is the final and most striking example of the Poet's cultivation of harmony through difference.[44]

But a (deconstructive) contradiction is embedded in those last two lines. The fantasizing mind, rather than maintain difference in the face of its object, seeks to appropriate it, to make it its own. La Fanfarlo in her "sacred" nudity would elicit Samuel's consciousness of differences; la Fanfarlo as Colombine appeals to his thirst for an erotic presence that alien flesh must always destroy.

Appeals to but does not slake. For only *différance*, the very principle and origin of difference, makes possible his being reflexively conscious at all. *Différance*, as Derrida explains in his essay "La Différance," is "the possibility of conceptuality"; it is "what makes the movement of signification possible," given the apparently ever-prevailing conditions of consciousness—"only if each element that is said to be 'present,' appearing on the stage of presence, is related to something other than itself but retains the mark of a past element and already lets itself be hollowed out by

[44] "The Poetics of Irony in Baudelaire's *La Fanfarlo*," *Neophilologus*, LIX (April 1975), 166, 167.

Charles Nodier · Charles Baudelaire

the mark of its relation to a future element."[45] La Fanfarlo,
as a creature of space and time, is perforce subject to the
play of differences: in short, to *différance*. But Samuel's quest
is, I think, a quest for a presence that is ultimately frustrated by the differences he perceives. And if he seems
somehow to have arrived at a rapprochement with the
dancer, one that was impossible with Madame de Cosmelly, it is because the intervals of difference have been
shrunken by fantasy, drawing him closer to the presence he
seeks. "*A* presence," "*the* presence": it is important that we
distinguish his object from "presence" itself. For I want to
argue, contrary to Wing's Derridean assumptions, that that
object is not fundamentally illusory (however, admittedly,
unattainable), that we may glimpse a special reality behind
this word that now languishes *sous rature*.

To understand both his quest and its goal, we should
begin, like Wing, with Baudelaire's *surnaturalisme*, to which
Wing opposes *différance*. "There are moments of existence,"
Baudelaire writes in *Fusées*, "when time and space are more
profound, and one's consciousness [*sentiment*] of existence
immensely increased" (*JI*, 23). Wing defines these moments as "ecstatic" experiences of "unity between the self
and a universal presence, which occur [. . .] in a time of
pure presence."[46] In another curious note from the *Fusées*,
Baudelaire records his desire to express this unity in a pantomime:

> Conceive a scenario for a lyrical or fairytale-like buf-
> foonery, for a pantomime, and translate that into a
> serious novel. Drown everything in an abnormal and
> dream-like atmosphere—in the atmosphere of *brilliant
> days of light* [*des* grands jours]. There should be some-
> thing soothing [*berçant*] about it—and even a strain of
> serenity running through the passion. Regions of pure
> Poetry. (*JI*, 33)

The word *berçant* betrays the identity of those "*Régions de
la Poésie pure*": they constitute the serene lap of the *mer*/

[45] Jacques Derrida, "Differance," *Speech and Phenomena, and Other Essays on Husserl's Theory of Signs*, tr. David B. Allison (Evanston: North-
western University Press, 1973), pp. 140, 142.
[46] "Poetics of Irony," p. 166.

95

mère, the sight of which is "so eternally agreeable" (*JI*, 85) to Baudelaire, the cradling lap upon which the poet is rocked in, for example, "La Chevelure." The source of that "*atmosphère anormale et songeuse*" is the inarticulate (and inarticulable) union with the mother to which Baudelaire always aspired. That he should have related this aspiration—for which the evidence is clamorous—to the pantomime suggests his profound intuition of the nature of that union: for it was not primarily an oedipal marriage, as René Laforgue has assumed.[47] Its goal, according more recently to Hélène Fredrickson (who has studied the letters to Madame Aupick with care), was identity with the maternal body, in a retreat to the wordlessness of the womb. He dreams of a return to earliest infancy, "in which every wish would be obeyed and every need filled on the instant," signifying "the abolition of literary creation and of the fame it can confer, since it would render all language useless."[48] A recovery of profound and infrangible silence, and of the warmth of the maternal sun, his ideal is not so much of "presence" as of blind confluence with the One.

It is an obliteration of the self in the Other—a kind of death about which we will have more to say when we turn to Gautier and Banville. The death is of single, hence personal, consciousness, an entering into a fullness that is a *non*-presence—at least as the term is usually understood. "Presence" traditionally implies self-presence, a Husserlian communion with the content of the mind "in a silent and intuitive consciousness."[49] But Baudelaire desires neither self-presence nor the "presence" of an independent Other: he, rather, thirsts for a mute Being that transcends (or subtends) personal consciousness itself. (*Surnaturalisme* is a *sentiment*, not a *conscience*, of existence.) It is a state very like that described by Uri Lowental in a recent study of "Dying, Regression, and the Death Instinct." Lowental's clinical observations of the terminally ill suggest that "the process of dying brings about a regression to infantile idea-

[47] *L'Echec de Baudelaire: Etude psychanalytique sur la névrose de Charles Baudelaire* (Paris: Denoël, 1931).
[48] *Baudelaire: Héros et fils: Dualité et problèmes du travail dans les lettres à sa mère* (Saratoga, California: Anma Libri & Co., 1977), p. 139.
[49] Derrida, "Differance," p. 146.

tion, object-relationships, and to the earliest pattern of emotional response." A nostalgia for "the unitary matrix of the primary affective constellation," this drive towards regression is "for a symbiotic reunion [with the mother], be it at the expense of [one's] own discrete existence." And Lowental concludes that "It is a regressive wish for non-being."[50]

Although Lowental refers to this wish as the "death instinct," as Thanatos, we should not confuse it with the "repetition compulsion" of Freud. The very ground of that compulsion, of a repeated deflection toward *Unlust*, it is— as we shall see in connection with Banville—a nostalgia for the "narcissism" of infancy. Freudian repetition, as Derrida has suggested, is in fact "an *economy* of death," the deferral that is *différance*, by which life paradoxically protects its integrity while betraying the self-destruction with which it is instinct. It is only by such a realization that we may conclude, with Freud, "that life *is* death, that repetition and the beyond of the pleasure principle are native and congenital to that which they transgress."[51] Our authority is this series of reflections in *Beyond the Pleasure Principle*:

> Under the influence of the ego's instincts of self-preservation, the pleasure principle is replaced by the *reality principle*. This latter principle does not abandon the intention of ultimately obtaining pleasure, but it nevertheless demands and carries into effect the postponement of satisfaction, the abandonment of a number of possibilities of gaining satisfaction and the temporary toleration of unpleasure [*Unlust*] as a step on the long indirect road to pleasure. (*SE*, XVIII, 10)

The pleasure principle intends, in short, the destruction of the self; but, since every organism "wishes to die only in its own fashion" (*SE*, XVIII, 39), it is opposed by the principle of "life," of repetition, deferral, *différance*. But we are dealing here not so much with an opposition of terms as with the dynamism of a single impulse. That impulse is

[50] *The Psychoanalytic Review*, LXVIII (fall 1981), 363.

[51] Jacques Derrida, "Freud and the Scene of Writing," *Writing and Difference*, tr. Alan Bass (Chicago: University of Chicago Press, 1978), p. 203.

différance itself, the "union of Eros and Thanatos,"[52] the protection of life as a movement towards death that is ever self-deferred.

But it is not the protection of life that motivates Baudelaire's principal fantasy. Upon the stage of the Baudelairean psyche is one object only, resplendent but inhumanly mineral: "What has always seemed to me, both now and in my childhood, the most beautiful thing in a theater," he writes in the *Journaux intimes*, "is *the chandelier* [le lustre]— a beautiful, luminous, crystalline, complicated, circular, and symmetrical object" (*JI*, 61). A mandala symbolizing the icy perfection of death (as *différance*, life is not capable of perfection), *le lustre* enters, by way of a casual admission, Samuel Cramer's description of la Fanfarlo: "[. . .] she danced, not with earrings, but with pendants hanging from her ears: I'd almost venture to say 'lusters' [*des lustres*]" (*F*, 78). The proximity of the actress inspires Samuel with the desire to translate himself to the luminous heart of those crystals. In her bedroom, he is overcome by what seem the poisonously heavy scents—and by a wish for self-extinction: "[. . .] the air, laden with bizarre miasmas, made one want to die slowly there, as if in a hothouse" (*F*, 87). When he calls for Colombine, he is, in effect, summoning the mother grown young, "*le rêve de ses jours les plus anciens*" (*F*, 83), a fantasy-object in which he may recover a primordial life-in-death. It is not difference he is cultivating but what Derrida calls, dismissively, a "transcendental signified" that would precede *différance*: the "presence" (or "absence": all words betray the vision) of the non-personal self at the nonoriginary origins of life. He seeks what Lacan calls, simply, the "real."

But *différance* is what he gets. For Colombine is for Samuel also the mother as genital object, source of both attraction and fear. "My mother is fantastical," writes Baudelaire in *Fusées*; "she must be feared and pleased" (*JI*, 30). Pleasing her promises the regressive pleasures of *bercement*, pleasures upon which—anticipating Freud—he implies that others, more dangerous, are propped:

[. . .] what is it that the infant loves so passionately in his mother, his nurse, his older sister [he asks in a

[52] Ibid., p. 331*n*.

letter to Poulet-Malassis]? Is it simply the being who feeds, combs, washes, and rocks him? It's also the caress and the sensual voluptuousness. For the infant, this caress is expressed unbeknownst to the woman, by all the woman's graces. He loves his mother, his sister, his nurse, then, for the pleasant tickling of satin and fur, for the perfume of her breasts and hair, for the jingling of jewelry, for the play of ribbons, etc.: for all this *mundus muliebris* beginning with the chemise and expressing itself even by the furniture, where the woman leaves the imprint of *her sex*.[53]

Consciousness of that imprint signals the awakening of the infant's oedipal sexuality, and, with it, consciousness of an insuperable *différence*.[54] Henceforth, union with the mother is subliminally a genital union, and the images by which this fantasy is elaborated undergo the displacements of sexual difference. For Baudelaire, forever haunted by the fantasy, the displacements assume an air of the grotesque: where once was asexual identification with the maternal body are now the neurotic compromises of perversion. Samuel can achieve that identification, for example, only by imagining himself androgynous: he who believes that "The angels are sterile and hermaphroditic" (*F*, 89) writes under a feminine *nom de plume*. For the same reason, la Fanfarlo acquires a penis: "She never wore those insipid gauzy dresses that allow everything to be seen and nothing to be imagined. She liked fabrics that make some noise, long, crackling skirts bespangled with tin plates, which have to be lifted very high by an energetic knee, the dresses of a *saltimbanque* [. . .]" (*F*, 78). That her uplifted knee is an erected penis accords with Samuel's fetishism: la Fanfarlo's leg is, "for Samuel, the object of an eternal desire" (*F*, 79); in leaving

[53] April 23, 1860: Charles Baudelaire, *Correspondance*, ed. Claude Pichois and Jean Ziegler ([Paris]: Gallimard, 1973), II, 30.

[54] "Insuperable" but not, to my mind, originary. Lacan would of course date the infant's sense of separation from precisely this point, from his induction into the "symbolic order" by the *Nom-du-Père*. But, as his own remarks about the mirror-stage imply, the child's consciousness of *différance* occurs long before the oedipal trauma, with the dramas of jealousy and self-possession in the "imaginary" order. Thus my relocating narcissistic "presence"—and I think I follow Freud in this—in the "impossible" register of the "real."

the theater he applies fervent kisses to the dancer's feet and hands (*F*, 83). The homosexual overtones, as Sartre has argued, mask a significantly passive fantasy: "that of his [i.e., Baudelaire's] body beneath a male desire"; this, in turn, is a screen-metaphor for a kind of onanism:

> It is a matter of an intention of desire, of a phantom of desire, more than of a reality. And it is in this secret void that Baudelaire revels at first—for he is in no way endangered by it. And since the desired object pays it no regard, [. . .] Baudelaire remains alone, shut up in his onanistic avarice.[55]

Samuel, one recalls, "was often alone in his paradise, no one could share it with him [. . .]" (*F*, 89).

The solitary self is the ideal because—or, more precisely, to the extent that—sexual difference cannot be overcome. Samuel may begin by assuring himself that la Fanfarlo's performance is "*décente*," but that word suggests its own cancellation—one that acquires voice in the adjectives that follow: "*féerique, folle, enjouée*" (*F*, 82). From the modesty of Marguerite and Elvire, she passes (by means of a *changement féerique*) to the lubricious gaiety of Colombine. Thus Samuel's ambivalence in her room, "that ravishing little hole, which savored at once of the lower depths [*du mauvais lieu*] and of the sanctuary" (*F*, 87); thus, too, his desire both to fondle its objects, as an infant a breast, and to draw his hands safely back: "La Fanfarlo's bedroom was [. . .] very small, very low, cluttered with things that were soft, per- fumed, and dangerous to touch [. . .]" (*F*, 87). Although irresistibly attracted to the dancer, he notes her abundance of heavy hair (*F*, 80), the obsessive meaning of which in Baudelaire has been analyzed by Charles Mauron. Later as- sociated with the tresses of the exigent Jeanne Duval, with the monster's "rubber appendage" in the poet's famous dream of 1856, with the enormous Chimera under which every back is bowed in *Chacun sa chimère*, it is a symbol of the mother as Other—as burden, *blessure*, and tomb: "The pet- rified Chimera is separated from the son, who had wished

[55] J.-P. Sartre, *Baudelaire* (Paris: Gallimard, 1947), pp. 178, 145-46.

to identify himself with it, and weighs him down."[56] It should not be surprising, then, that Samuel, who expresses the wish to die slowly near la Fanfarlo, as in a hothouse, is relieved that her chambers are small—that he will not be constrained, like the châtelains of old, "to make love in great bedchambers that had an air of the cemetery, in vast catafalques that happened to be called beds [. . .]" (*F*, 86-87). Woman as the all-encompassing One invites his impersonal death; woman as the sexual Other threatens an all-too-personal castration.

It is Samuel's intuition of the dangerousness of his fantasy that ensures his self-possession. His is a paradoxical position: driven to invest his object with all the attractions of fantasy, he is compelled to hold it off. And in failing to do so at the end of the tale, he suffers a predictable fate: as la Fanfarlo prospers, grows fat and fertile, he withers, unmanned, into sterility. He is less the Arlequin "not yet *poli par l'amour*" described by Francis Heck[57] than the Clown from "the misty realms of Spleen" in Baudelaire's essay "De l'essence du rire" (1855, revised 1857). There the poet recalls an English panto at the Variétés in which Clown, "le Pierrot anglais," is guillotined.[58] The parody of an *enfant sauvage*—an image everywhere touched by *différance*—Clown seems, like Samuel, a sexually ambiguous victim. The ribbons bedecking his costume "performed the office, about his jubilant person, of the feathers and down of birds, or of the fur of angoras" (*OC*:B, II, 538). Fantastically neither male nor female, he is that familiar of Baudelaire's reveries, the manly woman-with-a-penis, whose furs conceal her appendage. His object is "the same as that of the Pierrot known by everyone: insouciance and neutrality, and consequently the accomplishment of all his gluttonous and rapacious fan-

---

[56] *Des métaphores obsédantes au mythe personnel: Introduction à la psycho-critique* (Paris: Corti, 1962), pp. 59-60, 136.

[57] "Baudelaire's *La Fanfarlo*: An Example of Romantic Irony," *The French Review*, XLIX (February 1976), 335.

[58] "De l'essence du rire et généralement du comique dans les arts plastiques," *Oeuvres complètes*, ed. Claude Pichois, II ([Paris]: Gallimard [Bibliothèque de la Pléiade], 1976), 538-41. The *Oeuvres* will be cited throughout this chapter as *OC*:B, with appropriate volume and page numbers.

tasies, to the detriment now of Harlequin, now of Cassandre or Léandre" (*OC*:B, II, 539). Such, in general, is Samuel Cramer's goal: to gratify his fantasies while maintaining from his object an ironically respectful distance (*"insouciance et neutralité"*). Thus, given its structure as a compromise-formation, his drama has "something terrible and irresistible" (*OC*:B, II, 539) about it. For Clown, alas, too much of the terrible: he loses his head to the (castrating) blade.

What Baudelaire found irresistible in the pantomime, however, and why he chose it as la Fanfarlo's *métier* is suggested by Clown's blithe response to his beheading: "But suddenly the stumpy torso, set in motion by the irresistible monomania of thievery, stands up, makes off victoriously with its own head like a ham or a bottle of wine, and—much shrewder than the great Saint Denis—sticks it in its pocket!" (*OC*:B, II, 539). Clown is, in Jean Starobinski's words, a *"joyeux revenant,"*[59] courting disaster out of the safety of immortality. He is immortal because, however numerous his fantasy-transgressions, he is the ward of an eternal asexual mother. All of the characters, as Baudelaire implies, Harlequin, Cassandre, Léandre, Pierrot, are her agents in a world of *différance*, separated from her (by sexuality?) but ultimately secure in her Edenic protection: "All of their gestures, all of their cries, all of their looks say: The fairy has wished it, destiny urges us on, I'm not troubled about it: let us go! let us run! let us fly! And they fly through the fantastic work, which properly speaking, begins only there [i.e., after the prologue]—that is to say, on the frontier of the marvelous" (*OC*:B, II, 541). Baudelaire makes it clear that here, at the *"frontière du merveilleux,"* in the "absolute comic," we are as close as is humanly possible to his *"rêve d'union magique."*[60]

Throughout his essay, he preserves a distinction between two realms, the prelapsarian and the fallen worlds, those of the *surnaturel* and *différance*. The first is the realm of joy: "It is a plant-like joy. Also, generally, it is the smile rather [than the laugh], something analogous to the wagging [*balancement*] of dogs' tails or the purring of cats" (*OC*:B,

[59] *Portrait de l'artiste en saltimbanque*, p. 85.
[60] Fredrickson's phrase: *Baudelaire: Héros et fils*, p. 143.

II, 534). Here, with the evocation of the subhuman—the vegetable unconscious—and of the Baudelairean *balancement*, we are again at the heart of the *lustre*, in the lap of the *mer/mère*. The second realm is of laughter, partaking of the contradictions of compromise: "[. . .] as laughter is essentially human, it is essentially contradictory; that is, it is at once the sign of an infinite grandeur and of an infinite misery: of an infinite misery relative to absolute Being, of which it possesses the conception, and of an infinite grandeur relative to the animals" (*OC*:B, II, 532). Joy, he explains, "is *one*. Laughter is the expression of a double, or contradictory, consciousness [. . .]" (*OC*:B, II, 534). Significantly, however, there are two categories of laughter, of what Baudelaire calls "the comic": man's sense of superiority over other men is expressed by "the significative comic"; his sense of superiority over nature is limned by the grotesque, "the absolute comic," of which the pantomime is "the refinement," "the quintessence" (*OC*:B, II, 535, 540). In name and form, *le comique absolu* approaches closest for "fallen humanity" to "*l'absolu définitif*," where "there is no longer anything but joy": "[. . .] the absolute comic, drawing much nearer to nature [than the significative comic], presents itself under a *unified* aspect [*sous une espèce* une], one that demands to be seized by the intuition" (*OC*:B, II, 536). It is in the pantomime, he implies, that we draw closest in fantastic terms to our first Colombine, *la fée*—to our wished-for union with the One.

For Baudelaire, the approach is vertiginous. Once the fairy has pledged her protection and the prologue concludes, "Immediately a sense of vertigo has entered, it circulates in the air; one breathes it, it fills the lungs and sends the blood pumping through the heart" (*OC*:B, II, 540). He stands, as it were, on the edge of psychic space, his very being whipped by the winds of dissolution. It is a moment of exhilaration and of self-loss, when one is warmed to a kind of inhuman molecular dance. Perhaps this is why Champfleury seemed to find Baudelaire shuddering always on the brink of evaporation, like the volatile Sprite of English pantomime:

> Physically and intellectually I wouldn't know how
> to describe Baudelaire better than to compare him to

a certain *Sprite* [sic: Sprit] of an English pantomime that we saw performed together. This *Sprite*, which ran all through the play and appeared usually with his legs in the air and his head below his heels, was especially remarkable for the brilliant flame he had at the end of his nose. From time to time I looked over at the stall beside mine, wondering whether Baudelaire hadn't made off without my knowing it to take up the role of that singular *Sprite*.[61]

A more banal image may be more appropriate—that of the moth beating with excitement about the flame, repulsed by the heat, fascinated by the light, suspended in a frenzied agony. Between Spleen and Ideal, Baudelaire would have had it. Between la Fanfarlo and *la fée*, in our own *termes funambulesques*.[62]

[61] Champfleury, *Souvenirs et portraits*, pp. 145-46.

[62] Baudelaire made another significant incursion into the pantomime with *Une Mort héroïque* (1863), for, "Although the narrative evokes an imaginary Renaissance," as Starobinski observes, "the art of Fancioulle is that of Deburau" (*Portrait de l'artiste en saltimbanque*, p. 86). I have, however, nothing important to add to the interpretations of this much-discussed prose-poem offered by Starobinski (ibid., pp. 86-92), Charles Mauron (*Le Dernier Baudelaire* [Paris: Corti, 1966], pp. 116-17), and especially Leo Bersani (*Baudelaire and Freud* [Berkeley: University of California Press, 1977], pp. 132-44). For a general discussion of Baudelaire's fools and *saltimbanques* who stand only on the fringes of the pantomime, see, in addition to Starobinski (ibid., pp. 92-99), Henri Leyreloup, "Baudelaire: Portrait du Poète en Saltimbanque," *Revue du Pacifique*, II (spring 1976), 33-41.

IV

Pierrot *posthume*:
Théophile Gautier

[. . .] Molière est avant tout un poëte, et un poëte fan-
taisiste; avec quatre pierrots plus ou moins pris à la Co-
médie italienne, il vous donne l'impression de la vie; mais
la vie, jamais; c'est trop laid [. . .].

GAUTIER TO EMILE BERGERAT,
in the latter's *Théophile Gautier:*
Entretiens, souvenirs et correspondance (1879)

L'esthétique n'est jamais loin d'une érotique.

MICHEL CROUZET
"Gautier et le problème de 'créer' " (1972)

"Shakspeare aux Funambules": the title of Gautier's most
important tribute to the pantomime is more than an affectionate irony conferred upon an entertaining popular stage.
It identifies that stage as "the fantastic, extravagant, impossible theater"[1] of which d'Albert dreams in *Mademoiselle de
Maupin.* "If Shakespeare's *Midsummer-Night's Dream, Tem-
pest,* or *Winter's Tale* can ever be produced in France," writes
Gautier of the Boulevard theaters in "Shakspeare aux Funambules," "rest assured that it will be only on these
wretched, worm-eaten stages, before these ragged spectators" (*OC,* XXIX, 56). For the drama of d'Albert's naïve
Shakespeare is of pantomimic *désinvolture:*

Everything is tied up and unraveled with an admirable carelessness: the effects have not the least cause,

[1] Théophile Gautier, *Oeuvres complètes,* éd. déf., IV (Paris: Charpentier,
1883), 238. This edition will be cited throughout this chapter as *OC,*
with appropriate volume and page numbers.

105

and the causes have not the least effect; the most intelligent character is the one that babbles the most
foolishness; the stupidest says the wittiest things [. . .].
The most extraordinary adventures occur one after the
other without explanation: the heavy father arrives ex-
pressly from China in a bamboo junk to acknowledge
an abducted little girl; the gods and fairies do nothing
but go up and down in their machines. The action
plunges into the sea beneath the topaz dome of the
waves and wanders about on the bottom of the ocean,
through the forests of coral and madrepore, or it soars
into the sky on a lark's or griffon's wings. (*OC*, IV,
242)

The costumes are bizarre, and the dialogue (like the mime's)
is "*très-universel*"; as for the characters, they are—familiarly—"all these charming types, so false and so true, that
soar on the particolored wings of whimsy over coarse reality, and in whom the poet personifies his joy, his melancholy, his love and his most intimate dream under the most
frivolous and unconstrained of appearances" (*OC*, IV, 242,
243).

Flamboyant, irrational, erotic, "*le théâtre fantastique*" is,
for both poet and public, precisely what Gautier called the
pantomime classique: a "visible canvas [. . .] filled in by an
interior improvisation."[2] Indeed, the latter, in its silence,
all the more closely approximates the ideal:

The great advantage of the pieces performed at the
Funambules is that no one talks in them. [. . .] While
this silent poem unfolds in front of you, your mind is
at work, your imagination in ferment; you follow with
an indefatigable attention these mysterious signs, living hieroglyphics that are sketched out and effaced with

[2] Review of *Pierrot et les Bohémiens* at the Funambules: *La Presse*, July
26, 1847. A great number of Gautier's reviews in *La Presse* were collected
and published as the *Histoire de l'art dramatique en France, depuis vingt-
cinq ans* (Paris: Magnin, Blanchard et Cie, 1858-59), 6 vols, but the pieces
in that collection are often fragmentary, mutilated, and marred by mis-
quotation. My references, which will appear throughout this chapter as *P*,
appropriately dated (month.day.year), are drawn, as in the first two chapters, from Gautier's original reviews in *La Presse*.

the rapidity of lightning.—It's delightful! [. . .] nothing fixes your thought, nothing arrests your reverie.
The pantomime shares this advantage with music, that
it is vague, indefinite, immense, obscure, and yet comprehensible to all: the coarsest and the finest minds
take an equal pleasure in it. (*P*, 7.26.47)

Private yet universal, comprehensible yet obscure, the hieroglyphics of the pantomime transcribe "immense" interior
dramas, their translations always differing from mind to
dreaming mind: "Nothing exists in absolute terms; it is the
spectator who constitutes the landscape, and the dreamer
the pantomime: that means everything—or nothing."[3]

For Gautier himself, the dream seems, at first, disap-
pointingly thin:

Cassandre represents the family; Léandre, the stupid
and wealthy fop who suits the parents; Colombine,
the ideal, the Beatrice, the dream pursued, the flower
of youth and beauty; Arlequin, with his monkey's mug
and serpent's body, his black mask, his particolored
lozenges, his shower of spangles, [symbolizes] love,
wit, mobility, audacity, all the brilliant qualities and
vices; Pierrot, wan, lanky, dressed in his pale costume,
always hungry and always beaten, [is] the ancient slave,
the modern proletarian, the pariah, the passive and
disinherited being who assists, with gloomy cunning,
at the orgies and follies of his masters [. . .]. (*P*, 1.25.47)

Georges Poulet has accustomed us to just such a response.
For the poet who seeks in the stability of Form an escape
from the ravening worm, these types of wholly conventional appearance and meaning have a nearly irresistible allure. What Poulet calls "the purely objective, aesthetic, and
epicurean typology of Gautier"[4] in fact informs almost all
of his later work, from the Moliéresque masks of *Le Tri-
corne enchanté* (1845) to the stock figures of romance in *Le*

---

[3] Gautier, review of *Les Carubins* at the Folies-Nouvelles: *Le Moniteur
Universel*, November 2-3, 1856. All references throughout this chapter to
Gautier's reviews in *Le Moniteur Universel* will appear as *MU*, with appro-
priate dates (month.day.year).

[4] *Trois Essais de mythologie romantique* ([Paris]: Corti, 1966), p. 125.

Capitaine Fracasse (1861-63). That this typology serves to allay a subtle psychic anxiety is suggested by Gautier's dissatisfaction when the conventions are disturbed. "In the comedy of masks," he writes apropos of Champfleury's *Pantomime de l'avocat*, "the types, in our opinion, must be invariable; it is not permissible to change anything in their character or in their costume" (*MU*, 12.4.65). A Pierrot who has abandoned his white *casaque*, who has been sired by Cassandre or married to Colombine; a Pulcinella whose dress is unfaithful to Gautier's notion of the Neapolitan type—all elicit at least a paragraph of half-playful reproach in his reviews.[5] His objections, when they are given, seem always somewhat off the point ("These are impersonal figures, of an absolute generality" [*MU*, 12.4.65]); more significantly, when he has important reasons for doing so, he does not hesitate to betray them himself. As spectator, however, he prefers, like the child, to watch the same comedy again and again, enlivened by an invariable family of masks.

Recently, Michel Crouzet has seen in Gautier's predilection for the type the manifestation of an "*esthétique du* Faux," an aesthetic by which the poet addresses an obsession that subsumes and supersedes what Poulet calls his "obsession with death": "the problem of 'creating.'" Any act of writing, Crouzet explains, paraphrasing the psychoanalyst Janine Chasseguet-Smirgel, betrays either authentic or inauthentic gestures of the "*moi créateur*." The latter repose upon "the magical acquisition of a false autonomous phallus, owing nothing to the identification with the father—that is to say, created by the subject himself outside of the founding principle of filiation." The subject thereby imagines himself able to "*leap*, by the invention of an absolute power," over the snares of "*son Oedipe*," especially his fears of castration: "The false object is made, not engendered; it is born of the fetish, itself reposing upon a pact with the False."[6] The

---

[5] See, for example, in addition to his review of *La Pantomime de l'avocat*, his criticisms of *La Gageure* at the Funambules (*P*, 8.31.46), of Scribe and Duveyrier's *Polichinelle* at the Opéra-Comique (*P*, 6.18.39), and of Fernand Desnoyers's *Le Bras noir* at the Folies-Nouvelles (*MU*, 2.11.56).

[6] Michel Crouzet, "Gautier et le problème de 'créer,'" *Revue d'Histoire Littéraire de la France*, LXXII (July-August 1972), 660-61.

fetishistic object (it is also Poulet's phrase),[7] *le Faux*, the type: they offer Gautier an incarnation of selfhood that permits an evasion of "interior truth."[8] Thus his transcribing *le rêve funambulesque* in unequivocally conventional terms: the pantomime is a shadow-play, not of private passions, but of publicly literary signs.

But there is every indication that Gautier was conscious of their signifying in a literary world alone. The "true human comedy" of the pantomime he likens to Balzac's massive romance; the types he describes comprise "a complete microcosm [. . .] sufficient for all the evolutions of thought" (*P*, 1.25.47)—but not necessarily of dream. The true dreamer beneath the thinker seems attracted at once by the artificiality of the types and by their essential *lack* of correspondence with the so-called real world:

> Cassandre, Colombine, Arlequin, and Pierrot [. . .] flutter like light phantoms blown about by the breath of Caprice, and never is their feet dirtied by the mire of the Real [*aux fanges réelles*]. If you should find anything that differs even more from mankind than these charming masks—painted, powdered, floured, or blackened—your puppets will be well-received, and we will say to them, like Hamlet to the players: "Welcome, masters, to Elsinor!" (*MU*, 12.24.55)

In his review of Maurice Sand's *Masques et bouffons*, Gautier again emphasizes the division between "*la vie réelle*" and the fantastic landscape of the *commedia dell'arte*, averring that, in the latter, "You are propelled outside of real life, into the fullness of art—into an atmosphere of caprice and fantasy where the imagination has plenty of elbow-room, and where it reproduces not the world itself but a shadow-theater of the world, much more exact than the copy made laboriously after nature" (*MU*, 11.21.59). It is more exact because it respects the mind's collaboration in giving sub-

---

[7] Georges Poulet, *Etudes sur le temps humain* (Edinburgh: Edinburgh University Press, 1949), p. 308. The sense that Poulet gives here to "*objet-fétiche*" is obviously not identical to that in Crouzet's analysis; but the equally provocative discussions of Crouzet and Poulet are, I think, complementary in fundamental ways.

[8] Crouzet's phrase: "Gautier et le problème de 'créer,' " p. 662.

stance to the shadow: as in *le théâtre fantastique* of d'Albert, the perceiver is invited to improvise—or to choose not to improvise, as we shall see very shortly—upon the stuff of his senses. "Nature," observes the narrator of *Fortunio*, "somewhat resembles those great symphonies that each interprets after his own fashion" (*OC*, XII, 95); so, too, does *le monde pierrotique*: "A pantomime is like a symphony in which each pursues his dream across the general design" (*P*, 7.26.47).

If these remarks simply turn us back to those at the beginning of this essay, they also instruct us in Gautier's own elusive aesthetics, in the way he manages to evade Crouzet's category of *le Faux* even as he seems to fall into it. In point of fact, *le rêve pantomimique* of Gautier is both more revealing than a conventional literary typology and more subtle than *le Faux* can suggest.

It seems to be founded, first of all, upon the grand nostalgia of all the Romantics—the nostalgia for the naïve. For Gautier, the naïve has primarily a perceptual (and existential), not a spiritual, value: to be naïve is to be free from the self-implicating and essentially self-defining task of interpreting the world. Such naïveté—of the mind at rest in sensation—results in one of the hero's rare moments of happiness in what Crouzet calls the *Confessions* of Gautier, *Mademoiselle de Maupin*:[9]

> [. . .] my satisfied and nonchalant gaze traveled, with an equal pleasure, from a magnificent pot all covered with dragons and mandarins to the house-slipper of Rosette, and from there to the corner of her shoulder that gleamed beneath the batiste; it hung on the trembling stars of the jassemine and on the blond hair of the willows on the riverbank, crossed over the water and strolled about on the hill, and then returned to the room to settle on the pink bows in the bodice of some shepherdess. (*OC*, IV, 124)

The gaze pregnant with its object and undisturbed by reflection is the *desideratum* of all of the poet's aesthetes: of

[9] "Introduction" to his edition of *Mademoiselle de Maupin* ([Paris]: Gallimard, 1973), p. 27.

the embryonic Des Esseintes of *Fortunio*, of the eponymous marchioness of the "joyous eighteenth century" in *Le Chien de la marquise*, of the speaker in the early "Jardin des Plantes," impatient with the "*Vains projets*" of thought ("Forgetting prose and verse, with my ardent eyes/I follow the young girl [. . .]/[. . .]/And I return with my sheet completely blank").[10] Gautier the *feuilletoniste* delights in spectacles of utter uninterpretability—such as those at the Folies-Nouvelles:

> There the sentimental and tearful genre is prohibited: no grand tirades, no melodramatic action, but a mad and capricious gaiety that laughs with an unbuttoned belly, without knowing why—which is the best and perhaps the only way to laugh. [. . .] To see *Les Deux Gilles* and to eat a green sugar-stick at the Folies-Nouvelles is a quite pleasant way to pass one's evening. (*MU*, 9.10.55)

Gilles is, as here, an especially congenial subject because he is a creature of the most unalloyed naïveté. Such was not, of course, the creation of Deburau, whose mask oscillated between the naïve and the "*réfléchi*" (*P*, 5.6.39); and if Gautier is severe on the sentimental type of Paul Legrand, he is hardly less critical of Baptiste:

> With him, the role of Pierrot was widened, enlarged. It ended by occupying the entire piece, and, be it said with all the respect due to the memory of the most perfect actor who ever lived, by departing entirely from its origin and being denaturalized. Pierrot, under the flour and blouse of the illustrious Bohemian, assumed the airs of a master and an aplomb unsuited to his character: he gave kicks and no longer received them; Arlequin now scarcely dared brush his shoulders with his bat; Cassandre would think twice before boxing his ears.

The old Pierrot, "the Pierrot so timid and cowardly," would have been fearful of such "audacities"; and Gautier concludes that the actor has betrayed the type:

[10] *Poésies complètes de Théophile Gautier*, ed. René Jasinski, nouv. éd. (Paris: Nizet, 1970), I, 69, 70. This edition will be cited throughout this chapter as *PC*, with appropriate volume and page numbers.

Et du Pierrot blafard brisant le masque étroit
Le front de Debureau [sic] perçait par maint endroit.
(*P*, 1.25.47)

[And out of the pale Pierrot, shattering the tight mask,/
The forehead of Deburau broke through in many
places.]

It is a Pierrot anterior to Baptiste's conception that is
most attractive to Gautier, a Pierrot unmindful of the mastery to which Deburau's type aspired. Gautier's is a wholly
unreflective *naïf*—"he, the independent *flâneur*, he who
shook his sleeves in the good Lord's sun like a bird its
wings, who inhaled the perfume of the rotisseries in a con-
templative ecstasy, who stretched out on the benches,
yawning at butterflies, or who followed in a dream the
spangle-covered skirt of Colombine [. . .]" (*MU*, 7.28.56).
In a review of Cormon and Trianon's *Le Trésor de Pierrot*,
an *opéra-comique* of 1864, he makes appeal to this type of
an earlier tradition in criticizing its Pierrot-*avare*:

> We hardly know [. . .] whether Pierrot, with the mo-
> bile and infantile mind that tradition lends him, is ca-
> pable of following logically an *idée fixe* through the
> whole course of two acts, as the authors of the new
> play have him do. That, for this bird-brain, is an im-
> possible task: Pierrot is a purely instinctive being; if
> he steals some money, it is assuredly not to hoard it
> up or to invest it at a fat interest rate; it is to pick a
> quarrel with Cassandre or to buy the wherewithal to
> satisfy his insatiable appetite and his inextinguishable
> thirst. Calculation is not his forte. (*MU*, 11.7.64)

But calculation is certainly the forte of Gautier himself.
A writer who began his career in self-conscious confession
and self-referential mockery seems far from the candor of
the type. Is his affection for Pierrot *le naïf*, then, but another manifestation of *le Faux*? Like d'Albert, who is terrified by "distractions without object" (*OC*, IV, 134), fearing a glimpse of *les laideurs* of his depths when his mind is
not rich with sensation, Gautier may be seeking in the ingenuous Gilles a mask behind which he may hide from
himself. Certainly there is the ever-present horror—in Onu-

phrius as in d'Albert—of detecting, "with the aid of the microscope, worms in the healthiest of aliments, serpents in the clearest of liquids" (*OC*, XVI, 69-70): the temptation to turn away from the interior (*vide* the Molière of our epigraph) to the naïve Pierrots of public fantasy was almost, for Gautier, an overmastering urge. But it was only "almost"—or, better, *apparently*—so. *Le Faux*, like every other paradox in this fascinating writer, acquires definition by the light of *le Vrai*. There is a point at which the two are, in fact, inextricable—when public fantasy becomes private improvisation, when the naïve is indistinguishable from self-examining calculation, when "the opening flower and the thinking mind" (*PC*, II, 120) enjoy an identity behind the self's superficial defenses. And beneath the ugliness of its depths.

In the course of his review of Champfleury's *Pierrot pendu*, Gautier embarks upon an historical and interpretive digression. What is Pierrot's origin? he asks: "Is it not as interesting as all the arcana that have excited the curiosity of the Bocharts, the Father Kirchers, the Cluveriuses, the Champollions, the Creutzers, the Francks?"[11] Two texts, of *"une origine ancienne*," supply various clues. The first, preserving the sketch of an incident in Pierrot's early life, has been handed down by generation after generation of schoolboys, who inscribe their grammars and dictionaries with "a mysterious hieroglyphic representing a Pierrot hung on a gibbet, beneath which one reads, as a kind of admonition, this meaningful legend in macaronic Latin":

> *Aspice Pierrot pendu*
> *Quod librum n'a pas rendu;*
> *Si Pierrot librum reddidisset*
> *Pierrot pendu non fuisset.*

[11] *La Presse*, January 25, 1847; all quotations in this and the following paragraph are from the review. Samuel Bochart (1599-1667), French Orientalist and Biblical scholar; Father Athanasius Kircher (1601-1680), German Jesuit, student of sciences, languages, and antiquity; Philipp Cluverius (1580-1622), German geographer and archeologist; Jean-François Champollion (1790-1832), French Egyptologist, decoder of the Rosetta Stone; Georg Friedrich Creuzer (1771-1858), German philologist and archeologist; Adolphe Franck (1809-1893), French philosopher of logic, law, and religion.

[Behold Pierrot hanged/For not having returned a
book;/If Pierrot had returned the book/He would not
have been hanged.]

The inference is easily drawn: at one point in his history
"that no one can determine, and that is lost in the night of
time," Pierrot stole a book, or failed to return a borrowed
one ("*le texte n'est pas très-explicite*"). The severity of the
punishment suggests the former crime. It seems a puzzling
incident, since "the traditions do not present us with a let-
tered Pierrot; it is nowhere apparent that he has pursued
any studies: he is ignorant though artful, credulous though
skeptical, and his social position consists in receiving slaps
from Cassandre."

But the second text unarguably supports the first. It, like
the latter, rests upon unimpeachable folk authority: it is a
ballad, "*bien connue*":

> *Au clair de la lune,*
> *Mon ami Pierrot,*
> *Prête-moi ta plume*
> *Pour écrire un mot.*

[By the light of the moon,/My friend Pierrot,/Lend me
your pen/To write a word.]

"From this stanza it is obvious that Pierrot possessed a pen
and that he was known for doing so, since, when a lover
needed to scribble a billet-doux by moonlight, he addressed
himself to friend Pierrot." If he had a pen, he knew how
to write, and if he knew how to write, he knew how to
read: he was not "devoid of all instruction." The conclusion
is, in fact, ineluctable that Pierrot was a scribbler of sorts.
His writing by moonlight, while his master was asleep, would
explain his pallid complexion. But his works are lost—and
"*quel dommage*," for it is a loss as regrettable for the eye as
for the mind: "How fine an effect Pierrot's works, bound
in white vellum, would have produced on the library book-
shelves!"

The analysis is pure Gautier. The elaboration, both artful
and affectionate, of a tiny, near-negligible subject, the "uni-
fication of the rational and the sensuous in the play in-

stinct,"[12] the mock neutrality of tone—all confer Gautier's particular stamp upon it. (Only Banville, a writer who, as we shall see, resembles *le bon Théo* in more ways than one, could possibly be mistaken for its author.) What is most characteristic about it—and central to our understanding of its every other aspect—is its irony. As the analysis progresses, we feel subtly (and pleasurably) implicated in an act of simultaneous creation and dissolution. Even as the argument unfolds, it is crumbling, disintegrating, falling away: for Gautier is, like Nodier, a *déconstructeur d'avant la lettre*. In a fascinating study of *Tristram Shandy*, Peter Conrad suggests that irony, specifically romantic irony, "reconstitutes the double plot" of Shakespearean tragicomedy "inside the paradoxical romantic mind: the tragic half is sentiment, the comic half the sport of that sentiment which Carlyle, in an account of Jean Paul Richter, likened to 'the playful teasing fondness of a mother to her child' [. . .]."[13] So even as Uncle Toby is tenderly escorting flies to the window-sash, Sterne's all-pervasive irony is holding that tenderness up to ridicule. The *littérature pierrotique* is full of precisely such sport. This line from Laforgue's "Complainte de Lord Pierrot," for example: *"J'ai le coeur triste comme un lampion forain* [I have a heart as sad as a Chinese carnival-lamp]," fuses the melancholy and the mocking, dissolving the first with the second in order to ensure, paradoxically, the invulnerability of the too-tender heart.

But Gautier's irony is, curiously, of a different sort. What is dissolved is not the sentiment but the very procedures by which that sentiment is evoked. Gautier's method is to adopt the perspective of a naïve empiricist, a dispassionate *tabula rasa* before the *données* of his "texts," and to compose from that perspective, with a pen of vanishing ink, a creature of independent (and personable) life. Pierrot blossoms into being—like one of those Japanese paper flowers that so charmed Proust's Marcel—out of a veritable nothing, acquiring history and character by the pressure of what we can only call the calculations of naïveté. It seems no more

---

[12] P. E. Tennant, *Théophile Gautier* (London: The Athlone Press of the University of London, 1975), p. 102.

[13] *Shandyism: The Character of Romantic Irony* (New York: Barnes & Noble, 1978), p. 23.

than a happy accident that he, like Gautier, is a writer; that his productions would have delighted Gautier's painterly eye; that, though a writer, he is (as Gautier wished to be) "*ignorant*" and "*credule*." These are inescapable implications of the "texts"; there is nothing of "invention" about them: they are facts, rationally deduced, verifiable.

Facts that dissolve. For they are, of course, those veritable nothings by which Pierrot struggles into life: facts of the imagination alone. The "texts" themselves are inventions—a bit of schoolboys' doggerel, a song of *le peuple*. But even as this objection raises its mocking voice, yet another dissolution is occurring. Are these texts in any way similar to the hieroglyphic enigmas of Bochart, of Father Kircher, of the eminent Champollion? How close are these exegetes' glosses upon antiquity to the deductions of Gautier? What in short distinguishes an (uninterpretable) *invented* text from an (interpretable) *discovered* one? To the utter *naïf*, for whom an understanding of history is conjectural (or, as for the author of the *Histoire du romantisme*, little more than a series of anecdotes), the distinction cannot be made.

But there is more than playful confusion behind this modest *mise en abyme*: there is the suggestion, as elsewhere in Gautier, that invention and discovery are one, that what the mind makes of the world is all that we may ever know of its essence. "Nothing exists but in ourselves," he observes in *Jean et Jeannette*, that dramatization of the ambiguous interplay between invention and discovery, artfulness and naïveté, mask and face: "it is our gaiety or our sorrow that renders our horizons smiling or sad" (*OC*, XXXI, 328). For Gautier—a man for whom the visible world certainly did *not* exist outside the theater of the mind—all horizons are interior horizons, all dramas interior dramas, played out in what Conrad calls the Palaces of Thought. In moving them indoors, he complicates considerably our view of his phenomenology of the naïve. For (as the comic sleuths of *Militona* illustrate) an act of "simple" perception becomes then inseparable from calculation. The naïve thus dissolves, collapses as an artificial category, an illusory state of mind. But in its very dissolution it permits the discovery of a process by which it may in part be recovered: it comes to signify that frail, momentary self-liberation when, through the wayward calculations of play, the mind subverts its own improvisations—relegating them by *le Faux*, as it were, to *le Faux*.

The result, as "Shakspeare aux Funambules" suggests, is *le Vrai*. Here, too, the mind is at play upon a text. Like the texts in the review of *Pierrot pendu*, it is an invention, this time one of Gautier's own. (So artful an invention is it that it has been interpreted as an account of an actual performance, seducing the Bocharts and Father Kirchers of the pantomime into speculations of lamentable effect.) And like most of Gautier's productions, it is a text wholly prefigured by conventions—those of the *pantomime-réaliste*, first of all, with its traditional types and *cascades*. Superimposed upon a succession of Pierrot's strokes of audacity—his murder of a peddler and theft of his garments, his courtship of a duchess as a *jeune seigneur*—is a legendary drama of revenge: like the specter of Banquo or the statue of the Commander, the peddler's ghost everywhere haunts his murderer, until, at the wedding of Pierrot and the duchess, both sink into the flames of hell.[14] The pantomime itself is presented within

---

[14] In his *Théophile Gautier: Auteur dramatique*, Claude Book-Senninger (who erroneously accepts the long-standing interpretation of Gautier's essay as a review of *Marrrchand d'habits!*) notes that among the "Manuscrits trouvés dans les papiers de Th. Gautier," now in the Bibliothèque Spoelberch de Lovenjoul at Chantilly, there is a scenario that recounts the same plot as *Marrrchand d'habits!* but that "the author of this pantomimic scenario is unknown" (p. 337*n*). There are, in fact, two scenarios that recount that plot (C515, ff. 22-25 and ff. 26-39), though neither recounts the same details and both diverge in important ways from "Shakspeare aux Funambules." The first, in a copyist's careful hand and a clumsy prose, is untitled; it follows Pierrot through a series of events obviously inspired by Gautier's *feuilleton* but climaxed by the peddler's sudden (and unexplained) return to life and offer to his murderer of an honest living in the ragseller's business. The second, entitled *Habits-Galons, pantomime en cinq tableaux* and including, verbatim, long passages from "Shakspeare aux Funambules" in several scenes, seems a revision of the first. Its most important change is a more credible ending: now after enduring the persecution of the peddler's ghost and being reduced, as in the cruder version, to a suicidal despair, Pierrot is saved by *"une gracieuse femme ayant sur la poitrine cette phrase écrite en lettres d'or*: [. . .] je suis le pardon *et portant en outre une riche bannière avec cette inscription*: Crime expié/est oublié" (f. 39, paragraphing simplified). Its plot is clearly that described by L.-Henry Lecomte in his summary of *Mort et Remords, ou les Inconvénients d'assassiner*

the framework of another set of conventions, that of the dramatic review. Gautier describes his nostalgia at returning to the theater, ten years after *le beau temps* of *Le Boeuf enragé* and of *Ma Mère l'Oie*. He confesses to a certain uneasiness, inspired by the renovations to the *salle* ("it was almost clean: that alarmed me") and by the five or six cornets in the orchestra ("vague apprehensions of comic opera passed through my head" [*OC*, XXIX, 57]). But the rising of the curtain putting an end to his fears, he follows the piece with uninterrupted delight.

After several paragraphs of summary, Gautier turns, as convention dictates, to analysis. This *parade*, "with its mixture of laughter and terror," he declares, "conceals a myth that is very profound, perfectly whole, and highly moral, a myth that need only be formulated in Sanskrit to give rise to a swarm of commentaries" (*OC*, XXIX, 64, 65). Coming from the author of the "Préface" to *Mademoiselle de Maupin*, that "highly moral" makes us recoil in distrust; and in the explication that follows we are suspended *sans relâche* between credulity and disbelief. For the "myth" of the *parade* is an interior drama, at apparent odds with the knockabout of pantomime. An allegory of a soul's descent into remorse, the action is wholly symbolic: the peddler's second-hand sword is Opportunity, offering its hilt to "tempted and vacillating" minds; the peddler's spirit is Remorse itself, driving Pierrot to disorder, early sorrow and death (*OC*, XXIX, 65). The stage is, consequently, the skull of the victimizer-victim, of a Hamlet *funambulesque*, whose engagements transpire in a kind of deep mental space, its furniture the machinery of the mind. But at the same time

---

un marchand d'habits grêlé, a version of *Marrrchand d'habits!* by Paul Legrand and Charles Bridault produced at the Folies-Nouvelles in 1856 (see Lecomte, *Les Folies-Nouvelles*, pp. 65-67). This fact, together with the notation of cast members on the Lovenjoul manuscript (Legrand as Pierrot, Laurent as Léandre, etc.), identifies *Habits-Galons* as an early version of *Mort et Remords*. But what explains the presence of these two pieces among Gautier's papers? Perhaps the poet was asked by the authors to look over the presumably earlier scenario, both as a tacit acknowledgment of his collaboration in the project and as a polite solicitation of his own scene-writing energies. The result was then *Habits-Galons* (produced as *Mort et Remords*), enriched by Gautier's suggestions—and prose, now plagiarized by permission.

Pierrot is, paradoxically, the pure *naïf*: "When Pierrot took the sword, he had no other idea than of pulling a little prank!" (*OC*, XXIX, 65). His murder of the merchant was purely instinctive, and his subsequent encounters with the ghost elicit the naïve reactions of a *fantoche*.

Between the opaque Gilles of the summarized plot and the transparent Hamlet of the analysis—between, that is, candor and calculation, the naïve and the manipulative, the uninterpretable and the interpreted—Gautier's irony leaves us nothing to choose. Which is precisely as it should be: choice, as it is understood in the practical world, has no meaning in the realm of play. Play's first condition is mobility of mind, and to choose is to step outside this mobility into the sobriety of rationality or self-delusion (are they one?). This is not to imply, as Gautier seemed to assume, that play scorns *les fanges réelles*. As Freud suggests in *Jokes and Their Relation to the Unconscious*, the kind of psychic economy characteristic of play, by which apparently unreconcilable elements are unified, is directed by two impulses from the reality within, the one attempting to elude the critical faculty (*die Kritik*), and the other to substitute a pleasurable, child-like mood for the adult's habitual state of mind (*SE*, VIII, 129). In "Shakspeare aux Funambules," *die Kritik* is eluded in that mobility I have spoken of— while the real is recovered in a descent to *la boue*. Not, certainly, to the mudflats that Crouzet spies out in d'Albert's interior, "that country of his desires that he describes as a jungle or as a bestial and rotting bog, 'a country flourishing and splendid in appearance, but more saturated with putrid and deleterious miasmas than that of Batavia' ":[15] Gautier's "*porqueries*" (as he described his own sport in this *pays*)[16] are confined, as literature, to his libertine verse alone. It is a descent, rather, to the primal mud of his earliest being, far beneath the *laideurs* of the self—back to what Crouzet calls "the desired Form, image of the uniquely desirable, and of power also, image of the first and complete

[15] "Gautier et le problème de 'créer,' " p. 680.

[16] See, e.g., his *Lettres à la Présidente*, ed. Pascal Pia (Paris: La Bibliothèque Privée, 1968), pp. 58, 65, 91.

great Object from which nothing is separated": the pre-oedipal, phallic Mother.[17]

Effectively (and affectively) it is, like Baudelaire's *surnaturalisme*, a willful descent into death. "This is how I imagine supreme happiness," writes d'Albert:

> —it is a great square building without windows to the outside: a great courtyard surrounded by a colonnade of white marble; in the middle, a crystal fountain in the Arabian style with a jet of quicksilver; alternating tubs of orange- and pomegranate-trees: above it all, a very blue sky and a very yellow sun. Big greyhounds with pike-like snouts would lie sleeping here and there; from time to time barefooted blacks with gold rings around their legs and beautiful slender white serving-women dressed in rich and whimsical garments would pass through the rounded arcades, shallow little baskets on their arms, amphoras on their heads. And I: I would be there, immobile, silent, under a magnificent canopy, surrounded by piles of cushions, a great tame lion beneath my elbow, the naked bosom of a young slavegirl under my foot for a hassock, smoking opium in a large jade pipe. (*OC*, IV, 203-204)

As an image of infantile contentment, the vision is complete: power, pleasure, unreflective self-sufficiency—all constitute a preoedipal paradise. And for the worshipper of plastic Form, *tout est luxe, calme et volupté*, the very symbol of *le Beau. Mais tout est aussi mort. "Sa pensée-maîtresse"*— such is death, declares one of Gautier's critics,[18] thereby fusing *la Mort* and *la Mère*. Like the awesome white figure rising up at the end of Poe's *Pym*, she draws him ineluctably towards the abyss: "What a pleasure it would have been,"

---

[17] "Gautier et le problème de 'créer,' " p. 668. Crouzet's instincts are correct here, although he considerably deforms Chasseguet-Smirgel's argument. (For a more faithful reproduction of that argument, see below, pp. 165-66). Crouzet would have found more sympathetic support for his remarks in H. van der Tuin, *L'Evolution psychologique, esthétique et littéraire de Théophile Gautier: Etude de caractérologie "littéraire"* (Amsterdam: Holdert & Co., 1933), especially pp. 21-38.

[18] A. Fontainas, "Les Poésies de Théophile Gautier," *MF* (September-October 1911), cited in Tennant, *Théophile Gautier*, p. 47.

he exclaims in the *Voyages en Russie*, "to fly at full speed back towards the Pole, with its crown of Northern Lights, at first through the pinewoods heavy with frost, then through the half-buried birch forests, then across the white and immaculate immensity, over the sparkling snow, that strange floor that would lead you to believe, by its silvery sheen, that you are journeying over the moon, through the sharp, cutting air, as icy as steel, in which nothing corrupts, even death!" (*OC*, IX, 112). What the aging Gautier most feared, according to his son-in-law Bergerat, "was ugliness. To be ugly in death: that was his supreme preoccupation [. . .]."[19] To return to the Mother was to recover a time incorruptible, outside duration and decay: it was to find a wholeness and perfection of selfhood ("is it my existence that desires to complete itself?" asks d'Albert of his friend Silvio [*OC*, IV, 41]) in the fullness of *Néant*.

So the Pierrot of "Shakspeare aux Funambules" is condemned secretly—and rather shockingly—by Gautier's wish. His end is not wholly without precedent: the Pierrot antedating Baptiste's conception sometimes blundered his way towards oblivion. In, as we have seen, *Le Génie rose et le génie bleu* (1817), his crimes sweep him into the jaws of hell; even in Deburau's pantomimes he often shuddered in a devil's embrace. There was, in fact, just enough play in the popular traditions to make possible the pale hero's death—a dénouement that would later be denied to Gautier when he tried to entomb Sigognac of *Le Capitaine Fracasse* in the Château du Misère. If Baptiste had discovered an unknown audacity in the type, he had not delivered him completely from helpless *malheur*: his Pierrot had the makings of Scapin or of Hamlet. Both are summoned up by "Shakspeare aux Funambules," and both coalesce into one.

It was the poet's *pensée-maîtresse* that encouraged that coalescence. As Conrad points out, the naïve and the thought-obsessed (for him, Falstaff and Hamlet) share a subtle identity: "Apparently opposed, the tragic mind against the comic body, the chafing ineradicable intellectual being against comfortable, contented absorption in the flesh, Hamlet and

---

[19] *Théophile Gautier: Entretiens, souvenirs et correspondance*, 2nd ed. (Paris: Charpentier, 1879), p. 223.

Falstaff are secretly alike." Both aspire "towards a romantic state of self-forgetfulness, which they approach by different disciplines": Hamlet, by withdrawing from the sensible world "and the nauseous unceasing conscious life it imposes"; Falstaff, by "sinking down through the flesh" to a state of "profound carelessness and inanition." They are, of course, self-forgetful in a double sense. On the one hand, they are "moving towards that mystic state of extinction of will which Schopenhauer described," in order to "descend into the numbness and prostration of the inert, Lethean Hamlet or Falstaff babbling of green fields"; on the other, they are justifiably forgetful of the very extinction towards which they are moving, for, "Having become voluntary, death is no longer final. Resurrection is always possible [. . .]."[20] For Gautier, extinction and resurrection are indistinguishable: the self-obliterating union with the Mother is the self-perfecting recovery of life. And he enjoys this paradox by virtue of another: that naïveté is recoverable by calculation. "Between the opening flower and the thinking mind," he asked in "A un jeune tribun," "Between nothingness and nothing, what is the difference?" (*PC*, II, 120). *La différence* to the mind at perfect rest—or at ironic play—is none.

As these remarks imply, Gautier's is essentially a comic vision; if his *pensée-maîtresse* is death, it is death robbed of its sting. Certainly, he is always horrified by the prospect of death as decay. As Serge Fauchereau observes, "death confronts Gautier like a charm, being at once repulsion and attraction."[21] But outside the *frissons* that darken—somewhat theatrically—the earlier poetry, the attraction seems always the stronger; and this is so because death is associated (by one of the mind's bland paradoxes) with his most profoundly instinctive life. For the same reason, Gautier is most serious when he is most at play, when his irony has freest rein: it is no accident that "Shakspeare aux Funambules" figures, in Fauchereau's words, "among his best pages."[22]

20 *Shandyism*, pp. 8-9.
21 *Théophile Gautier* (Paris: Denoël, 1972), p. 66.
22 Ibid., p. 85.

These reflections prepare us for a reading of *Pierrot posthume* (1847), the poet's versified contribution to *la scène funambulesque*, being what Claude Book-Senninger calls a "*pantomime parlée.*"[23] It is a characteristic piece. Superficially devoid of originality, it owes its conception to another's idea and its plot to an earlier *parade*.[24] Pierrot seems at first only the *naïf* of tradition, the connoisseur of rotisseries and the gull of his pantomimic confrères. The victim of Turkish pirates, he is, predictably, hanged at sea ("*Aspice Pierrot pendu*"); but he escapes death when the rope is cut too soon and he is plummeted into the waves. On returning to Paris, he is convinced by Arlequin (who is enamored of his wife) that the hanging has done him in. The Doctor concurs with this judgment, attributing his apparent corporality to the unnatural health of a vampire. For a certain sum, an antidote is suggested—and the happy Pierrot is, in the closing scene, joined with Colombine, his *femme*.

Beneath this "*farce éternelle aux mêmes personnages*" (*OC*, XV, 203) is a private *comédie de la mort*. Like the hero of "Shakspeare aux Funambules," Pierrot has a paradoxical underside. A *naïf* and dupe in his relations with the world, he is a Hamlet in his dialogues with himself—a Hamlet whose too solid flesh has at last resolved itself into a dew:

> *Je battrais Arlequin, je reprendrais ma femme . . .*
> *Mais comment? avec quoi? Je ne suis plus qu'une âme,*

[23] *Théophile Gautier: Auteur dramatique*, p. 275.

[24] According to a letter from the director of the Vaudeville, Lefebvre, to *Le Corsaire* (October 8, 1847), "The idea of this piece had blossomed in my mind during the happy times when I was able to live in the country, several months before I was to take over the management of the Vaudeville. [. . . B]ut I told myself that this work, written purely and simply in prose, would furnish my good friends the opportunity to apply the label *Funambules* to my theater, and I quite frankly devised the means to have it executed in verse by one of our justly renowned writers. I went to Théophile Gautier" (cited by [Charles V.M.A.] de Spoelberch de Lovenjoul, *Histoire des oeuvres de Théophile Gautier* [1887; Geneva: Slatkine Reprints, 1968], I, 379-80; paragraphing simplified). In reviewing the comedy, T. Sauvage noted the similarity of *Pierrot posthume* to a vaudeville at the Théâtre de la Rue de Chartres, *Gilles en deuil de lui-même* (*Le Moniteur Universel*, October 11, 1847). Although Siraudin is often named as a coauthor of the piece, his role was apparently only that of a "*carcassier*," limited, as Book-Senninger observes, to offering "a few bits of advice" (*Théophile Gautier: Auteur dramatique*, p. 299).

Théophile Gautier

Un être de raison, tout immatériel;
L'hymen veut du palpable et du substantiel . . .
On se rirait de moi, mon trépas est notoire,
Et c'est un fait acquis désormais à l'histoire.
Pourquoi vouloir, objet de risée ou d'effroi,
Rester dans ce bas monde où je n'ai plus de moi?
Quelle perplexité! pour sortir de ces doutes,
Suicidons-nous, là, mais une fois pour toutes.

(*OC*, XV, 193)

[I'd give Arlequin a beating, I'd take back my wife . . ./
But how? with what? I'm no longer anything but a
soul,/A rational being, of no substance at all;/Wedlock
requires something palpable, material . . ./I'd be a
laughing-stock: they all know I'm dead,/And that's a
fact belonging henceforth to history./Why desire, O
object of derision or fright,/To remain in this world
here below where I no longer have a self?/What perplexity! To put an end to these doubts,/Let's put an
end to myself, now, once and for all.]

To be or not to be is still the question, but it is playfully
subverted by a more fundamental one: Is there an "I" who
is? Significantly, it is not the Doctor's antidote that restores
his sense of self—though promised, the potion is never
produced—but his reunion with the matronly Colombine.
"You cannot stay," she tells Arlequin, "Pierrot has come
back": and she receives her spouse with the same teasing
fondness that a mother shows her child: "I'll coddle you,
caress you . . ." (*OC*, XV, 202, 200). At the end of the
play, Pierrot, the *"fantôme blanc,"* remains ambiguously between life and death;[25] the fact that dissolves his existential
perplexity—dissolves it by diminishing its importance—is
Colombine's embrace. To ensure the future of his preoedipal bliss (he was always, says Colombine, *"un mari bien*

[25] When, in 1863, the play was performed *chez* Gautier as part of the
poet's fifty-second birthday celebration, Gautier *fils* as Pierrot was, according to Jules and Edmond de Goncourt, "cold, glacial, funereal—and too
dead in his posthumous role" (*Journal: Mémoires de la vie littéraire*, ed.
Robert Ricatte [Paris: Fasquelle-Flammarion, 1959], I, 1128). The author of the play—he took the role of the Doctor—was doubtless responsible for his son's strangely preternatural moribundity.

froid" [*OC*, XV, 186]), he invites Arlequin to share their ménage: henceforth Pierrot will be satisfied, Arlequin will be, in his words, "*vertueux,*" and Colombine (so she says) will be "*sage.*"

"In a piece whose title we have forgotten," wrote Gautier in his review of *Le Sylphe d'or*, a *féerie* of 1839,

> Deburau, with his intelligent face of plaster, spotted with two little eyes, black with malice and reflection, is walking with his hands in his pockets down that double-forked road that leads to virtue or to vice. To steal or not to steal a pâté: that is the question.—All of a sudden, a trapdoor opens, and out of a whirlwind of spirits of turpentine flashes a black and monstrous face. Deburau, a bit surprised, looks at the little devil, who tells him in a menacing tone: "I am your evil genie!" Without the least concern, he goes into a corner to fetch an axe, pushes up his sleeves, spits in his hands, and, with that reflective and cunning air that is so familiar, cuts his evil genie very cleanly in two and throws the pieces into the still open trap. The evil genie dispatched, now a fairy sparkling with spangles, a bit of red tinsel in her hair for a star, steps from a cloud and introduces herself to the clown by saying: "I am your good genie!" Deburau picks up his axe again, spits in his hands, and cuts the good genie into three pieces.—But he eats his pâté and the action continues as if nothing had happened. This scene well deserves to be placed at the beginning of every theatrical extravaganza. (*P*, 5.6.39)

Gautier set this scene before almost all of his own productions. Not only were Good and Evil usually dismissed in favor of the sweets of the senses, but the conventions, like these genii of Deburau's pantomime, were, though present, always subtly betrayed. As a writer, Gautier could not create without the assurances implicit in Form, but neither could he accede to those assurances without first investing Form with wish. What, therefore, he deplores as passive spectator, he without apology admits to his work: Pierrot perishing beyond the apparent hope of appeal, or married shamelessly to his rival's Colombine. His is a very private aesthetic, for all its appearances of conventionality. Founded upon the void that is a plenum, it is the aesthetic of a primal thirst, forever slaking itself in the well of infancy, imbibing the energy for play.

V

Pierrot *narcissique*:
Théodore de Banville

[. . .] ces vers toujours funambulesques de Banville, comme c'est le talent d'un jongleur de lettres, qui n'a que des mots dans la cervelle!

Goncourt Journal, October 18, 1890

Ce soir, Daudet faisait le portrait de Banville, disant que c'était l'homme qui avait peur de tout, peur d'une attaque de journal, peur d'un duel, peur de l'enfer, peur des coins d'ombre d'une chambre. Une peur qui l'avait empêché de sortir et de mettre en circulation le fond de son âme, qui était mauvais, acerbe, méchant. Une peur qui, par son universalité, devenait presque grandiose! Toute sa vie, dans son existence, Banville avait été le Pierrot funambulesque.

Goncourt Journal, March 15, 1891

"The old Spectacle des Funambules on the Boulevard du Temple," wrote Banville towards the end of his life, "[. . .] was certainly one of the most charming and entertaining things that Paris had to offer, and if I except the incomparable joys of poetry and love, the hours I spent in that little smoke-filled hall were without a doubt the best of my life."[1] His remark expresses more than nostalgia: it betrays

[1] Théodore de Banville, *Mes Souvenirs*, p. 215, cited throughout this chapter as *S*, with appropriate page numbers. Unless otherwise indicated, the standard Charpentier-Fasquelle edition is that to which all future parenthetical citations refer. The *Poésies complètes* (1883-88), comprising the following titles, will be cited, conventionally, by Roman numerals (dates in parentheses are those of the first edition): I: *Les Cariatides* (1842), *Les Stalactites* (1846), *Le Sang de la Coupe* (1857), *Roses de Noël* (1878); II: *Les Exilés* (1867), *Odelettes* (1856), *Améthystes* (1862), *Rimes dorées* (1869), *Rondels* (1874), *Les Princesses* (1874), *Trente-six Ballades joyeuses* (1873);

Banville's thirst for a charmed interior space. For *"cette pe-tite salle enfumée"* was clearly, for the poet, the stage for plays of the secret mind. Of the mind's dimensions, his Funambules was *"extrêmement petit,"* small enough to be held "in the hand" (*AP*, 21). Nestled in an "Eden," a *"jardin enchanté,"* it attracted "all of Balzac's Paris, drunk with love, with madness, with voluptuousness, with spirit, with joy" (*AP*, 24, 25)—passions unbridled by the fastidious claims of what Freud called "the higher systems," for, "there, the working-people, and also the urchins, the loafers, the scamps of the street, came as they were, in rags, in dirty jerseys, with unwashed hands, with dirty feet, without socks" (*AP*, 25). Insouciant children of the id, oblivious to dirt and dress, confounding the pleasurably real with the imagined, they saw there, "not in approximation, but in their absolute reality, the palaces of rubies and lapis lazuli, the skies of turquoise, the waterfalls streaming down in cascades of diamonds, in a ravishing display of coalescent metals, opals, and pearls" (*AP*, 26).

The hostile world outside was by no means excluded; indeed, *"monstrueux et abominable,"*[2] it appeared infused with what Banville called in his preface to the *Odes funambulesques* "the great character of our complex age"—with "an extreme degree of intensity," with *"le Paroxysme"* (III, 11). *La vie réelle, c'était la pantomime même*:

> It is familiar to those grown old—to come in by the window or fall down through the chimney, to receive passers-by on your head, to fill your glass so that another can empty it, to surrender to a barber who cuts off your nose, to submit to rain, storm, war; to follow after, go elbowing through, revile, confront a crowd,

---

III: *Odes funambulesques* (1857), *Les Occidentales* (1869), *Idylles prussiennes* (1871). Among the remaining volumes, the following (1882-1902) will be cited by abbreviations of title: *L'Ame de Paris: Nouveaux Souvenirs* (1890) as *AP*, *Le Baiser* (1887) as *B*, *Comédies* (1852-77) as *C*, *Contes féeriques* (1882) as *CF*, *Dans la Fournaise* (1892) as *DF*, *Lettres chimériques* (1885) as *LC*, *La Lanterne magique* (1883) as *LM*, *Marcelle Rabe* (1891) as *MR*, *Sonnailles et Clochettes* (1890) as *SC*.

[2] So Banville described *"le drame de la vie tel qu'il est"* in a review of Molière's *Georges Dandin* at the Théâtre-Français: *Le National*, February 16, 1874.

to be a crowd yourself, to not know where you are going and to howl for not getting there, to listen to a mad musician who, pulled about, beaten up, broken into pieces, torn into bits, continues to play his tune without noticing a thing; to roll around, to tumble down, to come popping up, to hide yourself, to fall asleep and be awakened with a start, to spill into a coach, to spring onto a train, to empty and fill your trunks, to make somersaults only to fall back in a chair and, finally, not have the time to sit there; to be wounded with unexpected sores, adorned with inexplicable humps, caught between doors, fleeced, crushed, pilloried, beaten, hugged, bussed, quartered, shaken like a puppet whose invisible strings are worked by an ironic hand: that is precisely life as it is.[3]

And yet the pantomimes of the Funambules "realized [a] double goal of making one forget Life and of representing it all the same" (S, 216), for through this farcically terrible spectacle, deprived of humanity and sense, "the shimmering Arlequin and the svelte Colombine, egoists like love itself, made their escape, took their leave, went running away, ecstatic, happy, hand in hand, drunk with springtime, youth, and dreams [. . .]" (S, 217). Like all emanations of the wish-expressive mind, they enjoy magic sympathy with an obliging object world. So the Sprite suggests in describing their flight in *Les Folies-Nouvelles* (1854), Banville's prologue for the opening of that little theater:

> Le feuillage s'éclaire au bruit de leurs chansons;
> Un repas sort pour eux du milieu des buissons;
> Sur leurs pas, que dans l'air suivent des harmonies,
> Des barques et des chars, poussés par les génies,
> Leur offrent un abri sous des voiles flottants,
> Et tout leur réussit, parce qu'ils ont vingt ans!
>
> (III, 88)

[3] Théodore de Banville, "Préface" to [Richard Lesclide], *Mémoires et pantomimes des frères Hanlon Lees* (Paris: Reverchon et Vollet, [1880]), pp. 12-13. Although Banville is alluding here to specific pieces of business in the Hanlons' pantomimes, his description is obviously applicable to many pantomimes of the Funambules.

[The foliage lights up at the sound of their songs;/A meal appears for them from the middle of the bushes;/In their footsteps, accompanied by aerial harmonies,/Barks and carriages, pushed by the genii,/Offer them a shelter under billowy veils,/And everything succeeds for them, for they are twenty years old!]

Neither Cassandre nor Pierrot can part them: the first, "*sot comme la raison*" (III, 87), a comic figuration of "*l'autorité*" (*AP*, 19), the superego incarnate, is impotent before their naked eminence of desire; the second, for reasons that will require later elaboration, pursues them "with a complete indifference, with a profound disdain, with the most skeptical dandyism, knowing the prodigious futility of all human effort, and having merely the point of view of a performer throughout nature [*et n'ayant d'autre point de vue que d'avoir lieu à travers la nature*], while preserving on his spotless clothes and on his face, as bloodless as the Gods', the whiteness and the glorious uselessness of the lily" (*S*, 218). For the meaning of the two lovers' courtship, Banville offers an allegory that is both banal and provocative:

> *Voyez! c'est Arlequin avec sa Colombine,*
> *Ce joli couple en qui le poète combine*
> *L'âme avec le bonheur se cherchant tour à tour,*
> *Et l'idéal avide, en quête de l'amour!*
> (III, 87)

[See! it is Arlequin with his Colombine,/This charming couple in whom the poet combines/The soul with happiness, seeking each other by turns,/And the avid ideal, in quest of love!]

The provocation is to accept their drama, as the couplets literally suggest, as a play of interior forces—to see the object of lithe Arlequin's love not as a creature outside the desiring mind but as a symbol of the omnipotent, illimitable *demand* for love on the part of the mind itself.

But to understand fully their wordless passion, we must first understand the figure who makes the demand. Of whom or what is Arlequin a symbol? Here, as elsewhere, Banville is explicit: he is "*Un don Juan de hasard*" (III, 87), "*autre don Juan"* (*LM*, 136), a character whose significance the poet unfolded in a number of intriguing articles in the press:

> [. . .] today [he wrote of Molière's libertine], if Sga-
> narelle were to ask Don Juan, "What do you believe
> in?" Don Juan would have something better to answer
> than this:
> "I believe that two and two make four."
> He would respond:
> "I believe in living and thinking matter, always re-
> newing itself, eternally young, blossoming, luminous,
> in flower; I believe that, in loving with my heart all
> human creatures, I love in them both God and myself;
> for I aspire incessantly, uncriminally, to mingle [*à me
> confondre*] with all this living nature, which is God
> Himself, and in which I will live and think eternally
> under all the forms of being."[4]

The legendary rake is, "like the Eros of the Greeks, a symbol of Desire, of the universal expansion."[5]

Here we encounter the Banville about whom Baudelaire
and Mallarmé wrote with such admiration: the poet whose
whole "interior being [. . .] soars up into the air by virtue
of too much lightness and dilation, as if to attain a higher
sphere."[6] His own "apotheosizing" (the word is Baudelaire's) of men, landscapes, palaces, expresses precisely Don
Juan's wish, to dissolve the self in their light: "to mingle
[*confondre*] everything," as Mallarmé observed, "in a poetic
kiss."[7] In this, Juan is at one with Banville's clowns and
saltimbanques—with Madame Saqui, whose head is "lost in
the azure and in the stars";[8] with the Pierrot-waif of the
cartoonist Willette, who is said to take wing "up to the/
Stars" (*DF*, 127); and with the acrobatic clown of "Le Saut

---

[4] Article of September 3, 1849, in Théodore de Banville, *Critiques*, ed.
Victor Barrucand (Paris: Charpentier-Fasquelle, 1917), p. 186.

[5] Article of February 21, 1870: ibid., p. 191.

[6] Charles Baudelaire, "Théodore de Banville" (1861), in *Oeuvres complètes*, II, 164.

[7] Stéphane Mallarmé, "Théodore de Banville" (1892), in *Oeuvres complètes de Stéphane Mallarmé*, ed. Henri Mondor and G. Jean-Aubry (Paris:
Gallimard [Bibliothèque de la Pléiade], 1945), p. 520. (Mallarmé is quoting from his earlier *Symphonie littéraire* [1865].)

[8] Banville, "Théâtres" (*Revue Fantaisiste*), III, 248.

du Tremplin," whose desperate cries seem the most movingly passionate in all of Banville's poetry:

> [*"*]*Plus haut encor, jusqu'au ciel pur!*
> *Jusqu'à ce lapis dont l'azur*
> *Couvre notre prison mouvante!*
> *Jusqu'à ces rouges Orients*
> *Où marchent des Dieux flamboyants,*
> *Fous de colère et d'épouvante.*
> [. . .]
> *Plus haut! plus loin! de l'air! du bleu!*
> *Des ailes! des ailes! des ailes!"*
> (III, 177)

["Higher still, up to the pure sky!/To that lapis lazuli whose azure/Covers our moving prison!/To those rosy Orients/Where blazing Gods walk about,/Mad with anger and fright.//[. . .]/Higher! farther! air! the blue!/Wings! wings! wings!"]

What Baudelaire and Mallarmé found to praise, however, has charmed few modern readers. Today Banville is hardly read at all. And at least one of the reasons for this neglect lies precisely in the purity of his aspiration: "The flight towards the regions of pure ideality," Jean Starobinski complains, "gets lost in an abstraction without content."[9] But that abstraction is, I think, only apparently without content. Banville's "ideality" is more problematical than his few commentators have realized,[10] and to analyze it with precision will help explain not only the love of his "*don Juan de hasard*" for svelte Colombine but also the dynamics of Banville's whole enterprise as a writer.

We should begin by noting that his aspiration partakes exactly of that quality that Baudelaire saw in it, of "obsession":[11] "In this final poem," wrote Banville of "Le Saut du Tremplin," "I have tried to express *what I feel the most*:

[9] *Portrait de l'artiste en saltimbanque*, p. 40.
[10] See, e.g., Russell S. King, "The Poet as Clown: Variations on a Theme in Nineteenth-Century French Poetry," *Orbis Litterarum*, XXXIII (1978), 240: " 'Le Saut du tremplin' is a sustained elaboration of [a] comparatively simple theme"—of aspiration "from reality to ideality, from the physical to the spiritual."
[11] "Théodore de Banville," *Oeuvres complètes*, II, 164.

the attraction of the gulf from above [*l'attrait du gouffre d'en haut*]" (III, 225, my italics). The attraction appears in poem after poem, and yet it often has a disturbing resonance that the cries of his ecstatic trampolinist have obscured. Madame Saqui is also drawn by "the voluptuous appeals of the abyss," but *le gouffre* is clearly death, not "ideality": "[. . .] if her feet were to stop, if they were to drowse for the hundredth part of a minute under the kisses of the invisible tarantula, the gulf is below, and the ballerina would be swept away by the voluptuous appeals of the abyss!"[12] In one of the *Odelettes*, addressed to Joseph Méry, Banville compares—rather predictably—Saqui's performances on the rope to the poet's before his audience:

> *Dans les nuages vermeils,*
> *Au beau milieu des soleils*
> *Qu'elle touchait de la tête*
> *Et parmi l'éther bravé,*
> *Elle songeait au pavé.*
> *Tel est le sort du poète.*
> (II, 176)

[In the rosy clouds,/In the very middle of the suns/ That she touched with her head/And amidst the bravèd ether,/She mused upon the pavement./Such is the fate of the poet.]

The theme anticipates that of the better-known "Saut du Tremplin," written two years later, but here *l'attrait du gouffre* holds out no possibility of apotheosis:

> *Dans l'azur aérien*
> *Qui le sollicite, ou bien*
> *Sur la terre nue et froide*
> *Qu'il aperçoit par lambeau,*
> *Il voit partout son tombeau*
> *Du haut de la corde roide.*
> (II, 177)

[In the aerian azure/That beckons him, or else/On the cold, naked earth/That he glimpses here and there,/He

---

[12] Banville, "Théâtres" (*Revue Fantaisiste*), III, 250.

sees, everywhere, his tomb/From the height of the tightrope.]

Finally, "L'Attrait du Gouffre" in *Les Exilés*, composed after the *saltimbanque* poems, gathers up all these associations— the thirst for the Ideal, the lure of the azure firmament, the imminence of self-extinction—and fuses them with the oceanic imagery to which the Romantics turned instinctively to express one of their most familiar and obsessive nostalgias:

> *Ces yeux où les chansons des sirènes soupirent,*
> *Océans éperdus, gouffres inapaisés,*
> *Bleus firmaments où rien ne doit vivre, m'inspirent*
> *La haine de la joie et l'oubli des baisers.*
>
> *Les yeux pensifs, les yeux de cette charmeresse*
> *Sont faits d'un pur aimant dont le pouvoir fatal*
> *Communique une chaste et merveilleuse ivresse*
> *Et ce mal effréné, la soif de l'Idéal.*
>
> (II, 115)

[These eyes in which the songs of sirens sigh,/Distraught seas, unquenched gulfs,/Blue firmaments where nothing is to live, inspire in me/Hatred of joy and forgetfulness of kisses.//The pensive eyes, the eyes of this enchantress/Are made of a pure magnetic attraction, whose fatal power/Imparts a chaste and wonderful drunkenness/And this unrestrained ache, the thirst for the Ideal.]

The "oceanic feeling" (Romain Rolland gave it its name) that is evoked here with such reluctant intensity was analyzed at length by Freud in *Civilization and Its Discontents*, as a recovery of the primordial and paradisiacal ego-state of earliest infancy, when the world and the self are one. "An infant at the breast," Freud writes, "does not as yet distinguish his ego from the external world as the source of the sensations flowing in upon him. He gradually learns to do so, in response to various promptings" (*SE*, XXI, 66-67). Those "promptings" are occasioned by losses of his sources of pleasure—"among them what he desires most of all, his mother's breast" (*SE*, XXI, 67)—losses which effect, gradually, a "detachment" of his ego from the world.

> If we may assume [Freud continues] that there are many people in whose mental life this primary ego-feeling has persisted to a greater or less degree, it would exist in them side by side with the narrower and more sharply demarcated ego-feeling of maturity, like a kind of counterpart to it. In that case, the ideational contents appropriate to it would be precisely those of limitlessness and of a bond with the universe—the same ideas with which my friend [Rolland] elucidated the "oceanic" feeling. (*SE*, XXI, 68)

"Limitlessness," "a bond with the universe"—and the annihilation of the personal self: all are concomitants of Banville's *attrait du gouffre*. Holding out the promise of both death and ecstasy, it is the lure of the great sweet mother: "Like a moist lip, it draws me near with a kiss,/And my cowardly reason trembles at drowning there" (II, 116). Hers is clearly not the lip of a lover, at least to a mind preconsciously vigilant against the "*folie*" of an oedipal transgression: "[. . .] I cannot, without finding madness,/Seek your pearl, Love! in this immensity" (II, 116). It is, rather, the lip of his "nurse," who "was no miser/Neither of milk nor of kisses" ("A ma Mère" [II, 85]), just as "*les yeux de cette charmeresse*" derive from those eyes described in the *Roses de Noël*:

> Mère, tes yeux aussi réfléchissent l'azur,
> C'est pourquoi tu seras pareille à ce flot pur
> Qui reflète le ciel et qui n'a pas de rides!
> (I, 415)

[Mother, your eyes also give back the azure;/That is why you shall be like this pure billow/That reflects the sky, without a wrinkle.]

Banville ("*ton fils, non, ton enfant*" [I, 419]) is drawn by these eyes and lips to dissolve his being in their caress, to relinquish selfhood and allow his heart, like his clown's of "Le Saut du Tremplin," to be "devoured" (III, 178) by a suprapersonal love.

Seen in this light, the formerly much-ridiculed verses beginning "*Coupe! Sein! Lyre!*" of the early "Songe d'hiver" lose all their air of obscurity.[13] Visionary outbursts by Don Juans "hungry for the Ideal" (I, 101), they celebrate instinctively the "*synthétisme/Originel*"[14] of the inebriating cup, the apotheosizing lyre, and the death-nourishing breast. *Sein* is probably to be understood in all of its senses here—as "breast," "bosom," "heart," "womb," "gulf"; it is described in lines veiled in ambiguity and evasion, associating, cryptically, both *le gouffre* and the featureless obliteration of a lava flow with the transfiguration of a suckling dreamer. "*Marbre esclave*," it serves "The old titan Desire, tyrant of the universe" (I, 102):

> *Sein! marbre esclave!*
> *Gouffre que lave*
> *Le flot de lave!*
> *Spasme auguré!*
> *Le corps qui rêve*
> *Par toi s'achève*
> *Et se relève*
> *Transfiguré!*[15]

[Breast! enslaved marble!/Gulf laved/By the laval wave!/Augured spasm!/The dreaming body/By you is perfected/And resurrected/Transfigurèd!]

To lie at the breast in a perfecting, transfiguring dream, and there to enjoy a satisfaction of desire possible only to the unbounded self: such is Banville's fearsome wish. It is the wish that underlies the project he outlines for "*l'homme moderne*" in the preface to *Les Stalactites* ("To reconquer the lost joy [. . .] that is the ceaseless aspiration of modern man" [I, 213]), and that to which Baudelaire is unconsciously alluding when he calls his poetry "a very willful return to-

[13] Maximilien Fuchs cites the verses as exemplifying the obscurities of Banville's youthful style: *Théodore de Banville (1823-1891)* (1912; Geneva: Slatkine Reprints, 1972), p. 65.

[14] Théodore de Banville, *Les Cariatides* (Paris: Pilout, 1842), p. 193. I cite the original edition for both this phrase and the fragment of the song that follows: Banville completely revised the section in which these passages appear for subsequent editions.

[15] Ibid., p. 194. Cf. Banville's "Sachons adorer! Sachons lire!" (I, 143).

wards the paradisiacal state."[16] It is the wish that drives Don Juan to a conquest of the azure—and that unites Arlequin with Colombine. A late poem from *Dans la Fournaise*—the "Variations" of its title must be quoted in full—illustrates the implications of this nostalgia with touching naïveté:

> *Colombine, mon coeur, viens, au clair de la lune*
> *Qui brille dans l'azur céleste, comme l'une*
> *De tes soeurs! Viens errer tous deux, au clair de la*
> *Lune. Allons-nous-en, seuls et charmés, par delà*
> *Ces jardins frémissants où la lumière argente*
> *L'étang poli, glacé d'une moire changeante.*
> *Allons-nous-en bien loin, mon amoureuse, au clair*
> *De la lune. L'éclair divin, le doux éclair*
> *De tes yeux d'or, qui fait ma joie et mon désastre,*
> *Brillera dans la nuit sereine, comme un astre,*
> *Et je me pencherai pour baiser tes bras, au*
> *Clair de la lune! Ainsi qu'un flexible roseau,*
> *Quand les parfums du soir empliront ta narine,*
> *Ton corps svelte et charmant ploiera sur ma poitrine.*
> *Une haleine de rose est éparse dans l'air,*
> *Et le délicieux rossignol chante, au clair*
> *De la lune. Ote un peu ton masque de théâtre;*
> *Sous les rayons pensifs de la lune folâtre*
> *Laisse-moi voir ton front de lys, que modela*
> *Pour moi le fol Amour, et viens, au clair de la*
> *Lune. Allons vers Cythère ou bien vers Pampelune,*
> *A travers la forêt bleue, au clair de la lune!*

(DF, 72)

[Colombine, my heart, come, in the light of the moon/ That shines in the celestial azure, like one/Of your sisters! Come to wander, we two, in the light of the/ Moon. Let us go out, alone and enchanted, through/ These quivering gardens, where the light silvers/The smooth pond, glazed with a shimmering moiré./Let us go far, far, my beloved, in the light/Of the moon. The divine sparkle, the gentle sparkle/Of your golden eyes— my joy and my disaster—/Will shine in the serene night,

---

[16] "Théodore de Banville," *Oeuvres complètes*, II, 168.

like a star,/And I will bend to kiss your arms, in the/ Light of the moon! Like a pliant reed,/When the perfumes of evening fill your nostrils,/Your slender and lovely body will fold over my breast./A breath of rose is loosed upon the air,/And the delicious nightingale sings, in the light/Of the moon. Lower a little your theater mask;/Under the pensive beams of the playful moon/Let me see your lily-white forehead, sculpted/ For me by madcap Love, and come, in the light of the/Moon. Let us set off for Cythera or else Pampelune,/Across the blue forest, in the light of the moon!]

Maximilien Fuchs has analyzed this poem in detail, noting the "rigorous" symmetry of these variations (the opening and closing lines end with the theme *"Au clair de la lune,"* framing couplets of alternating feminine and masculine rhymes, the latter of which ring changes upon *"au clair de la,"* *"au clair,"* and *"au"* before repeating the process in inverse order) and commenting, with some perplexity, upon the "somewhat strange mood" of this *"simple"* but complex *"jeu"*:

> These perpetual enjambments somehow blur and efface the rhythm, thereby giving an impression analogous to that which a landscape vaguely illuminated by this *"obscure clarté"* would create; finally, [. . .] the logical element is sacrificed completely to the emotion: this song, with its insistent *leitmotif*, does not present to the mind a coherent argument, but it evokes certain images, by its resonant sonorities. It has an expressive meaning peculiar to itself, independent of the sense of the words that it contains.[17]

Evoking both a charmed landscape and an *état d'âme*, enclosing a suprahuman world of moonlight within the fugal symmetry of a canonical mind, yet preserving the formless fluidity of that world by its sonorities and perpetual enjambments, the poem is a fascinating experiment in Banville's *oeuvre*, and a perfectly oxymoronic expression of *l'attrait du gouffre*. It describes a dissolution of the line of demarcation, a gathering of this magical world into the

[17] *Théodore de Banville*, pp. 477, 479.

self, a complete dispersion of the self through that world. That the dispersion is both beatific and self-destructive is suggested by the motive of Banville-Arlequin for calling up this *chant*. Wandering "sadly, pursued by the eyes/Of the brilliant moon with its pallid face" (*DF*, 71), he has mounted, death-haunted, the stairs "*Chez Raoul*," from whom he begs the variations on his violin: he wishes "to savor to the last drops the madness/And the drunkenness of the moonlight" (*DF*, 71). The union with Colombine ("*ma joie et mon désastre*") marks a return to the pure pleasure-ego, a miraculous satiation of desire, a fulfillment of the self's illimitable demand for love—and a confusion of the dreamer with the dream.

"Primary narcissism" is the phrase often used, perhaps erroneously, to describe the ideal of this union.[18] In Banville, its wished-for and courted recovery is an accompaniment (if it is not a cause) of a "secondary" narcissistic project, in which the anxious confirmation of his selfhood is an endless, albeit unconscious, pursuit. His mind's movement is apparently double—instinctively towards *l'abîme*, the loss of boundary and demarcation, and willfully towards all that would confer differentiation, identity, and integrity upon his *moi infiniment peureux*. The *attrait du gouffre*, in its various associations, manifests, as I have shown, Banville's ambivalence towards the former attraction. His ambivalence towards the latter is suggested by a word that he uses almost synonymously with *le gouffre* or *l'abîme*: *l'indifférence*. "They have taught me, these billows with their bloodthirsty pallor," he writes in "L'Attrait du Gouffre," "The

---

[18] Ben Bursten objects that, during the (very early) developmental stage at which this union is literally experienced, the infant can not be called "narcissistic" since he "has no locus (inner or outer) of [the] experiences" he undergoes: "In the mind of the infant, these are experiences, if you will, but not 'his' experiences" ("The Narcissistic Course," in Marie Coleman Nelson, ed. *The Narcissistic Condition* [New York: Human Sciences Press, 1977], p. 109). But such an argument ignores the important point: that there is an obvious connection, as Bursten himself assumes, between the early "boundaryless state" (to adopt his own terminology) and later, "secondary," narcissistic disorders. "Primary narcissism" is a phrase so often used to describe this state—see, e.g., Esther Menaker's discussion of "The Ego Ideal" in the same collection (p. 251)—that I do not hesitate to retain it.

voluptuous delights of calm and indifference" (II, 116).
But *l'indifférence* does not always intoxicate. Defending, under the guise of "Monsieur Figaro Barbier," the apotheosizing tendencies of Balzac, Banville betrays an intense fear
of losing the self, like Don Juan in the trap, through a loss
of faith in his vision:

> Superficial minds have leveled a specious criticism at
> Balzac. In his books, they say, all the characters have
> genius. He shows us a lawyer's clerk; this lawyer's clerk
> has genius. Is it a matter of a porter? It is a porter of
> genius.
>
> O hasty and trifling judges, it is precisely in this that
> Balzac, engaged in painting *la vie parisienne*, has shown
> his supreme good sense. In Paris, in this prodigious
> Babel-Athens in quest of the grandiose absolute and
> ideal perfection, whoever lacks genius has no *raison
> d'être*.
>
> Let that disappear!—a trap is opened under his feet,
> a thousand times more terrible than that through which
> Don Juan sinks in the fifth act, and this trap is called:
> indifference.[19]

And *l'indifférence* outside the self is as frightening as *l'indifférence* within. The Funambules was an ideal "theater"
for Banville—I think the word's dual meanings are applicable—because, there, as he insists again and again, the
spectacle and public shared a mutual regard. The conventional theater offers no such bond, and it inspires in Banville a loathing close to terror: "[. . .] a solitude, a desert,
an abyss, a terrifying space that nothing can fill: that is the
theater as it is" (*S*, 216). His terms are so strong, I think,
because he feels acutely the relevance of the spectacle he is
describing to his own self-authenticating project: "[If it were
only] that these people are strangers to me," he writes of
the characters of *l'Ecole de Bon Sens*, of those "bourgeois
born in a box,"

[19] Théodore de Banville, ed., *A Figaro, Salons de coiffure, Figaro Barbier
à ses clients et à tout le monde, Boulevard Montmartre, 12, Entrée par le Bazar
Européen* (Alençon: Poulet-Malassis et de Broise, n.d.): this pamphlet, "*à
peu près introuvable aujourd'hui*," as Fuchs describes it, is quoted in his
Théodore de Banville, p. 447.

that would as yet be nothing; what is worse is that *I* am profoundly a stranger to *them*. They know nothing about me, they do not love me, they do not pity me when I am disconsolate, they do not console me when I cry, they would hardly smile at what makes me burst out laughing. (III, 9)

Relevant here, of course, is Banville's own explanation for his disgust—that the modern theater in general has lost the communal spirit of Aristophanes' stage. But equally relevant are the facts that belie his own republican sentiments. *Le peuple*, if not *le public*, was always more symbol than reality for the poet; as John Charpentier has pointed out, Banville was "*au fond très aristocrate*."[20] This is perhaps nowhere more apparent than in his comedies inspired by Molière and the *commedia dell'arte*, in which Scapin and Léandre, *scélérats* both, permit him an uninhibited play of personae. Amoral, sensual, self-absorbed ("*Je m'aime*" [*C*, 224], Scapin engagingly declares), they are, like Arlequin and Colombine, "egoists like love itself," true aristocrats of the unconscious.[21] In fact, in describing the elegant stuffs of their costumes, Banville ignores one of his own fundamental beliefs—that the theater should *suggest* sartorial *largesse*, never show it (*AP*, 31-32)—and revels, like Gautier, in their ornament, textures, and hues (*C*, 468-70). Splendidly colored and peopled with rogues, these comedies solicit the regard of the people for no communal aim: they, rather, confer upon their creator the glory of the gaze.

Apparently all that Banville sought from both his work

---

[20] *Théodore de Banville: L'Homme et son oeuvre* (Paris: Perrin, 1925), p. 141.

[21] Léandre is of course the title-character of *Le Beau Léandre* (1856), and Scapin appears as the victim of his own famous *lazzi* of the sack in *Les Fourberies de Nérine* (1864). In an unpublished "*farce italienne*," *Le Petit Mezzetin*, produced at the Folies-Nouvelles in 1855, and for which a censor's copy survives in the Archives Nationales de France (as *Mezzetin*: F^{18} 1023, MS 3420), Banville created a Pascariel who rivals even the former rogues in unmitigated egoism. "*Bête et vicieux*" (p. 1), but easily the most interesting character in the play, he is a gourmet and gourmand of enviably solitary pleasures: "What joy to eat alone, like a glutton," he muses aloud, "without giving a thing to anyone; to stuff yourself to the point of splitting your skin, and to drink like a pit, till your nose is purple and your forehead scarlet!" (p. 20).

and his public—the *délices du gouffre*, the self-confirming gaze, the sanction of aristocratic aloofness that the narcissist craves—all seem to have been enjoyed by a single figure whom he never tired of celebrating: the Pierrot of the Funambules. *"Le beau, le gracieux, le svelte, l'ironique Jean-Gaspard Deburau"* (*S*, 218) had the authority of an alter-ego for the writer, and he did so because he appeared to contain and express the ambivalences of Banville's own psyche. On the one hand, he seemed dispassionately (and defensively) aloof, "like the cat, having no other care than to stay clean, pure, spotless, as immaculate as the snow on the peaks" (*AP*, 17);[22] he moved through the pantomime with exclusively oral decision, "eating and drinking of the best/And taking interest in nothing, like the sages" (III, 90). His pursuit of the lovers was disdainfully half-hearted because their drama of desire was an allegory, for Banville, of Pierrot's own *comédie narcissiste*. Always separate yet united by a mysterious and lyrical bond, both Pierrot and the lovers were instruments of an interior *chanson d'amour*: "The settings changed, Arlequin and Colombine passed by, tremulous with love in the light, and in the middle of the turbulent and busy crowds, he, the Pierrot with pale face and snow-white vestments, he, the great Jean-Gaspard Deburau, he told upon the beads of mute scenes that were at once deliciously lyrical and buffoonish the innumerable rhapsodies of his poem" (*S*, 221).

But however distant from the crowds or the lovers and however impregnably aloof, Pierrot never ceased to bask in the gaze of an admiring public. Not only was there an instinctive kinship between the clown and *le peuple*, but between them was an identity of reciprocal regard, enviable in its self-authenticating mutuality—a regard very like that between a mother and infant: "[. . .] both mute, attentive, always understanding each other, feeling and dreaming and responding together, Pierrot and the People, united like two twin souls, mingled their ideas, their hopes, their ban-

[22] Cf. Freud's remark: "The charm of a child lies to a great extent in his narcissism, his self-contentment and inaccessibility, just as does the charm of certain animals which seem not to concern themselves about us, such as cats and the large beasts of prey" ("On Narcissism: An Introduction," in *SE*, XIV, 89).

ter, their ideal and subtle gaiety, like two Lyres playing in unison, or like two Rhymes savoring the delight of being similar sounds and of exhaling the same melodious and sonorous voice" (*AP*, 28). This unequivocal confirmation and amplification of self was accompanied by a control that approached the omnipotent. No easy dupe of Cassandre, Pierrot was equal to the wiles of all authority: he could vanquish both sickness and death. In his *Souvenirs* Banville describes with revealing particularity two scenes that summed up for him Deburau's art: in the first, Pierrot-baker takes pity on a pair of old women who come to him with their flour—"two old, old women, bald, disheveled, decrepit, with quivering chins, bent towards the earth, leaning upon gnarled sticks, and showing in their sunken eyes the shadows of years gone by, more numerous than the leaves in the woods."

> "Really now! there's no common sense in this!" exclaimed (in mute speech) the wise baker Pierrot: "to allow women to come to such a state is unthinkable. So why hasn't anyone noticed they need to be melted down, remade, rebaked anew?" And immediately, in spite of their protestations, he seized them, laid them both on his shovel, popped them right in the oven, and then stood watch over his baking with faithful care. When the number of desired minutes had elapsed, he took them out—young, beautiful, transformed by brilliant tresses, with snow at their breasts, black diamonds in their eyes, blood-red roses on their lips, dressed in silk, satin, golden veils, adorned with spangles and sequins—and modestly said then to his friends in the house: "Well now, you see? It's no more difficult than that!" (*S*, 221-22)

In the second scene, Pierrot is a doctor who administers to a "young Parisian lord, bored, anemic, wan, having no strength to live, and disgusted even with his boredom" (*S*, 222). He slices open the sufferer's skull to flush from it a terrified mouse.[23]

---

[23] Banville is remembering at least one of these scenes with characteristic imprecision: here, as elsewhere, he makes little of the malice that motivated almost all of Deburau's business in the *féeries*. The first scene is

Théodore de Banville

A master of the marvelous, vanquishing misery and *ennui*, manipulating the responses of the Paradise by his irony and extraordinary finesse, strolling with "a complete indifference" through "an intrigue always interesting because it was always the same" (*S*, 218, 217), Pierrot was for the poet a reassuring symbol of self-possession and self-containment, and of grandiose self-sufficiency and control.[24]

from *Pierrot partout* (1839), and Pierrot is neither a baker nor the compassionate cavalier of Banville's recollection. He has just abducted Colombine from Arlequin, and he, Cassandre, and Léandre have come upon a fabulous oven that rejuvenates old women. Léandre and Cassandre hope to restore their fiancées, Isabelle and Angélique, through its powers: Arlequin's magic bat has reduced them to ugly decrepitude. I translate from the censor's manuscript in the Archives Nationales (F[18] 1085, MS 2692), regularizing punctuation and capitalization:

[Isabelle and Angélique] refuse [to enter the oven], finding themselves fine as they are. Pierrot brings in Colombine and wants to burn her alive, too, if she continues to resist his advances; she struggles; the two others succeed in thrusting Isabelle and Angélique inside; Pierrot helps them. Meanwhile, Arlequin sticks his head up through the emberbox and signals to Colombine to run off with him. Pierrot sees him; Léandre pushes the lid down, hard, and sits on top of it. But hardly has he done so than the box sinks into the ground, swallowing him up.

Pierrot tries to put Colombine inside. He opens the oven door; Isabelle and Angélique come out, young and fresh; they are delighted. Isabelle looks for Léandre. A moaning comes from the oven. It is Léandre, who has been shut up in it, and who emerges half-baked and furious. They clean him up. Meanwhile, Arlequin has come back in; he makes Colombine step down—she was already on the shovel—and seizes Pierrot. The wicked genie appears and helps Arlequin. They pinion the poor Pierrot and are going to throw him into the oven, when a gong announces the [good] fairy [. . .]. (pp. 15-16)

Pierrot disguises as a doctor in several pantomimes, and I have been unable to identify with certainty the source of Banville's second scene. Perhaps it is *La Naissance de Pierrot* (1843), in which Pierrot's (doubtlessly malicious) ministrations are concluded by a typically hair-raising rout. Again, I quote the manuscript (AN document F[18] 1087, MS 4844):

Several sick people arrive, to whom Pierrot gives advice. —During this scene, the heads of Arlequin and Lisa become visible in the mirror; Pierrot, furious, seizes a gun and shatters the mirror; a devil leaps out; Pierrot, who has taken up a halberd, runs him through; two other little devils arrive and fall upon Pierrot in order to avenge the death of their companion: a comic scuffle; the devils drag Pierrot off. (sc. 4 [unpaginated])

[24] "Grandiose" has a somewhat technical meaning here; I am using it

But, predictably, this symbol served Banville's tendencies towards regression as well as his techniques of defense. While praising the skill of the Hanlon-Lees, a troupe of English mimes schooled precisely in Deburau's art, Banville describes a scene from *Le Voyage en Suisse*, a pantomime in which a flask is sent flying "under the very eye of its owner with so much agility and precision that it is physically impossible for him to see [the] movement [of those tossing it about]." The finesse of the jugglers inspires a vision of oceanic bliss:

> These actions, which correspond with one another so harmoniously and so cleanly, communicate the same voluptuous well-being that you are given by the high-lighted color of Delacroix—a blue that is reproduced from one end of the canvas to the other, when the soul is thirsty for it![25]

Le bleu, l'azur—and *le blanc*: they are synonymous for Banville, as his next two sentences, betraying the proximity of his obsessions, suggest: "And how charming these Hanlon-Lees are, the Pierrots especially! Their white heads are gentle, ingenuously *spirituelles*, boundless with love, for no artist would know how to give me pleasure if I did not feel he loved me!" Like the precision of his *geste*, the whiteness of Pierrot's blouse appeals to the subtleties of the poet's ambivalence. On the one hand, it is a visible symbol of self-definition, an image of what psychoanalysts call an "ego-ideal," usually the "introject" of an idealized parent. For Banville, the ideal is of purity, innocence, spiritual naïveté ("Lys sans tache" is the title of a poem addressed to Madame de Banville in *Roses de Noël*). "My function is to be/

---

in the sense intended by Heinz Kohut in his description of the "narcissistic course": "The equilibrium of primary narcissism is disturbed by the unavoidable shortcomings of maternal care, but the child replaces the previous perfection (a) by establishing a grandiose and exhibitionistic image of the self: *the grandiose self*; and (b) by giving over the previous perfection to an admired, omnipotent (transitional) self-object: *the idealized parent imago*" (*The Analysis of the Self: A Systematic Approach to the Psychoanalytic Treatment of Narcissistic Personality Disorders* [New York: International Universities Press, Inc., 1971], p. 25). For the "idealized parent imago" in Banville's work, see below, p. 145.

[25] Article of September 8, 1879: in Banville, *Critiques*, p. 389.

White" (*B*, 11), the Pierrot of *Le Baiser* confides to Urgèle, and in his "*nouveaux souvenirs*" the aging (and resignedly disappointed) poet[26] describes the full range of this function:

[. . .] those who did not see him with their own eyes will never know how white Deburau was! Whiter than the marble of Pentelikon, reserved for the statues of the Gods; whiter than the Lily, of which Hugo says so well: *The lily like unto God!* whiter than the snow of the peaks, virgin of human footprints; whiter than the plumage of swans gliding over calm waters, awaiting the supreme hour when they will savor the joy of song and death. [. . .] But what gave [his costume] its ideal purity, its angelic and lily-like candor, was the soul of the man who wore it, exempt from every hypocritical or cruel thought. For in this great mime lived the soul, also white, of the People, valiant and resigned [. . .]. (*AP*, 35)

But, as those ecstatically singing swans suggest, the white-frocked Pierrot is obviously, like Banville's Delacroix, also a *chercheur du gouffre*. His whiteness is that of primordial innocence, of unbounded and limitless ego, of the self lost to the world. Paradoxically, the self-defining ideal invokes a nostalgia for undifferentiated origins: "Your sole appearance," Banville laments of the vanished Pierrot in a late "*lettre chimérique*," "consoled me for everything that is not white—that is to say, sir, for everything [. . .]" (*LC*, 107).

That "everything" includes, of course, art. "The representation of primary narcissism well deserves its name of *infans* [L. "not speaking," whence F. *enfant*]," writes Serge Leclaire: "It does not speak, nor will it ever speak. It is in the exact measure that one begins to kill it [within oneself]

[26] Banville's personal discouragement, implicit in the final line of the quotation that follows, was revealed to the fatherly Hugo in a series of letters published by Gustave Simon in 1923. In the first (November 11, 1864), he "*dare[s] tell Victor Hugo that I am put in mind each day of the bitterness of the fruitless martyrdom to which those who have not betrayed the cause of true poetry are consigned, and of how insurmountable are the obstacles against which they must struggle*" (*La Revue de France*, 3rd Year, II [March-April 1923], 517).

that one begins to speak [. . .]."[27] For those in whom the
infant will not die, the mammarial blank page speaks more
satisfyingly than any words upon it—and Pierrot was for
Banville "as white as the blank paper, alas! on which I am
writing [. . .]" (*LC*, 107). When, in "Ancien Pierrot," the
clown is transformed into *un homme en habit noir*, he is
conscious of suffering, as from a crippling burden, "*cette
infirmité stupide, la parole*" (III, 166). It is stupid because
superfluous: "Love is there," observes Banville of Paul Legrand's silent *jeu*, "to replace/All vain literature" (*DF*, 248).
The emergence of literature marks the death of the infant;
it arouses in Banville (though screened, typically, with irony)
an obviously anal disgust:

> [. . .] ceaselessly occupied in blackening, in piling up
> pages of copy, in beginning again when he has fin-
> ished and in finishing when he has begun, [the man
> of letters] is always a prisoner in a room, in the com-
> pany of a quire of foolscap and an inkwell full of a
> liquid as black as the tide of Cocytus.
> [. . .]
> But, sir, your snowy visage, your candid costume, your
> hands whiter than those of Cidalise—can you see them
> soiled and stained by that horrible stuff called ink? No,
> you are not a man of letters [. . .]. (*LC*, 109-10, 111)

And yet "*le Verbe*" is, as Banville repeatedly insists, "*l'outil
divin*" (*LC*, 109)—apparently because it is attached to origins,
both of his body and of his sustaining conceptions of self:
"The WORD that, in the beginning, created the world and
the infinite and the universes, and that then produced the
humble masterpieces of man, has this unique quality: it has
always retained the ineffaceable stamp of its divine origin"
(*LC*, 244). Like his very self-conceptions, both distress-
ingly and gratifyingly ambiguous, the word teeters on the
line that divides the grandiose from the meaningless, the
divinely ample from the empty, the writer from the *infans*.
To speak more precisely, it professes the essential and insuperable ambiguity of *le gouffre*—to be both All and Noth-

---

[27] *On tue un enfant: Un Essai sur le narcissisme primaire et la pulsion de
mort* (Paris: Editions du Seuil, 1975), p. 22.

ing. Thus Jean Starobinski can describe the Banvillian *saut*, "his vertical flight outside of disappointing (and deceptive) 'reality' [*hors du réel décevant*]," as "one of the best possible symbols for the intoxication peculiar to *romantic irony* [. . .]."[28] Irony is in fact the only authentic manner for a poet of Banville's obsessions. Between a conception of the word as expressing "*Tous les frissons de la Lyre*" (*DF*, 101) and that which regards it as an "*infirmité stupide*" must mediate the word as *saltimbanque*, incessantly aspiring to recover—and yet acknowledging its own inability to recover—what Baudelaire called "*l'état paradisiaque*." Such a conception informs, for example, a late poem, "Lecture": "The words that form the parade [in reading]/Are all comedians" (*DF*, 102). "*Comédiens*"[29] because their ultimate reference both comprises and rests on *le gouffre*: "To leap out with agility and confidence across space, over the void, from one point to another," wrote Banville towards the end of his career, "that is the supreme skill [*science*] of the clown, and I imagine that it is also the only skill of the poet."[30]

So, in the *Odes funambulesques*, Banville's most admired collection, the reader is made to see, in Maximilien Fuchs' words, "that he is being given irreproachable verses and, at the same time, that it is absurd to versify what is being recounted."[31] If Edmond de Goncourt thought that words alone filled Banville's head, it is because the world to which they refer is a void—or a great *corps maternel* of self-gratifying fantasy. In this way we may explain the rather bizarre frequency with which the pantomimic types invade his work. Among the *Camées parisiens*, portraits of Pierrot and Polichinelle stand beside those of Corot and Baudelaire; Scapin is identified with Bismarck in the *Idylles prussiennes* ("Scapin tout seul" [III, 406]); and Polichinelle—cruel, stupid,

---

[28] *Portrait de l'artiste en saltimbanque*, p. 40.
[29] The word's context suggests that it means more than "actors" here:

> *Tel, qui parmi nous émigre,*
> *Nous vient du pays latin,*
> *Et tel autre est, comme un tigre,*
> *Plus rayé que Mezzetin.*
>
> (*DF*, 103)

[30] Article of May 12, 1879: in Banville, *Critiques*, p. 422.
[31] *Théodore de Banville*, p. 191.

grasping, but at bottom a harmless *pantin*—serves as symbol for the most detestable of the poet's foes: the *académicien* ("Polichinelle Vampire" [III, 137]), the bellicose general ("Madame Polichinelle" [III, 319]), the gullible citizen ("Chez Guignol" [III, 314]), the self-righteous bourgeois ("Deux Polichinelles" [*LM*, 71-72]), the unscrupulous entrepreneur ("Les Huit Sous de Pierrot" [*CF*, 173-81], "Un Auteur chez les marionnettes"[32]). These identifications seem to be more than merely tropes; there is the persistent feeling, in reading Banville, that the types are as real to him as the figures they signify: more precisely, that all persons, at bottom, are types, are—as lovers, poets, rogues—*these* types.[33] In the pantomime (as, relatedly, in Watteau) Banville encountered a drama that encouraged the constellation of his own psychic forces, a constellation that was in turn projected upon the world. The privateness of his obsessions reveals itself in small but significant ways. A late poem, "La Lune," in *Dans la Fournaise*, presents a parade of masks that is, for Fuchs, "quite dull":

> *Voilà Pulcinelle*
> *Avec Arlequin!*
>
> *Voilà Scaramouche*
> *Et don Spavento,*
> *Et Scapin farouche*
> *Dans son vert manteau.*
> (*DF*, 115)

[There is Pulcinella/With Arlequin!//There is Scaramouche/And Don Spavento/And fierce Scapin/In his green cloak.]

He concludes that "This dry enumeration of proper names," as well as the poet's cryptic response to it, creates an effect

---

[32] In Théodore de Banville, *Les Pauvres Saltimbanques* (Paris: Lévy, 1853).

[33] This is interestingly illustrated in Banville's late (and only) novel, *Marcelle Rabe*, whose physician-hero, Daniel Mathis, falls in love with a woman of Pre-Raphaelite ethereality and of secret, insatiable appetites. Early in their affair, Daniel is entertained by a pantomime at one of his mistress's soirées, in which Colombine is tirelessly unfaithful to a distraught Pierrot. "*Quoi! est-ce donc ainsi, l'amour?*" (*MR*, 239), asks the lady of her guests. Several minutes later, Daniel finds her in an embrace with a mustachioed Latin.

149

that *"n'est pas heureux."*[34] He is right, it is both dull and dry. But for Banville the names themselves, rich in signification, were, I think, enough.[35]

But it was not as a *funambule* that he wanted to be remembered. Unlike Gautier, he was not liberated by his own irony: he aspired to sublime, univocal utterance. *Les Exilés* is in fact the collection in which Banville professed to put "the most of myself and my soul" (II, 3), the book he hoped would live after him. But in rereading these always predictable tales of gods and heroes, these tributes to contemporaries in which the abstract and the conventional seem to vie tediously for precedence ("*La Matière, céleste encor même en sa chute,/[. . .]/Pâture du Désir, jouet du noir Remord* [. . .]" ["Baudelaire," II, 134]), we are impressed not with amplitude, which the rhetoric is striving ceaselessly to invoke, but with emptiness. It is, rather, in his ironically playful verse, which often seems about nothing, that the amplitude begins to emerge—as in this little "caprice," "Sérénade," from the *Cariatides*:

> *Las! Colombine a fermé le volet,*
> *Et vainement le chasseur tend ses toiles,*
> *Car la fillette au doux esprit follet,*
> *De ses rideaux laissant tomber les voiles,*
> *S'est dérobée, ainsi que les étoiles.*
> *Bien qu'elle cache à l'amant indigent*
> *Son casaquin pareil au ciel changeant,*
> *C'est pour charmer cette beauté barbare,*
> *Que remuant comme du vif-argent,*
> *Arlequin chante et gratte sa guitare.*
>
> (I, 182)

---

[34] *Théodore de Banville*, p. 477.

[35] In a review of *Le Petit Mezzetin*, Théophile Gautier remarked that Banville was "enamored to the point of mania with all this particolored world of the old Italian comedy" (*Le Moniteur Universel*, October 15, 1855). And that mania extended even to proprietorship. Towards the end of the century, when Félix Larcher was soliciting support for the Cercle Funambulesque to revive interest in the pantomime, he reported to Paul Hugounet that Banville "didn't like anyone touching the pantomime: you were made to believe this was his domain, and he wanted it to die with him" ("Comment fut fondé le Cercle Funambulesque," *La Plume*, IV [September 15, 1892], 407).

['Las! Colombine has closed the shutter,/And vainly the pursuer spreads his sails,/For the minx with the sweetly wanton wit,/Having lowered the veils of her curtains,/Has disappeared, just like the stars./Although she conceals from the indigent lover/Her short little gown (like the changing sky)/It is to charm this cruel beauty/That, moving about like quicksilver,/Arlequin sings and scratches his guitar.]

At least part of the charm of this piece, its intimations of Verlaine's moonlit *Fêtes galantes*, arises from the veiled psychic comedy beneath it: that of a mind whose chaste libido is courted by the importunate ego itself. Vaguely onanistic (*vide* the "quicksilver" and that guitar), the poem depicts a *spirituel* foreplay to which still greater delights will accrue. To enjoy those delights, to know the "joys of love and poetry" (they were one), was a wish that the pantomimic world, in fantasy, always granted to Banville: Arlequin invariably won his Colombine—and Pierrot kneeled to join them, as if assuaging his own psychic hunger, with an embrace. "*C'est un plaisir adorable/D'être un Pierrot de calicot*" (*SC*, 229), wrote the poet in "Carnaval." He had reason to think so: when he was most a poet (if not most a lover), he was most a charming Pierrot.

VI

Pierrot *emmerdant*:
Gustave Flaubert

Saint Antoine *est-il bon ou mauvais? Voilà par exemple
ce que je me demande souvent. Lequel de moi ou des
autres s'est trompé? Au reste, je ne m'inquiète guère de
tout cela; je vis comme une plante, je me pénètre de soleil,
de lumière, de couleurs et de grand air. Je mange: voilà
tout. Restera ensuite à digérer, puis à chier,—et de bonne
merde! C'est là l'important.*

Flaubert to his mother,
from Cairo, January 5, 1850

Produire, littéralement, c'est chier.

DOMINIQUE LAPORTE
Histoire de la merde (prologue) (1978)

[. . .] dès qu'on abandonne le silence, on est perdu.

JEAN-PAUL SARTRE
L'Idiot de la famille, II (1971)

Flaubert to Eugène Delattre, prescribing conduct appropriate to the provinces:

Terrify the bourgeois by your extravagances and
desolate your family by your talk! If you're invited out
to dinner, stuff yourself! and belch at dessert! Maybe
they'll be offended? Doesn't matter! You'll answer: "It's
the way things are done in Paris." Caress the serving-
maids, take snatch off the ladies, excite the adolescents
[. . .] and the provincials to bestiality! In a word, be
sleazy: that's the way to please![1]

[1] Gustave Flaubert, *Correspondance*, ed. Jean Bruneau, II (Paris: Gallimard [Bibliothèque de la Pléiade], 1980), 828. Throughout this chapter,

One of course turned a public face to *maman*: "We have adopted the principle," wrote Flaubert to his mother from Alexandria of his tour with Maxime DuCamp, "of listening to the advice of competent people and of conducting ourselves like two little saints" (*C:P*, I, 530). But when curtained within his study, confiding, insouciant, to a friend, he was *l'Excessif, le Géant*, the wild "Folbert," committing the enormities of the *Correspondance*. So, too, when he bent over *Salammbô* or *La Tentation de saint Antoine*. "Excess has always attracted me [. . .]" (*C:P*, I, 383), Flaubert confessed to Louise Colet. An admirer of Nero, Rabelais, and the Marquis de Sade, he unhesitatingly equated genius with *la force* and great art with the superhuman elements of nature: to write was quite literally to rattle the windows in a thunderous *gueulade*. *Madame Bovary*, as "excessive" in its own way as any of his other novels, was a prodigious exercise in self-restraint, the monkish labor of a man condemned, as it were, to the chair. "There are two men in me," Flaubert remarked to the Goncourts: "One, you see, narrow-chested, with a butt of lead, the man made to be bent over a table; the other, a traveling salesman, with the genuine gaiety of the salesman on the road, and with a taste for violent activity!"[2]

It was, in fact, during a respite from that first long martyrdom, "the *Bovary*," the very title of which had become synonymous in his young niece's mind with toil, that the *commis-voyageur* broke out at his most violent and most gay. In the summer of 1854, Flaubert was nearing the end of his novel and planning to join his friend Bouilhet in Paris: there they would abandon themselves to a drunken collaborative prose: "Just one more year, and we'll be all set up [*piétés*] down there, together, like two bronze rhinocer-

---

the first two volumes of the (incomplete) Pléiade edition will be cited as *C:P*, with appropriate volume and page numbers. For citations from the rest of Flaubert's correspondence, I have used volumes XIII-XVI of the recent *Oeuvres complètes* (Paris: Club de l'Honnête Homme, c. 1971-75), titled and numbered separately as *Correspondance*, II-V. The latter will be cited throughout this chapter as *C:C*, with appropriate volume and page numbers.

[2] Edmond and Jules de Goncourt, *Journal*, II, 261. The *Journal* will be cited throughout this chapter as *J*, with appropriate volume and page numbers.

oses.—We'll do the *Ballet astronomique*, a *féerie*, panto-mimes, the *Dictionnaire des idées reçues*, scenarios, *bouts-rimés*, etc.—We'll be a real pair, I promise you" (*C:P*, II, 561). By November Flaubert was in the capital, where he stayed until the spring of the following year. How many of his projects were undertaken it is impossible to say, but appar-ently at some point during that winter—sometime, that is, between November of 1854 and February or March of 1855[3]—the two friends finished a pantomime, a work that Flaubert would have called "*hénaurme*." For the hero of *Pierrot au sérail* is, though hardly of *le genre commis*, a *vo-yageur* of his mad ideal.

A schoolboy who has carried off all the class prizes, Pier-rot is rewarded with a trip to the Levant. He smuggles Colombine aboardship in his trunk, and in Act II we find them astride a camel, Pierrot devouring a jar of brandied plums, Colombine cowering at his back. Immediately she is abducted by Arabs; Pierrot, unconscious after attempting suicide (by igniting the explosive cotton in his ears), is car-ried away by a battalion of Turks. The next act discovers them both in the gardens of the seraglio of the Grand Turk. Pierrot—quite innocently—attracts the eye of the favored Sultana ("one must submit to fate,"[4] he subsequently rea-sons); Colombine struggles gamely to keep her man. In Act IV, the Sultan surprises all three in a scene of disputatious ardor, and Pierrot is condemned to death:

[. . .] a stake, a huge saber, and a long well-rope are brought in, and the latter is attached to the limb of a tree.

Pierrot, whose immediate decision is demanded, goes at first to put his head through the noose; gives it a little tug; makes a face; and expresses clearly that he would rather not.

[3] The first reference to *Pierrot au sérail* in the *Correspondance* is in a letter to Alfred Baudry, written from Paris and dated by Bruneau as February or March 1855 (*C:P*, II, 572). See note 8 below.

[4] Gustave Flaubert [and Louis Bouilhet], *Pierrot au sérail, pantomime en six actes, suivie de l'apothéose de Pierrot dans le paradis de Mahomet*, in *Oeuvres complètes*, VII (Paris: Club de l'Honnête Homme, 1972), 567. All subse-quent references to the *Oeuvres* throughout this chapter will appear as *OC*, with appropriate volume and page numbers.

Two blacks lift him up and hold him over the stake. He goes through tortuous motions with his rump so that it can be stuck into his butt. His horror at the initial sensation. Finally, he declares that he prefers the saber.

So he goes up to the saber; tries out the edge on his thumb; and, after hesitating a long moment, again declines the invitation.

The Sultan, however, is losing his patience. He bears precipitately down upon Pierrot and orders the slaves to finish him off. (*OC*, VII, 569-70)

The captive adroitly leaps aside as the blade falls, however, and the Grand Turk receives the blow. Pierrot distributes the latter's wealth among the soldiery and, in the next act, is invested, grandly, as the Sultan himself. He is intoxicated with his role: repulsing the Sultana with a flourish of his chibouk and Colombine by a kick in the bum, he stuffs himself with food and drink; he embroils the odalisques in a battle for his favors; when his father and schoolmaster appear to vent their astonishment and indignation, he makes them dance the cancan then thumbs his nose at their solemn oaths. But his gustative riot gradually takes its toll: when the sixth act opens Pierrot cannot move from his chair. Doctors attend to his now enormous person. An epic *lavement* is prescribed. But in a final gesture of defiance, he flings the syringe at his attendants and begins to feast "with heedless immoderation" (*OC*, VII, 574). Suddenly his belly splits open: out of it spill bottles of wine, pâtés, black puddings, fruits, a melon, a live rabbit, a lobster. His *crevaison* finally translates him to Paradise, where the trees are festooned with sausages, where acrobats raise their bocks among the arbors, and where Mohammed welcomes him with open arms. Bengal lights blaze brightly; the *Marseillaise* strikes up. *Tableau*.

We are familiar with such impudence from these collaborators: the more solemnly outrageous *Découverte de la vaccine* (1846-1847) was composed in much the same spirit as *Pierrot*. But Bouilhet's hand is all but absent from the pantomime. Although Flaubert refers to it as their common property in a letter of September 1855, the *brouillons*

that survive (and they are all that survive) are almost entirely in Flaubert's script.[5] And virtually every element of
its meticulously detailed plot may be traced to an event (or
obsession) in Flaubert's own life. His "Orient," that fabulous Near East to which he was often and irresistibly drawn,
offers everywhere the same face as in *Pierrot au sérail*: the
immense desert traversed by dromedaries, the romantic seraglio of *"secret voluptuary chambers"* (*OC*, VII, 572)—such,
for example, was the East of his long-meditated but never-
written *Conte oriental*, actively occupying his mind just before his visit to Paris in the fall of 1854.[6] And he seems to
have early associated its landscapes with those of Corsica,
through which he had traveled, like Pierrot in the "Orient,"
as a triumphant recipient of his *bac*; for it was of the East
(and of himself as, significantly, a kind of Pierrot-*tyran*)
that he began dreaming after his return from Corsica to
France: "I was born," he wrote to Ernest Chevalier, "to be
emperor of Cochin China, to smoke pipes thirty-six fath-
oms long, to have 6000 wives and 1400 young catamites,
scimitars to lop off the heads of people whose faces dis-
please me, Numidian mares, marble pools [. . .]" (*C:P*, I,
76). When, ten years later, he recorded his first impressions
of the Nile, he opened "A bord de la cange" with recollec-
tions of that initiatory voyage to the south. The pantomime
conflates, then, two journeys that were twinned in Flaubert's mind.

   And as with scene, so with character. It is not difficult

---

[5] The fair copy was apparently lost. Manuscripts of the pantomime exist—as rough drafts bearing numerous additions and cancellations—in three
forms, all bound together and codified in the Bibliothèque Nationale,
Paris, as MSS n.a.fr. 14153: (1) a one-page summary, in eight acts (f. 1);
(2) a version bearing the short title *Pierrot au sérail* (ff. 2-20); and (3) a
third version bearing the full title (see previous note), first published in
1910. Between versions (2) and (3) there are occasional discrepancies: a
few of the animals are omitted from the list of characters in (2); in the
latter, Pierrot's family is entertained in the first act by four drummers and
a drum-major, a piece of business that does not appear in (3); also in (2),
all of Pierrot's doctors confer before prescribing the *lavement* of Act VI,
a courtesy they do not extend to the Pierrot of the published version. As
these examples suggest, the differences are minor and negligible.

[6] See his letter to Bouilhet of August 7, 1854 (*C:P*, II, 564). What we
know of the *Conte oriental* has been assembled by Jean Bruneau, *Le "Conte
Oriental" de Gustave Flaubert* (Paris: Denoël, 1973).

to see Pierrot's father, lecturing the schoolboy on the com-
portment of the good traveler, as a parody of Achille-Cléo-
phas, giving advice to his Corsica-bound son ("Profit from
your trip and remember your friend Montaigne, who has
it that one travels in order to bring back principally an
acquaintance with the dispositions of nations and their
manners [. . .]" [C:P, I, 68]). Nor is it difficult to glimpse
Flaubert himself through the grotesqueries of the extant
drafts. He is certainly the "white bear" that at one point
lumbers improbably across the desert: *l'Ours Blanc* is one
of Flaubert's favorite self-conferred sobriquets in the *Correspondance*. He is also, of course, Pierrot himself, suffering
the *"désirs immenses et insatiables,"* as well as the *"ennui atroce"*
(C:P, I, 76), that afflicted Flaubert as much as his hero in
their reluctant skirmishes with life. Pierrot's high-handed
treatment of Colombine—indeed, of all the women in his
sérail—recalls the recent (if not imminent) rupture with the
exigent Louise Colet. And his illness, his bout with the
physicians, seems to have been inspired by an experience of
his creator's shortly before the pantomime took form:
"Laxatives, purgatives, derivatives, leeches, fever, salivation,
diarrhea, three nights without sleep, gigantic annoyance of
the bourgeois, etc., etc.," wrote Flaubert to Bouilhet in
August of 1854, "that's been my week, my dear sir" (C:P,
II, 562). Less ferociously proud than Pierrot, however, he
submitted to the cure: "Finally, *by means of purgations*, of
leeches, of douches (!!!), and thanks, also, to *my strong con-
stitution*, I am quit of it" (C:P, II, 564). *Pierrot* is, by contrast, a portrait of the artist heedlessly immoderate in all
things.

Flaubert was unusually eager to unveil that portrait to
the public. After his return to Croisset, he pressed Bouilhet
to negotiate for the production of the pantomime at the
Folies-Nouvelles.[7] The theater had opened only a few days

[7] May 9, 1855: "Do you have any news of *Pierrot?*" August 15, 1855:
"As for the Folies-Nouvelles, yes: I hold to it, and strongly!/What would
it cost you to go there?/Go: and *intelligently*." August 17, 1855: "Don't
forget the Folies. *Deploy* a Napoleonic energy." August 30, 1855: "Go
then to the Folies-Nouvelles, you damned holy dimwit, and find out what
this 'reversal' meant. I'd give a hundred francs to know." September 13,
1855: "I have the intimate conviction that there was some dirty work,

before Flaubert had arrived in Paris, and it is likely that he and Bouilhet, drawn by the little stir it was making, had attended one or more of Legrand's performances. That the mime's art was, by nature, ephemeral (even trifling, in the public mind) probably enabled Flaubert to overcome his usual scruples about publication: an inconsequential *jeu d'esprit*, his pantomime would appear for several days, at best, and be forgotten in as many weeks. But it may have been just those scruples that prevented the piece from being read with any receptivity. In 1855 Flaubert's name meant nothing to the administrators of the Folies-Nouvelles. After a negligent silence, apparently, Louis Huart responded in a letter dated only by the "185-" of its letterhead:

> I am extremely sorry for the delay brought about in the answer that you have been expecting. Monsieur Altaroche, my associate, promised me to write you a word on the subject of your play, and he unfortunately forgot to do it. There are in our fileboxes, at this moment, three manuscripts bearing the title of *Pierrot au sérail*. The first act of your pantomime is good, but the rest of the piece would have to be changed.
>
> If you wish to oblige us by spending a day at the theater, you may come to an arrangement on this subject with Monsieur Altaroche, who would explain to you his ideas about your play.
>
> If you are willing to give us a time and a place for a meeting, we will be there, Altaroche and I.[8]

---

unknown to us, connected with the *Pierrot* business, which you're not bringing to light [sic: *que tu ne te tires pas à clair*], I don't know why, despite my repeated pleas." September 19, 1855: "You'll see that they'll end up by stealing *Pierrot* from us. We'd have to get back the manuscript, as well as that of *Agénor*. It's easy" (*C:P*, II, 574, 586, 589, 590, 592, 596).

[8] MS H1363, f. 472, Bibliothèque Spoelberch de Lovenjoul. This letter may well have preceded Bouilhet's negotiations with the theater. In his letter to Baudry in which *Pierrot* is first mentioned, Flaubert remarks: "As for *Pierrot*, you don't know, then, that it has been accepted *conditionally*; but that [i.e., the production?] won't be until this summer, if we want to make changes in it—which I hardly care to do" (*C:P*, II, 572). It is possible, of course, that the theater that had accepted *Pierrot* "conditionally" was not the Folies-Nouvelles. Whatever the case, there is no evidence that the pantomime was ever produced.

Little in this letter would have been welcome to Flaubert: and yet the criticisms, both explicit and implied, have a certain vague justice. Flaubert's humor, as he himself realized, was always rather heavy, often even conventionally so. That his Pierrot was but one of several travelers in the Levant of the Folies-Nouvelles suggests the somewhat worn currency of his conception. There is much in Flaubert's scenario that is patently *vieux jeu*—the scene of Pierrot's thoughtful selection of the machinery of his death, for example, a scene that recalls the *lazzo* of suicide so ubiquitous in the *littérature pierrotique*.[9] And yet, for all its conventionality, this scene (and others like it) is irresistibly amusing, and I suspect that Huart's allusion to the three manuscripts is a feint: little in Legrand's pantomimes was truly ever "new," but contributors, nevertheless, could be reproached with a lack of originality if they grew impatient, like Monsieur Flaubert.

The more serious criticism is the more explicit one: that everything following the first act had to be changed. *Pierrot au sérail* actually gains in originality—and interest—as it nears its apotheosis, a fact of which Huart was probably aware. After its first act, however, it is no longer Legrand's kind of piece. The leave-taking of the opening is both sentimental and satiric, with its portraits of warm devotion in the lovers, of dissembled self-importance in the bourgeois. But once Pierrot arrives in the seraglio and begins to indulge his savage appetites, he becomes the kind of Satan *bouffe* with whom we are familiar in Baptiste. Deburau, in other words, seems to be behind the last five acts of *Pierrot au sérail*. Although the Funambules is never mentioned in Flaubert's letters, Henry Gosselin, of the first *Education sentimentale* (1845), sometimes goes there with his friend Morel (*OC*, VIII, 126). Henry's experience is doubtless Flau-

---

[9] Flaubert performs a variation upon that *lazzo* earlier in the pantomime, when, after Colombine's abduction, Pierrot falls into despair: "With a rapid movement, he seizes all the [brandied] plums at once and swallows them, at the same time sending a multitude of kisses in the direction in which Colombine disappeared. He then tries to strangle himself with his cravat: that hurts; he stops. He pulls out his knife, thrusts it into his clothes; then he closes the knife and puts it back in his pocket," etc. (*OC*, VII, 566).

bert's own, when, in the early 1840s, Flaubert studied law in Paris: an ardent lover of the theater, a *cabotin* in early youth, he would not have lived two years in the capital without seeing one of the most celebrated actors of the age.

But Baptiste was less a model for the Pierrot of Flaubert's pantomime than an invitation to the *commis-voyageur* to disport his wicked self. Pierrot is an avatar—and an important one—of his creator; he is one of those selves, both fictive and revealing, that mark the stages of the "great straight line" (*C:P*, II, 205) of Flaubert's career. He, in fact, connects in very interesting ways one of the first and the last of the writer's creations, the Garçon of his schooldays and the posthumous *Bouvard et Pécuchet*. How and why he does so suggest, I think, much about Flaubert— suggest, in particular, why he insisted that "The artist must contain a *saltimbanque*" (*C:C*, V, 339), that he himself was a *saltimbanque, au fond* (*C:P*, I, 278). It was more than simply *tours d'agilité* that attracted the novelist to the latter: *la force* of a very special kind admitted the *saltimbanque* to Pierrot's paradise: the perfect Forms incarnated by the acrobat[10] were, quite literally, *tours de force*. And to explore the origin, meaning, and structures of this strength, we must start with le Garçon.

"Montdory," "Descambeaux"—le Garçon seems to have had several monikers; but of them all "le Garçon" is the best. For he was a creation that transcended the specific: a primordial, superhuman figure, uncircumscribable by the society of names. A "modern Pantagruel,"[11] in Jonathan Culler's words, he was a colossus, of immense appetites and *bêtise*. Although he was apparently a collaborative invention, he was a lifelong obsession of Flaubert's: in February of 1880, *le maître* wrote to Laure de Maupassant: "Since

[10] That Flaubert associated the feats of the *saltimbanque* with artistic form is evident from the letter to Colet in which he professes his kinship with the acrobat: "Fundamentally, I am, whatever anyone might say, a *saltimbanque*. [. . .] Even now, what I love above everything else is form, provided that it's beautiful, and nothing beyond that" (*C:P*, I, 278).

[11] *Flaubert: The Uses of Uncertainty* (Ithaca: Cornell University Press, 1974), p. 162. As my subsequent remarks will suggest, I am deeply indebted to this brilliant book.

the middle of November I've lived completely alone, and how many times, at the corner of my fire, in ruminating over the past, haven't I thought of him (le Garçon!) [. . .]" (*C:C*, V, 318). That the creation of a few *collégiens* of fourteen should accompany Flaubert all of his life, that his exploits should be detailed with such memorable enthusiasm to Flaubert's friends, suggests that le Garçon was what D. L. Demorest early suspected: "an infinitely complex being, representing all sorts of 'Freudian' instincts in [his] creator."[12] Sartre corroborates the suggestion when, in *L'Idiot de la famille*, he writes that "le Garçon takes the place of an *I* to which Gustave does not want to give voice, or cannot give voice."[13]

But Sartre clearly emphasizes the first of those alternatives. In over a hundred brilliant pages, he analyzes le Garçon as a merciless self-parody of his creator, as an instrument of destructive self-mockery, created in defense of Flaubert's frail self-esteem: "At the source of le Garçon, there is an unhappy child who believes himself to be a washout, and whose pride impels him to dissociate himself [*se désolidariser*] from his failure by laughter, thereby making himself something other than what he is." The Rabelaisian laughter of le Garçon, a laughter cosmically directed at the All, is, for his incarnator, an "Imaginary laughter, laughter 'that is not laughter' but that receives a certain consistency from the fact that he who laughs is already *laughable* in his own eyes for having been *constituted such* by the terrible gaze of the surgeon-in-chief, his original superego, and for having consequently been the object of the collective laughter of his comrades (or for having believed that he was that object)."[14] Moving with the mechanical mindlessness of the bourgeois and exulting in the misfortunes of the weakly hypocritical, secure in his gargantuan vanity and scornful of the machinations of men, le Garçon is all that Gustave threatened to become, projected upon an object of derision and fear.[15]

[12] *A travers les plans, manuscrits et dossiers de* Bouvard et Pécuchet (Paris: Conard, 1931), pp. 68-69.

[13] Jean-Paul Sartre, *L'Idiot de la famille: Gustave Flaubert de 1821 à 1857*, II (Paris: Gallimard, 1971), 1223.

[14] Ibid., II, 1298.

[15] Ibid., II, 1251-57, 1261-67.

But, as powerfully compelling as this argument is, it does not fit the "tone" of the figure. The Garçon upon whom Flaubert brooded towards the end of his life revived none of the pain of his youth; he, rather, seems to have recalled the Gustave of Sartre's final paragraph on the figure, conceding Flaubert's occasional abandonment to "the game": "Then he is bewitched like his comrades, fascinated by his character; he becomes animated, gesticulates, gets drunk on his paradoxes, revels in his gigantic strength as much as in his debasement. [. . .] In these moments, author, actor, and director, he exults, he returns to his old passion, the theater, he plays le Garçon as he played Pourceaugnac: the malicious intention is relegated to the background; the essential thing is to have genius."[16] I suspect that *"l'intention maligne"* was always *"au second plan,"* if it had any real place at all: *"l'essentiel,"* indeed, was *"d'avoir du génie"*—which, for Flaubert, meant *d'avoir de la force*.[17] Le Garçon was a creation by which Flaubert could enjoy an almost metaphysically perfect strength, a superiority that was utterly invulnerable. If he laughed at the unfortunate, it was less out of malice than a sense of *grandeur*, of the unassailability of his own position. This is the meaning of le Garçon's famous laughter when the *censeur des études* is apprehended in a bordello:

> It gladdens me, amuses me, delights me, does me good in my chest, in my belly, in my heart, in my bowels, in my viscera, in my diaphragm, etc. When I think of the look on his face, the *censeur* caught in the act and going at it with his file, I give a shout, I laugh, I drink it up, I crow ha ha ha ha ha ha and le Garçon's laughter rings out, I pound on the table, I tear out my hair, I fall helpless to the ground, it's so good. (*C:P*, I, 23)

It is the heady transport of the weak overtaking the strong, a transport to which le Garçon offered unlimited access. A materialist, he was on the side of the verifiable; a bourgeois, he was of the complacently dominant class; a glut-

---

[16] Ibid., II, 1329.

[17] Flaubert to Louise Colet, July 15, 1853: "I believe that the greatest quality of genius is, above everything else, *la force* [strength, power, force, intensity]" (*C:P*, II, 385).

ton, he had the indomitable robustness of a bull; a paragon of all of the vices, he revealed the essential, that is to say appetitive, man; both a purveyor of cant and its critic, he exposed all possible enthusiasms as *blagues*; a breathing image of *bêtise*, he reigned supreme in the superior life:[18] "To be stupid, to be egoistical, and to have good health," wrote Flaubert to Louise Colet, "those are the three conditions requisite for happiness" (*C:P*, I, 298).

He was also quite violently obscene. To make "the entrance of le Garçon" was to "smash and shatter everything, belch behind the door, upset the ink-stands, and shit in front of H[is] M[ajesty]'s bust" (*C:P*, I, 460). Flaubert told the Goncourts that le Garçon kept a Hôtel des Farces, whose corridors echoed, at the "Fête de la Merde," with cries of: "Three buckets of shit to number 14! Twelve dildos to number 8!" (*J*, I, 729-30). In a letter to Edmond Laporte, Flaubert asked, coyly, "At the Hôtel des Farces, where does the cheese that is consumed there come from?" and added, "An easy problem to solve!" (*C:C*, IV, 526). To the Goncourts, all this smacked darkly of Sade, who seemed to bound Flaubert "like a horizon"; to Sartre, it expressed Flaubert's horror of the natural functions and, ultimately, his horror of himself:

> Le Garçon belches and farts, his comrades are shocked and, while he laughs, discover the laughable absurdity of their indignation: *in the name of what* can I—I who am a bag of stinking odors—dissociate myself from this other bag of filth? He releases his stench and I hide it? Then *I* am the funny one. In short, le Garçon's obscene and scatological stupidity manifests itself only to expose the stupid hypocrisy of our material determination which takes itself for a pure spirit and whose ends have no meaning unless it regards its ephemeral, relative, and finite being as an Absolute.[19]

Sound existential logic, certainly, but opposed to almost everything we know of Flaubert. It is not for nothing that Dominique Laporte's provocative *Histoire de la merde* is

---

[18] See *C:P*, I, 67, 69, 98, 138, 784; II, 657; *J*, I, 729.
[19] *L'Idiot de la famille*, II, 1268.

dedicated to "the young Flaubert": shit was a profound source of fascination for the writer, and one of his most respectful metaphors for art.

"*J'aime l'ordure* [. . .]" (*C*:P, II, 119), rhapsodizes Flaubert to Louise Colet. A work of art that stinks of urine and incense, in which bestiality is wedded to mysticism, is—and the word is Flaubert's highest praise—*bête*, like Nature, turning a blank face to the cosmos. The poetry of Corneille, writes the schoolboy Gustave, deserves to mount up to the heavens: and, in a redoubling of praise, he appends "la belle explication de la *fameuse* constipation," describing "*la production du trou fameux.*"[20] Fifteen years later, to encourage Le Poittevin in his work, he exhorts him to "shit us some good turds" (*C*:P, I, 222); when Bouilhet has done so, with two "Greek pieces," he congratulates him on *la production: "En résumé, voilà deux bonnes merdes* [. . .]" (*C*:P, I, 749). In another letter to Bouilhet, he broaches a common concern: "I suffer, like you, at the idea of the disinfection of shit (your morsel on that theme is brilliant, it farts like a man and it farts like a beast [. . .])" (*C*:P, I, 681). His aesthetic is neither mimetic nor expressive; it is, for the writer young and old, expulsive: "You have to drink up oceans and piss them out again" (*C*:P, II, 86), he declares to Louise Colet. (The poor writer, like Lamartine, "has never passed anything but clear water" [*C*:P, II, 299].) His mode of composition is to stuff himself "to vomiting" with other writers' works, and then to spill out his prose: "I don't feel any intellectual desire to do so," he confesses to Louis Bouilhet, "but a kind of physical need" (*C*:P, II, 755). Only when a book is going badly, when the labor seems sterile, does Flaubert "masturbate [his] poor head in vain" (*C*:C, III, 156); when, as in the writing of *Salammbô*, he is intoxicated by his own power, his metaphors usually revert to a lower plane: "I'm sweating blood, I'm pissing boiling water, I'm shitting out catapults, and I'm belching out balls for the sling" (*C*:C, III, 83). Sweat, piss: his terms are various (Edmond de Goncourt remarked that Flaubert grew expansive in discussions of bodily excretions [*J*, II,

[20] In Jean Bruneau, *Les Débuts littéraires de Gustave Flaubert, 1831-1845* (Paris: Colin, 1962), p. 41.

1256]), but his favorite "*grand mot*," the word with which "one consoles oneself for all the human miseries," is *merde* (*C:P*, I, 237).

Grand, perhaps, because erotic. In a remarkable letter to Louis Bouilhet, written from Patras in early 1851, the sight of a fragment of sculpture elicits a dithyrambic description of breasts: Flaubert's catalogue ends with "the pumpkin-tit, the formidable and sluttish tit," which "pleases a pig like me." Such a *téton*, he declares, "makes you want to shit over it" (*C:P*, I, 754). Sartre notes that le Garçon "is willingly scatological but, curiously, is hardly tempted by pornography—at least according to the information that we have about him."[21] Like Flaubert before his vision of "*le téton citrouille*," he expresses his potency by *la merde*. But then why, Sartre asks, at the Fête de la Merde, are dildos requested by his celebrants? Sartre's answer rests upon his earlier analysis—too intricate to be done full justice here— of Flaubert's fantasy-relationship with his mother. Always *bête*, as a child, in his relations with the world, Flaubert imagined erotic satisfaction as masturbatory, as passive gratification by a valorizing Other: the ideal partner was his mother, "provided on the occasion with an imaginary phallus."[22] The celebrants at the Fête are then asking to be sodomized, to be taken, in fantasy, by "*une femme virilisée*,"[23] who will enjoy them with a rubber penis. Although Sartre obviously errs in ascribing an historical reality to this "festival"—he suggests that the schoolboys equipped whores with real dildos—its underpinnings in fantasy are undeniable. But there is a more economical explanation for those dildos, I think, one that accords with the function of le Garçon as I have described it, with the psychology of Flaubert analyzed subtly by Sartre, and with the scatology of the Fête de la Merde.

From her study of paranoiacs, Janine Chasseguet-Smirgel has hypothesized that the child for whom the phallic mother-imago is particularly "bad" is unable to identify with the father: he is unable to transfer his narcissistic projec-

---

[21] *L'Idiot de la famille*, II, 1318.
[22] Ibid., I, 696.
[23] Ibid., II, 1318.

tions from her (fantasized) penis to that of the imago-*père*.
The paternal penis is, consequently, for him "an erotic and
aggressive object but is not a bearer of his ego-ideal." It is
as a result of this inhibition that he fabricates the "false"
penis to which Crouzet ascribes the formalizing passion of
Gautier. Having no share in his father's authority, "The
subject will elaborate [. . .] fantasies and a behavior that
aim to demonstrate that he has already in his possession a
penis of absolute power and perfection." This magical appendage acquires its power by association with the infant's
unique creative act: defecation. And as an essentially fecal
instrument of authority, it is invulnerable to any threat:

> In effect, by comparison with genital castration, anal
> castration (insofar as it applies to the fecal *bâton*) is
> not a definitive and absolute mutilation. The fecal *bâ-
> ton* renews itself, in fact, indefinitely. It is indeed the
> only penis that grows back, the phoenix that is reborn
> from its ashes.[24]

Although Chasseguet-Smirgel contends, as we have seen,
that its possessor is a prisoner of *le Faux*—of a false art for
the writer, not "engendered" but "made"—the more accurate (because less judgmental) word would be Sartre's:
"*l'imaginaire*." The artist possessed of the *bâton fécal* has no
intercourse with the True or the False. Having been dis-
couraged in the assumption of a clear ego-ideal, he resides
freely among transvalued Forms.

Such, of course, is the Flaubert of Sartre's analysis. Un-
derloved by the mother in whom he sought his gratification, he took revenge in fantasies of cruelty: she became
the "bad" mother, the victim of the juvenilia, whose punishment is a kind of castration. The father remained ever
alien, a menacing butcher-surgeon, as in the dream Flaubert recorded in his *Mémoires d'un fou* (1838).[25] The result,

---

[24] "Le Rossignol de l'Empereur de Chine: Essai psychanalytique sur le
'faux,' " *Pour une psychanalyse de l'art et de la créativité* (Paris: Payot, 1971),
pp. 189, 190, 213.
[25] The dream (*OC*, XI, 483) was analyzed by Freud himself as expressing fear of castration by the father: see Theodore Reik, *Flaubert und seine
"Versuchung des heiligen Antonius," ein Beitrag zur Künstlerpsychologie*
(Minden: Bruns, 1912), p. 99.

in part, was the creation of le Garçon—not, as Sartre argues, so that the boy might "abolish himself, in order to carry out the orders of the Father,"[26] but rather to confront that Father, at least in unconscious fantasy, with an image of his own invincible power. Le Garçon is a phallic god, whose authority emanates from his anus; he reigns, like Ubu, with a "*croc à merdre*," and, like Ubu, reigns supreme. Those dildos, I am suggesting, in the Fête de la Merde, are merely variants on his buckets of turds: at once proliferate and false, they symbolize the limitless power of *l'imaginaire*. It is, in fact, the purely imaginary status of le Garçon himself that Sartre sees as important for Gustave:

> The real is not *true*, the unreal is not *false*. Then, one will say, le Garçon is not a *false* image of man? He [Flaubert] does not intend to deceive his comrades? Let us say that *for Gustave* this character is neither true nor false: he is unreal, that is all.[27]

But that "*c'est tout*" gives us pause. Flaubert is indeed conscious of le Garçon's unreality; but he is drawn, by reasons he could not have explained, by his secret, fantasmatic power.

And it is this very power—to close up our lengthy parenthesis—that animates Flaubert's Pierrot. When invested as Sultan, he literally bristles with phallic strength: the aigrette on his turban "rises to infinity," his upper lip sprouts a "gigantic mustache" (*OC*, VII, 570). He wields his chibouk like a mace, his saber like the scimitar of Flaubert's fancies. When lectured upon his immorality, he "waves away the author of his years with an indifferent air"; then when, heated, his father enjoins him to remember his duty, "Pierrot answers that he is the master" now (*OC*, VII, 571-72). But, a master with a fecal phallus, he sins only in his *régime*: in the desert, he rejects Colombine's kisses in favor of his brandied plums; in the harem, he obviously prefers *la cuisine turque* to his eager odalisques. The "alimentary obsession" that has been remarked in Flaubert[28] is at the service

[26] *L'Idiot de la famille*, II, 1263.
[27] Ibid., II, 1327.
[28] Jean-Pierre Richard, "La Création de la forme chez Flaubert," *Littérature et sensation* (Paris: Editions du Seuil, 1954), p. 120.

of Pierrot's authority. And when that authority is threatened, significantly, by an enormous enema-tube, his response is to enlarge the *bâton* by which he rules in an orgy of food and drink.

Pierrot differs from le Garçon in that, like Baptiste, he lives partly by ruse. Le Garçon is never menaced, mainly because he is so *bête*: "Le Garçon believes that the Parmesan cheese is the painter of all the pictures designated under the name of the Parmesan," writes Flaubert to DuCamp from Venice; "and every time he sees some Parmesan he pays it compliments and talks painting with it" (*C:P*, I, 784). A creature of such monumental stupidity knows nothing of the world without: any threat must seem an incomprehensible madness and, hence, alien to both person and self-esteem. And, supreme egoist that he is, he is thus relieved of a social existence. Without family, occupation, in effect without class (*le bourgeois* was simply anyone whom Flaubert claimed to detest), he enjoys the atemporality—and irrepressibility—of myth. Pierrot, on the other hand, suffers Baptiste's uncertainties, now exulting in the strength of an ego inflated by wish, now acceding to the external temporalities of power. Before becoming Sultan, he is humbled to all fours—literally, when he first follows the Sultana into the harem; figuratively, when he is faced with the instruments of his death. With Pierrot, *le réel* has seeped into *l'irréelité* of le Garçon's world; and his cleverness is an indication of, and response to, its presence.

Flaubert's ultimate response is the violent climax, in which Pierrot's belly bursts in a *crevaison*. The image is, I think, compromised by what could be shown on the stage: I suspect it is not Pierrot's belly but his sphincter that has let go. To defend my emendation, as well as to suggest its full value for Flaubert, we should turn to le Garçon's last avatar—not a character, exactly, but a projection of his creator, the odd persona that fabricated *Bouvard et Pécuchet*. There *le réel*, as it were, achieves parity with le Garçon, and Flaubert must muster his full strength to subdue it. But the struggle is complicated by certain ambiguities upon which we have not yet touched. Flaubert's Ubu has no equal—but one, and that is Flaubert himself.

1. Jean-Louis Barrault as J.-G. Deburau Paying Court to the Moon: still from Marcel Carné, *Les Enfants du Paradis* (1945).

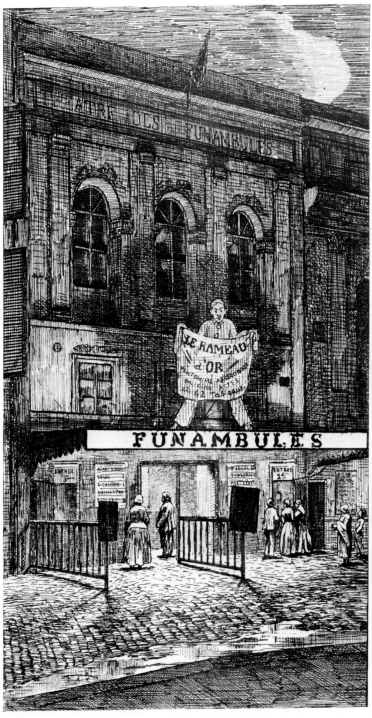

2. Charles Patémont: The Théâtre des Funambules in 1862: engraving in the
Bibliothèque Nationale.

3. Auguste Bouquet: *Le Repas de Pierrot*: J.-G. Debureau as Pierrot-Gourmand: engraving in the Harvard Theatre Collection.

4. Eustache Lorsay: Four Caricatures of J.-G. Deburau in *Satan, ou le Pacte infernal* (*c.* 1842): from *Le Musée Philipon, album de tout le monde* (*c.* 1842).

5. Cham: Caricature of J.-G. Deburau in *Pierrot en Afrique* (*c.* 1842): from *Le Musée Philipon, album de tout le monde* (*c.* 1842).

6. Eustache Lorsay: Caricature of J.-G. Deburau in the Apotheosis of a *Féerie* (*c.* 1842): from *Le Musée Philipon, album de tout le monde* (*c.* 1842).

7. Hutchisson: Madame Saqui at Vauxhall (1820): engraving in the Bibliothèque National

GALERIE PAUL LEGRAND

FOLIES-NOUVELLES

Pierrot Carotier   Ni hommes ni femmes   Legrand Poucet   La sœur de Pierrot   Pierrot bureaucrate   Pierrot Gribouille   La fausse Douairière
                                           Pierrot Marquis   L'œuf blanc et l'œuf rouge   Le petit Cendrillon   Robinson

8. F. Robineau and G. Levilly: *Galerie Paul Legrand* (1858): Legrand in His Most
Memorable Roles at the Funambules and Folies-Nouvelles: engraving in the
Theatre Collection of the New York Public Library at Lincoln Center.

POLICHINELLE.

Des services!…. Vous seriez donc?…

LA MORT.

La Mort.

POLICHINELLE.

Brrrr!… Madame, enchanté de
faire votre connaissance…. Ah!
vous êtes la Mort! Eh bien, ça
me fait plaisir de vous voir….
Vous vous portez bien?

9. Louis Morin: Polichinelle in an Encounter with Death: from Champfleury, *Les bons
contes font les bons amis* (Paris: Truchy, n.d.).

0. Adrien Tournachon: Charles Deburau (*c.* 1858): photograph in the Bibliothèque
Nationale.

11. Anon.: A Late *Féerie* at the Funambules: *affiche* in the Bibliothèque de l'Opéra.

2. Jules Chéret: Paul Legrand at the Tertulia (1871): poster reproduced in Ernest Maindron, *Les Affiches illustrées: Ouvrage orné de 20 chromolithographies par Jules Chéret* Paris: Launette, 1886).

13. Charles Baudelaire: La Fanfarlo: pencil-drawing in Jacques Crépet, ed., *Dessins de Baudelaire* (Paris: Gallimard, 1927).

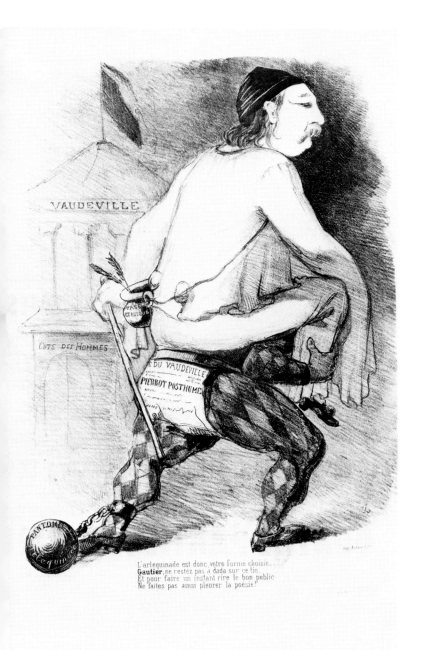

VAUDEVILLE

COTE DES HOMMES

DU VAUDEVILLE
PIERROT POSTHUME

PANTOM
arlequina

L'arlequinade est donc votre forme choisie....
Gautier, ne restez pas à dada sur ce tic,
Et pour faire un instant rire le bon public
Ne faites pas ainsi pleurer la poésie!

4. Nadar: "So the Harlequinade Is Your Chosen Form . . . /Don't Stay Astraddle This
Hobbyhorse, Gautier;/and Just To Give the Good Public a Momentary Laugh/Don't
Make Poetry Cry This Way!": Caricature of Gautier as Pierrot, After the Production at
the Vaudeville of *Pierrot posthume*: from *Le Charivari*, October 20, 1847.

15. Anon.: The Hanlon-Lees in the Scene with the Flask from *Le Voyage en Suisse* (1878): poster in the Theatre Collection of the New York Public Library at Lincoln Center.

5. Georges Rochegrosse: Pierrot Abandoned by the Fairy Urgèle: frontispiece to Théodore de Banville, *Le Baiser* (Paris: Charpentier, 1888).

Oh! Banville, n'abandonnez pas vos pierrots,
votre Pierrot « plus pâle que de coutume »

17. Adolphe Willette: "Oh! Banville, Don't Abandon Your Pierrots, Your Pierrot 'Uncustoarily Pale' ": from *Le Pierrot*, March 20, 1891.

18. Anon.: The Hanlon-Lees in the Drunken Scene from *Le Voyage en Suisse* (1878): poster in the Theatre Collection of the New York Public Library at Lincoln Center.

19. Anon.: The Hanlon-Lees in *Superba* (1890): poster in the Theatre Collection of the
New York Public Library at Lincoln Center.

20. Jules Chéret: *Pierrot sceptique*: title-page for J.-K. Huysmans and Léon Hennique, *Pierrot sceptique* (Paris: Rouveyre, 1881).

21. Adolphe Willette: *Deux Pages d'Amour* (I): Pantomime in Pictures: from *Le Chat Noir*, January 17, 1885.

22. Adolphe Willette: *Deux Pages d'Amour* (II): Pantomime in Pictures: from *Le Chat Noir*, January 17, 1885.

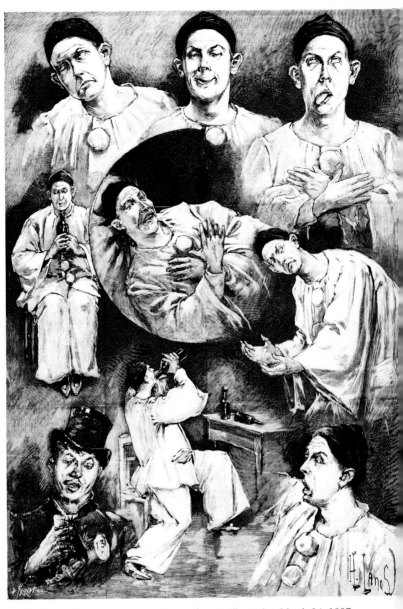

23. H. Lanos: *Pierrot assassin de sa femme*: from *L'Illustration*, March 26, 1887.

24. Adolphe Willette: *Pierrot assassin de sa femme* (*c.* 1888):
from Adolphe Brisson, *Nos Humoristes* (Paris: Société d'Edition
Artistique, 1900).

25. Adolphe Willette: *Pierrot assassin de sa femme*: from *Le Pierrot*, December 7, 1888.

26. Atelier Nadar: Sarah Bernhardt in the *Pierrot assassin* of Jean Richepin (*c.* 1883): photograph in the Bibliothèque Nationale.

27. Anon.: Raoul de Najac as Pierrot: frontispiece to Raoul de Najac, *Souvenirs d'un mime* (Paris: Emile-Paul, 1909).

28. J.-M. Le Natur: A Rehearsal at the Cercle Funambulesque: from Félix Larcher and Paul Hugounet, *Les Soirées Funambulesques* (Paris: Kolb, [1890-93]).

29. Adolphe Willette: *L'Enfant prodigue* (1890): poster reproduced in Ernest Maindron, *Les Affiches illustrées (1886-1895)* (Paris: Boudet, 1896).

20. Jules Chéret: *Le Miroir* (1892): poster reproduced in Ernest Maindron, *Les Affiches
illustrées (1886-1895)* (Paris: Boudet, 1896).

31. Happichy: Séverin in *Chand d'habits!* (1896): poster in the Theatre Collection of the New York Public Library at Lincoln Center.

L. Damaré: Séverin in *Plaisirs d'Amour* (1907): poster in the Theatre Collection of
New York Public Library at Lincoln Center.

33. Anon.: Séverin in *Chand d'habits!*: photograph in *The Drama*, August 1923.

34. Anon.: Georges Wague as Père Pierrot in the Film Version of *L'Enfant prodigue* (1906): photograph reproduced in Tristan Rémy, *Georges Wague: Le Mime de la Belle Epoque* (Paris: Girard, 1964).

35. Anon.: Igor Stravinsky and Vaslav Nijinsky as Petrouchka (*c.* 1911): photograph in the Bettmann Archive.

For, like most anal erotics, Flaubert suffered familiar ambivalences.[29] On the one hand, his art was a "letting go," the bawling *gueulade*, the deliberate *emmerdement* of the first *Tentation*. On the other hand, after the chastisement of his literary big brothers, it was an extreme, obsessive control. "Art," Flaubert wrote to Ernest Feydeau in November of 1859, "[. . .] requires calm white hands" (C:C, III, 12), unsoiled, apparently, by *l'ordure*. The first Flaubert is the bronze rhinoceros, the enthusiast of Sade, whose contagious violence astonished Edmond de Goncourt: "So much nervousness, so much pugnacious violence emanates from Flaubert," he wrote in his *Journal* of 1873, "that the surroundings in which he finds himself soon become stormy, and a certain aggressiveness lays hold of everyone" (*J*, II, 956). It was a violence that, with Flaubert, was habitual. Translated into an indignation at life and symbolized by an anal *bâton*, it gave him, both as man and as writer, his strongest sense of a personal self:

> Flaubert was saying today, rather picturesquely [again I am quoting Edmond de Goncourt]: "No, it's indignation alone that sustains me! Indignation for me is the rod that dolls have up their butts, the rod that makes them stand up. When I'm no longer indignant, I'll fall flat!" And he sketches out the silhouette of a Polichinelle collapsed on a floor. (*J*, II, 927)

But his strength, at bottom, was powerless, as he confessed to Louise Colet: "[. . .] I have nothing to sustain me but a kind of permanent rage, which weeps sometimes from impotence, but which is continual" (C:P, II, 75). As a func-

---

[29] For a classic discussion of the anal character, see Ernest Jones, "Anal-Erotic Character Traits," *Papers on Psycho-Analysis*, 5th ed. (Boston: Beacon Press, 1948). Jones's description was given empirical validation in an early study by Halla Beloff, "The Structure and Origin of the Anal Character," *Genetic Psychology Monographs*, LV, 2nd Half (May 1957), 141–72. In referring to Flaubert as an "anal-erotic" personality, I do not mean to set limits to the extraordinarily rich repertoire of Flaubertian fantasy. For a discussion of the narcissistic and oedipal impulses that also direct his work, see Charles Bernheimer, *Flaubert and Kafka: Studies in Psychopoetic Structure* (New Haven: Yale University Press, 1982), and William J. Berg, George Moskos, and Michel Grimaud, *Saint/Oedipus: Psychocritical Approaches to Flaubert's Art* (Ithaca: Cornell University Press, 1982).

tion of *l'imaginaire*, of the penis "made" not "engendered," his power, as he suspected, was threatened by its own hollowness—and his self by a polichinellesque collapse.

Such an intuition was perhaps responsible, at least in part, for the ambivalence of the "second" Flaubert, of the exemplar of self-control. Not the conduit of the diarrheal *Tentation*, he was—in the terms of our first epigraph—*le faiseur de bonne merde*. But what distinguishes *la bonne merde* from *la mauvaise*? Flaubert's own answer was a vaguely Platonic one: the former, as Art, resides in the realm of Forms; it participates in *le Beau*. But, in doing so, it surrenders its worldly power. Flaubert, as Victor Brombert has observed, was "convinced of the impossibility of language"[30]—which is to say that, for him, it presented a paradoxical face. On the one hand, it was associated with the profoundest fantasies of his strength. "Our Normand," wrote Edmond de Goncourt, "is very logomachical by nature" (*J*, II, 933). Words were supremely important because they, in effect, constituted Flaubert's very self: they were not simply the medium but the source and sustainer of his "rage." In a curious letter to Louise Colet, he defended himself against her reproaches by avowing that only in the act of writing was he alive to his own sensations:

> You tell me that I seriously loved that woman: that's not true.—Only when I was writing to her, with the faculty I have of being moved by my pen, did I take my subject seriously, but *only while I was writing*. A lot of things that leave me cold, either when I see them or when others talk about them, excite my enthusiasm, annoy me, wound me if I talk about them and especially if I write. That's one of the effects of my clownish nature [*ma nature de saltimbanque*]. (*C:P*, I, 380)

To write, exclaimed the young author of *Un parfum à sentir* (1836), "is to feel one's thought being born, growing, living, standing erect on its pedestal, and remaining there forever" (*OC*, XI, 260). Words, in short, gave to the thinking self the life (and power) of an erected phallus.

[30] *The Novels of Flaubert: A Study of Themes and Techniques* (Princeton: Princeton University Press, 1966), p. 24.

But of a phallus *imaginaire*. For, on the other hand, language, like his anal *bâton*, was impotent. Moreover, it often seemed—like, again, that *bâton*—as much an object of disgust as consolation. "I think I've embarked upon a dirty piece of work!" wrote Flaubert of his struggle with *Salammbô*: "[. . .] there are days when it seems to me I'm navigating on the high seas of shit [. . .]" (*C:P*, II, 735). Here speaks the slave of the rigid routine, the writer whose work is a *pensum*, the retentive payer-out of words, the hoarder of manuscripts, for whom language is like money, both precious and filthy. "*Moi, je déteste les mots!*" (*J*, II, 932), Flaubert declared to Edmond de Goncourt. And yet he had remarked to Louise Colet: "I'd like to produce books for which one would have only to *write sentences* (if one can say that), as, in order to live, one has only to breathe the air" (*C:P*, II, 362). The ideas are less far apart than they seem: the Flaubert who conceived the impossible project, of a book about nothing, sustained by its style, was an artist for whom words had no strength in the world.

These considerations are important in reading *Bouvard et Pécuchet*, for the latter was Flaubert's last thunderous volley in his struggle with that world. *La merde contre la merde*: such, characteristically, were the terms of his struggle. "It's been said that we're dancing on a volcano [. . .]," he wrote to Eugène Delattre in January of 1859: "Not at all! we're stamping about on the rotten seat of a vast latrine" (*C:C*, II, 654). With the passing of years, the shit got higher, until, finally, with the cataclysm of the Prussian War, it seemed to be lapping at his walls. "I have always tried to live in an ivory tower," he wrote to Turgenev in 1872; "but a flood of shit is beating at its walls, threatening to bring it down" (*C:C*, IV, 181). The enemy was, of course, the object of his intense fascination (because, in a sense, the object of his desire): *la bêtise*. He wrote to the Princesse Mathilde: "As far as I am concerned, I'm terrified by the universal stupidity. It has the effect of the Flood on me, and I feel the terror that the contemporaries of Noah must have suffered when they saw the inundation overrun every summit in turn" (*C:C*, IV, 307). At times the spectacle gave rise to his wish to "drown humanity under my vomit," to "vomit out my hatred, spit out my gall, ejaculate my anger, purge myself of my indignation" (*C:C*, IV, 20, 170). Under its most considered forms, however, his response seemed a vast *emmerdement*: "*Sacré nom de Dieu!*" he exclaimed to Louise Colet: "we have to harden ourselves and besmear with shit the humanity that's besmearing us!" (*C:P*, II, 367). Later, to Bouilhet, he conceived the exact terms of his revenge:

> In the face of the stupidity of my age I feel waves of hatred that are suffocating me. Shit rises up to my mouth, as in strangulated hernias. But I want to keep it down, congeal it, harden it. I want to make a paste of it with which I'll besmear the nineteenth century, as they glaze Indian temples with cow-dung [? *bougée de vache*]; and who knows? maybe it will last? (*C:P*, II, 600)

The book with which he wanted to dirty the face of his century caused him, understandably, immense trepidation: its writing implicated the whole of his psychic self. To Madame Roger des Genettes he remarked that he was not free to choose another subject, even should the book cost him (as it would) long years of exasperating labor (*C:C*, V, 60). He regarded the whole project as an almost terrifying audacity, fearing, early on, that he might be run out of France, and aiming, once he had begun, to frighten his readers, or bewilder them to the point of madness (*C:C*, III, 156; IV, 338; V, 116). He complained of becoming "idiotic" during its composition, of having intruded into an "abyss (wasps' nest or latrine)" from which he could not retreat (*C:C*, IV, 329, 582). Such remarks strike us as puzzling when applied to *Bouvard et Pécuchet*, or even to the notes for the more aggressively acerb *Copie*. The effect is, in general, of rather benign tedium, relieved, in the former, by a slowly expiring humor; a sense of impotence pervades the whole. What Flaubert had conceived as a club to fend off *la bêtise* is, in fact, the hollow *croc à merdre*, flourished in vain against a more powerful cloacal reality.

The characters to whom he entrusts that *croc* are, to begin with, comic types, unfit, as Lionel Trilling has observed, for any of "the large enterprises of the spirit." To that much vexed question "Bouvard et Pécuchet sont-ils des imbéciles?" Trilling has made the sanest reply: their intelligence is actually beside the point; they are, from conception, *impotent* men and can merely "catalyze" the "foolishness of others." They are impotent because they are funny, and they are funny

> because they are what they are, because they are middle-aged, because one is fat and one is thin; because they wear strange garments; because they are unmarried and awkward in love; because they are innocent; because they are clumsy and things blow up in their faces, or fall on them, or trip them up; because they are gullible and think they are shrewd; because they are full of enthusiasm. Being funny in themselves, being comically *not* the men for high enterprises, they are therefore funny when they undertake the intellectual life. Their comicality is *a priori*, it does not grow out of their lack of intelligence.[31]

And in their comicality, they are helpless in the face of the *bêtise* that they catalyze. In one of the *plans* of the conclusion, the whole town rises up against them, in the manner of an Ionesco farce. At first threatened with prison, they are defended by several citizens "*avec une pitié insultante.*" Finally, they are treated as harmless madmen: "Thus everything has snapped in their hands."[32]

Flaubert's project, as he had told Bouilhet, was to harden the shit rising up to his mouth and then use it to besmear his age. This is, in a sense, and in a limited way, what his *bonshommes* seem to do. Like Flaubert before the hundreds of sources for his novel, they ingest, then excrete, *la bêtise*. But to put the matter in these expulsive terms suggests one more source of their impotence: their power is the enemy's own. "De défaut de méthode dans les sciences": Flaubert's subtitle for his book refers not simply to the two heroes' bungling but to the model of "method" to which both

[31] "Flaubert's Last Testament," *Partisan Review*, XX (November-December 1953), 615, 616.
[32] Gustave Flaubert, "Plan," *Bouvard et Pécuchet*, ed. Alberto Cento (Naples: Istituto Universitario Orientale, and Paris: Nizet, 1964), pp. 595-96. This edition will be cited throughout this chapter as *B&P*, with appropriate page numbers.

characters defer—to the authorities who seduce their spirit. The wise man contemns them all. "L'ineptie consiste à vouloir conclure" (*C:P*, I, 679), contends Flaubert in a famous phrase. But such wisdom begets only passiveness; it seems useless as *la force*. Thus Flaubert's terror before the *bêtise* both outside and *inside* his "*deux idiots*": he knows it is one and the same. It is the debilitating power of the Other. "Could it be," he asks of his niece Caroline, "that I'm too full of my subject and that the stupidity of my two *bonshommes* is invading me?" (*C:C*, IV, 335). To Madame Roger des Genettes, he is more definite: "Bouvard and Pécuchet fill me to such a point that I've become them! Their stupidity is mine and I'm dying of it" (*C:C*, IV, 379).

The actual results of their bungling have never been sufficiently remarked. Their little property at Chavignolles gradually assumes the aspect of a latrine. When all the water leaks from the ill-made pool in their garden, they are left with a basin of mud. The house itself is invaded by dim piles of refuse: "The ruins of the distillery, swept towards the back of the room, were discernible in the shadows as a vague heap" (*B&P*, 331). Their geological specimens are strewn everywhere—"along the steps in the stairway, in the rooms, in the hall, in the kitchen; and Germaine lamented over the abundance of dust" (*B&P*, 351). When they chat in the evenings, it is to the sound of foraging mice and to the smell of decaying vegetation. As one enthusiasm follows another, the mess is simply shoved aside, like the stone effigy of Saint Peter, heaved out a window onto the compost heap after Bouvard stumps his toe on its foot. The *bonshommes* seem not to mind the mounting *excreta*, but Flaubert himself is in subtle revolt. Brombert speaks of "a sense of clutter and obstruction" in the novel, citing Claudia Neuenschwander-Naef's characterization of the style as "unlivable."[33] It is unlivable because, as Jonathan Culler has ably argued, it seems so blankly uncomprehending of the clutter it describes. Stolid, inert—in short, *bête*—its prose is that of an almost mindless deposition. And, like that "vague heap" swept up in the corner or, better, the grotesque garden, which was, "in the twilight, something frightening" (*B&P*, 315), it disquiets by its dumb respect of the chaos.

[33] *The Novels of Flaubert*, p. 262.

But it is by that very style that Flaubert both expresses and annuls his revolt. For the style is an odd mastering of the chaos of which it declares itself masterless: it betrays, in a self-cancelling confession, the retentive's disgust at disorder and the expulsive's delight in *l'informe*. It is the hollow *croc à merdre*, the powerless instrument of power. And yet the man who wields that *croc* is not the ambivalent voice of the *Correspondance*, the *révolté* of the Goncourt *Journal*, for he seems no longer a victim of his disabling personal self. Thought, rage, even the thirst for meaning are dissolved in the self-sufficiency of *les mots*. In this style Flaubert seemed to find an equivalent for his long-coveted escape from the world. "You call me 'the Brahman,' " he wrote to Louise Colet:

> It's too great an honor, but I'd well like to be one. I have aspirations towards that sort of life powerful enough to drive me mad. I'd like to live in their forests, whirl like them in mystical dances, and exist in that endless absorption. (*C:P*, I, 433)

"To be matter!"—this is Anthony's much-quoted wish: and to share the consciousness of beasts or of Brahmans, those beings with whom Flaubert felt intense sympathy, was to adopt a material eye. Flaubert's mature style approaches that consciousness[34] and, in doing so, offers a final reply to *bêtise*.

Only when his two "idiots" learn the lesson of this style, only when they become genuinely *bêtes*, do they enjoy le Garçon's serenity. The answer, they discover, is not to work upon the shit that is strangling them, intolerant of *la bêtise*: the answer is to let it unobstructedly flow. When they return to copying they become, in effect, spotless conduits of *la merde*. Their rage for certainty is satisfied—to copy faithfully requires discipline of a high order—and yet they are no longer dabblers in the shit. What passes through them is now *purely* other, utterly alien from their being. Having accepted their impotence, they discover their strength, each

---

[34] We should recall Flaubert's remark to Maxime DuCamp: "I want to produce such an impression of lassitude and boredom that whoever reads this book might think it's been written by a cretin" (Maxime DuCamp, *Souvenirs littéraires*, II [Paris: Hachette, 1892], p. 390).

becoming, as Jeanne Bem has observed, like Flaubert, an impassive *"homme-plume."*[35] This explains their imperturbability in one of the final projected scenes:

> One day they discover (among the old papers from the mill) the rough draft of a letter from Vaucorbeil to the Prefect.
> The Prefect had asked him if B[ouvard] and P[écuchet] were not dangerous madmen. The letter from the doctor is a confidential report explaining that they are two harmless imbeciles. In summing up [. . .] all their actions and thoughts, it should be, for the reader, the critique of the novel.
> "What are we going to do with it?"—Don't think about it! Let's copy! The page must be filled, "the monument" finished.—Equality of everything, of the good and the bad, the beautiful and the ugly, the insignificant and the characteristic. Nothing is true but phenomena.
> Finish with a scene of the two *bonshommes* bent over their desks, copying. (*B&P*, 124-25, capitalization and punctuation regularized)

Words are merely part of the phenomena and, being equal to everything else, are valueless. But they will now declare their own lack of value; they will not entrap the two friends in the fray: the page, Flaubert observes in a significant reflexive, will fill itself up (*"la page s'emplisse"*), the "monument" will be completed. At the end of *Bouvard et Pécuchet, la bête de la parole* has triumphed over *la bêtise*.

We seem to have wandered from *Pierrot au sérail,* but we have not actually wandered very far. Pierrot, too, thrashes about, like Flaubert's *bonshommes,* in a world of *idées reçues.* Exploiting the self-parodying tendencies of Legrand's pantomime, Flaubert at first deconstructs that world. "To denote clearly that one is in the desert," for example, he sends an ostrich—on casters—across the footlights (*OC*, VII, 566). His Arabian warriors, clad in stage-cliché dress, "come

---

[35] *Désir et savoir dans l'oeuvre de Flaubert: Etude de* La Tentation de saint Antoine (Neuchâtel: La Baconnière, 1979), p. 240. The allusion is to a letter from Flaubert to Louise Colet, January 31, 1852: "I'm a man-pen. I feel with the pen—because of it, with respect to it, and a lot more with it" (*C:P*, II, 42).

gamboling in on cardboard horses of all colors (the horses are finished off with cloth bodies, from which the warriors emerge at the waist)" (*OC*, VII, 566). His Turks carry "gilt paper sabers" (*OC*, VII, 566); the Sultan needs a black boy to hold up his pipe. In the seraglio itself, we breathe the air of the Koran, where, according to the *Dictionnaire des idées reçues*, "*il n'est question que de femmes*."[36] Pierrot's illness, one suspects, is the result of a metaphorical overindulgence: the *bêtise* of this world has filled him, quite literally, to bursting. And when he ensures his *crevaison* by calling for more food, we hear his master meditating his last terrible book: "Yes, I'll finally unburden myself of what's stifling me. I'll vomit over my contemporaries the disgust that they inspire in me, even if my breast is to burst from it; it will be abundant and violent" (*C:C*, IV, 167). In writing that book, he will "*purge*" himself, "and be afterwards more Olympian, a quality that I absolutely lack" (*C:C*, IV, 192). Expressing his wish in one word to a correspondent, he summons up Pierrot's final fate: "I desire only one thing: namely, *to die* [crever]" (*C:C*, IV, 198).

That fate is given its ultimate expression in a bizarre doomsday fantasy, in Flaubert's apocalyptic vision of an immense *emmerdement*. "What a nice subject for an ode the strike of the cesspool-cleaners would make!" he exclaims to Jules Duplan in a letter of 1865: "The shit is about to boil up in the overfull cellars and so splinter the houses, etc." He then sketches out a detailed scenario:

> Seriously, you could do some fine things with this idea; and what a charming Chorus the cesspool-cleaners would be, at rest, all seated in broad daylight, in the shadow of the soil-tubs, like shepherds under the vine, etc.
>
> [. . .]
> I
> Chorus of shit
> Et les étrons disaient, rêvant dans leurs caveaux,
> Quand aurons-nous fini de combler les tonneaux?
> Désolation.
> [*And the turds, dreaming in their little vaults, were*

---

[36] Jean Canu's alert observation: *Flaubert: Auteur dramatique* (Paris: Les Ecrits de France, 1946), p. 24.

*saying:/When will we have finally overtopped the tanks?/O
Sorrow . . .*]

At least, in the Old Man's day [i.e., the day of the
Marquis de Sade], they ate us, etc., but now they're
disinfecting us. We don't feel like ourselves anymore.
They're torturing us, they're roasting us in sugar.

II

Chorus of cesspool-cleaners

III

Joy of the kikes. Schoolboys' exuberance.

Eruption of Vesuvius. *Tableau* of Paris buried under
the shit, like Herculaneum under the lava.

In the last strophe, the thinker walks about among
the ruins in a reverie. (*C:C*, III, 239)

As his last line suggests, this *emmerdement*—I am using my
words in their root senses here—is also an *embêtement*: that
dreaming *penseur* is Flaubert's ideal reader, who stands before Nature and great art *en rêvant*.[37] The shit-covered world
now presents him with an inscrutable face—like Homer or
Shakespeare, or like the Acropolis's blank wall before which
Flaubert once stood dreaming, longing to produce its "effect" in a book (*C:C*, IV, 446). *Emmerdé*, the world has
become *bête*; it has been subdued, as it were, and its *bêtise*
vanquished, by an expense of Flaubertian force. And it is
at precisely this point that we intuit both the fantastic identity and practical separateness of *les mots* and *la merde*. If
the latter was the weapon of an infantile Flaubert, the former were the eyes of the Olympian adult. And yet both
offered him the paradoxical opportunity to master and evade
the world. Together their powers constitute an ideal self,

[37] See his letter to Louise Colet of August 26, 1853: "What seems to
me the highest (and most difficult) thing in Art is neither to incite laughter or tears nor to put the reader in a rut or a fury, but to work as nature
does—that is to say, *to induce reverie* [faire rêver]. And the most beautiful
works have this quality. They are serene of aspect and incomprehensible.
[. . .] Homer, Rabelais, Michelangelo, Shakespeare, Goethe seem to me
pitiless. It's all bottomless, infinite, multiple" (*C:P*, II, 417). To these remarks should be compared two lines in an earlier letter to Colet: "Masterpieces are stupid [*bêtes*].—They have a tranquil aspect, like the productions of nature herself, like the great animals and the mountains" (*C:P*,
II, 119).

majestic, invulnerable, like the ideal book, hanging freely by a thread in the void.

Such is the site of Pierrot's apotheosis, in a paradise of imaginative force. His is, predictably, a heaven of sausages and acrobats—that is, of food and Form:[38] of the aliments of an anal power and the metaphors of an *écriture bête*. *La bêtise ennemie* has by no means vanished: Pierrot's ascent is to the brassy strains of the ubiquitous *Marseillaise*. But he will be wise if, anticipating Bouvard and Pécuchet, he lets it go in one ear and out the other, and, joining those acrobats on the wire, he masters its rhythms by his own. Wise, too, not to add to the clamor with speech. His dumb and insouciant silence, as Flaubert seems to have known all along, is best.

[38] *Panem et circenses?* suggests my colleague Naomi Ritter. Perhaps—as well as a nod towards the mythical *pays de cocagne*. But to identify Flaubert's "sources" does not explain why he thought it fit to translate Pierrot to their realms. Baudelaire, after all, would have couched him indolently beneath *vastes portiques*.

VII

Pierrot *glacé*:

Edmond de Goncourt

Je comprends peut-être aujourd'hui ce que doit être l'amour, s'il existe. Otez le côté charnel, le rapprochement du sexe, c'est ce qui existe entre nous,—qui fait que quand l'un n'est pas avec l'autre, il y a dépareillement comme dans un couple d'oiseaux qui ne peuvent vivre qu'à deux. L'un séparé de l'autre, il y a une moitié de nous-mêmes qui nous manque. Nous n'avons plus que des demi-sensations, une demi-vie, nous sommes décomplétés comme un livre en deux volumes, dont le premier est perdu. Voilà ce que je pense être l'amour: le décomplétage et la dépareillement dans l'absence.

Goncourt *Journal*, November 15, 1859

Notre maison glace ceux de nos amis qui ont le courage d'y venir.

Goncourt *Journal*, November 12, 1868

When, on December 27, 1876, Edmond de Goncourt first recorded in the *Journal* his intention to write the book that would become *Les Frères Zemganno* (1879), Parisian Boulevard pantomime was virtually lifeless. The old Funambules had been demolished in 1862;[1] the new, on the Boulevard de Strasbourg, had all but abandoned the *pantomime classique*. Hippolyte Hostein, manager of several theaters in

---

[1] The Goncourts had witnessed—and deplored—its decline into "realism." In a review of Charton's *Pierrot sorcier* in the sixty-fourth number of *Paris* (December 22, 1852), they noted that the piece "is no longer one of those vague pantomimes, without a precise date, that unfolded between heaven and earth, at the primordial crossroads; with *Pierrot sorcier*, the pantomime is received back into the bosom of the possible; M. Charles has driven out Dame Fantasy, that mocker of time, who takes pleasure in anachronism [. . .]."

the course of his busy life, described its repertoire at just about the time of Edmond's *Journal* entry: "In place of the melodrama and of the grandly spectacular pantomimes of the old repertoire, that of today offers the genre-comedy, the vaudeville with modern tunes, and finally the pantomime in one act or in a very small number of scenes, stripped of those changes of décor, of those transformations, of those ingenious tricks that the [. . .] theater of the Circus, its neighbor, did not disdain to come borrowing from it."[2] The great mimes were either dead or forgotten or performing elsewhere, far from the refashioned Boulevard du Temple. Deburau *fils* had died in 1873 after having taken his repertoire to Marseille and Bordeaux. His student and successor, Louis Rouffe, played only on the stages of southern France. As for the mime Dimier, known as Kalpestri, who had replaced the famous Pierrots at the old Funambules, he was to die in penury and neglect, a suicide, in 1884.[3] Legrand was still performing at the Tertulia, but, by the late 1870s, his art seemed already passé to the public. Writing in 1898 of a pantomime seen some eighteen years earlier, at the Variétés, Paul and Victor Margueritte recalled their admiration for that art, but noted that Legrand's name "seemed already at the time that of a survivor of a quite distant epoch."[4]

As Hostein's remark suggests, it was to the circus that the amateur had to turn to recover *l'esprit funambulesque*. The Goncourts had always been circus enthusiasts. "We go to one theater only," they observed in their *Journal* of 1859: "All the others bore and annoy us."

> The theater we go to is the Circus. There we see male and female tumblers, clowns, and ladies leaping through

[2] "Causeries d'un ancien directeur": undated article appearing in unidentified newspaper on occasion of publication of Champfleury's novel *La Petite Rose* (1877): in Ro 11521 ("Rec. fac. d'art. de presse, textes de pièces, arguments, progr., doc. icon. concernant le théâtre des Funambules"), f. 5, Bibliothèque de l'Arsenal.

[3] For an account of the careers of Rouffe and Kalpestri, see Hugounet, *Mimes et Pierrots*, pp. 162-84.

[4] Untitled article in unidentified newspaper, dated—by hand—April 22, 1898: in Ro 11590 ("Rec. fac. d'art. de presse, doc. et référ. concernant Charles Legrand [1816-1898], 1847-1898"), f. 56, Bibliothèque de l'Arsenal.

paper hoops, exercising their craft and their duty—the only talents in the world that are incontestable, absolute, like mathematics, or rather like a somersault. There are no actors or actresses there pretending to have talent: either they fall or they don't fall. Their talent is a fact.

We watch them, these men and women risking their necks in the air in order to fetch a few bravos, with a stirring of entrails, with an indefinable sensation of fierce curiosity and, at the same time, of sympathetic compassion, as if these people were of our race and as if all of us—Bobèches, historians, philosophers, puppets, and poets—were leaping heroically for that imbecile, the public.[5]

In conceiving a book that would pay homage to their collaboration—that of "*deux vies inséparées dans le plaisir, le labeur, la peine; de deux pensées jumelles*" (J, I, 27)—Edmond turned naturally to the trapeze-artists, or, more precisely, to those *artistes* who wittily dissembled their talents, the acrobatic clowns. The Paris circuses were prodigal of models. Jules Claretie remarked that Edmond's own favorite was Médrano ("Boum-Boum"), whose circus eventually bore his name.[6] Alidor Delzant, on the other hand, whose *Les Goncourt* had been overseen by Edmond, makes no mention of this clown; he alludes, rather, to the "*spleené-tique*" James Boswell, "who sometimes, in the middle of his acrobatics, giving in to a macabre whim, draped himself in some tawdry piece of finery and, imposing a tragic character upon his whitened comic mask, ran about the circus while declaiming, in a shrill and raucous voice, the most terrifying verses of Shakespeare."[7] Such clowning is indeed close to that of the nameless English artists whom the Zemgannos emulate. "A curious fact," observes Goncourt's narrator "—it has turned out that, in the birth-place of Hamlet, the genius of the nation has stamped this com-

[5] Edmond and Jules de Goncourt, *Journal*, I, 653. The *Journal* will be cited throughout this chapter as *J*, with appropriate volume and page numbers.

[6] *La Vie à Paris, 1906* (Paris: Charpentier, 1907), p. 381n.

[7] *Les Goncourt* (Paris: Charpentier et Cie, 1889), p. 221.

pletely English creation [the clown] with its phlegmatic and darkly bilious character, and that it has fashioned its gaiety— if the expression is permissible—with a kind of splenetic comic art."[8] One of Boswell's inventions seems certainly to have inspired Nello's taunting of "la Tompkins":

> He would [. . .] station himself in front of the star equestrienne as she basked in the audience's applause between turns. Icily staring at her in a frightful manner, he would recite from Hamlet's famous soliloquy, telling the now very nervous equestrienne of "the undiscover'd country from whose bourn no traveller returns." She understood nothing but continued to smile. Sometimes he would take pleasure in taunting her by abruptly pulling back the paper hoop just as she was about to somersault through it, a bizarre look on his face as he emitted a gutteral cry accompanied by a nervous hop.[9]

But neither Boum-Boum nor Boswell seems to have been uppermost in Edmond's mind when *Les Frères Zemganno* was written. Boswell died in 1859; though both clowns were excellent *sauteurs*, their acts bore no resemblance to pantomime: neither, unlike the Zemgannos, was mute. And both (if we discount Boum-Boum's elegant pig) most often worked alone. The acrobatic mimes upon whose craft Edmond drew are in fact acknowledged for their assistance in his "Préface": these were the English Hanlon-Lees, who practiced their art, in Edmond's words, "*comme des savants et des artistes*" (*FZ*, 12n).

Natives of Liverpool and Manchester, the six Hanlon brothers spent much of the 1860s touring Europe and America, billing themselves as the "Hanlon-Lees' Transatlantic Combination."[10] "Lees" was "Professor" John Lees,

---

[8] Edmond de Goncourt, *Les Frères Zemganno*, éd. déf. (Paris: Flammarion-Fasquelle, [1924]), p. 116. This edition will be cited throughout this chapter as *FZ*, with appropriate page numbers.

[9] John H. Towsen, *Clowns* (New York: Hawthorn Books, Inc., 1976), p. 168.

[10] For the most reliable account of their career, see Towsen, *Clowns*, pp. 175-86. When, in the following paragraphs, I depart from Towsen's account, I am drawing upon the clip-files devoted to the mimes in the Theatre Collection of the New York Public Library at Lincoln Center.

an acrobat under whose tutelage George, William, and Alfred Hanlon had made their début at London's Adelphi in 1847 as "entortilationists." When, in 1855, Lees died aboardship between Panama and Havana in the course of a worldwide tour, his students returned to England and joined brothers Thomas, Edward, and Frederick, with whom they reappeared before the public as gymnasts. They duplicated Jules Léotard's somersaulting feats on the flying trapeze and added "*une foule d'exercices nouveaux*"[11] to their repertoire. From their association—dating from around 1865—with the French juggler Henri Agoust, they began to develop what proved to be extraordinary comic and pantomimic talents. Agoust, who had had experience as a fencer, magician, dancer, and mime, rehearsed them in two pantomimes of Deburau *père*; and in 1867, "When they came to Paris with a show compounded of Deburau, the circus and the English pantomime [. . .]," as Maurice Willson Disher writes, "the real vogue of the circus began [. . .]."[12]

Hardly coherent by most dramatic standards, the Hanlons' skits seem to have gained their hold by little more than their mad, nightmarish power. Agoust revealed to Hugues le Roux the fertile source of that power: "The Hanlons were [of] Irish [descent], and were supposed to drink deeply sometimes after leaving the theatre. But if there were excesses they were utilised, for when they met on the following day, they related their dreams to each other and endeavoured to construct a play out of them."[13] Their plays were, in effect, the fantasias of a fermented unconscious. In *Le Frater de village*, a thwarted Pierrot-suitor decapitates several members of the bourgeois family to which his Colombine belongs, his stint as demon-barber concluding with "a sunburst of frenetic gestures from which slaps and kicks shoot out like sparks from a pinwheel."[14] The eponymous carpenter of *Pierrot Menuisier*, fallen upon slack times, mur-

---

[11] [Lesclide], *Mémoires et pantomimes*, p. 66.

[12] *Clowns and Pantomimes* (London: Constable and Co., Ltd., 1925), p. 194.

[13] Hugues le Roux and Jules Garnier, *Acrobats and Mountebanks* [orig. *Les Jeux du cirque et la vie foraine*, 1889], tr. A. P. Morton (London: Chapman and Hall, Limited, 1890), p. 295.

[14] [Lesclide], *Mémoires et pantomimes*, p. 111.

ders a young man in order to unload one of his coffins; when he fires upon the apparition that then rises up to haunt him—the corpse bearing the coffin on its back—he brings down a cat from a neighboring rooftop, and the storm of kittens that burst out of its belly furnishes the antagonists with ammunition for their battle.

Zola, in writing of one of their most celebrated triumphs, in Blum and Toché's *Le Voyage en Suisse* (1878), deplored the restriction of their talents within a conventional framework of farce ("My feeling quite frankly is that the movement of the play is too banal, too cold, and that, as soon as the Hanlons appear on the wings of their farcical lyricism, they introduce a false note"), observing that their art is an assault upon limitations, both formal and moral: "Fundamentally, it is the negation of everything, it is [the assertion of] human nullity."[15] A reviewer of the English version of this piece suggests the primitive power of the emotions to which the characters seemed absolute prey:

[. . .] ideas dawn slowly on their faces, both vacant as slates; by degrees they assume form and consistency and every feature is lighted up; the frame of each man is permeated by one idea. You can read it in every delicate modulation of gesture. It seems to absorb the entire being, to throb in every nerve, to quiver in every muscle. [. . . Their drunken scene] is so dreadfully true to nature, and withal so genuinely diverting, that one gazes on it with an enthralled interest which would be more fittingly applied to some burst of passion at the Lyceum.[16]

"*C'est toute une psychologie de l'ivresse*," Zola wrote of this scene, adding that he could imagine "with what an angry outcry a work of ours, of the Naturalistic novelists, would be received if we were to push so far the analysis of the human grimace, the satire of man in the grips of his pas-

[15] Emile Zola, "La Pantomime," *Le Naturalisme au théâtre* (1881), in *Oeuvres complètes*, ed. Henri Mitterand (Paris: Fasquelle, 1968), XI, 479, 480.

[16] Article in the monthly *Theatre*, cited in *What the Leading Papers of London Say Concerning the Hanlon-Lees and M. Agoust in* Le Voyage en Suisse! (Birmingham: James Upton, Printer, 1880), p. 36.

sions."[17] And that his judgment was no mere Naturalist's fancy is suggested by Théodore de Banville's equally provocative commentary. Writing in his "Préface" to the pantomimists' *Mémoires*, he remarks that, "All things considered, if anyone were to merit the name of Realist, it would be the Hanlon-Lees alone, for only they have reproduced life with that ravenous and senseless intensity without which it does not resemble itself."[18]

But Banville goes further, developing a point for which there are only hints in Zola's review. The latter had described the Hanlons' art as a combination of "*la finesse et la force*," isolating "*une férocité saxonne*" as the British contribution to these traits.[19] Without trying to identify the "Englishness" of their behavior, Banville simply remarks the curious disparity between their finesse—their phlegmatic self-possession—and their ferocity, and asks, with characteristically comic grandiloquence, "But since the Hanlons love grace, beautiful attitudes, the eurythmy of poses, how is it that they are as savage as bulls pricked by a thousand banderillas, as mad as kid-goats grazing on flowers, as infuriated as worms cut in half, as agitated as quicksilver, as frenzied as travelers with scouring-powder down their backs?"[20] Echoing perhaps his friend Baudelaire's "*deux postulations simultanées*," those impulses towards *Spleen* and *Idéal* described in *Mon Coeur mis à nu*, he explains "*leur jeu double*" as the expression of "two orders of ideas that are diametrically opposed":

> Notice, in effect, how the serene gentleness and celestial innocence of their faces contrast with the violence of their leaps, of their contortions, of their scuffles, and of their gambols! The contrast is owing to the fact that their faces declare their appetite for the ideal life, while their gymnastic ferocity, having no other aim than frenetic movement itself, represents precisely the terrestrial life, with its uproar, its bustle, its confusion, and its absurd tragedies.[21]

[17] "La Pantomime," *Oeuvres complètes*, XI, 482, 483.
[18] [Lesclide], *Mémoires et pantomimes*, p. 12.
[19] "La Pantomime," *Oeuvres complètes*, XI, 483.
[20] [Lesclide], *Mémoires et pantomimes*, p. 11.
[21] Ibid., p. 12.

Like his own trampolining clown in the *Odes funambu-lesques*, who "leaped so high, so high,/That he broke through the canvas ceiling," these knockabouts represent both "life as it is" and their aspirations beyond it: "[. . .] their innocent gaze, both friendly and malicious, tells you: 'Yes, that's how it is; but all the same, you see, I'm straining to take wing into the ether, beyond the birds and the azure—out there among the stars!' "[22]

It may have taken a Banville to glimpse such aspirations through the Hanlons' icy excess: they were certainly not visible to Edmond de Goncourt. In the "*glaçante bouffon-nerie*" of these clowns, Goncourt saw only "All of the shudders and anxious excitement to which contemporary things give rise" (*FZ*, 125, 124). Their pantomime was no longer "the sarcastic irony of a pierrot with a head of plaster, one eye closed and a single corner of his mouth turned up in a laugh" (*FZ*, 123); the wink of complicity was gone, and their dumbshow seemed somehow "terrifying." Goncourt's response should be quoted in full:

There is something terrifying about it for the spectator, something of which the terror is engendered from cruel little observations, from ferocious little notations, from pitiless little assimilations of what is ugly and crippled in life, then magnified, exaggerated by the caprice of ruthless caricaturists—something which, within the fantasy of the spectacle, assumes the form of a fantastic nightmare, and which gives you a hint of the sense of anguish that a reader takes away from "The Tell-Tale Heart" by the American Poe. A diabolical reality seems to have been put on the stage, lit up by a capricious and wicked ray of moonlight. And in the circus arenas and on the music-hall stages of Great Britain, these acts have been for some time only interludes, in which the leaps and gambols are no longer intended to please the eye but are contrived to induce uneasy astonishment, and emotions of fear, and almost painful surprise, all from this strange and unhealthy commotion of body and muscle where, mixed in with mocking bouts of pugilism, with hair-raising domestic

[22] Ibid., p. 13.

scenes, with lugubrious farce, unfold visions of Bed-
lam, of Newcastle, of the dissecting theater, of the
prison, of the morgue. (*FZ*, 124-25)

It is at this school, as the narrative makes clear, that the
Bescapés learn their art. But how curious, then, to turn the
page and discover that "The gymnastic pantomime of the
two brothers in no way resembled that of the latest English
clowns" (*FZ*, 126). All the more curious in that those clowns
share the Goncourts' *nervosisme*. It was, after all, the author
of "The Tell-Tale Heart," along with Heinrich Heine, whom
Edmond preferred among "the moderns." And in both
novelists—students of the morgue, the hospital, the asy-
lum—there was something of their character Anatole Bazoche, borne ineluctably by his tastes "towards the men of
funereal professions."[23] But, like Anatole's, their tastes were
furtive. The somberness of their own books surprised them.
"This is, to our own astonished eyes, the strangest book
we have done," they wrote of their first important novel,
La Soeur Philomène, "the book that for us is the least personal."

> A lugubrious book, even more distressing than horri-
> ble, one that cast a pall over us all the time that we
> worked on it. Today it's like a dead body that we have
> on our table and that we're eager to take outside . . .
> What is this book? To tell the truth I do not know
> [. . .]. (*J*, I, 888)

A book like *Soeur Philomène*, they observe in an earlier entry, "astonishes you, like something that was in you of which
you were unconscious" (*J*, I, 882).

Such books emerge from the "*fièvre hallucinatoire*" of
composition[24] the way the Hanlons emerge from the décor. Like the impassive "innocence" of their faces, that décor seems an impenetrable blank:

[23] Edmond and Jules de Goncourt, *Manette Salomon*, éd. déf. (Paris:
Flammarion-Fasquelle, [1925]), p. 403. This edition will be cited
throughout this chapter as *MS*, with appropriate page numbers.
[24] So, in a letter to Zola after Jules's interment, Edmond described the
brothers' habitual state of mind during the writing of their novels: the
letter is reproduced in Delzant, *Les Goncourt*, pp. 187ff.

[. . .] the usual décor of these gymnastics—what is it? A wall, a barrier wall under a suspicious light, a wall over which there still seem to be traces of an imperfectly effaced crime, a wall on the top of which appear, in black suits, these modern phantoms of the night, descending with protracted limbs that grow longer, and longer . . . like those seen by the opium-eaters of the Far East in their dreams; then before it, projecting their queer and dislocated shadows over this blank wall, which resembles a shroud serving as a magic-lantern screen, begin the maniacal *tours de force*, the idiot-like gesticulations, the agitated pantomime of a prison-yard for madmen. (*FZ*, 125)

That disturbing *mur de barrière* is clearly a psychic scrim, behind which sinister figures are lurking. Figures as figurations: Edmond is obviously aware of their source: "My vague and troubled state," he writes shortly before embarking upon his novel, "complicated by the filthy obsession that haunts my thoughts, intrigues me. I'm afraid that abnormal and destructive things are going on in my brain" (*J*, II, 1159). But his book is in flight from such things. Confessing himself in his "Préface" to have been "in a state of soul in which truth that is too true was antipathetic to me," he has written *Les Frères Zemganno* as "a venture into a poetic reality" (*FZ*, 13, 12). "Poetry," one suspects, for this novelist utterly indifferent to most poems, is synonymous with evasion. But from what is his novel in flight?

Homosexuality, declares Richard Grant, the only critic to offer a serious reading of the book. In the Zemgannos' pantomimic gymnastics Grant sees a psychodrama of sublimation, a confession of Edmond's coming to terms with an impossible incestuous wish.[25] On the face of it, the proposal seems uncomfortably plausible. Having banished from their *exercices* everything "*de* cimetiéreux, *de triste, de sombre*" (*FZ*, 126), his *artistes* invoke both "Shakespeare" and the old Italian comedy, fusing them into a kind of acrobatic romance. Goncourt provides a detailed account of one scenario. In a dream, the older Gianni is visited by "one of

[25] Richard B. Grant, *The Goncourt Brothers* (New York: Twayne Publishers, Inc., 1972), pp. 123-26.

those malevolent sprites"—that is, Nello—"dressed in colors of smoke and shadow, shot through with the somber ful-gurations of metals hidden in the bowels of the earth, of black mother-of-pearl sleeping in the depths of the oceans, and stirred to life by the butterflies of the night, fluttering their wings in sunless skies" (*FZ*, 140-41). The sprite crouches on Gianni's chest, "the physical image of Night-mare" (*FZ*, 141), and torments his sleep with a charivari on his violin. Awakening, Gianni pursues him on foot and in the air, finally grappling with him in "*une lutte corps à corps.*" But it seems less a battle than an engagement of bodies, "embracings and unclaspings of grace, a fight in which the sprite brought to the elegant and rippling display of his muscular development what painters seek to put into their pictures when they paint the physical battle of men with supernatural beings" (*FZ*, 143-44). At last vanquish-ing his opponent, Gianni produces a violin in his turn and begins to soothe the savage breast. As if undergoing a ter-rible exorcism, Nello passes through an agony of metamor-phosis:

> In this flesh in repose there occurred strange juttings of his shoulder-blades, hollowings of his loins; his backbone, as if having moved from the back to the front of his chest, bulged out like the crop of a wad-ing-bird from an unknown planet, and in the sprite's limbs there seemed to be those sudden currents of muscular life that momentarily fill the flaccid skins of snakes. For every eye it was apparent that the wingless fluttering, the creeping, the larval squirming of the an-imals of malediction and fabulous legend: the *beast* was disappearing and leaving, driven from the interior of the sprite, who finally, in a rapid succession of plastic poses, showed on the graceful canvas of his body, now unbound and set free, the harmony and the glory of the beautiful movements and the beautiful human ges-tures of man in the statues of antiquity. (*FZ*, 144-45)

As the lights begin to brighten, both take up their violins and play an aubade to the awakening day.

As a naïve hymn to sublimated sexuality, this little piece hardly needs comment here. But I am not convinced that it is indeed such a hymn—or at least that this reading is its most interesting "solution." We should begin by noting that Edmond's own affection for his brother was not without its ambivalences.[26] Their fraternity was, on the surface, an idyll; but a parapraxis seems to have troubled its depths. Approximately a year before Jules's death, both had been involved in an accident: a drunken coachman had driven them into a wagon, and Edmond, pitched into the glass of the window before him, had nearly lost an eye. Jules recorded the incident in the *Journal*, adding that, afterwards, Edmond "told me this quite bizarre thing: that a moment before the collision, he had had a presentiment of the accident; only, by a kind of transposition of fraternal second-sight, it was I whom he had seen injured, and injured in the eye" (*J*, II, 492). A year later, after Jules's death, Edmond insisted (as he would often thereafter) that it was he who had caused that death, driving Jules to labors of collaborative creation that had enfevered and destroyed his mind. At the same time, he feared going blind. "Always the fear of blindness [. . .]" (*J*, II, 890), he wrote in April of 1872. That fear was still, over fifteen years later, an obsession, an "*idée fixe*" (*J*, III, 747). This seems magical retribution for an obsessive unconscious wish—a wish that had had its source in the intimacy of the two brothers' relationship and in the family that they hardly knew. "You alone have given me low instincts," says la Faustin of her sister Bonne-Ame, "[. . .] and it's you, always you, who drag me at times into the mud [. . .]. Oh, the slime, the slime that you're made of, completely . . . and of which I have a little myself!"[27] Is this Edmond speaking to Jules? Again, the *Journal* suggests an answer: "There is," writes Jules of himself, "a fundamental piggishness [*un fond de porc*] in me, which I don't think has reached its full development." And he continues his entry as follows:

> I don't have the same aspirations as the other one of us. The core of his life, if it weren't what it is, would

---

[26] Grant hints of it when he speaks of "the ambiguity of desire-rejection" in the Zemgannos' pantomime: *The Goncourt Brothers*, p. 125.

[27] Edmond de Goncourt, *La Faustin*, éd. déf. (Paris: Flammarion-Fasquelle, [1923]), p. 107.

be a home, the bourgeois dream, the ideal of lifelong communion with a sentimental woman. I'm a melancholy body; he's a sensitive and melancholy flame [*Moi, je suis un matériel mélancolique; lui, un passionné tendre et mélancolique*]. (*J*, II, 194)

In this light, Gianni's "exorcism" of Nello's *malfaisance* seems an expression of secret antipathy.

For the profoundest source of that antipathy—as well as for the source of his genuine affection—we must look at Edmond's relation with Jules vis-à-vis their early familial life. They had no such life as adults: "When I'm with my family," they write in 1852, "it seems to me I'm inside an injection of laudanum" (*J*, I, 53). The man of letters, they declare, should assume a pseudonym "to disinherit his family of his name" (*J*, I, 251). Their "true family" was the Louvre (*J*, II, 5), its art the real objects of their love. It is a rare character in their books who is not an orphan or, at the very least, a familial outcast: Sister Philomène, Germinie Lacerteux, Madame Gervaisais, Chérie—all lose their mothers to death or madness at a very early age; Madame Mauperin pays only mechanical attentions to her daughter, Renée, after her son is killed in a duel; Elisa abandons her midwife mother for the less odious life of prostitution. With the exception of the kindly Monsieur Mauperin, the fathers die young or disappear or are callously indifferent to their offspring. The Goncourts were literally orphans themselves by the time that Jules was eighteen. But Edmond had been orphaned in spirit, apparently, many years before.

Of his emotional relationship with his father, an officer under the Empire who died before Edmond was twelve, we know very little. Edmond recalled once escaping a thrashing with a horsewhip when, his nurse coming between him and his father, she maintained in the face of Edmond's guilt that she had eaten an apricot intended for dessert. (The horsewhip fell upon her.)[28] The idealized portrait in the *Journal* (*J*, IV, 213-15) is a purely external one, suggesting little intimacy between father and son. Toward his mother he obviously felt great tenderness, but his

[28] See André Billy, *The Goncourt Brothers*, tr. Margaret Shaw (London: Deutsch, 1960), p. 14.

affection was never returned. Her love was reserved—or so he always thought—for the *"enfant chéri et préféré"* (*J*, II, 566), the younger, more charming Jules. "A kind of impassioned and exclusive love,"[29] he called it in a note to one of Jules's letters. And her preference persisted through the hour of her death: "I see her again without the strength to speak," recalled Edmond in 1892, "putting my brother's hand into my own, with that unforgettable look of a mother crucified by her anxiety over what will become of the still very young man, left at the threshold of life master of his passions and not yet a journeyman on the road of a career" (*J*, IV, 217). This could not have been written without a bitter memory of his own struggle: "I think of my vocation as a painter, of my vocation as a student at the Ecole des Chartes," he had written twenty years earlier, "destroyed [. . .] by the will of my mother" (*J*, II, 791). It is hardly surprising that when she appears in Edmond's dreams, as she does with suggestive infrequency, she is "a being who stands as if stricken with catalepsy, making no reply whatsoever to my words, indifferent to the catastrophes in which I am floundering, almost hostile" (*J*, IV, 849).

If Stépanida of *Les Frères Zemganno* is a romanticized portrait of Madame de Goncourt, she is also a psychologically accurate one. Estranged from all save her second-born, she seems "a woman only half-awake from a dream, living on the earth not wholly certain of her own existence in an otherwise real world" (*FZ*, 35). Her attachment to Nello is "violent and savage," but is also oddly impersonal: he is an object "whom she neither kisses nor caresses, but presses frantically against her breast in embraces strong enough to smother him" (*FZ*, 66). Gianni in his turn is acutely conscious of being a *mal-aimé*: "Stépanida Roudak had been a mother to her first-born, but a mother without tenderness, without inner warmth, without excited happiness when he was around her, a mother whose care seemed the performance of a duty, nothing more" (*FZ*, 65). The *"inégal partage d'affection"* is painful to him—but it is also, he claims, "completely natural" (*FZ*, 66). He has none of his sibling's

---

[29] Edmond de Goncourt, ed., *Lettres de Jules de Goncourt*, éd. déf. (Paris: Flammarion-Fasquelle, [1930]), p. 37*n*.

beauty; he is temperamentally morose; "The very signs of his filial love were clumsy" (*FZ*, 66). He feels not the slightest jealousy for young Nello. And he obviously protests too much. In a sense, the whole course of the novel is towards Gianni's crippling of his brother: before the latter's ill-fated leap, Gianni perceives his great danger, but decides to proceed with their trick.[30] Goncourt of course attributes his decision to the importunity of circumstances. His research would have ruled this unlikely; but the "poetic realism" of the novel gave him license to do what the Goncourts always did: choose their "facts" by the inclination of instinct. And that instinct dictated, in this case, that Nello be obscurely punished. But that he be crippled, not killed: thus Edmond's ambivalence is served. A disabled Nello may be humbled but, still living, enjoy his brother's proofs of love.

But this argument, as I am aware, does not rebut Grant's assertion—that theirs, however ambivalent, is a homoerotic bond. It does not, in particular, take into account the fear of women that pursued Edmond all of his life. Grant cites two dreams recounted in the *Journal* to suggest the depth of that fear: in the first, he is ill in bed when a woman arrives in mourning; from the train of her gown a priest leaps out to coerce him into a marriage *in extremis* (*J*, IV, 170). In the second, a friend, ignoring Edmond's pleas for help, abandons him to waltz off with a woman, leaving him alone and terrified in an unfamiliar town (*J*, IV, 565). "Fear of women" is, of course, vaguely suggested by both; but such a phrase begs more questions than it answers. It certainly takes no account of either the contexts or the complexity of the dreams. A little over a week before dreaming the first, Edmond had had to shake off an importunate suitor—had been "obliged to write a brutal letter, to strike a blow to a heart that loves me perhaps," an act which "has made me unhappy all day" (*J*, IV, 166). His dream seems then as much a cruel self-punishment as an expression of anxiety. The second dream, unusually long and detailed, and rich in intriguing incident, resists abbreviation of such kind: it would, in fact, need an essay of its own if we were to begin to unravel its latencies.

[30] And, like Edmond, he later blames himself for his brother's tragedy: *FZ*, 240-41.

Grant's point seems better made by another of Edmond's dreams, recorded July 14—a significant date—of 1883. Since its phrasing and details are important, I reproduce Edmond's account in full:

> I was dreaming last night that I was at a soirée in white tie. At this soirée I saw a woman come in, a woman whom I recognized as an actress in one of the boulevard theaters but without being able to associate a name with her face. She was draped in a scarf, and I was merely remarking that she was completely naked when she jumped up on the table, where two or three young girls were drinking tea.
>
> Then she started to dance and, while dancing, to do the splits, which showed her private parts to be armed with the most terrible set of jaws imaginable, opening and closing just like the dentures on display in the streets. This spectacle had no libidinal effect on me but filled me with an atrocious jealousy, giving me—whose own teeth are beginning to go bad—a fierce desire to appropriate hers. (*J*, III, 268-69)

Those formidable teeth seem unambiguous—if, again, one ignores the context of the image. We should note Edmond's reaction—jealousy, amounting to "fierce" envy—and take into account his surroundings: he has arrived at a soirée in white tie and tails, on an obviously dignified occasion, at which women would not be expected to mount the tables to dance and do the splits. This disparity, his response, the woman's "licentious" profession—as well as the date itself, the Quatorze Juillet in France—all suggest what Charles May has described as the pornographer's typical wish: to enjoy the "woman's" role in intercourse, to abandon oneself to ecstatic pleasure, to surrender dignity to the dance of *jouissance*.[31] Those teeth, in their aggressive *terribilità*, would seem to belie this reading, but I suspect that they excite no fear in Edmond because they are actually not "teeth" at all. Nearly a year after recording the dream, Edmond described his first glimpse of lovemaking,

---

[31] Charles E. May, "Perversion in Pornography: Male Envy of the Female," *Literature and Psychology*, XXI (1981), 66-74.

a glimpse that was no doubt crucial in his orientation towards the sexual act. He had opened a door upon a cousin's room, and there, "her head tilted back, her legs lifted and spread, her behind raised on a pillow, [she] was ready to be mounted [or "forked": *enfourchée*] by her husband." His nights were thereafter haunted by visions of "that pink behind on a pillow bordered with large scallops [*à grandes dents festonnées*]" (*J*, III, 341). It is probably the "*dents*" of this pillow, billowing around the girl's rosy thighs, that have become the "*mâchoire*" of Edmond's dream: the pun has permitted the primal memory of his cousin—the very image of self-abandonment—to spawn an oneiric judgment about himself.[32]

About himself and women in general. If he is too cold, too correct (as indeed he always was in life), they are, in his eyes, too unpredictable. It is here that his fears have their source: the secret energies of women disturbed—often terrified—both him and Jules. "*Toute femme est, de nature, secrète et ténébreuse*" (*J*, II, 464): the *Journal* rarely makes this sort of concession. For the most part, their *femme* is an *idée reçue*, the caricatural butt of the Magny dinners, a body without a brain, a baby-machine, who found her sentiments in cheap novels and religion. They of course wished to believe this was so, since caricature is more manageable than mystery. But the mystery would keep breaking through. As Jean-Pierre Richard has observed of their fiction, "woman becomes a formidable enigma, a sphinx, a source of unknown dangers, and—see *Charles Demailly* or *Manette Salomon*—a constant possibility of ruin."[33] When they dis-

[32] For a discussion of the recent dream-theory that seeks out such punning superimpositions, see below, pp. 226-27.

[33] "Deux Ecrivains épidermiques: Edmond et Jules de Goncourt," *Littérature et sensation* (Paris: Editions du Seuil, 1954), p. 267. As for those sympathetic heroines who give their names to the majority of the Goncourts' novels, Enzo Caramaschi is surely right in seeing them as their creators' self-projections: "More changeable, more sensitive, more fragile than man, women lend themselves better in seizing to their profit the perceptions in which these highstrung artists excel and the reactions that are familiar to these '*sensitives*.' And that is why these misogynists, when they are not putting themselves directly onstage (*Les Hommes de Lettres* [*Charles Demailly*, in the second and subsequent editions], *Les Frères Zemganno*), invariably place women figures at the center of their novels" (*Réalisme et impressionnisme dans l'oeuvre des frères Goncourt* [Paris: Nizet, and Pisa: Goliardica, n.d.], p. 287).

cover that their old servant Rose had led a double life—the source for Germinie's secret transgressions—they are horrified, not by her betrayals or degradations, but by her fathomless depths of deceit:

> On top of that, a strength of will, of character, a power of secrecy, to which nothing can be compared; a secret, every secret kept deep within, hidden, without ever betraying herself to our eyes, to our ears, to our observant senses, even in her hysterical attacks, which I had seen her suffer in coming back from the dairy; a secret maintained till death, one that she must have thought would be buried with her, so deeply had she buried it inside!

This rumination is followed by an even more revealing one: "Our thoughts returned to our mother, so pure, for whom we were everything; then, from there, going back to the heart of this Rose, who we thought was completely ours, we felt as it were a great disappointment, realizing that there had been a whole other side of her life that we had not filled. Distrust of the entire female sex has entered our souls for the rest of our lives" (*J*, I, 1121). And that sex includes, as the comparison both denies and yet clearly confirms, their mother.

Little wonder, then, that the shadowy villainess of *Les Frères Zemganno* should be so like the good Stépanida. Insular, exotic, possessive, she seems the dark obverse of the mother that the brothers claim to love.[34] And in her "dec-

---

[34] In a recent article, Floyd Zulli argues that Miss Tompkins was modeled upon Adah Isaacs Menken (c. 1835-1868), an American equestrienne, actress, and poetess, who had become the talk of Paris after a performance at the Gaieté in 1867. Zulli's evidence is not wholly convincing. Noting that Goncourt describes her speech as a "*français nègre*," he remarks that the phrase "aids immeasurably in the identification. Menken spoke French fluently, but she spoke it with a southern American accent which she doubtless acquired in Louisiana" ("Edmond de Goncourt's American Equestrienne," *The French American Review*, III [winter 1979 and spring 1979], p. 55). But "la Tompkins" hardly speaks fluent French (". . . *vous tranquille . . . moi continuer à fumer*" [*FZ*, 194]); Goncourt obviously intends the phrase to mean "pidgin" (i.e., "*petit nègre*"). If he had had a model in mind, he undoubtedly would have produced her name to answer the charges of incomprehensibility leveled at his creation.

adence," she exerts with the other creatures of her despised sex a powerful effect upon her creator: she fascinates. She is like the women of the "corrupt" eighteenth century: "[. . .] secret and profound, impenetrable and invulnerable, they bring to dalliance, to vengeance, to pleasure, to hatred, a cold-blooded heart, a collected wit, a liberated manner, a queenly cynicism, mixed in with a lofty elegance, a kind of implacable lightness of touch." And the Goncourts cry with one voice: "*Figures étonnantes qui fascinent et qui glacent!*"[35] They fascinate for the same reason that the century itself attracts them: beneath the elegance or frivolity of surface they glimpse dizzying, intoxicating depths. As their analysis of eighteenth-century love begins to impinge upon the excesses of Sade, they betray as much febrile ardor as revulsion. And yet, by an apparent act of will, they draw up short at the analytical threshold:

> Enough: let us descend no deeper, let us probe no farther into the rotten entrails of the eighteenth century. History must stop at the garbage pit. Beyond, there is no longer any humanity; there is no longer anything but miasmas, where it is impossible to breathe, where the light would die out of its own accord in the hands that would seek to hold it.[36]

But their real subject lies there—"beyond," where the light does not reach. "One's passion for things does not come from the goodness or pure beauty of those things," they confide to their *Journal*: "One adores only corruption" (*J*, II, 275).

The "corruption" was, of course, neither in woman nor

He in fact eagerly welcomed the congratulations of Léon Hennique for having created the fictional "double" of an *artiste* unknown to him, one Lucia Morgantini (see Hennique's "Postface" to *FZ*, 282). Delzant, whose source was probably Edmond himself, notes that the caprices of Miss Tompkins are those of Ludwig II of Bavaria, the "mad Wagnerian," who at the time was annoying Goncourt with reiterated requests to allow his collection of drawings to be copied (*Les Goncourt*, p. 221*n*). That this source seems so superficially unlikely suggests, of course, that the figure's origins are in the depths of a psychic reality.

[35] Edmond and Jules de Goncourt, *La Femme au dix-huitième siècle*, éd. déf. (Paris: Flammarion-Fasquelle, [1929]), I, 203.

[36] Ibid., I, 206.

wholly in the age: it was in the Goncourts themselves. "When we sound ourselves to the depths," they write in 1862, "we seem to be émigrés from the eighteenth century. We're déclassé contemporaries of that refined, exquisite society, with its supreme delicacy, its ferocious wit, its adorable corruption [. . .]" (*J*, I, 1193). What they meant by "corruption" is explained by the quotation above: "*il n'y a plus d'humanité.*" It is the ignorance (or abuse) of "object relations," as a psychoanalyst would say. This is not to imply that the Goncourts were incapable, as their detractors have protested, of any but the feeblest of "human feeling." They themselves were aware of the intensity of their own emotions: "Deep within us, and escaping to the outside in our excitement, there is a fund of ill-humor, of contempt, of burning rages, repressed by our politeness and an excellent education" (*J*, I, 1008). But their profoundest emotional instincts were repressed by neither delicacy nor their schooling: they seem to have been restrained by fear. They are haunted by visions of arrested violence:

> I was recalling the other night, still awake, the impression of a panoramic battle scene, a strange, profound, and terrifying impression. It's like a suspended, immobilized storm, a frozen tempest, a dead, mute chaos. The bombs bursting in the air don't move, they remain bursting eternally, in the filtered and softened and luminous northern light. The cavalrymen rush forward, the infantrymen engage, the arms lift, the gestures convulse, the wounded fall, the mobs clash, Victory soars overhead, without a sound, without a cry, in a fierce and sinister immobility of violence. (*J*, II, 6)

That this violence lies within is suggested by their fascination with—and fear of—the mannikin:

> I don't know of anything more terrifying among the falsehoods of life than wax dummies. That frozen movement, that living death, that fixity, that immobility, that silence of gaze, that petrifaction of figure, those hands hanging clumsily from the ends of the arms, those black, straggling wigs on the men's foreheads,

those long eyelashes framing women's eyes—a silken grill behind which flits a velvet bird—that bluish-white flesh: it is all poignantly macabre. (*J*, I, 199)

And to these quotations may be added their account of a dream, in which, beyond a dark chamber inhabited by glacial figures, inexplicable violence erupts:

Dream. Three statues of death. One, a skeleton; another, a consumptive body bearing a big ridiculous head, such as one sees at carnivals; the other, a statue of black marble. All three on a pedestal in a room, while in the shadow of a corridor, vague, fearful shapes are locked in a struggle. One after the other, coming down from their pedestal and trying to catch me, taking me by the arms and pulling me to themselves, they dispute over my person like streetwalkers. (*J*, I, 228)

I suspect that the disputed person is Edmond's.[37] There is no confirming the suspicion with certainty, of course, but it accords with the terrifying anxiety-dreams he records in later life. And it goes far towards explaining both his hatreds and his fears. If woman is secretly—and savagely—unpredictable, it is because he is afraid that he is so himself. Similarly, if he harbors unacknowledged hatred for his brother, it is because Jules reminds him of the *fond de porc* in his sentimental idealism. Edmond's psychology may be best characterized, I think, by a concept given currency by Lacan: the so-called "mirror-stage." Lacan argues that, at the age when the child first recognizes his image in a mirror, before his sense of self is "objectified" in a dialectic with the Other, his ego is turned in a "fictional direction" towards the "Gestalt" in the glass—that the latter, in short, acquires symbolic value for him as "the mental permanence of the *I*." The image, reversed and reduced in size, seems in manageable contrast with "the turbulent movements that the subject feels are animating him." It is therefore both an

[37] In a note to the passage, Robert Ricatte observes that Edmond added the following words and phrases when this section of the *Journal* was published in 1887: "a consumptive body bearing," "ridiculous," "black," and the end of the last sentence, beginning with "taking me by the arms. . . . " Are the skeleton and consumptive figure on the pedestal two versions of the sick child of Edmond's childhood memory (see below, p. 201-202)?

object of desire and a fantasized defense, both an image of anticipated wholeness and a self-alienating icon of transcendence. Lacan describes it succinctly:

> The *mirror stage* is a drama whose internal thrust is precipitated from insufficiency to anticipation—and which manufactures for the subject, caught up in the lure of spatial identification, the succession of phantasies that extends from a fragmented body-image to a form of its totality that I shall call orthopaedic—and, lastly, to the assumption of the armour of an alienating identity, which will mark with its rigid structure the subject's entire mental development.

The stage comes to an end when the "specular *I*" is deflected into the "social *I*" by "the identification with the *imago* of the counterpart and the drama of primordial jealousy [. . .], the dialectic that will henceforth link the *I* to socially elaborated situations."[38]

For Edmond, the link was never fully made. A *mal-aimé* as an infant, he seemed to suffer his adulthood in flight from the turbulence of desire. Having been deprived of the avenues of relationship through which the turbulence could find expression and discipline, he sought the specular image of a permanent self in the all-too-human Jules. Lacan observes that the "fragmented body" feared by the subject who seeks the safety of such a defense "usually manifests itself in dreams when the movement of the analysis encounters a certain level of aggressive disintegration in the individual. It then appears in the form of disjointed limbs, or of those organs represented in exoscopy, growing wings and taking up arms for intestinal persecutions [. . .]."[39] In a *Journal* entry for 1888, Edmond analyzes the influence of an uncle on his taste for "*la japonaiserie*," and is then led to an obsessive memory of his childhood:

> It's very strange, I don't have any memories of my childhood, or at any rate I have only one, but it's always with me and I see it again in every detail of its

[38] Jacques Lacan, "The Mirror Stage as Formative of the Function of the I as Revealed in Psychoanalytic Experience," *Ecrits: A Selection*, tr. Alan Sheridan (New York: Norton & Company, Inc., 1977), pp. 2, 4, 5.
[39] Ibid., p. 4.

reality when I think of it, and it's connected with this uncle. I had had the whooping-cough; Doctor Tartra—yes, I'm fairly sure that was his name—would not believe it was the whooping-cough, and it had developed into consumption, which made everyone afraid I wouldn't recover. I was lying in my mother's big bed— it was in the daytime—and I see him, my handsome uncle—for he had kept the beauty of his youth—I see him sitting between the bedside and the wall, and I see him speaking words in a soft, soft voice to my mother, who was crying, and who suddenly, with a sob, threw back the sheet that covered me and showed him my poor little skeleton's body. (*J*, III, 848)

This haunting image of a ravaged, insufficient self—the skeletal victim of internal "persecutions"—was probably born of fear rather than physiological fact. There is, in any case, no factual basis for the mature Edmond's terrible fantasies: "A state full of anxiety," he writes in 1882: "the fear at every moment of fainting with a feeling of the collapse of all the solid parts of my body; it seems to me that the secret elaboration of a general paralysis is operating in me" (*J*, III, 169). To lose control of his body, to be mastered by dark interior forces—this is Edmond's persistent dread. His first glimpse of lovemaking was a classic primal scene, in which his cousin was "*enfourchée*" by her husband. The brutality of that verb expresses the view of sexuality that Edmond retained all of his life. He of course envied, in his secret depths, the expression of such brutality, as his dream of the dancing actress suggests; but he was to remain, in both dreaming and waking life, the observer *en habit noir*, disgusted by his own bouts of sensuality, seeking wholeness in the mirror of Jules. Women as sexual partners were ugly creatures of disjointed limbs, like the first woman with whom he made love—"an enormous woman with a rhomboidal torso, fitted with two little arms and two little legs, which in bed made her resemble a crab turned over on its back" (*J*, II, 1196). By contrast, his companionship with his brother was the very model of spiritual harmony: "Imagine, if you can," they wrote in 1859, "two men [. . .] leaning upon and drawing strength from each other, buttressed by each other, having no need to reveal themselves to others or to mix with them, opening their hearts in private: a chain-shot in which the cannonballs move together, even in describing a curve" (*J*, I, 599).

It is in this light—we may now answer Grant—that we should view the Bescapés' fraternity. Their pantomime is a double allegory—first, of what its surface suggests: the "nightmare" within the dreaming Gianni is subdued and sublimated into art; and, second, of the two brothers' relationship: it is through the young Nello that Gianni's self-mastery is both mirrored and accomplished. Nello's grotesque dislocations of body recall graphically the dream-images of Lacan; and when he is transformed into a figure of Grecian grace, he in effect transfigures the dreamer, bringing harmony out of discord, serenity out of turbulence, sweet dreams out of *cauchemar*. But it is only by an act of Gianni's will that all this is brought about: he creates, as it were, his own mirror, exorcising the sprite's malevolence—Nello's *fond de porc*—so that his own might then be exorcised. So Edmond himself has transformed the brutal pantomimes of the Hanlon-Lees: out of the violence of their *gambades* (the truth of which he never denies) he has fashioned a "Shakespearean" comedy, an idyll *à la* Watteau. It has dramatically the same "destination" as that which both Goncourts attributed to the painter: the "smiling Arcady" of *l'Amour paisible* and its "eyes without fever, embraces without impatience, desires without appetite, and pleasures without desire." The summer landscape described by the Zemgannos' violins is the site of his *fêtes champêtres*, where all love is merely platonic and "where the riot of the senses has been stilled."[40]

To what extent Jules was aware of being implicated in—or of contributing to—such a drama we can but vaguely surmise. It is tempting to ascribe biographical value to those *"petits phénomènes anormaux"* (*FZ*, 155) with which Nello is visited while loitering in the wings of the circus. There, "in a state at once vague and exalted, and as if in the middle of a light effacement of the reality around him and of an

[40] Edmond and Jules de Goncourt, "Watteau," *L'Art du dix-huitième siècle*, éd. déf., I (Paris: Flammarion-Fasquelle, [1927]), p. 13.

enslumberment, as it were, of his daytime thoughts, the clown reached a point of having nothing in his head (as in that empty head from which one sees the ideas scooped by a spoon, one by one) but the reflection of his white face sent back by the mirrors, the images of the monsters that his eyes encountered on his costume, and the murmur that still remained in his ears of the diabolical music from his violin" (*FZ*, 156). A mask without a face, a body without a self, he is nothing but a repository of reflected images, a mirror relieved of its depths. Such was the character of Anatole Bazoche—probably a figure of Jules's invention[41]—in the earlier *Manette Salomon* (1865): "Anatole presented the curious psychological phenomenon of a man who is not in possession of his individuality, of a man who feels no need for a life apart, a life of his own, of a man whose tastes and instincts lead him to attach his existence to that of others by a kind of natural parasitism" (*MS*, 394). A bohemian, a mimic, a *blagueur*, Anatole is sometimes driven by his "*sens de l'invrai*" (*MS*, 395) to nihilistic displays. At a masked ball he sheds his costume, of the "*saltimbanque classique de baraque*," and "he reappeared in a white tie and black suit, with the floured face of a Pierrot" (*MS*, 248, 249). A kind of parody of the clerical Edmond and of the dandy drained of self, he launches into a dance that, in its frenzy, betrays the *porc* behind the glass. A piece of the Goncourts' bravura writing, the passage should be quoted entire:

> It was impossible to know what sort of sardonic spirit was running the length of his spine. From every part of his person shot out cruel caricatures of infirmities: he gave himself nervous tics that disfigured his face, imitated the limps of bandy- or wooden-legged men, simulated, in the middle of a stride, the jiggling foot of an old man stricken by apoplexy on the sidewalk. He had gestures that spoke, that murmured: "*My angel!*" that said: "*And your sister!*" which seemed to throw off filth, slang, disgust. He fell into stupid beatitudes, idiotic ecstasies, sodden states of bewilderment, cut off

[41] Most of the Goncourts' critics attribute the scenes and characters of lively wit in the early novels to Jules: see, e.g., Robert Ricatte, *La Création romanesque chez les Goncourt, 1851-1870* (Paris: Colin, 1953), p. 377.

by sudden bestial cravings that made him beat his chest like a native of Tierra del Fuego. He raised his eyes to the ceiling as if he were spitting at the heavens. He had looks that seemed to fall from paradise to the beer-joint; he placed his hands on the forehead of his dancing-partner in benedictions *à la* Robert Macaire. He kissed the place where the woman opposite him had stepped; he made himself graceful, deformed himself, reached out to seize some ideal on the wing, stamped about as if upon a tarnished illusion, sucked in his chest, humped up his shoulders, played Don Juan, then Tortillard. He set a machine in motion with one circling hand, and, cranking in the void, he appeared to grind out a tune that seemed Juliette's song of the lark on Fualdès's barrel-organ. He parodied woman, he parodied love. The poses, the swayings of amorous couples, consecrated by the masterpieces, the statues and the pictures; the immortal and divine lines of endearment that go from one sex to the other, that greet woman and long for her; the embrace that takes her by the waist and that knots itself to her heart; the pleading, the kneeling, the kiss—the kiss!—he caricatured everything with an artist's strokes, in poses taken from the tops of clocks and from the lore of troubadours, in derisory attitudes of supplication, of modesty, and of respect, mocking, with one of Cupid's fingers on his lips, all the tender sentimentality of man. [. . .] It was the infernal cancan of Paris—not the cancan of 1830, naïve, violent, sensual, but the corrupted cancan, the sneering and ironic cancan, the epileptic cancan that spits, like a blasphemy of pleasure and of the dance itself, at all the blasphemies of the times. (*MS*, 249-51)

If Anatole is led, by his very selflessness, to degrade piggishly the affairs of the self, the persona Edmond created, after Jules's death, to ensure his continued self-mastery abandoned human affairs almost completely. Sustained by the vision, in Enzo Caramaschi's words, of his "pietas *de survivant*,"[42] Edmond retreated more deeply into the mar-

---

[42] *Réalisme et impressionnisme*, p. 289.

tyr's role in which both brothers had cast themselves. And he grew fonder of sequestration: "The sweet sensation, upon entering one's study in the morning," he exclaimed in 1879, "of having the prospect of twelve hours of work, without going out, without visitors, without interruptions, in the perfect pleasure [*jouissance*] and inner exaltation of solitude!" (*J*, III, 52). Even in the company of others (save the ingratiating Alphonse Daudet) he was alone, receiving his guests coldly, suffering contradiction or an imagined affront only to excoriate the offender, in the silence of his chambers, on the sympathetic leaves of his *Journal*. He was happiest when the Grenier was empty, and he was left to his bibelots and books. "My 'castle in the air,'" he wrote only two years before his death,

> would be to have a gallery like the great hall in the Saint-Lazare station, with, all around, books chest-high, then glass cases of bibelots stacked over my head. A balcony going all around would make up the first floor, hung with three rows of drawings; another balcony would make up the second floor, its walls covered all the way to the roof with bright eighteenth-century tapestries. And I'd like to work, eat, and sleep there, inside [. . .]. (*J*, IV, 653)

Nothing better illustrates the desperate insularity of his life, or better suggests why his books—including those on which Jules collaborated—seem "*fruits incomplets*," in Robert Ricatte's words,[43] or why his most characteristic work is the two-volume description of the furnishings of his house, *La Maison d'un artiste* (1881). Without Jules, that house was his armor, its *objets d'art* affirming the taste and genius with which he pathetically credited himself. But it was obviously inadequate. Those nightmares that tormented his years alone betray his hopeless fear and confusion: "I no longer have any dreams but one," he writes in 1887, "a unique dream, which is always, necessarily, a nightmare: it involves a departure for a vague place and the loss, at the train station, of my luggage, my money, my coats; and, in the midst of the anxiety produced by these terrible discoveries and es-

---

[43] *La Création romanesque*, p. 9.

pecially by my fear of the cold during the trip, the sudden movement of the train" (*J*, III, 635). The cold had begun to descend in 1870, when Jules, having abandoned him for death, was lost even in the labyrinths of his dreams, leaving Edmond always searching like a pitiable K. for the center of his life. It is Jules who has been translated into the lost possessions of the anxious dreaming Edmond.[44] Such a reflection, sending us back to the deprivations of their childhood, robs the disclaimers of the Goncourts of their justice: it is not "insufficient humanity" that prevents their work from achieving its "fullness."[45] Its faults are the issue of a humanity betrayed.

[44] Cf. Edmond's entry in the *Journal* for December 29, 1883: "When I find my brother again in my dreams, it's always on railway journeys, in which I lose him at the station [. . .]" (*J*, III, 296). For a detailed account of such a dream, in which Jules's loss sends Edmond on a frustrating, labyrinthine search, see *J*, III, 185.

[45] As Caramaschi, among others, claims: *Réalisme et impressionnisme*, p. 98.

VIII

Pierrot *oedipien*:
J.-K. Huysmans

—Vous n'allez plus au théâtre, n'est-ce pas?
—Je n'y ai pas remis les pieds depuis je ne sais combien
d'années. Le public qu'on y subit me répugne et toutes les
pièces qu'on y joue m'indiffèrent. Je ne comprends guère
que la féerie avec la lumière électrique, de séduisantes
étoffes et des femmes. De la musique intéressante, si c'était
possible—et d'extraordinaires mimes. Une sorte de . . .
d'onanisme oculaire.

HUYSMANS TO GUSTAVE COQUIOT,
in the latter's *Le Vrai J.-K. Huysmans* (1912)

In a playful pseudonymous self-portrait for Léon Vanier's
series *Les Hommes d'Aujourd'hui*, Huysmans described the
heroes of his novels as "one and the same person, transported into different milieux," then added: "And very obviously this person is M. Huysmans [. . .]." With the solemn deprecation of the true hack, he went on to deplore
how far we are "from that perfect art of Flaubert, who
effaced himself behind his work and created characters so
magnificently diverse."[1] But we are not, of course, so far as
Huysmans pretended to suppose; his own self-portraiture
is simply more explicit than that of the Master of Croisset.
And as the self-dramatizations of an "autobiographical"
novelist, his heroes are rather generously diverse. There are,
in fact, at least three personae in Huysmans's work—the

---

[1] The study was published in 1885 under the pseudonym "A. Meunier"
(after Anna Meunier, a friend and sometime mistress of Huysmans): rpt.
[Pierre Cogny, ed.] *Mélanges Pierre Lambert consacrés à Huysmans* (Paris:
Nizet, 1975), p. 19.

splenetic anchorite seeking the peace of books and fireside, the spiritual adventurer attracted to both satanism and sainthood, and the dispassionate artist, the recorder and inventor. They are present in almost all of the important novels, sometimes distributed among two or three characters, sometimes distilled into one. The heroes of the middle works, Des Esseintes, Jacques Marles, and the Durtal of *Là-bas* (1891), are clearly syncretic figures—albeit unstable ones—who play out the Huysmansian roles at various pitches of intensity, while the Durtal of *L'Oblat* (1903), at the end of the Catholic trilogy, finds, through his conversion, a definitive means to unify all three.

In the early novels, particularly *Les Soeurs Vatard* (1879), *En ménage* (1881), and *A vau-l'eau* (1882), Huysmans seems still to be experimenting with the first two personae, each in isolation. André Jayant and Monsieur Folantin are novices in what Pierre Cogny wittily calls *"la religion de la pantoufle et du placement sûr"*;[2] Cyprien Tibaille, who appears in both *Les Soeurs Vatard* and *En ménage*, is a man of quite another faith: "a man who was depraved, enamored of all the nuances of vice, provided they were complicated and subtle."[3] They are clearly *"une seule et même personne"*—but how different are their masks. Both André and Folantin, timid, self-effacing, are happiest in an atmosphere of "pacifying quietude" (*OC*, V, 72). André, like the dyspeptic clerk of *A vau-l'eau*, "hesitated—in the simplest circumstances of life—to take part, vacillated, saw difficulties everywhere, resolved them sometimes with the bravado of a coward, and regretted, two minutes later, the decisiveness of which he had given proof" (*OC*, IV, 132). Whereas Folantin—and André—enjoys nothing more than a comfortable evening alone in his rooms, surrounded by "the engravings of Ostade, of Teniers, of all the painters of real life he loved" (*OC*, V, 71), Cyprien aggressively seeks out "the leper-house of nature" (*OC*, IV, 125), the sensational, *"le moderne,"* in both art and life:

[2] *J.-K. Huysmans: A la recherche de l'unité* (Paris: Nizet, 1953), p. 41.
[3] J.-K. Huysmans, *Les Soeurs Vatard*, in *Oeuvres complètes de J.-K. Huysmans*, III (Paris: Crès et Cie, 1928), 158. This edition will be cited throughout this chapter as *OC*, with appropriate volume and page numbers.

Frail and nervous to excess, haunted by those dull ardours that rise from tired organs, he had come to dream only of carnal pleasures seasoned with perverse grimaces and baroque accoutrements. In the matter of art, he understood only the modern. (*OC*, III, 158-59)

What unites these figures psychologically, and in fact reconciles their superficial differences in temperament, is their complementary attitudes towards women. The Cyprien of *Les Soeurs Vatard* finds pleasure in young girls of the street, on whom the profession is beginning to tell: "At bottom, the *fille*, young and worn-out, with a complexion already dulled by long evenings, her breasts still elastic but softening and starting to droop, her face seductive and nasty, licentious and painted, attracted him" (*OC*, III, 161). As a painter, he disdains the "irreproachable forms of the paintings known as 'nudes,' " and represents on his canvases that woman "faded like the majority of those who have had children, or who have indulged too freely in alcohol or fights, [. . .] with slack breasts, a glittering eye, a drooling mouth" (*OC*, III, 162). Like the Degas of Huysmans's *Certains* (1889), he seems determined to "vilify" in his painting "the idol constantly put on a pedestal: Woman" (*OC*, X, 22). And that Cyprien's painterly ideal inspires an acute private disgust, despite its offering a perverse sexual attraction, is suggested by his response towards the end of the novel to Céline's vulgar manners and temperament:

One fine day, he stopped taking her to the restaurant. With her mania for ordering rabbit and sharpening her teeth on the carcass, with her way of hitching up her napkin, of filling the glasses to the brim, of giggling and fidgeting around on her chair, of fishing about in the dishes with her fork for the little onions, she exasperated him.

Another fine day, he also stopped taking her to the theater. Her childish raptures, her clapping, her jumping around on the banquette, her bobbing over the balustrade, her clumsy kicks against the seats, her way of meddling with the lorgnette and smearing it up, her purchases of apple-sugar and oranges, made his flesh creep. (*OC*, III, 216)

Even as he takes a kind of depraved delight in her overripe body, Cyprien revenges himself in his art upon this incorrigibly naïve animal. Significantly, what Freud would call his "choice of object" ensures his taking such revenge again and again: the women to whom he is drawn are simply destined to be vilified.

As for André and Folantin, they desire retreat, not revenge. When woman distracts André from his quietude—from "the peace of a man always unbuttoned and slippered"—it is, in his eyes, a "*crise juponnière*" (*OC*, IV, 148, 149). His need for woman's company affects him as an "indefinable malaise that grows more and more acute, resulting in a kind of *spleen*" (*OC*, IV, 149). And yet he denies that his body craves satisfaction: "He desired Woman, not for the carnal embrace of her body, but for the rustling of her skirt, the tinkling of her laughter, the prattling of her voice, for her company, for the air, in a word, that she emanated" (*OC*, IV, 152). His liaisons (which seem hardly contracted for the sake of the lady's "*société*") all end, like his marriage, in disillusionment or failure; but even after he has lost his mistress, Jeanne, with whom he is reasonably happy, he finds an odd contentment in his solitude: "Then there were no longer lancinating bouts of anguish, hot fevers, *idées fixes*, no longer mad moments of faintness and frightful starts, but a kind of charming languor like that of a convalescence, a gradual lulling of thought, a complete resignation, a wan quietude, a melancholy and smiling reverie, a tender and consoling feeling like that which one sometimes feels on the day of Commemoration, before a friend's grave that has long been closed" (*OC*, IV, 304-305). *La vie en pantoufles* is, for both André and Folantin, a kind of protracted convalescence, a sweet and pacific mourning, in which sex is a painful distraction. Like Folantin's lameness, which excuses him, conveniently, from the world that exhales "*Tout un fumet de femme*" (*OC*, V, 16), it is an avenue of escape, of withdrawal: it offers the sort of sanctuary that Durtal, of *En route* (1895), spies out in the Church, that "hospital of souls": "You're received there

211

[. . .], you're put to bed, you're cared for [. . .]" (*OC*, XIII, 43).

If woman has a secure place in the lives of any of these characters, it is in fact as a nurse, as a mother tending her sick or frightened child. André is thankful that his first sexual experience was "an almost maternal welcome" (*OC*, IV, 162), and Cyprien is fortunate in finding, at the end of *En ménage*, a mistress who nurses him tenderly through a debilitating illness, one who, finally, "fulfills [. . .] all the conditions of a last ideal that kept me going: to find a mature, calm, devoted woman, without amorous needs, without coquetry, without pose—in a word, a strong and pacific cow" (*OC*, IV, 338). With this woman, André, too, feels profoundly, childishly, at ease:

> Mélie's good humor, which from time to time made his throat dance with deep laughter, delighted him. He felt at home. His legs splayed full-length under the table, his behind slid to the edge of the chair-seat, his head almost propped on the back, his hands in his pockets, he relaxed, torpid with the food he had put away and the wine. (*OC*, IV, 352)

"Mélie is exceptionally maternal," Cyprien tells his friend, happy at having finally established "a sincere comradeship" with this woman, both "dissociating [themselves] from [their] sex" (*OC*, IV, 339, 333).

The obviously oedipal overtones of these relationships have at least part of their source in Huysmans's own childhood. H.-M. Gallot, who, surprisingly, makes little appeal to the novelist's early books, describes the precipitating crisis in his *Explication de J.-K. Huysmans*:

> When the father dies, only to be immediately replaced, the step-father becomes a veritable intruder, and the little boy finds himself, quite against his will, in a situation that works to greatest effect against the liquidation of the oedipus complex—for his sharing of the mother is all the more unacceptable since, from the time of the father's death, she has belonged completely to the child.[4]

[4] Paris: Agence Parisienne de Distribution, 1954, p. 42.

J.-K. Huysmans

Even Huysmans's biographer, Robert Baldick, who thinks "we may safely discount [. . .] these Freudian fantasies," admits that "there can be no doubt that [. . .] Georges was outraged when his mother married again, and embittered when she later neglected him in favour of Juliette and Blanche, her two daughters by this second marriage."[5] Baldick adds that Huysmans's "revenge" was to "banish" his mother and stepfather from his autobiographical novels, an assertion made by both Gallot and Cogny with respect to the mother alone. But, as I have tried to suggest in my brief discussion of André and Cyprien, surrogate mothers are certainly present here: they are, in fact, everywhere in Huysmans's novels, from Cyprien's tender "comrade" to "Our Lady of Sorrows" in the Catholic works. Cogny shrewdly assesses the latter's psychological function for the writer: "An old orphan who has never truly known the treasures of maternal love, [. . .] he cries out his distress to the Virgin because, according to the prayer of Saint Bernard, she is the only one who does not abandon those who come to her in appeal [. . .]."[6]

Huysmans's *"fixation névrotique à la mère"*[7] helps explain not only his heroes' attraction to idealized maternal figures but also their fear of and disgust for "normal" sexuality— explains their neurotically reiterated desire to stretch out in bed alone, *sans gêne*.[8] "Above all," Gallot observes, "[Huysmans] fears physical lovemaking, an act hedged about by the strongest taboos."

> Indeed, he had mistresses, a number of them, but if he was obsessed by the flesh and if he succumbed, it was always with a kind of self-disgust, which sometimes resulted in a semi-impotence or, more precisely, in an obsession with impotence, to which Pierre Cogny has justly drawn attention.[9]

[5] *The Life of J.-K. Huysmans* (Oxford: Clarendon Press, 1955), p. 5.

[6] *J.-K. Huysmans: A la recherche de l'unité*, p. 157.

[7] Gallot's phrase: *Explication*, p. 43.

[8] A desire expressed by both Cyprien and André in *En ménage* (*OC*, IV, 10, 192, 196), by Monsieur Folantin in *A vau-l'eau* (*OC*, V, 33, 43), and by Jacques Marles in *En rade* (*OC*, IX, 245).

[9] *Explication*, p. 43.

"At once adored and hated,"[10] woman is the force that separates the Andrés from the Cypriens in Huysmans's work: the diffident from the aggressive, the abstinent from the perverse, the monkish from the satanic. And she is the force that unites them in their general malaise. Huysmans's familiar *horreur de la vie*, as well as that of his characters, has its fundamental source in his neurosis: "His very hypochondria, his pessimism, and his ennui are only the epiphenomena of his underlying anxiety."[11]

If his struggle as a man and as a writer was to subdue his anxiety, to sublimate neurosis in a conversion amenable to both reality and spirit, it was, fortunately for literature, a dynamically protracted struggle of naïve, if often short-lived, victories. One thinks of the audaciously uncompromising gestures of Des Esseintes, of Gilles de Rais, of Saint Lydwine of Schiedam—for Huysmans all gestures in the field of fantasy, where the mind can liberate itself to its most compelling obsessions. The reason he gave for his withdrawal from Zola's *médanistes* ("I was vaguely seeking an escape from the cul-de-sac where I was suffocating [. . .]" [*OC*, VII, xi]) accords perfectly, in fact, with his frequently expressed delight in the *féerie*, an entertainment unnaturalistically aglitter with the crude promise of wishes fulfilled. That those wishes were, at bottom, sexual for Huysmans is suggested by his hesitant admission of my epigraph. And so it should not be surprising that, even in the most sober of the autobiographical novels, a world of explicitly infantile self-abandonment—of self-indulgence and self-abuse—always beckons, a world usually having ties with the *féerie* as well as other spectacles of the popular stage, of the music-hall, the pantomime, and the circus.[12] When, for ex-

[10] Ibid., p. 42.

[11] Ibid., p. 51.

[12] Throughout his prose-poems and art criticism, and especially in the pages of *L'Art moderne* (1883) devoted to Degas, Huysmans's love for "certain corners of Parisian life—balletic gymnastics, the foolery of clowns, the skits of English mimes, the interiors of hippodromes and circuses" (*OC*, VI, 14)—is everywhere apparent. In 1888, the novelist became a founding member of the Cercle Funambulesque, a professional dramatic society that had conceived the program of producing plays in the manner of *commedia dell'arte*, farcical *parades*, comedies from the repertoire of the Théâtre-Italien, and modern pantomimes. See Hugounet, *Mimes et Pierrots*, p. 238, and below, Chapter XI.

ample, Durtal awakens from dreams of demons, luring him *là-bas*, he describes them to himself as "A band of mystical female clowns, hanging head-downward and praying with their feet together [. . .]" (*OC*, XII, 117). And, later, in *En route*, whenever he lapses "into dreams,"

> it was then, especially, that *idées fixes* wandered through his head; they ended by playing out *féeries* for him behind the lowered curtain of his eyelids, plays whose scenes hardly ever varied. Always nude figures went dancing through his brain, accompanied by the singing of psalms [. . .]. (*OC*, XIII, 37)

The fantasist of most elaborate and sustained invention is, of course, Des Esseintes, who reigns over his "refined Thebaïd," in Gallot's words, as "a tyrannical child," wanting "to liberate himself from all emotional and social constraints so as to comply with nothing but his elementary instincts, whatever they might be."[13] Before settling in his château at Fontenay, he indulges some of these instincts in flesh as well as fantasy: having fitted out a boudoir with "little pieces of furniture, sculpted in pale Japanese camphorwood, under a kind of tent of pink satin from the Indies," he invites women "to dip their nakedness into this warm, fleshcolored bath" and to inhale with him the aromatic odors (*OC*, VII, 15-16). Whore's bedroom and infant's nursery, this room gives Des Esseintes "singular joys, pleasures that were heightened and quickened, in some sense, by memories of past misfortunes, of dead torments" (*OC*, VII, 16). He locates his motive for sexual depravity in his unhappy childhood, particularly in "all the constrained and silent evenings in his mother's company," and when his memories of those days are disrupted—when, in other words, he is reminded that his wishes can neither regain nor alter the past—he is nearly overcome by his thirst for vengeance and desperate gratification:

> [. . .] then, with the jerks of the woman he was mechanically caressing and whose words or laughter was breaking into his vision and carrying him rudely back to reality, into the boudoir, down to earth, a tumult

[13] *Explication*, p. 105.

rose in his heart, a thirst for vengeance for the time of sadness he had suffered, a rage to defile family memories by acts of baseness, a frenzied desire to pant upon cushions of flesh, to drain the most vehement and bitter of carnal follies to their last drops. (*OC*, VII, 16-17)

First in his "defile of mistresses" is Miss Urania, "one of the most celebrated acrobats of the Circus" (*OC*, VII, 156). In watching her perform, Des Esseintes is powerfully attracted by her masculine strength, and he is soon longing for her "athletic brutalities" (*OC*, VII, 159), "panting just like a sickly young girl after the coarse muscleman whose arms could crush her in an embrace" (*OC*, VII, 157-58). (Cyprien Tibaille—that "des Esseintes in embryo," as Baldick calls him[14]—also has fantasies of embracing "a woman dressed in the rich costume of a *saltimbanque* [. . .] in a room hung with Japanese fabrics [. . .]" [*OC*, III, 159].) Outside its obvious suggestions of homosexuality, his fantasy is clearly a masochistic one, for, "added eventually to this sudden admiration of brute force, formerly repulsive, was the exorbitant charm of defilement, of the delightfully base prostitution of paying dearly for the vulgar endearments of a pimp" (*OC*, VII, 158). Freud invokes the wish lurking behind this perversity when he remarks that "the masochist wants to be treated like a small and helpless child, but, particularly, like a naughty child." His elaboration of this notion is especially interesting for the light it throws on the second relationship that Des Esseintes recounts—that he enjoys with the nameless lady ventriloquist:

> But if one has an opportunity of studying cases in which the masochistic phantasies have been especially richly elaborated, one quickly discovers that they place the subject in a characteristically female situation; they signify, that is, being castrated, or copulated with, or giving birth to a baby. (*SE*, XIX, 162)

After Des Esseintes has abandoned Miss Urania and taken up with the ventriloquist-*artiste*, he eventually "had recourse to the most effective adjuvant for an old and spo-

---

[14] *Life*, p. 43.

J.-K. Huysmans

radic itch—to fear" (*OC*, VII, 164). He persuades the young woman to throw her voice beyond the door of his bedroom and to bluster in the tones of an outraged husband, threatening to force the lock and so surprise his wife in a criminal embrace. From his participation in this little drama, which strongly suggests the castration fantasy of a child sharing his mother's bed, Des Esseintes derives "unprecedented joys" (*OC*, VII, 164)—joys doubtlessly intensified by guilt.

The " 'new perfumes, [the] larger flowers, [the] untasted pleasures' " (*OC*, VII, 163) that Des Esseintes seeks from both these women are, in effect, pleasures foretasted in infancy and lost, long ago, in childhood. It is altogether appropriate that not only Des Esseintes but also a number of Huysmans's other heroes should look to the world of the circus for these satisfactions, a world that for so many nineteenth-century writers seemed, in Jean Starobinski's words, "a shimmering isle of marvels, a fragment of the land of childhood that has been preserved intact."[15] For to reimagine that *pays*, to make it over, to reenter it for the sake of avenging oneself on the imagoes that people its landscape—this seems to have been the function of the incidental fantasies weaving in and out of Huysmans's work.[16] It is clearly the impulse behind that extended and most intriguing of fantasies in the canon, *Pierrot sceptique* (1881).

"He didn't like the theater," Léon Hennique once remarked of Huysmans, "but he liked the pantomime a lot,"

and often, after dinner, we'd go to the Folies-Bergère together: that's how our collaboration on *Pierrot sceptique* came about. As a matter of fact, at that time there were some English mimes who were enjoying a very

[15] *Portrait de l'artiste en saltimbanque*, p. 8.

[16] André Thérive observes that "it is not difficult" to explicate "*le fantastique*" in Huysmans, especially the dreams of Jacques Marles, along psychoanalytic lines (*J.-K. Huysmans: Son Oeuvre* [Paris: La Nouvelle Revue Critique, 1924], pp. 64-65). Nor is it difficult to see similarities between Des Esseintes's reign as an "*enfant tyrannique*" at Fontenay and Durtal's curious fantasy of Chosroes's self-deification in *L'Oblat* (*OC*, XVII, 39-43). But these fantasies, as well as others having no connection with the pantomime, lie outside the scope of this chapter.

keen success: the Hanlon-Lees. Huysmans said to me one evening, after watching them: "It'd be fun to do something along those lines, what do you say?" We worked out the scenario together. I wrote the pantomime, I passed it on to him, and he made the changes he wanted.[17]

Pierrot sceptique was born, then, of a double collaboration, one with Hennique, the other with the Hanlon-Lees. Hennique's contribution was, I suspect, less than his actual writing of the scenario might lead one to suppose. The pantomimes he later published under his name alone, *Le Songe d'une nuit d'hiver* and *La Rédemption de Pierrot*, are the fruits of a rather banal inspiration, merely vulgar in conception, precious in language, conventional in sentiment and dramatic effect.[18] *Pierrot sceptique* breathes out a different kind of spirit—one that infected audiences everywhere at the end of the nineteenth century, in the presence of the Hanlon-Lees.

Huysmans must have seen several of the Hanlons' performances.[19] In the opening section of his *Croquis parisiens*

[17] Cited in Frédéric Lefèvre, "Une Heure avec Léon Hennique," *Les Nouvelles Littéraires*, May 10, 1930; cited in O. R. Morgan, "Huysmans, Hennique et 'Pierrot sceptique,' " *Bulletin de la Société J.-K. Huysmans*, No. 46 (1963), 103.

[18] In *Le Songe d'une nuit d'hiver* (Paris: Ferroud, 1903), Pierrot reenacts the crimes he had read about in his newspaper during an early scene of the play—then awakens with relief from his nightmare before the final curtain. In *La Rédemption de Pierrot* (Paris: Ferroud, 1903), the clown is turned from his evil ways when a statue of the Virgin in a church that he is burgling comes to life and dissuades him from further sin. James B. Sanders has recently published a third pantomime by Hennique, *Pierrot à Stamboul* (*Revue de la Société d'Histoire du Théâtre*, XXXII [July-September 1980], 237-47), but this scenario is no improvement on the other two. The pantomime is little more than a single extended joke: Pierrot has fled prison in a woman's garb; when he is sold as a slave, the Sultan conceives a passion for "her" person, and Pierrot's desperate wriggling constitutes the feeble action of the piece. Hennique's enthusiasm for the Hanlon-Lees was apparently not so great as Huysmans's, since, according to his daughter, Hennique "recognized as a worthy interpreter [of Pierrot] only the inspired [*génial*] Deburau"—that is, Baptiste's son Charles, who died in 1873 (Nicolette Hennique-Valentin, *Mon Père: Léon Hennique* [Paris: Editions du Dauphin, 1959], p. 289; cited in Morgan, "Huysmans, Hennique et 'Pierrot sceptique,' " p. 104).

[19] They were still vivid to him in memory twenty years after the composition of *Pierrot sceptique*. In 1900, he compared several novices' gam-

("Les Folies-Bergère en 1879"), he describes but does not name a pantomime recounted in the brothers' *Mémoires et pantomimes* as *Le Duel*. *Pierrot sceptique* suggests that he saw at least two other pieces—*Pierrot menuisier*, described in the last chapter, and *Pierrot terrible*. In the latter playlet, two Pierrots amuse themselves by measuring a dandy for a new suit of clothes ("not without strangling him, bullying him, roughing him up, and planting leveling-staves in his shoulders"), bury a butcher under his own beefsteaks before they sack his shop, then make war on the peripatetic sweets that evade their grasp in a bakery. When all the boutiques have closed, they invite, "*comme Don Juan*," an unresponsive statue on the streetcorner to dinner, finally deciding to spend the night in a neighboring house, "where there are probably a few people who do not fully occupy their beds." There, they have a number of distressing encounters—with "the white shoulder of Madame Colombine" ("virtuous, Pierrot shrinks back, all atremble") and a troupe of enormous rats. One of the Pierrots inadvertently sets fire to the house, and "Thus commences the final pandemonium of all healthy pantomimes." When, amid the confusion, the Pierrot sees that an old doorkeeper is menaced by the conflagration, "he rushes upon her, raises her, snatches her, rolls her, wrests her from the flames, and sends her plunging headfirst into the bass drum of the orchestra." For this "*acte généreux*," he mounts to heaven, transfigured, "in a sparkling aureole."[20]

Pierrot sceptique begins, like *Pierrot menuisier*, with a coffin in full view: the body of Madame Pierrot, "*dead in the flower of her years*" (*OC*, V, 100), awaits its final rites. Her widower is being fitted out, in the bedroom above, with a suit of black percaline (black, too, were the unconventional vestments of the Pierrots in *Le Duel*); he pays his tailor with a kick in the rear, which sends him flying into a wall-cupboard. At a hairdresser's shop, he has his bald pate pomaded with black bootpolish ("Pierrot knows what one

---

boling over his house at Liguté, decorating it for a religious celebration, to the frantic exercises of the Hanlon-Lees (letter of June 22, 1900, to the Abbé Mugnier; cited in Lucien Descaves, *Deux Amis: J.-K. Huysmans et l'Abbé Mugnier* [Paris: Plon, 1946], pp. 90-91).

[20] All quotations describing *Pierrot terrible* are from [Lesclide], *Mémoires et pantomimes*, pp. 119, 121, 122, 123, 125-26.

owes to the dead. It must be *black* pomade—pomade of mourning!" [*OC*, V, 107]), and when his head begins to burn, he throws himself savagely upon the hairdresser, who must take to his heels through the street. At the funeral, he awaits his guests "Gravely, in a Napoleonic pose" (*OC*, V, 109), his wife's syringe in one hand. He kisses the women, ignores the men, finally drives them all away with squirts from his weapon, then dances gaily into a corner bar. When he staggers out, his eye is caught by "*a silent and precious mannikin* [sidonie]" (*OC*, V, 100) who stands in the window of a wigmaker's shop, "her physiognomy placid, divine in her bride's dress, like one of those madonnas that stand commandingly in the tabernacles, in daylight subdued by the vaults, emerging radiantly from a background of gold" (*OC*, V, 112). He makes her, unsuccessfully, several propositions, then, like the importunate Pierrots of *Pierrot terrible*, invites this statue to dinner. Vanquished, the *sidonie* joins him in his rooms, ominously at her breast a bouquet of Dame Pierrot's immortelles—and Pierrot begins his assault. ("The immediate goal is to rape her, but the attack is perilous, the *sidonie*'s biceps very hard" [*OC*, V, 117].) He snatches a pigsticker from the wall, threatens her with violence, but, distracted by the tailor's commotion in the *armoire*, serves him instead several thrusts through the door. After two other nightmarish interruptions—from the tombstone-cutter and an audacious dandy, who easily wins two kisses from the captive—"Pierrot's saber whirls about, falls on the *sidonie*" (*OC*, V, 122), and she drops to the floor: "This execution calms the dandy. Suddenly adopting elegant manners, he picks up the lady, lays her on the bed, covers her with the sheet, says goodbye to Pierrot—and bumps into an old woman coming in" (*OC*, V, 123). The woman being "abominably drunk," Pierrot "overwhelms her with kicks" (*OC*, V, 124). She recovers from her abuse and stupor long enough to rouse the *sidonie*, then she collapses in a sodden heap. Pierrot disposes of her body in a corner and again lays siege to his guest. When it is apparent that "Nothing can heat up this glacial body" (*OC*, V, 125), he punningly sets fire to the room, thus initiating the "final pandemonium" of the pantomime. The *sidonie* perishes, the tailor's skeleton tumbles out of the closet, and Pierrot makes off to a dressmaker's shop, from which he rapes its dummy. Amid shouts of distress and clangs of the tocsin, he kisses his cardboard captive "with wild abandon" and "flees with her far from the disaster" (*OC*, V, 127).

What has been borrowed here from the Hanlon-Lees's skits is of course far less interesting than what has been unleashed by their license. Neither "virtuous" nor "generous," Pierrot *sceptique* is an almost disturbing portrait of the artist "in grips with his passions"[21]—*ses passions oedipiennes*. Here woman is ambiguous, both madonna and whore ("Women are corruptible," Pierrot thinks, "he knows that only too well" [*OC*, V, 113]); she inspires Pierrot's contemptuous cruelty with her wholly unconscious allure—even the wish for her death. (Her murder, of course, relieves him of his tabooed attraction even as it articulates his erotic rage.) Banville notes with fair accuracy that, aside from broad caricatures and travestied men, "There are no women in the Hanlon-Lees's pantomimes." His explanation for their absence suggests the gulf between the Hanlons' mad, random energy and the secret purposiveness of *Pierrot sceptique*: "In effect, wherever woman can be found, there love is also; through her divine and supernatural power, the imparadised man escapes his troubles, his torments, the vulgar brutalities of his frightful life, and consequently *la comédie est finie* [. . .]."[22] For the *pierrotiste* of less conventional energies, *la comédie* has of course just begun. Sustained by a kind of compelling dreamwork, with a logic not found in its models, *Pierrot sceptique* makes the fortuitous seem subliminally meaningful: the comic frustrations of Pierrot's heated suit, the doubling of assailants into spectator and dandy, who, unlike the former, can vulgarly enjoy the girl's favors; the self-willed drop of Pierrot's phallic blade and the silent withdrawal of the toff from the scene—all resemble the evasions of dream displacement, not simply the accidents of farce. That Pierrot's erotic "objects" are inanimate dummies, at once manipulable and intractable, betrays, somewhat icily, the forbidden tenor of his passion.

---

[21] Zola's phrase: see above, pp. 185-86.
[22] "Préface" to [Lesclide], *Mémoires et pantomimes*, pp. 13, 14.

J.-K. Huysmans

"*Froide folie*" Huysmans had called the Hanlons' art (*OC,* VIII, 23), thus uniting in an oxymoron what Banville had described as "their double style of acting." The style of the outrageous Pierrot *sceptique* is equally "double," for this terrorist is also a dandy. Faultless in dress, impeccable in form (with "his hand rounded like a lorgnette" he watches his wife's mourners flee [*OC,* V, 111]), he is, like the toff who crudely mirrors his passions, a perfect mimic of manners. And as a mere copyist, he is form without substance, untouched by his own acts of terror. Experientially innocent of his crimes—*septique,* so to speak, as well as *sceptique*—he aspires through his pose to Banville's realm of the transcendent "*vie idéale*." For the dandy is—as Baudelaire well knew—a saint. (Huysmans and Hennique had planned to follow *Pierrot sceptique* with a number of other pantomimes, among them a *Tentation de Saint-Pierrot*.)[23] In Freudian terms, Pierrot's *dandysme* is a kind of "undoing," a gestural fending off of *der Wunsch*: it both permits and denies the expression of the wish that lies latent in this *jeu d'esprit*.[24]

[23] According to Lucien Descaves's note to *Pierrot sceptique* (*OC,* V, 130), this pendant was to have been illustrated by Degas. With its title reminiscent of Flaubert's eccentric masterpiece—one of Des Esseintes's enthusiasms—and with sketches by the painter whom Huysmans seems to have regarded as an ardent misogynist, this little playlet, simply as an unrealized project, sets one dreaming (as Des Esseintes would have said).

[24] For an interesting interpretation of the scenario that is completely opposed to my own, see Brunella Eruli, "Huysmans al circo: 'Pierrot sceptique,' " *Paragone: Letterature,* XXV (October 1974), 54-68. According to Eruli, the circus was for Huysmans "the triumph of the artificial" (p. 60), and *Pierrot sceptique* "exemplifies perfectly the line of investigation that connects, in content and form, the *Croquis* and *A rebours*" (p. 61). Eruli concludes: "The construction of a privileged world (which is that of the spectacle) favorable to the revelations created by the play of the liberated imagination, subverts the relationship between life and performance, between fiction and reality, presenting a series of emotional states, simultaneous and changeable, which the artist, the ideal spectator, can develop without limit" (p. 65). It may strengthen my argument to call attention to a factual error in this otherwise excellent essay: it is not J.-L. Forain "who will illustrate *Pierrot sceptique*" (p. 67*n*) but Jules Chéret, the illustrator and *affichiste* whom Huysmans praises in *Certains* for his "neurotic joy": "M. Chéret has, first of all, the sense of joy, but joy that can be understood without being debased—frenetic and cunning joy, as if frozen by the pantomime, a joy heightened by its very excess, which car-

Not surprisingly, Pierrot himself acquires disquieting, if incidental, symbolic force in the writer's subsequent novels and criticism. Referring, for example, to a "shocking" Japanese print in the course of his essay on Rops, Huysmans describes a woman clasped in the erotic embrace of an octopus, her face (a "long Pierrot's visage with an aquiline nose") registering both loathing and indecent joy:

> [. . .] with its tentacles, the horrible beast milks the nipples of her breasts and probes her mouth, while the head itself drinks from the lower parts. The almost superhuman expression of anguish and of grief that convulses this long Pierrot's visage with an aquiline nose, and the hysterical joy that seeps, at the same time, from this forehead, from these eyes closed like a corpse's, are admirable! (*OC*, X, 80)

In *En rade* (1887), the district postman tries to interest Jacques Marles in adopting a baby tawny-owl, a creature that had frightened Jacques and his wife on their first restless night at Lourps—that, moreover, seems somehow to embody the obscure disgust they share as sexual partners, for which the decaying château is a symbol. Huysmans's description of the owl suggests both its fascinating appeal and its grotesque repulsiveness:

> [It was] a strange beast, fitted with enormous gray hooked feet, and crowned—on a very small body rolled up in white down—by a frightful, grimacing head, with unblinking round eyes and an eagle's beak, which knitted this face like an old scared monkey's into a frown. (*OC*, IX, 135)

When Jacques refuses to have anything to do with the creature, the postman gathers him up, thoughtlessly christening him "Pierrot."

But the most interesting and significant reappearance of the clown—once more in a quasi-circus context—occurs in *A rebours*. Des Esseintes has spent the day supervising the

---

ries it almost to the point of anguish" (*OC*, X, 53, 49). Such joy seems to me less likely to issue from "the liberated imagination" than from a mind "in the grips of its passions."

delivery of scores of exotic plants to his château at Fontenay; he feels overcome by his exertions and the heavy, hothouse atmosphere, and soon falls into a sleep fevered by nightmare. He dreams he is walking through the woods beside a bizarrely dressed woman who "had the air of a carnival *artiste*, the appearance of a *saltimbanque* of the fair" (*OC*, VII, 144). He feels a profound kinship with her, feels that she has been "lodged already for a long time in the most intimate part of his being and in his life" (*OC*, VII, 144), but can recall nothing definite of "this inexplicable and yet undeniable liaison" (*OC*, VII, 144). Suddenly, a figure on horseback appears before them, hideous, with skeletal limbs and a face disfigured with pustules: Des Esseintes identifies it as the Pox. Both are terrified, the woman even more than he, and they seek escape in a nearby summerhouse. Once inside, the woman begins to cry and complain that she has lost her teeth in their flight; to replace them, she smashes a few clay pipes she has been carrying in her apron pocket and stuffs the pieces into her gums. They fall out immediately, as Des Esseintes indeed predicts. When they hear the horse approaching the house, Des Esseintes must strangle the woman to stifle her cries. He tries to escape through an unlatched door, but is stopped by the spectacle of a crowd of Pierrots jumping about like rabbits in a vast clearing before him:

> "I'd be trampled to death," he thought; and, as if to justify his fears, the group of gigantic Pierrots grew bigger; their somersaults now completely filled the horizon, the whole sky, which they bumped against alternately with their feet and their heads. (*OC*, VII, 146)

Des Esseintes becomes aware of the rider's horse snuffling at his back, behind a window in the passageway, and he sinks to the floor, helpless and defeated. When he opens his eyes, after what seems a very long time, he is facing a desolate landscape bathed in an eerie phosphorescent light. A woman, naked except for a pair of stockings, is on the ground before him. As he gazes at her, she seems to take on the physical characteristics of both the Pox and the grotesque fleshy plants that now fill his rooms. Both fascinated and repulsed, he is drawn into her embrace—then, "wild-eyed, he saw the savage Nidularium opening in the depths of her raised thighs, its bloody swordblades agape" (*OC*, VII, 149). He feels himself on the point of death, then awakens in terror.

It is impossible to account for every detail of this dream: only if Des Esseintes were to consent to a session on the analyst's couch (an enthralling prospect) could all of its associations be clarified. But in its major aspects, it obviously both confirms and enlarges the hypothesis I have been developing. In that bizarre *saltimbanque* and that silk-stockinged woman we once more encounter the Mother. The creature on the horse, a totemic Father, has been disfigured by the very threat that he poses: his powers of castration have been turned back on his person, rendering him, paradoxically, wasted and feared. Des Esseintes clearly relates his mother's death ("of exhaustion," we are told [*OC*, VII, 3]) to those powers: the teeth and pipe-stems that drop from her gums suggest common dream-fantasies of castration.[25] In throttling the woman, Des Esseintes hopes to deliver himself from the temptation that elicits the threat; but those leaping Pierrots—symbols, as we have seen, of both infantile self-indulgence and neurotic self-absolution—hold him rooted to the spot. His approach to the woman on the gullied plain (evocative, in its emptiness, of those "immense high-ceilinged rooms [. . .] where [Huysmans] spent an icy childhood")[26] is both horrible and irresistible, climaxed by a vision of castration so intense that Des Esseintes is awakened from the dream.[27]

[25] See Freud, *The Interpretation of Dreams* (1900), *SE*, V, 357, for the dream-equation of castration with the losing of teeth—an equation given graphic illustration by Des Esseintes's feeling of nightmarish violation in the episode with the dentist (Chapter IV). On the psychological connection between castration and death, as well as the empirical evidence behind the theory, see Irving Sarnoff and Seth M. Corwin, "Castration Anxiety and the Fear of Death," *Journal of Personality*, XXVII (1959), 374-85; rpt. Seymour Fisher and Roger P. Greenberg, *The Scientific Evaluation of Freud's Theories and Therapy: A Book of Readings* (New York: Basic Books, Inc., 1978), pp. 214-24.

[26] Baldick, *Life*, p. 4.

[27] In his article "Le Cauchemar de Des Esseintes" (*Romantisme: Revue du dix-neuvième siècle*, XIX [1978], 79-90), Michel Collomb thickens the

In the light of Stanley Palombo's recent information-processing model of dreaming, it is of great significance that Des Esseintes takes up this same fantasy material in the following chapter, when he returns in imagination to Miss Urania and his former "defile of mistresses." Palombo argues convincingly that a dream is not the fulfillment of a wish—not the "hallucinatory gratification" that Freud thought it to be—but is rather the superimposition of images (either perceived or imagined) from the dreamer's immediate and childhood past in order to determine where new "day residues" are to be stored in the permanent memory. If the superimposition is coherent—that is, if the recent images prove to match, in their affects, the affect-laden memories to which they are being compared—then an associative bond is created between the nodes to which they are assigned in the memory tree. If for any reason the superimposition is incoherent, the matching process is carried out in subsequent dreams, usually aided by waking reflection upon the dreamwork, until a "correction dream" provides the proper match. "The decision to introduce the representation of a new experience into the permanent memory," as Palombo explains, "is based in large measure on its relevance to the fulfillment of the subject's wishes."[28] But, at the same time, the process does not serve exclusively the narcissistic interests of the "archaic adaptive ego," the agency that Freud called the id. For "it also creates new nodal points and new pathways in the already complex representation of [parental figures], through which dissociated aspects of the older image[s] may become reconnected, or possibly connected for the first time."[29] Dreaming, in short, is an adaptive activity, only incidentally a self-gratifying one.

But the anxiety dream, such as Des Esseintes experiences, is maladaptive: the dream censor "has prevented the match-

---

texture of this reading by pointing out the "masculine" and phallic qualities of both women, qualities that lead him to conclude that Des Esseintes's fear is not only of castration but also of "feminization" (p. 87). Such profound sexual confusion is usually attendant, of course, upon an unresolved oedipal conflict.

[28] Stanley R. Palombo, *Dreaming and Memory: A New Information-Processing Model* (New York: Basic Books, Inc., 1978), p. 170.

[29] Ibid., pp. 90-91.

ing mechanism of the memory cycle from producing a successful correction dream, which would normally introduce
new linkages between the traumatic past event [or fantasy]
and related but less threatening experiences which would,
in turn, have been successfully matched with the new day
residue." Palombo goes on to suggest how the censorship
operates in such a case:

> The imagery of a new day residue is always included
> in the composite formed by the matching process. But
> the new day residue is not the significant current ex-
> perience originally selected for the matching. It is a
> substitute introduced by the censorship. For this rea-
> son it tends to be overshadowed by the vividness of
> the traumatic past experience with which it is eventu-
> ally matched, or by the representation of earlier dreams
> in which that experience had been incorporated.[30]

In Des Esseintes's nightmare, the interference of the censorship has allowed the "vividness of the traumatic past" to
overshadow the immediate experience under evaluation: the
day residues that have been introduced—images of his recently acquired hothouse plants and the associations they
have called up in him of venereal disease—are clearly substitutes for the "significant current experience" that should
have been matched with memories incorporating the early
fantasy material. Des Esseintes's returning to such memories (which relate the fantasy-trauma to "less threatening
experiences") by way of reflection on Miss Urania and the
ventriloquist gives evidence of his innocently working over
their obsessive content in preparation for a "correction
dream." The latter, coherent, benign, adaptive, is rarely remembered by the dreamer, performing its work of association—and restitution—secretly.

That it ultimately succeeds in its work is suggested by
Des Esseintes's sudden renunciation of his narcissistic self-
indulgence at the end of the novel, and by his appeal to
God for grace. Huysmans himself has commented in his
famous twenty-year-after "Préface" to the book upon "the
perfectly unconscious nature of the last cry, the religious

[30] Ibid., p. 165.

appeal on the final page of *A rebours*" (*OC*, VII, xxv). It is a cry whose source was necessarily unknown to the writer, expressing as it does the work of the quietly dreaming mind coming to terms with obsession. But once it was uttered, it pointed the way, as Huysmans realized, to the work of complete adaptation: to Durtal's (and Huysmans's) serious preoccupation with the occult, to his retreat with the Trappists described in *En route*, and to his investiture as an oblate at "Val des Saints." Only in *En rade*, that bizarre and understandably anxiety-ridden book, does Huysmans turn away from this path—perhaps because he is not yet aware he is on it. He describes in his "Préface" the indistinctness of the implications of the climax of *A rebours*:

> If we look at it, as I do, from the standpoint of a conversion, it is, in its beginnings, impossible to make out; certain corners are discernible, perhaps, but the others are not: the subterranean work of the soul eludes us. There was, doubtless, at the time when I was writing *A rebours*, a moving of earth, a drilling in the soil, so that foundations could be laid, all of which I was insensible to. God was digging a pit for his plumbline, and He worked only in the shadow of the soul, in the night. (*OC*, VII, xxvi)

After *A rebours*, Huysmans's future as man and artist was to realize a psychic reconstitution of himself, the creation of a selfhood that would neither deny nor fall victim to the tyranny of childhood wish. Still the boy importuning the mother, he became a postulant before the Mother of God. But in the differences lay all the importance: though inaccessible to the senses, She now offered infinite love; if She yet served the Father, She acted as intercessor for His sons; to the anguished, She counseled chastity, abstention from the sexual life. Gallot is both right and wrong when he says that the novelist "had to remain till his death the man that his childhood drama [. . .] had created."[31] That drama was unvarying in its *dramatis personae*—but not in their relationships each to each. For the plot in which they worked out their destinies issued from the resourcefully creative

---

[31] *Explication*, p. 199.

mind, a mind working in both darkness and light to accommodate wishes to the imperatives of reality. Huysmans's triumph was to find an adaptive mean between that latter moral world and those dark wishes that disturbed its surface, manifest in Durtal's lewd fantasies, in Des Esseintes's bad dreams, and in his own regressive delight in the circus.

IX

Pierrot *pubère*:

Paul Verlaine

Mon amitié est pure. Mon coeur est d'un enfant, d'une innocence absolue. Je n'ai rien de double, je suis naïf comme tout [. . .].

VERLAINE TO F.-A. CAZALS
January 19, 1889

L'examen de Verlaine, hélas, n'est pas difficile.

ANTOINE ADAM
Le Vrai Verlaine (1936)

Un paysage choisi. Or *retrouvé*, the landscape of these *Fêtes galantes*. For the shudders rippling across its pools, dissolving the soul into the vague languors of its pines, are the *frissons* of an infant's body, curled, blissful, about the breast. It was one of the primal fantasies of Verlaine.[1] As it was of his *ami* Pierrot: "I am the infant suckling at/The breast," declares the eponym of Georges Lorin's *Pierrot voleur!* (1896), the full moon in his hands at last, "from which one drinks the milk of tomorrows."[2] That moon hangs heavy over the *Fêtes galantes*, entrancing the birds into reverie, convulsing its fountains with sobbing sighs, offering the milk of ecstasy. Owing nothing to the solar fantasy of Watteau,[3] it is a magical trace of the maternal presence, the

[1] See Antoine Adam, *Le Vrai Verlaine: Essai psychanalytique* (1936; Geneva: Slatkine Reprints, 1972), pp. 38, 69, 75.

[2] *Pierrot voleur! comédie en 1 acte, en vers* (Paris: Ollendorff, 1896), p. 27.

[3] Verlaine had identified the moonlight of "Clair de lune" as the "*calme clair de lune de Watteau*" in the first version of the poem (*Gazette rimée*, February 20, 1867). When Anatole France then asked, in the *Chasseur bibliographique* of March 1867, where the poet had seen moonlight in

230

source of that *"atmosphère anormale et songeuse"* that Baudelaire called *surnaturalisme*. And like the latter it eludes the grasp. Grave, solitary, distant, it presides *"triste"* over this Versailles of the dreaming mind.[4] The masks and bergamasks that pass beneath it seem disbelieving of their own happiness; the ecstasy towards which their senses thrill engenders doubt, fear, despair. Verlaine's is not the ambivalence of Baudelaire, or of Banville, those mentors of his youth: it is not sexuality itself that disturbs him, or any threat to his integrity of self. He suffers as an adult before the garden of infancy, at whose gate whirl the flaming swords of consciousness. J.-P. Richard has, as usual, articulated the essential terms of the paradox: "His impersonal ego introduces him to strange ecstasies, but his personal sensibility can only declare the distance that still separates him from these ecstasies, and from that other self more himself than it."[5]

And yet the two selves are one; their inextricability gives rise to the ambiguities of these poems: that which separates seems to promise strange ecstasies. The mask, for example, that agency of self-liberation and self-imprisonment. Or the rococo dress and manners of the maskers. (David Kunzle has suggested that the whalebone of a closer-corseted age was an erotic instrument for the young lady constricted, however formidable a fortress for her suitor.)[6] And the little slaps exchanged for stolen kisses, the "very dry" looks of reproach—these are the transparent ploys of the game of love, cancelled by a "somewhat lenient *moue*" ("A la promenade" [*OPC*, 109]). The reproof, the gloved hand,

---

Watteau, *"le peintre ensoleillé,"* Verlaine responded by altering the line—but keeping the moon. See Jacques-Henry Bornecque, *Lumières sur les* Fêtes galantes *de Paul Verlaine, avec le texte critique des* Fêtes galantes (Paris: Nizet, 1959), pp. 88, 153.

[4] "Clair de lune," *Fêtes galantes*, in Paul Verlaine, *Oeuvres poétiques complètes*, ed. Y.-G. Le Dantec, rev., completed, and presented by Jacques Borel ([Paris]: Gallimard [Bibliothèque de la Pléiade], [1977]), p. 107. This edition will be cited throughout this chapter as *OPC*, with appropriate page numbers.

[5] Jean-Pierre Richard, "Fadeur de Verlaine," *Poésie et profondeur* (Paris: Editions du Seuil, 1955), p. 178.

[6] *Fashion and Fetishism: A Social History of the Corset, Tight-Lacing and Other Forms of Body-Sculpture in the West* (Totowa, New Jersey: Rowman and Littlefield, 1982), pp. 22-23, 28-40.

the masked face: all sharpen the tooth of desire in the *Fêtes galantes*, even as they frustrate its intentions. But the frustrations go deeper, gaining intensity as desire recedes to its primitive source. Its goal is a pleasure beyond the pleasure principle, and such ecstasy life does not know. Creatures of flesh and language, of space and duration, Verlaine's lovers are victims of their first Separation, and their love, like their creator's, is "made of the anguish of being alone."[7]

They are separated by time. The old faun of terracotta presages, by his laughter, "an unhappy/Sequel to [. . .] serene moments" ("Le Faune" [*OPC*, 115]). The lover of "Lettre" envisages a time when "My shadow will melt forever into your shadow"—but the pathetically banal phrase that follows suggests how close are all earthly souls to eternity: "*En attendant, je suis, très chère, ton valet*" (*OPC*, 117). Human love is frugal of privileged moments, and is jealous of few. "Do you remember our old ecstasy?" asks the gallant of "Colloque sentimental," and the reply comes, icily, "And why do you want me to remember it?" (*OPC*, 121). To melt, to merge, to blend, to swoon into ecstasy: the lovers, like the suave poems themselves, aim at an inarticulate singleness, the form of no form; but the limitations of passion—as well as its very practical exigencies—interpose solid walls:

> *Et l'Amour comblant tout, hormis*
> *La faim, sorbets et confitures*
> *Nous préservent des courbatures.*
> ("Cythère" [*OPC*, 114])

[And, Love gratifying all, except/Hunger, sherbets and jams/Preserve us from body-aches.]

And as food preserves their integrity of body (how desirable is a Dorimène with lumbago?), so language ensures their integrity of self. "The 'indolents' are separated only by a metaphor," observes Jean Gaudon, "but that is sufficient to paralyze them":

"Let us die together," says the boy Tircis, who is well-read. Dorimène, who is no more sensitive to poetry

---

[7] Adam, *Vrai Verlaine*, p. 43.

than Mathilde Mauté will be, opts unfortunately for
the literal sense and makes fun of this caprice. This
important divergence of interpretation causes them to
put off "an exquisite death"—a "little death," as others
call it—thereby provoking the mocking laughter of the
sylvan creatures and of the poet-commentator.[8]

But the laughter of the poet is more than a comment upon
her confusion, for *la petite mort*, here as elsewhere in the
Fêtes galantes, is clearly an invitation to *la grande*. His
laughter is the dandy's laughter, acknowledging the vital
supremacy of the surface: "Autumn," declares the lover seduced by the "heavy voluptuousness" of summer winds,

> *L'Automne, heureusement, avec*
> *Son jour froid et ses bises rudes,*
> *Vint nous corriger, bref et sec,*
> *De nos mauvaises habitudes,*
>
> *Et nous induisit brusquement*
> *En l'élégance réclamée*
> *De tout irréprochable amant*
> *Comme de toute digne aimée . . .*
> ("En patinant" [*OPC*, 113])

[Autumn, happily, with/Its cold light and rough winds,/
Came, brusque and dry, to turn us/From our bad habits,//And briskly inducted us/Into the elegance de-
manded/Of every irreproachable lover,/As of every
worthy beloved . . .]

Acceding, by their distance, to the fate of being two, they
are "*Sans enthousiasme—et sans peine!*" (*OPC*, 112). Others
are not so intelligent. "Half-close your eyes," instructs the
grave voice of "En sourdine," counseling his mistress to
banish all counsel:

> *Croise tes bras sur ton sein,*
> *Et de ton coeur endormi*
> *Chasse à jamais tout dessein.*
> (*OPC*, 120)

[8] "Préface" to Paul Verlaine, *Fêtes galantes, La Bonne Chanson, Romances
sans paroles, Ecrits sur Rimbaud* (Paris: Garnier-Flammarion, 1976), p. 12.

[Cross your arms over your breast/And from your slumbrous heart/Forever rout all design.]

For such deliberate seekers of ecstasy, the nightingale of the evening can sing only of despair.

In another part of the park are characters of less ambitious design. *Fantoches*, Verlaine calls them: marionettes, masks of pantomime. Indeed, they seem inhumanly limited of gesture: Pierrot leaps a bush with alacrity, drains a flagon, cuts a pâté; Arlequin pirouettes four times and plots the abduction of Colombine; the Doctor gathers simples in the grass. They are characters that in fact seem defined by their gestures, as if few others were possible for them. Hence the sharpness of focus in "Pantomime," "Fantoches," "Colombine." There is (as Hallam Walker has observed) little merging with the landscape here.[9] The moon works no magic: Scaramouche and Pulcinella hatch their plots with clean gesticulations, "black against the moon" ("Fantoches" [*OPC*, 114]). Such simple creatures are not to be explained by an appeal to their "sources"[10] but to their role in the dynamics of the poems. Like the speaker of "En patinant," they are self-sufficient, *contents*—but very

[9] "Visual and Spatial Imagery in Verlaine's *Fêtes galantes*," *PMLA*, LXXXVII (October 1972), 1010, 1012, 1014.

[10] Although those "sources" have occasioned much discussion. Jacques-Henry Bornecque cites, in addition to Watteau's tributes to the Comédie-Italienne, Janin's *Deburau*, Aloysius Bertrand's "Viola de Gamba" in *Gaspard de la nuit*, Gautier's "Variations sur le Carnaval de Venise" in *Emaux et camées*, Banville's "Arlequin et Colombine" in *Les Stalactites* (*Lumières sur les* Fêtes galantes, pp. 36, 40-44); Antoine Adam calls attention to Maurice Sand's studies of the *commedia dell'arte* and singles out a specific model for Verlaine's Pierrot: "The pierrot of 'Pantomime' is clearly that of Banville in *Les Folies-Nouvelles*" (*Verlaine* [Paris: Hatier, 1970], p. 99). Such precision seems to me misleading: to look for "sources" behind Verlaine's uncomplicated *fantoches* is akin to seeking out a literary source for Santa Claus in a contemporary American children's story. The *commedia* types were ubiquitous in nineteenth-century Paris: even Mathilde Mauté, that unlettered Dorimène, tried her hand at a *pantomime-pierrotade*, *La Croqueuse de coeurs* (see André Vial, *Verlaine et les siens, heures retrouvées: Poèmes et documents inédits* [Paris: Nizet, 1975], pp. 93-109). Richard Whitmore's contention that all of the types in "Pantomime" are "divorced from their own traditional, characteristic identities" ("Verlaine's 'Pantomime,'" *The Explicator*, XXXIV [May 1976], item 71) is equally misguided: the types were never so sharply delineated or so static as Whitmore assumes.

unlike in their powers of reflection. They, in short, have no such powers; gesture is both character and self for these puppets: they have been delivered from the deliberations of consciousness. Utterly determined by their roles, they enjoy an utter freedom of self-realization; what Antoine Adam finds impossible for the other characters (as well as for Verlaine himself) these pantomimic masks embody: "simplicity," "spontaneity," "naturalness."[11]

But there is a serpent in their garden, and its name is Colombine. In the masks' final appearance, she (*"implacable enfant"*) leads them all a merry dance, doubtless towards certain destruction. The *"Désastre"* is apparent in her eyes. Perverse, like the green orbs of cats, they

> *Gardent ses appas*
> *Et disent: "A bas*
> *Les pattes!"*
> ("Colombine" [*OPC*, 119])

[Defend her charms/And say: "Down/With those paws!"]

Those eyes threaten eternal estrangement—even as her uplifted skirt promises *la petite mort*. Significantly, she is the only one of the *commedia* characters to hold a kind of intercourse with the landscape: in "Pantomime," she "dreams,"

> *surprise*
> *De sentir un coeur dans la brise*
> *Et d'entendre en son coeur des voix.*
> (*OPC*, 107)

[Surprised/To feel a heart in the breeze/And to hear voices in her heart.]

In "Fantoches," a nightingale crying *"à tue-tête"* sends her in quest of her Spanish corsair (*OPC*, 114). What I am suggesting is that she mediates between the two worlds of these poems—between that of the *fantoches* and their self-pleasuring self-sufficiency, and that of the "indolents," who seem to sense in the landscape what they seek in an em-

[11] Adam, *Vrai Verlaine*, p. 105.

brace: the possibility, ever frustrated, of regaining the ecstasy that is a remembrance of *l'enfance perdue*. She will
conduct her retinue from carelessness to consciousness, from
the autoeroticism of Pierrot's *friandise* to the inevitable disappointments of object-love and of its tantalizing attendant
fantasy.

In a late poem from *Epigrammes* (1894), Verlaine describes the business of pantomime:

> *Jeux de silence et de mystère*
> *Que la musique rend déjà*
> *Plus muets, et dont l'art va taire*
> *Mieux le secret, qu'il ne lâcha*
>
> *Qu'à l'oreille de Colombine*
> *Ou de l'indolente Zulmé.*
> (*OPC*, 857)

[Motions of silence and mystery/That the music is already rendering/More mute, and of which the art is
going to silence/More effectively the secret—which it
imparted//Only to the ear of Colombine/Or of the in-
dolent Zulmé.]

One is reminded of that earlier "Pantomime," in which
Colombine is inducted into both outer and inner mysteries,
unshared by her bergamask companions. Here music is in
complicity with those mysteries—as it always was in Verlaine's verse. His impulse towards musicality in the earlier
poetry is analogous to the merging with the landscape of
his characters: the voice of the mellifluous confidences is,
as Jacques Gaucheron suggests, *"un aspect de l'érotique ver-
lainienne."*[12] Banville understood this instinctively: "Sometimes you skim so close to the shores of poetry," he wrote
of *Jadis et naguère*, "that you risk falling into music."[13] To
"fall into music" is to merge irrevocably with the landscape,
and to enjoy a death by drowning in the water of life at
the soporific breast.

Such reflections may help explain why "Pierrot," a son-

---

[12] "Verlaine," *Europe: Revue Littéraire Mensuelle*, Nos. 545-46 (September-October 1974), 18.

[13] Cited in C. Chadwick, *Verlaine* (London: The Athlone Press of the
University of London, 1973), p. 116.

net of 1868, does not appear in the *Fêtes galantes*. Contemporaneous with other poems of the collection, it was probably rejected from the volume for which it had been intended, then published (by *Paris-Moderne* in 1882) when need silenced the voice of scruple. An anomaly beside "Pantomime," "Fantoches," "Colombine," it does not share what Verlaine called their "savory tones of velvety tartness and of winning malice."[14] Nor is it consistent with their delineation of the *commedia* masks. But the scruple was, I think, as much a psychological as a formal and aesthetic one. If, as Jacques-Henry Bornecque suggests, the *Fêtes galantes* promised a "*salut*" to its anguished author, that salvation lay not wholly in the "words of altruism and fervor" of its first poem, "Clair de lune."[15] His *fantoches*, as I have remarked, enjoy, in their simple self-sufficiency, a salvation of a less precarious kind. "Pierrot" illustrates the danger of abandoning that self-sufficiency, of aping wan Clitandre, of sacrificing the simple pleasures of cheap wine and pâté for the less dependable *délices* of Colombine. It is a portrait of Pierrot after the "*Désastre*," when his isolation has acquired a consciousness and his figure the lineaments of tragic desire:

> *Ce n'est plus le rêveur lunaire du vieil air*
> *Qui riait aux aïeux dans les dessus de porte;*
> *Sa gaîté, comme sa chandelle, hélas! est morte,*
> *Et son spectre aujourd'hui nous hante, mince et clair.*

> *Et voici que parmi l'effroi d'un long éclair*
> *Sa pâle blouse a l'air, au vent froid qui l'emporte,*
> *D'un linceul, et sa bouche est béante, de sorte*
> *Qu'il semble hurler sous les morsures du ver.*

> *Avec le bruit d'un vol d'oiseaux de nuit qui passe,*
> *Ses manches blanches font vaguement par l'espace*
> *Des signes fous auxquels personne ne répond.*

---

[14] "Conference faite à Anvers" (1893), in Paul Verlaine, *Oeuvres en prose complètes*, ed. Jacques Borel ([Paris]: Gallimard [Bibliothèque de la Pléiade], 1972), p. 904. This edition will be cited throughout this chapter as *OEP*, with appropriate page numbers.

[15] *Lumières sur les* Fêtes galantes, p. 70.

Paul Verlaine

Ses yeux sont deux grands trous où rampe du phosphore
Et la farine rend plus effroyable encore
Sa face exsangue au nez pointu de moribond.
                                        (OPC, 320-21)

[This is no longer the lunar dreamer of the old song/
Who laughed at his ancestors at the top of the door;/
His gaiety, like his candle, alas! is dead,/And his specter haunts us today, thin and luminous.//And so it is
that amidst the terror of a long flash of lightning,/His
pale blouse has the aspect, in the cold wind that carries
it away,/Of a windingsheet, and his mouth is gaping,
so/That he seems to scream under the gnawings of the
worm.//With the sound of a passing flock of night-
birds,/His white sleeves make vaguely through space/
Mad signs to which no one responds.//His eyes are
two great holes where phosphorus creeps,/And his flour
renders more frightful still/His bloodless face with its
pinched nose of one near death.]

Now signaling hopelessly to the Other across empty space,
Pierrot has fallen into a world of human coordinates, of
social space and psychic duration, having relinquished the
self-determining gestures of the gayer "Pantomime." He
has also fallen into the depths of Verlaine's insidious *musique.* He seems threatened to be entombed there, among
the grave cadences, the dark internal assonances, the sonorous uvular rhymes. The cosmic wind tearing at his blouse,
the elegiac music of the verse: with both he is merging,
dissolving, but like a corpse under the worm, as if in a
black hole of estrangement and despair. Here the *voix érotique* inducts him into a moonless landscape, one riven by
lightning, where, motherless, he will obviously die alone.

"Pierrot" has a precedent—perhaps has a source—in *Pierrot*
(1860), a novella by Henri Rivière. Inspired by Deburau's
méchanceté and by Pierrot's criminality in "Shakspeare aux
Funambules," it tells the tale of one Charles Servieux, a
mime driven by madness to decapitate his rival during one
of his own fantastic *féeries.*[16] Its romantic extravagance seems

[16] For a full discussion, see my "Verlaine's Pierrots," *Romance Notes*, XX
(1979), 223-30.

both *en arrière* and *en avant* in the year of its publication: too late to exploit the sensationalism of a Pétrus Borel, it is yet too early for "decadent" fashionability. Similarly, the Pierrot of Verlaine's sonnet seems to stand in an ambiguous relationship with his other *rôles bergamasques*: "Pierrot" offers no *salut*; it, rather, inscribes the poet within its irredeemably pathetic hopelessness. A role with which Verlaine is not content. No Baudelaire, he rarely lingers long in the sloughs of self-laceration. *Sagesse, Bonheur*: the titles of his collections suggest the goals that he set himself, often in deplorable contravention of his own poetic gifts. In the years surrounding the composition of "Pierrot," he was experimenting with other masks, in fact, in which despair is forestalled by an ideal pose. In "Le Clown" (1867) it is the impassability of the *poète parnassien*, invulnerable in his "white satin armor," his eyes lifeless mirrors behind their "clay mask," disdainful of "*le peuple bête et laid*" (*OPC*, 324). In "Le Pitre" (1869) it is the ingenuousness of an engaging *baladin*, as light and drifting of wit (and affections?) as the butterfly that circles his wig.

In both poems, however, the poet is still alone. Contemptuously aloof in "Le Clown," estranged by his performance in "Le Pitre," his spectators "stamping before him in the mud" (*OPC*, 327), he has won serenity at the cost of his own passionate gregariousness. "*J'ai la fureur d'aimer*," Verlaine will declare in "Lucien Létinois" (*OPC*, 445). But he has great fear of love, as well: the presence of the Other, as I have been trying to show, is always a declaration of absence. "Absence" is, of course, in one sense what Verlaine professed to seek—an absence of the self in the wholly embodied pleasure of infancy. "Flesh! Love!" he exclaims in his sonnet "Invocation":

> ô tous les appétits *vers l'Absence,*
> *Toute la délirance et toute l'innocence* [. . .].[17]

[O *all the appetites* towards Absence,/All the deliriousness and all the innocence . . .]

---

[17] Paul Verlaine, *Correspondance*, ed. Ad. van Bever, I (Paris: Messein, 1922), 100. The sonnet was later revised and published in *Jadis et naguère* as "Luxures."

But, as in the *Fêtes galantes*, as in "Pierrot," the quest for this Absence leads to the realization of its unattainability—to an "absence" of a more absolute sort. And yet to abandon the quest is impossible, for the mere absence of the Other is intolerable. "Oh, absence!" he cries in *La Bonne Chanson*, "the least merciful of all evils!" (*OPC*, 148). And he returns to this theme in *Dans les limbes*:

> *J'ai dit jadis que l'absence*
> *Est le plus cruel des maux;*
> *On s'y berce avec des mots,*
> *C'est l'horreur de l'impuissance*
>
> *Sans la consolation*
> *Du moins de quelque caresse.*
> (*OPC*, 838)

[I once said that absence/Is the cruelest of evils;/One deludes oneself with words on that score:/It is the horror of powerlessness//Without the consolation/Even of a caress.]

Each of Verlaine's erotic relationships, as Antoine Adam has argued, was an abortive attempt to escape *l'impuissance*. Modeled upon the primary affective bond, it cast the lover into the role of mother and nurse, Verlaine into that of the child.[18] The poet's homosexuality seems to have been the definitive response to his dilemma: taking his own body as his ideal erotic object, he enjoyed his moments of self-presence as, paradoxically, moments of self-absenting *jouissance*.

But, as a poet, he sought a public role, one in which he could be "absolutely sincere," undisguisedly "himself," without of course confessing to what Lepelletier called "*moeurs contre nature*."[19] To speak more precisely, he sought a role that was not a mask, one that would deliver him from "*l'Enfer*" of absence (*OPC*, 397) but—unlike the lovers' masks of the *Fêtes galantes*—would not frustrate as it promised to facilitate his *salut*. How to enjoy the Other (and recover one's primordial self) in a presence unvitiated

[18] *Vrai Verlaine*, pp. 43, 75.
[19] Edmond Lepelletier, *Paul Verlaine: Sa Vie, son oeuvre* (Paris: Mercure de France, 1907), p. 27.

by Separation? To answer this impossible question (*vide* the evasions of Baudelaire), he turned once again to Pierrot.

He apparently first did so in the *Mémoires d'un veuf*, that uneven collection of heterogeneous prose sketches that he published in 1886. Pierrot seems misplaced there, even amid its heterogeneity, for he appears in a scenario, "Motif de pantomime." An "Apologie" defends its inclusion: "[. . .] if I have melted but not melded [*fondu et non confondu*] some apparently theatrical fragments into these 'memoirs' "—there is also a "Scenario pour ballet" featuring Gaspard Hauser—"who is to say that I didn't have my reasons?" (*OEP*, 84). Those reasons, he implies, are consistent with his choice of title. To the reader who would object that "this part of the book does not have the character of memoirs, as that word is ordinarily understood," he answers:

> "Autobiographically speaking, no; but I have the very clear right to make use of a word that is convenient, broad, traditionally elastic, to designate a series of impressions, reflections, etc., etc., emanating from a man who would be as free, independent, unconstrained—as disinterested as he is egoistical, and the spectator *par excellence*, for example—as a widow." (*OEP*, 84-85)

"*Libre, indépendant, dégagé, aussi désintéressé qu'égoïste*"—his words recall the Pierrot of the *Fêtes galantes*. Indeed, the *gamin* of "Motif de pantomime" has much of the latter's insouciance. But there are some very significant differences: first, he lives in Paris, not in a park *à la* Watteau. Born in a working-class quarter of the city, "*de parents tout petits marchands*" (*OEP*, 120), he has been transposed from what Octave Nadal calls vaguely "*le songe*" of the poet[20] to a world of verifiable "reality." Such a transposition would seem to bode little good. The earlier Pierrot of "Pantomime" seemed a creature of contentment precisely to the extent that he was a fantastic *fantoche*. Once liberated from his happy predestination of gesture and inducted into the

[20] *Paul Verlaine* (Paris: Mercure de France, 1961), *passim*.

human world, he lost, as "Pierrot" illustrates, both his independence and his joy. And yet "independence" is what Pierrot promises, apparently, to the author of the *Mémoires d'un veuf*. He does so because of a second difference, a difference to which we should devote some space.

This Pierrot is an adolescent: "Twelve years old, palish, tallish, rather thin" (*OEP*, 120). The precision of age is important: he is obviously a pre-pubescent *enfant*, his features still childishly unformed: "The face is long: vague features on a puny neck, a mediocre nose betraying disproportionate nostrils" (*OEP*, 120). That he is of any age at all is unusual: most Pierrots, as appropriate to their fantasy functions, are ageless. Perhaps Verlaine was inspired by the cartoons of Adolphe Willette, whose Pierrot was a ubiquitous *flâneur* of Parisian streets throughout the 'eighties and 'nineties. A brat, a bohemian, a *fumiste*, he appeared in every guise—but always strongly particularized—in the illustrated papers that Verlaine habitually read. And yet, for the aging poet, *le gamin* was Pierrot's only avatar. Certainly part of the attraction was in the appeal of youth, its audacity, liberty, and exuberance. In "Motif de pantomime," Pierrot is a careless waif, trailing his untied shoes through the mud of the gutters, plunging his fingers into a kitchenboy's gravy (after first having tripped him, *bien entendu*), "borrowing" the curé's surplice and skullcap for Shrove Tuesday, stealing pralines and prunes to please Colombine. But such delinquency is the province of all Pierrots. Why specifically, then, "Pierrot gamin"?

The answer lies in what we might call the sexual register of his youth. This Pierrot enjoys a peculiar relation to sexuality: at the end of his latency period (Verlaine's realism permits us such an apparently odd remark), he is still innocent of sexual fantasy. What this means may be explained by the nature of sexuality itself. In one of the most persuasive recent readings of Freud, Jean Laplanche has observed that, in the early *Project for a Scientific Psychology*, sexuality is identified as "the repressed *par excellence*."[21] Asking, Why is it our sexuality alone which is repressed? Freud answers that there must be some "characteristic of sexual ideas that can explain how it is that sexual ideas are alone subjected to repression" (*SE*, I, 352). That "characteristic" is a function of the conditions under which sexual "ideas" are obtained. The case of "Emma" illustrates those conditions clearly:

> Emma is subject at the present time to a compulsion of not being able to go into shops *alone*. As a reason for this, [she produced] a memory from the time when she was twelve years old (shortly after puberty). She went into a shop to buy something, saw the two shop-assistants (one of whom she can remember) laughing together, and ran away in some kind of *affect of fright*. In connection with this, she was led to recall that the two of them were laughing at her clothes and that one of them had pleased her sexually.
>
> [. . .]
>
> Further investigation now revealed a second memory, which she denies having had in mind at the moment of Scene I. Nor is there anything to prove this. On two occasions when she was a child of eight she had gone into a small shop to buy some sweets, and the shopkeeper had grabbed at her genitals through her clothes. In spite of the first experience she had gone there a second time; after the second time she stopped away. She now reproached herself for having gone there the second time, as though she had wanted in that way to provoke the assault. In fact a state of "oppressive bad conscience" is to be traced back to this experience. (*SE*, I, 353-54)

In the second scene (chronologically the first), Emma is ignorant of the sexual meaning attached to the shopkeeper's actions: the event, writes Laplanche, "has no immediate sexual effect, produces no excitation, and provokes no defense [. . .]."[22] The scene is, in Freud's words, "sexual-presexual." Of the first scene, Laplanche remarks,

> we might also say that it is equally lacking in sexuality, since it involves apparently banal circumstances, the fact that two shop assistants laugh at an adolescent's

---

[22] Ibid., p. 40.

clothing. No doubt, we might expand on the underlying sexual atmosphere of the scenario (convulsive
laughter, flight, etc.). What is beyond question is that
there is no sexual assault. Now that scene, however it
may, in fact, have transpired, will reactivate the memory of the first scene, and through the mediation of
that memory, "trigger" or "release" (*entbinden*) a sexual reaction in its double form: both a physiological
excitation and a series of ideas that young Emma, now
in puberty, will henceforth have at her disposition.[23]

In other words, as a prepubescent young girl, Emma was
"incapable of linking what happened to anything *corre-
sponding* to it within her": she was utterly without a sexual
consciousness. Only after she had passed that temporal barrier which inscribed the scenes *"in two different spheres of
meaning"* was she able to understand—and respond to—
the sexual dimension of the assault. "Between the two
scenes," writes Laplanche, "an entirely new element has appeared—the possibility of a sexual reaction."[24]
   And yet I think it is possible—indeed, necessary—to read
Freud's texts with somewhat more critical attention. The
Emma of the earlier scene does not, in fact, seem ignorant
of its sexual meaning. Laplanche himself observes:

> there has undoubtedly been a sexual assault by the adult
> but it might also be said that, inversely, there has been
> seduction by the little girl, since she returns to the
> store, clearly in order to submit again to the same kind
> of act. To the extent that memory and fantasy can con-
> dense into a single scene several successive events as
> well as *distribute* into a temporal sequence the simul-
> taneous elements of an experience, nothing prevents
> us from wondering whether the girl, *on the very first
> occasion*, had not gone into the store, moved by some
> obscure sexual premonition.[25]

When Freud summarizes his hypothesis, he refers to Emma's reaction in the later scene as evidence of a *different*

[23] Ibid.
[24] Ibid.
[25] Ibid., p. 39.

"understanding" on her part, not of a dissipation of ignorance: "Here we have the case of a memory arousing an affect which it did not arouse as an experience, because in the meantime the change [brought about] in puberty had made possible a different understanding of what was remembered" (*SE*, I, 356). The "affect" which is excited seems to differ in only one important respect from Emma's initial reaction: it has been *deflected by fear and guilt into neurotic behavior; it has acquired a fantasmatic character.* Her sexuality, in short, has become *subject to the deformations* of repression.

The implications of this turn may be appreciated when we recall a later Freudian text, a famous passage from the *Three Essays on the Theory of Sexuality*:

> At a time at which the first beginnings of sexual satisfaction are still linked with the taking of nourishment, the sexual instinct has a sexual object outside the infant's own body in the shape of his mother's breast. It is only later that the instinct loses that object, just at the time, perhaps, when the child is able to form a total idea of the person to whom the organ that is giving him satisfaction belongs. *As a rule the sexual instinct then becomes auto-erotic, and not until the period of latency has been passed through is the original relation restored.* There are thus good reasons why a child sucking at his mother's breast has become the prototype of every relation of love. The finding of an object is in fact a refinding of it. (*SE*, VII, 222, my italics)

Here Freud is proposing a radical distinction between the two principal epochs of prepubescent sexuality: the early, so-called "anaclitic" period, comprising the familiar infantile phases "propped up" on the vital functions, and a later autoerotic period, in which all such relations are severed. The suggestion is strong that the severing is of both real and fantasmatic relations, that the "breast" as a fantasmatic object is not "recovered" until the period of latency has been passed. Such a conclusion, of course, supports our remarks above about "Emma." We are led to assume, to extrapolate from both texts, that the "latency period" is a period of nonfantasmatic sexuality, or of fantasy in which the Other at best plays a feeble role. Such—to return to Verlaine and his "Motif de pantomime"—is the sexual position of Pierrot.

In this respect he is, of course, a counterpart of the Pierrot in the *Fêtes galantes*. Both are self-pleasuring, auto-erotic; more importantly, both are by definition (to use that word in its delimiting sense) without fantasmatic memory of the primordial matrix of desire. And, being innocent of infantile fantasy, they suffer no sense of separation, none of the anguish that suffuses "Pierrot." But, whereas in "Pantomime" Pierrot escapes this consciousness only by virtue of his role as *fantoche*, the Pierrot *gamin* of the *Mémoires d'un veuf* is a creature who is demonstrably of the world. Having emerged from *le songe* of the early poetry, he promises a human *salut*. Verlaine has, in part, answered the question that we posed at the end of the first section of this essay, and done so by reducing its terms. Since the primordial self is affectively irrecoverable without an attendant consciousness of its loss, it is to be struck from psychic life altogether: what Richard calls Verlaine's "impersonal ego," which recalls the strange ecstasies of his past, is to be no longer an agency of memory, knowledge, or desire. Hence his late poetic principle, described in the "Critique des *Poèmes saturniens*" (1890): "Sincerity and, in the satisfaction of its ends, *the impression of the moment followed to the letter* are my preferred rule today" (*OEP*, 720, my italics). The moment without a past is the moment without regret. It is the moment of *bonheur*, when, *sans arrière-pensée*, Pierrot licks the gravy from his fingers.

And yet such a role, even were it possible to enjoy, has the failings of "Le Clown" or "Le Pitre": the poet is still alone. What of that moment when, in Freud's words, "the original relation [is] restored," when the Other appears—as it must to one who has a *fureur d'aimer*—on the scene of postpubescent desire? Verlaine broaches this problem uncertainly in an epilogue to "Motif de pantomime." There Arlequin, Pierrot, and Colombine are *"cette âge glorieux, Vingt Ans!"* The lovers, Arlequin and Colombine, live in a passionate present moment, "without tenderness, violent in its feelings"; Pierrot, on the other hand, seems furtive, "cowardly but prudent, libidinous but outwardly continent" (*OEP*, 123-24). His adult sexuality has been relegated to the wings of this pantomime; onstage he is still the self-indulgent *enfant*:

> Pierrot is their friend in a vaguely subservient capacity. He, too, is happy, wanting nothing, and eating everything, drinking everything [. . .]. Ah! he has pleasures of his own, little tricks he plays that are sometimes hard on them, corrected by a kick of a pointed toe, by a slap with beringed fingers. It makes no difference: he has had his fun, laughed, smiled. And then he has not a care. At times the others must still use guile to win a victory over existence. He lives in their wake like a fish in water. No remorse, no regret for anything at all. (*OEP*, 124)

But, as if this were an unsatisfactory position, Verlaine takes up the problem in "Pierrot gamin," a poem published in *Le Décadent*, September 14, 1886, two months before the appearance of the *Mémoires d'un veuf*. The first verse opens aggressively: "This is not an embryonic Pierrot"; it is a "Pierrot *gamin*, Pierrot *gosse*,/The green walnut outside of its shell" (*OPC*, 520). Here the sexual boundary has been crossed: Pierrot's features have sharpened, his appetites have declared themselves, and he is clearly ready to satisfy them:

> *Bien qu'un rien plus haut qu'un mètre,*
> *Le mignon drôle sait mettre*
> *Dans ses yeux l'éclair d'acier*
> *Qui sied au subtil génie*
> *De sa malice infinie*
> *De poète-grimacier.*
>
> *Lèvres rouge-de-blessure*
> *Où sommeille la luxure,*
> *Face pâle aux rictus fins,*
> *Longue, très accentuée,*
> *Qu'on dirait habituée*
> *A contempler toutes fins,*
>
> *Corps fluet et non pas maigre,*
> *Voix de fille et non pas aigre,*

Corps d'éphèbe en tout petit,
Voix de tête, corps en fête,
Créature toujours prête
A soûler chaque appétit.
(*OPC*, 520)

[Although hardly any taller than a yardstick,/The ro-
guish little devil knows how to put/The steely glint in
his eyes/That suits the subtle genius/Of his infinite
malice/As a grimacing poet-charlatan.//With lips as red
as a wound,/On which lasciviousness sleeps;/A pale face
lit by cunning grins,/Long, its features very sharp,/Ac-
customed (one might say)/To contemplating every
outcome;//A body slim but not scrawny,/A voice girl-
ish but not shrill/—The body of a young ephebus in
miniature,/A head voice, a body on holiday—/[He is]
a creature always ready/To slake every appetite.]

The headlong *vers impair*, the naïve toy-drum rhythms, the
exhilaratingly insistent repetitions ("*C'est Pierrot, Pierrot,
Pierrot!*" [*OPC*, 520]), all propel the reader (and poet) towards an utterly unreflective identification with this "*ca-
marade*," this "*frère*" (*OPC*, 521). They also imply an analogous spontaneity in the character of Pierrot himself. This
is a *gamin* so receptive to the immediate moment—at least
so Verlaine would himself believe—that the past has simply
ceased to exist. And without a past, Pierrot is without a
conscience: he can be both "vile" and "lofty," "noble" and
"base" (*OPC*, 521), because those oppositions have no
meaning within the ahistorical purity of the present. For
his creator, the severance is complete: not only have the
fantasmatic relations of infancy been repudiated, but the
frustration (and violence) that accompanied the grief of their
loss no longer evokes anguish or guilt. Both he and Pierrot
share "*innocents esprits*," the *gamin* a "symbol" of his "simplicity" (*OPC*, 521).

But the symbol is also a "grimace": Pierrot is a "caricature" of his creator here (*OPC*, 521). In the false intoxication of the pose, Verlaine seems to have descried the purely
literary character of the *salut*. And as if again seeking to
inscribe the role within reality, he undertakes a final experiment in *Gosses*, specifically the four sketches that appeared

under this title in *Art et Critique* of 1889.[26] Striking from the character the props of art—the theatrical premise of "Motif de pantomime," the rhetorical artificiality of "Pierrot gamin"—he conceives these sketches as a series of *histoires*, as portraits from life or as transcriptions of encounters between poet and streetwise waifs. Pierrot appears as a "Pierrot *noirouffe*" (*OEP*, 216), no longer a mask but a metaphor. He is a vehicle of meaning for a tyrant of the courtyards, a "*soldat en herbe*," whose mouth is equal to the fists of his companions, who is naïvely eager to fight the Boches. Still boyishly ugly (the women are waiting for him to make them "suffer"), he asks the poet for cigarettes in an "instinctively fraternal voice," adding "in a lisp that for you is natural but which you exaggerate, and with a broad, falsely emphatic gesture, borrowed from me, 'or a cigar, in a pinch' " (*OEP*, 216). For all his apparent crudity, this is a Pierrot of spontaneous warmth: "And then I have seen you crying, when your mother was ill, and make one day, while seated on the sidewalk (comfortably enough, at that), a big sign of the cross when a corpse passed by" (*OEP*, 216). What the poet admires in him is his "being so spontaneous in so simple a passion" (*OEP*, 217). In his way, this Pierrot has become a *fantoche vivant*, now worked by the strings of passionate impulse, by an *élan* "so ardent—and so exemplary!" (*OEP*, 217). "Simplicity," "spontaneity," "naturalness": these are also the qualities of his companion *gosses*—of the boy ("*cher enfant si joli* [. . .] *si affectueux*" [*OEP*, 215]) who helps the poet to his feet after a fall, or who abandons his homework "to seize the fork and spoon for a duty [*devoir*] that is, finally, natural" (*OEP*, 218). Later each will become, as Verlaine says of one, "*méchant, oh non! mais mauvais*" (*OEP*, 216). Meanwhile, in their nostalgically privileged sexuality—they tremble on the brink of pubescent maturity, too young to indulge in frustrating fantasy, too old to be ignorant of appetite—they live as insouciant *naïfs*.

For Verlaine they are both subject and object: roles in

[26] A fifth related sketch, first published in the *Oeuvres posthumes*, appears as the third of the series in *OEP*, 217; I draw upon this sketch in the remarks that follow.

which to project the self, mirrors in which to seize the Other. The affectionate voice of "Motif de pantomime," which was merely in anonymous complicity with its subject, is, in *Gosses*, assigned to the speaker "Verlaine" himself: there is now a dialogue between poet and Pierrot. And yet in this strategy to give a kind of social authenticity to his encounter with the type, one detects a retreat into fantasy far deeper than in the ambivalent *Fêtes galantes*. The Other now reflects not only body but psychic self, giving back to the poet a self-fabricated image of *salut*. One thinks inevitably of Verlaine's sexual companions—of the boyish Rimbaud ("a true child's head, plump and fresh, on a big bony body that seemed to betray the clumsiness of an adolescent who was still growing" [*OEP*, 974]), or of Lucien Létinois, with his ephebe's physique, "Like a lanky Pierrot on fatigue-duty" (*OPC*, 451), or of the "streetboys with lesbian eyes" (*OPC*, 509) in *Parallèlement*, or of the faceless *gosses* in *Hombres*. Standing before them as before the mirror of an ideal self, the poet has been gradually effaced from the world[27]—from precisely that world he had affected to enter. He has entered, instead, a mythology, in which the impossible goal of "simplicity" lures him on towards a factitious salvation. Treacherous, it has the sanction of public myth: only the *naïf*, for example, "*Simple comme un enfant*" (*OPC*, 260), may petition the grace of God. And it is but a single step from this (impossible) postulant to the (irrecoverably) naïve *pubère*: thus the vulgar logic of Pierrot's self-satisfaction in "Motif de pantomime." He is strolling down the sidewalk in the curé's stolen vestments, "and, having looked at himself in the mirror of a *charcutier*, the pale lad in disguise—neither more nor less than his God, yours and mine, on the evening of each day of Creation—rejoices in his costume, and sees that it is good [or "a good joke": *la trouve bien bonne celle-là*]" (*OEP*, 122).

As James Lawler has observed, with more acuity than he seems to realize, we are confronted, throughout Verlaine's

---

[27] Cf. the interesting discussion by Jeanne Bem, "Verlaine, poète lunaire: Mythe et langage poétique," *Stanford French Review*, IV (winter 1980), 379-93.

poetry, with the project of *"making oneself naïf,* in the same way as Rimbaud spoke of the need to 'make oneself a visionary.' "[28] Unlike Rimbaud, however, Verlaine will not admit defeat. From the "simplicity" of the spirit, he oscillates to the "simplicity" of the flesh, growing apparently more wearied with every disillusionment, until, at the end, his poetry seems merely a hollow patter of words. *"Posterity is entreated,"* he writes of *Epigrammes,* an "opuscule" conceived by *"a sick man wishing to distract himself," "to see nothing in this but a game"* (*OPC,* 849). At bottom he knows that the rules of his own game are against him; that he has no choice but to fail. "These new 'notes on my life,' " he observes, confusedly, in anticipation of Part II of his *Confessions,* "will be of a character at once literary and . . . social, of a darker and darker complexion, concerning, as they do, the existence—still less and less luminous as it emerges, alas! into the light—of this complicated self, one not at all to my liking, as an utterly simple and perhaps naïve man" (*OEP,* 491).

The *Livre posthume* (1893-94) is a clear-eyed admission of ruin: "The poet has finished his task./The man has not."

> *Pour l'homme,—le poète à part et lyre et luth*
> *Bien écartés,—mal occupé de son "salut"*
> *Peut-être autant que ce poète qu'est lui-même,*
> *Son rôle n'est joué qu'à demi, le problème*
> *De sa vie, il ne l'a résolu que si peu*
> *Qu'il n'est pas sûr de quoi que ce soit devant Dieu.*
>
> (*OPC,* 816)

[For the man—apart from the poet, and his lyre and lute/Quite aside—ill occupied with his "salvation"/Perhaps as much as this poet that is himself,/His role is only half played out, the problem/Of his life so little resolved/That he is not sure of his fate before God.]

He now seeks in his debilitated verse ("[. . .] *c'est curieux ce qu'il/Gagne en cordial de ce qu'il perd en subtil"* [*OPC,* 817]) the fantasmatic *"paradis"* that he had resisted: "A comfortable room, quite warm, quite fresh,/Fresh as an arbor, warm

---

[28] "Verlaine's 'Naiveté,' " *Essays in French Literature,* II (November 1965), 98.

as a creche" (*OPC*, 817). In love he surrenders himself to the "infinite weaknesses/Of a mama for her little brat" (*OPC*, 819). For his consciousness of Separation is weakening: "[. . .] nothingness is good for me,/For this absurd and fragile being;/It is what I need [. . .]" (*OPC*, 821). Only three years from death, he is moving towards the Absence he had coveted (*"Toi le souvenir, moi l'absence"* [*OPC*, 822]): he need struggle no longer against its elusive allure. These "Fragments" offer a glimpse of transcendent serenity in a life pathetically bent on embodying it. But they come too late to redeem him, or to regenerate the wasteland of his failed art.

Pierrot Vanishes:
Paul Margueritte and
Stéphane Mallarmé

[. . .] mais comment se conjuguaient les verbes de ce per-
pétuel présent qu'est la pantomime, et leurs nuances?

PAUL MARGUERITTE
Le Printemps tourmenté (1925)

[. . .] il n'est pas de Présent, non—un présent n'existe
pas . . .

STÉPHANE MALLARMÉ
"Variations sur un sujet:
L'Action restreinte" (1895)

Derrida's lecture "La Double Séance" brings together three
unlikely pieces—a passage from the *Philebus* of Plato, a
pantomime by Paul Margueritte entitled *Pierrot assassin de
sa femme* (1881), and "Mimique" by Mallarmé, a response
to his reading of Margueritte's pantomime in the text of its
second edition (1886). The latter two are actually offered
as a critique of the ideas in the first, for despite the puerility
of *Pierrot assassin de sa femme* and the brevity of Mallarmé's
"Mimique," both encourage, according to Derrida, a radical rethinking of mimesis. Plato, as Derrida reminds us,
conceives thought in the *Philebus* as a kind of mimetic writing: "It appears to me," remarks Socrates to Protarchus,
"that the conjunction of memory with sensations, together
with the feelings consequent upon memory and sensation,
may be said as it were to write words in our souls [. . .]."[1]

---

[1] Cited in Jacques Derrida, "The Double Session," *Dissemination*, tr.

These words are inscribed in the soul's "book," where they are read, in silence, as thought. The sensations transcribed, the memories recovered, the feelings experienced, or reexperienced, are, according to such reasoning, prior to all discourse; thinking, on the other hand, is subsequent to it, is synonymous with the reading of it. That discourse is, in turn, prior to the operations of a "second artist [. . .] in our souls," a "painter [. . .] who comes after the writer and paints [. . .] pictures of these assertions that we make" (*D*, 175). His *imitatio* is assigned an ambiguous status. On the one hand, having come *after* the writer, he is a mere illustrator, decorator, or re-presenter of the former's discourse about the world; on the other hand, he seems capable of purifying that discourse of its status as mere verbal commentary: "How do we make out," asks Protarchus of this painter, "that he in his turn acts, and when?" And Socrates answers: "When we have got those opinions and assertions clear of the act of sight [. . .] or other sense, and as it were see in ourselves pictures or images [. . .] of what we previously opined or asserted" (*D*, 175). True "in-sight" is then the achievement of a painterly translation or refinement of a discourse that declares itself "originary" and, therefore, superior to any such refinement or translation.

"So that in psychic writing," Derrida concludes, "between the *zōgraphia* and the *logos* (or *dianoia*) there exists a very strange relation: one is always the supplement of the other."

> In the first part of the scene, the thought that directly fixed the essence of things did not essentially need the illustrative ornament that writing and painting constituted. The soul's thinking was only intimately linked to *logos* [. . .]. Inversely, a bit further on, painting (in the metaphorical sense of psychic painting, of course, just as a moment ago it was a question of psychic writing) is what gives us the image of the thing itself, what communicates to us the direct intuition, the immediate vision of the thing, freed from the discourse that

Barbara Johnson (Chicago: University of Chicago Press, 1981), p. 175. Derrida's collection will be cited throughout this chapter as *D*, with appropriate page numbers.

accompanied it, or even encumbered it. Naturally, I would like to stress [. . .], it is always the *metaphors* of painting and writing that are linked in this way back and forth: we recall that, on another plane, outside these metaphors, Plato always asserts that in their literal sense painting and writing are totally incapable of any intuition of the thing itself, since they only deal in copies, and in copies of copies. (*D*, 189-90)

What such an analysis suggests is that there is no leaving the closed circle of imitation, that neither through the word nor through the image is "the thing itself" to be apprehended. "Perhaps, then," Derrida concludes, "there is always more than one kind of *mimēsis*; and perhaps it is in the strange mirror that reflects but also displaces and distorts one *mimēsis* into the other, as though it were itself destined to mime or mask *itself*, that history—the history of literature—is lodged, along with the whole of its interpretation" (*D*, 191).

It is within this strange mirror that he lodges "Mimique" and *Pierrot assassin de sa femme*. The mime, assiduously mimicking reality, in fact mimicks "nothing":

There is no imitation. The Mime imitates nothing. And to begin with, he doesn't imitate. There is nothing prior to the writing of his gestures. Nothing is prescribed for him. No present has preceded or supervised the tracing of his writing. His movements form a figure that no speech anticipates or accompanies. (*D*, 194)

The very image of *mimēsis*, he "mimes reference" itself; he "is not an imitator; he mimes imitation" (*D*, 219). Or so runs the boldest argument. Derrida qualifies it significantly at another point in his essay: "*There is* mimicry," he concedes, for both Margueritte and Mallarmé. Neither conceives the mime as the mere generator of nonmimetic gesture—as, for example, an Etienne Decroux, whose performance *in praesentia* is his only enigmatic "meaning." "We are faced then," he concludes, "with mimicry imitating nothing; faced, so to speak, with a double that doubles no simple, a double that nothing anticipates, nothing at least that is not itself already double. There is no simple reference" (*D*, 206). The qualifications are immensely important: between the assertions that the mime "imitates nothing" and that "there is no simple reference" lies more than a difference of degree. A Zeno among modern thinkers, reckless of the differential calculus of perception, memory, and desire, Derrida equates here, as he habitually does elsewhere, the specular with the phantasmal, the ambiguous with the indeterminate, the nonoriginary with nothing itself. But we must keep these two classes of phenomena apart. To confuse them is to elide important differences— not the least of which are those between "Mimique" and *Pierrot assassin de sa femme*. In "La Double Séance" the second anticipates the first, Mallarmé uncovering in Margueritte's little pantomime the principles set forth in "Mimique." But this is to simplify the relationship and to obscure Mallarmé's extraordinary achievement. Derrida clearly appreciates that achievement, but it will appear the more extraordinary if set in relief against Paul Margueritte's career, against the texts of his life and forgotten art.

He discovered the theater during his boyhood in Algeria, at a performance in Blidah of *Les Rendezvous bourgeois*:

I understand nothing of the dialogue, of the stage business, but an actor in tight nankeen breeches and a big cocked hat of the Directory, who slips through the casement-window or squeezes into the wall-cupboard, sends me into transports. I cause a scandal with my laughter; my mother has to calm me down. For eight days I declame, I write plays, I rig myself out in cheap finery: the very keen taste that I've retained of the theater and that has all but made an actor of me dates from that evening. Seized strongly by that artificiality of the sets, of the gestures, of the words, by the dazzle of the makeup, by the waking dream that I had lived, I will keep its imprint forever. I have anticipated the pleasure of transforming oneself, of creating illusory existences, of incarnating beings of fantasy, of legend, or of history: *Pierrot assassin de sa femme*, its white and tragic phantom, the pantomime that I have so much loved, our stages in the country at Valvins, at Samois, at Vétheuil: they've all come from that.[2]

Later, in Paris, working as a copyist in the Ministère de l'Instruction Publique but indulging, in his evenings, "*un goût très Jeune-France et Pétrus Borel,*"[3] Margueritte nursed vague ambitions of making his mark in literature or on the stage. Irresistibly, almost unaccountably, he was drawn to the moribund pantomime.

He had seen none of the illustrious Pierrots, neither Deburau *fils* nor Legrand nor Rouffe; his first scenarios were for the most part inspired by literary texts, such as his *Rétameur*, based upon Gautier's "Shakspeare aux Funambules." But, determined to give Pierrot palpable life, he began performing, in 1881, in a makeshift theater in Valvins, where the Margueritttes, like their relative, Stéphane Mallarmé, then took their summer retreats. Its *salle* was nothing but a converted painter's atelier in the upper loft of a barn. A plank floor upon trestles, illuminated by candles, constituted its only stage. Its curtains were bedsheets; its scenery, a few folding-screens covered with foliage. But for prompter, poet, and *metteur-en-scène* it had Paul's cousin and neighbor, Stéphane; for Colombine it had Mallarmé's daughter, Geneviève. For two summers both Paul and Victor, his brother, were to present Hugo, Gautier, and Banville to the villagers, and Paul was to incarnate Pierrot. Mallarmé, who had seen both Deburau *fils* and Legrand, "whipped up" Margueritte's "emulation" of these artists; he in fact advised him to see Legrand, then playing in a revue at the Variétés.[4] Neither the mime nor Banville, from whom he next sought encouragement, was sympathetic to his "Pierrot *satanique.*" But over the next several years, as he was becoming established as a novelist, Margueritte continued to write his "*monomimes,*" and to per-

---

[2] Paul Margueritte, *Souvenirs d'enfance: Les Pas sur le sable* (Paris: Plon-Nourrit et Cie, 1906), pp. 149-50.

[3] Paul Margueritte, *Le Printemps tourmenté* (Paris: Flammarion, 1925), p. 18.

[4] Paul Margueritte, "Le Mythe de Pierrot," *Nos Tréteaux: Charades de Victor Margueritte, pantomimes de Paul Margueritte* (Paris: Les Bibliophiles Fantaisistes, 1910), p. 15; Margueritte, *Printemps tourmenté*, p. 33.

form, whenever he was given the opportunity, *Pierrot assassin de sa femme.*[5]

In spite (perhaps because) of its puerility, it is an intriguing and powerful piece. Pierrot and a *croquemort* return from the cemetery where Colombine has just been buried. After several glasses of cognac (they gallantly lift them "to the health of the deceased," as she smiles from her portrait on the wall), Pierrot unceremoniously turns out his companion and begins to undress for bed. But a memory obsesses him: for it is he who has killed his wife. She had fleeced him, beat him, furnished his forehead with horns—"but what does all that matter?" He has killed her because it amused him to do so. His crime is undiscoverable (he congratulates himself): no rope, no knife, no phial of poison had disfigured her body or face. He had tickled the soles of her feet until she had quite literally laughed to death. (And Pierrot mimes the scene, leaping in and out of his great bed, playing victim and murderer, until, after an ambiguous "*spasme suprême*," Colombine gives up the ghost.) His exertions have tired him, he is ready for sleep; but suddenly he is seized by a tickling: Colombine is exacting a revenge. To escape, he invokes a "remedy": "the sovereign boon of drunkenness." Indeed, after one bottle, he grows spirited, fantastical, amorous: the next bottle he caresses like the hand of a woman; it "dances in his hand and gives him a spasm that excites, lasciviously, arms, head, and legs, a spasm that ends in a swoon." He again toasts the portrait, then casts a lecherous glance at the bed. But the champagne is wearing off; his gaiety ebbs away. He breaks the neck of one last bottle, drains it, and collapses in a heap. Suddenly bed and portrait seem to glow, and Colombine seems to be laughing. Pierrot gets up to investigate and, in his stupor, ignites the bedclothes with his candle. The room is run through with flames; Pierrot's feet are

[5] On the Théâtre de Valvins and Margueritte's relations with the pantomime in general, see the following titles by Paul Margueritte: "Notice," *Pierrot assassin de sa femme*, 2nd ed. (Paris: Lévy, 1886), pp. 5-9; *Le Jardin du passé* (Paris: Chailley, 1896), pp. 19-38; *Souvenirs de jeunesse: Les jours s'allongent* (Paris: Plon-Nourrit et Cie, 1908), pp. 236, 274-75, 284-86; *Printemps tourmenté*, pp. 22-60, 73, 75-78, 96-97, 157-60, 176-82; *Nos Tréteaux*, pp. 9-23.

again seized with an epileptic dancing; from his own throat bursts the laughter of his victim at her death. And after a violent seizure of all his person, he dies at the foot of the portrait, his arms extended like a cross.[6]

A "tragic nightmare *à la* Hoffmann or Edgar Poe" is how Margueritte described the pantomime; and he cited still other sources: "The reading of a tragic story by Commander [Henri] Rivière, as well as two lines by Gautier:

> *L'histoire du Pierrot qui chatouilla sa femme*
> *Et lui fit de la sorte, en riant, rendre l'âme.[7]*

[The tale of Pierrot, who tickled his wife/And thus made her, with laughter, give up her life.]

induced my satanic, ultra-Romantic, and yet very modern conception: a subtle, neurotic, cruel, and ingenuous Pierrot, uniting in himself all contrasts, a veritable psychical Proteus, a bit sadistic, willingly drunken, and perfectly villainous."[8] Such was Rivière's Pierrot, a "mysterious and redoutable Proteus," a "genius of evil," by turns "splendidly sinister" and "grotesquely base."[9] In this tale of a young mime unhinged by Poesque *supplices* and seduced by the cruelty of Deburau, the vulgar heartlessness of his Alexandrine—her extravagance, imperiousness, and infidelity—lead also to crime, remorse, and death. The tale even includes a reference to "those nameless convulsions of the wife whose husband ties one night to a bed, and whom he slowly murders in tickling the soles of her feet."[10] As Derrida remarks, a pursuit through "the back corridors and genealogies" of this piece of business—through Lassailly's *Les Roueries de Trialph, notre contemporain, avant son suicide* (1833), for example, or Webster's *White Devil* (1612) (or other plays ap-

---

[6] My quotations are from the text of the pantomime in *Nos Tréteaux*, pp. 100, 101, 103, 104, 105. The pantomime is given an introduction and excellent translation by Daniel Gerould (under the title "Paul Margueritte and *Pierrot Assassin of His Wife*") in *The Drama Review*, XXIII (March 1979), 103-19.

[7] Théophile Gautier, *Pierrot posthume*, in *Oeuvres complètes*, XV, 194 (slightly misquoted).

[8] *Nos Tréteaux*, p. 15.

[9] Henri Rivière, *Pierrot/Caïn* (Paris: Hachette, 1860), pp. 24, 26.

[10] Ibid., p. 47.

parently unknown to Derrida in which it is a matter of a ticklish death)[11]—would suggest that *Pierrot assassin de sa femme* is but one element in "a text extending far out of sight" (*D*, 204*n*, 203).

A text, he would add, that is limitless, bottomless, and reflexive. For to what do Pierrot's actions refer? Colombine's "spasm" is ambiguous. Is it merely an announcement of *la petite mort*? And is it not the spasm of Pierrot himself, of this murderer doubling for his victim? Does the "spasm," then, induced by that dancing bottle suggest that the "remedy" for his own "tickling" is suicide, a "sort of masturbatory suicide," in the words of Derrida (*D*, 201)? Colombine herself seems an expendable element in this ghostly mental play. "In the final analysis," Derrida concludes, "what happens is nothing, no violence, no stigmata, no traces; the perfect crime in that it can be confused only with the heights of pleasure [*jouissance*] obtainable from a certain speculation" (*D*, 201). The "speculation" is upon that "reality" residing outside all representation: "[. . .] reality, indeed, is death. It will prove to be inaccessible, otherwise than by simulacrum, just like the dreamed-of *simplicity* of the supreme spasm" (*D*, 206), which seems to unite the lover and his beloved—as it separates the murderer from his victim.

But even though she is dispensable, Colombine cannot be dismissed from the play. Derrida tries, sophistically, to deny that a murder has occurred. No crime has been committed, he declares: "Never, anywhere, not even in the theatrical fiction" (*D*, 200).

> There is only the memory of a crime that has never been committed, not only because on the stage we have never seen it in the present (the Mime is recalling it), but also because no violence has been exerted (someone has been made to die of laughter, and then the "criminal"—bursting with hilarity—is absolved by his own death), and because this crime is its opposite: an act of love. (*D*, 214)

Tell it to the poor girl's mother: Colombine—at least the Colombine of the "theatrical fiction"—is undeniably dead.

---

[11] Such as Fatouville's *Arlequin, Empereur dans la lune* (1684), in which Arlequin tries to tickle himself to death.

We know she is because of that undertaker's mute, an emissary from beyond Pierrot's lewd speculation, setting fantasy within the dark frame of "reality": "And here we've just come from out there, where we've put her in the ground."[12] If there has been no "crime," there has been an event; Colombine has been the victim of *jouissance*. Pierrot's motives are ambiguous, admittedly, but his actions do more than mime mimicry: they mime that event towards which the title implacably gestures: the murder of his wife. What they mime, in effect, is a writing for which there is a private text. For even when Margueritte is not inspired by tales of pedal terror, his Pierrot is murdering his wife. In *Colombine pardonnée* (1888), the most admired of Margueritte's pantomimes after *Pierrot assassin de sa femme*, Pierrot takes a knife to Colombine when she persists in playing the coquette. Taken together with Margueritte's other scenarios, these pieces suggest a structural necessity, of which the recurrent elements are three: a Pierrot loves a faithless Colombine; both are involved in a "crime" of erotically charged cruelty, usually initiated by Pierrot himself; Pierrot dies as a result of the crime. One of the elements is sometimes omitted (*Colombine pardonnée*); all three may be telescoped into an early scene of the pantomime (*Pierrot mort et vivant*); or the structure may be merely implicit, Pierrot's fear and death unexplained (*La Peur*).[13] The pantomime entitled *Au cou du chat* plays the most sophisticated variation on this structure. Here the capricious Colombine has three amusing *jouets*—her husband, Pierrot, her black cat, Mime, and her cigar-smoking lover, Arlequin. On a day heavy with summer heat she disports with all three in the garden: her cat she nestles between her breasts; her husband she tramples like a trampoline, skipping over his prostrate person ("*Encore!*" he cries in a martyr's ecstasy) within the "golden circle" of her rope. ("One would think," Margueritte un-

---

[12] *Nos Tréteaux*, p. 99.

[13] All of the pantomimes mentioned here appear, without dates of composition or first publication, in *Nos Tréteaux*; one pantomime, *Amoureux de la lune*, abandons the structure I describe to illustrate a more public sentiment: it gives voice (if such a phrase is permissible) to a *carpe diem* theme. Margueritte returns to the structure in *La Mort de Pierrot*, which appears in translation in *Pastels in Prose*, tr. Stuart Merrill (New York: Harper & Brothers, 1890), pp. 215-18.

necessarily explains, "that she danced in her own nimbus.") On a whim, this "Salomé *funambulesque*" then slips a gold circle—that is, one of her bracelets—over Mime's velvety neck: frightened, the cat disappears. Pierrot lures it back, and then—*ô horreur!*—Mime is spread out on a chopping-block, for the bracelet cannot be removed. As Colombine looks on with quivering nostrils, both "entranced and ter-rified," Arlequin brings down the cleaver: "The cat's head comes off like a champagne cork, and the bracelet, thrown up around a crimson fountain, goes rolling into the bloody grass." Triumphantly Colombine retrieves it: and wipes it on the "immaculate" blouse of Pierrot.[14]

Here, too, we are confronted with a text "extending far out of sight," through the "Hérodiade" of Margueritte's cousin Stéphane, through Jean Lorrain's poem "Salomé" (1884), in which Pierrot's head is produced on a platter, through the other *femmes fatales* of the Romantic Agony—and through the pages of Margueritte's life. One of the first of those pages is an apparently minor incident from his childhood. His father's orderly, Margueritte recalls in his *Souvenirs d'enfance*, "is mixed up in one of my great sor-rows, having told me that the cat has had several kittens, and that they are going to be drowned. Outraged, I bear a complaint to my mother, who explains to me (without con-vincing me of it) the necessity of this massacre."[15] The event was transposed to his first novel, *Tous Quatre* (1885), a book, as Margueritte was to declare in his last volume of memoirs, which "is to me what *David Copperfield* is to Dickens."[16] There the incident is given a symbolic func-tion. The young hero, Léon, has never known his mother, having been delivered from her corpse after she had died from a fall; now, at the age of seven, he begins to suffer "a sadness of spirit, a melancholy of the motherless child."

The following year was marked by a great event. A cat to which Léon had taken a fancy had her litter. By the commander's orders, the little ones were going to

[14] My quotations are from the text of the pantomime in *Nos Tréteaux*, pp. 127, 126, 129.
[15] *Souvenirs d'enfance*, p. 140.
[16] *Printemps tourmenté*, p. 112.

be thrown in the water, into the hollow ravine at the bottom of the garden, between the high banks where a wide stream flowed. Léon, in his ignorance, was overwhelmed. Drown these little kittens, so precious?

"Whatever for? Why? What would the mother-cat say: what would human mothers say if their little ones were thrown in the water? . . ."

The commander laughed at these questions and these wild supplications. Kittens were simply gotten rid of. Léon broke down, sobbed. Two days later, seeing the mother-cat playing in the sun, leaping about like a little mad thing, he became outraged, threw rocks at her, and, unable to forgive her, hardened his heart in hatred.[17]

Superimposed, the two versions articulate a subtext, betraying late oedipal aggression, frustration, and fear. The mother is both "present" and "absent"—(desirably) within reach but (infuriatingly) beyond possession—and an accomplice of the *commandant* in the destruction of exigent *chatons*. The fantasy this suggests—of castration by a powerful father, abetted by an ambiguously indulgent wife—is inscribed predictably within Margueritte's portraits of his parents. In his *Souvenirs d'enfance*, after giving an affectionate description of his grandfather, he recalls his memories of the man—a war hero, killed at Sedan—whom he had eulogized in *Mon Père* (1884):

With his upright bearing, his tanned and glowing complexion, the extraordinary impression of strength that he radiated, my father inspired in me a less familiar respect. His voice alarmed me, whether it was soft or loud (although my mother affirms the contrary, it is as loud that it has remained in my ears); its influence upon me was an immediate and mesmerizing weight: perhaps that's why I escaped it as often as possible. His foresight divined the danger: my love of dreaming and distaste for action. By gymnastics, rifle-practice, horseback-riding, marching, he strove to put me in

[17] Paul Margueritte, *Tous Quatre* (Paris: Giraud et Cie, 1885), pp. 29, 30.

touch with living reality; he wanted to see me play rather than read and moon about, he sought out companions for me. He frustrated my hazardous inertia. So I loved him with a complex fervor, mixed with fear.

With my mother, a good and gentle soul, who seemed very beautiful to me (I used to beg to see her dressed for the ball, and I recall a certain pink Chinese jacket and a bell-skirt of white satin), I quibbled, became evasive, made promises, counting on not keeping them and sure of her indulgence.

"It is curious," Margueritte naïvely adds, "that with such good parents my confidence soon came to an end. Did it happen on the heels of some innocent joke, of some mortifying reproach? I shut myself off early [. . .]."[18] So withdrawn, he rehearsed the fantasy of an aureoled Salomé, delivering her (erotically culpable) *petit* up to a martyr's cruel cat-stration.

He rehearsed it again and again. *Tous Quatre* was followed by two novellas: in *L'Impasse* (1886) a "beautiful and fatal woman"—I quote Margueritte's revealing summary— "a princess or duchess, incites pursuits in the street and, at the decisive moment, disappoints [or "dupes": *déçoit*] her pursuers by exposing, under her robe, a body sheathed in hermetic black tights."[19] In *La Confession posthume* (1886, rev. ed. 1890) a young man murders his unfaithful wife, then marries a woman who had, in the past, enigmatically rejected his suit; in the closing lines, she, strangely aged, leans over him to ask "with a terror that she seemed to enjoy": "And me, will you kill me too?"[20] A Pierrot duped

---

[18] *Souvenirs d'enfance*, pp. 221-22.

[19] *Printemps tourmenté*, p. 126. Margueritte erroneously identifies the novella as "L'Abdication," a short story that was paired, in 1890, with the second edition of *La Confession posthume* (as *L'Impasse* was paired with the first). The interdiction of which the tights are a symbol may be operating to repress Margueritte's memory of *L'Impasse*. The hero, in fact, is undeterred by those tights, but his success is his undoing: once he and the duchess have confessed to True Love, their passion seems, irredeemably, "worse than incest" (*La Confession posthume* [Paris: Giraud et Cie, 1886], p. 283). "L'Abdication" is, incidentally, another tale of lovers pathetically estranged by the Flesh.

[20] Hers are the concluding words in the text of the second edition (Paris: Flammarion, [1890]). In its first edition, the novella loses much of its

by a coy Colombine, or murdering her in an act of erotic gratification, an act that is equally an expression of frustration and infantile rage: so the young Margueritte invariably conceived his own mask. As "Paul Violas" he appeared as a mime in *Tous Quatre*, as the author and actor of *Pierrot bourreau et patient*. The latter is merely *Pierrot assassin de sa femme*; Violas's remarks about the pantomime are identical with those that Margueritte later made to the mimophile Paul Hugounet;[21] Violas is, like his creator, a "romantic," inebriated by his self-destructive art. It was, not surprisingly, as "Paul Violas" that Margueritte made his journalistic début.

As Pierrot, Margueritte seems to have been acceding, as it were, to the tyranny of his texts, to the stubborn powers of the roles that bespoke him. For though he often alludes, as in the quotation with which I opened this section, to the liberating effect of the mask, it is obvious that Pierrot was for him an "essential" self, the expression of a *"moi intime."*[22] "The control that this revelation of art exercised over me," he mused in *Le Printemps tourmenté*,

> resulted from the troubling disclosures of these peripeteiae without voice, this rhythm of emotions translated into a perpetual silence: the expressive anguish of beings who can't speak, who, in making themselves understood, cannot express everything, and who are therefore pursued by a tireless fatality: hence the pathos of this mask, behind which the powers of an agitated soul take refuge; hence the eloquence of these movements that, even in farce, borrow an indefinable poignancy from the drama, as if one were seeing the turmoil of convulsive sleepwalkers, figures both passionate and inane, or of the resurrected dead.[23]

---

disturbing power by continuing for several more pages: the motives of the mysterious second wife (who will be lured into infidelity by the spirit of experiment) are given a retrospective explanation in the terms of nineteenth-century psychological realism, and the tale comes slackly to an end with the studiedly casual death of a minor character.

[21] Cf. *Tous Quatre*, pp. 262-63, and Hugounet, *Mimes et Pierrots*, pp. 226-28.

[22] *"J'imaginai donc un Pierrot personnel, conforme à mon moi intime et esthétique"*: "Notice," *Pierrot assassin de sa femme*, 2nd ed., p. 6.

[23] Page 27.

To assume the mask was to recover, unfailingly, the pathos and eloquence of one's anguish—and to inscribe that anguish still more deeply upon the soul. The pantomime traced over an ancient writing; its reading gave both pleasure and pain.

But when it shifted its tense from the past to the "present," it laid out perilous traps for the writer. Margueritte told Edmond de Goncourt that his pantomime was "a violent distraction, a shaking off of his life's black ennui"; and Goncourt, automatically reading "distraction" as displacement, "sensed, in everything he said and in everything he did not say, a great deal of bitterness coming from his marriage [. . .]."[24] The disaster of Margueritte's marriage— passed over in his memoirs as one of his *"plaies trop intimes"*[25]—could only have been hastened by such a "distraction." Which may explain (as it does for Arthur Adamov) the political commitment of his late career. After his separation from his wife in 1896, he turned to the writing, in collaboration with his brother, of a series of novels entitled *Une Epoque* (1898-1904), set amidst the events of the Prussian War and the Commune. Its publication was punctuated by a *Histoire de la guerre de 1870-1871* (1903) and by a number of works celebrating the enlightened New Woman and calling for a reform of the divorce laws. Pierrot had no role in this earnestly adult activity. Or at least he did not show his face. One detects his presence, though, everywhere, trying soberly to mend his ways, assuming Père Margueritte's self-control as an officer and a gentleman, forgiving Colombine of her socially induced faults.

Once a Pierrot, for Margueritte (as his passionate *souvenirs* of the pantomime suggest), always a Pierrot. *Hélas.*

It was left to Mallarmé to disarm Pierrot of his tyrannical authority by robbing him of "present" life. He did so in "Mimique," which in its brevity may be quoted in full:

> Silence, sole luxury after rhymes, an orchestra doing nothing with its gold, its rustlings of thought and evening, but detailing its meaning like an unspoken ode,

[24] Edmond and Jules de Goncourt, *Journal*, III, 773.
[25] *Printemps tourmenté*, p. 155.

meaning which it is up to the poet, roused by a challenge, to translate! silence of the afternoons of music: I find it, with pleasure, also, before the ever-new reappearance of Pierrot [*la réapparition toujours inédite de Pierrot*] or of the poignant and elegant mime Paul Margueritte.

Such is this *Pierrot assassin de sa femme*, composed and recorded by himself, a mute soliloquy that is held throughout with his soul by both the face and the gestures of the phantom, as white as a page not yet written. A whirlwind of reasons, naïve or new, emerges, which it would be pleasant to grasp with assurance: the aesthetics of the genre situated closer to principles than any other! nothing in this region of caprice hindering the direct simplifying instinct. . . . Here they are: "The stage illustrates only the idea, not a real action, in a vicious but sacred marriage [*hymen*] (from which the Dream arises) between desire and accomplishment, perpetration and its remembrance: here anticipating, there commemorating, in the future, in the past, *under a false appearance of the present*. So operates [*opère*] the Mime, whose acting is restricted to a perpetual allusion, without breaking the glass: he thus creates [*installe*] a pure milieu of fiction." Less than a thousand lines long, the role—whoever reads it immediately understands the laws [or "the role, which reads him, immediately embraces the laws": *le rôle, qui le lit, tout de suite comprend les règles*], as if placed before a trestle-stage, their humble depository. Surprise, accompanying the artifice of a notation of sentiments by unproffered sentences, that, in the single case perhaps with authenticity, there still reigns, between the pages and the gaze, a silence, the condition and delight of reading.[26]

No "tragic nightmare *à la* Hoffmann or Edgar Poe" here. Mallarmé is not interested in the kinds of texts that animate Margueritte's Pierrot; his reflections are rather stirred by the nature of the pantomimic moment. What does Pierrot's

[26] Mallarmé, *Oeuvres complètes*, p. 310. The *Oeuvres* will be cited throughout this chapter as *OC*, with appropriate page numbers.

little drama represent? Not a real action but an "idea." The word should not conjure up (as Derrida insists) a "literary" (or Hegelian) idealism: in none of the three versions of "Mimique,"[27] in fact, is the "idea" hypostatized into the "Idea"—and Mallarmé is usually scrupulous in the conferring of metaphysical distinction.[28] Clearly, *l'idée* is (Freudian) "ideality": the pantomime represents an action that has been installed in Pierrot's mental life. Between the world and Pierrot (and his public) mediate the assassin's memory and desire. What we are confronted with, then, is their movement—into the past to recover the remembered event, into the future to reconstruct the event as desire would represent it. The "present" is the point of their dynamic convergence, a point in perpetual motion, erasing itself ceaselessly (and the self that it constitutes) as it, fleetingly, converts future to past. It is therefore a mere "*false appearance*," a space of pure "fiction," the ghostly "moving limit" of *Igitur* (*OC*, 435). Pierrot appears at its hypothetical center as "a page not yet written," both inscribed by and inscribing his gestures as that limit traces its arc. As one who "operates," he is like Mallarmé himself, the *opérateur* of his "Livre": "[. . .] he places his Idea before him, subjects it to every twist he likes, appoints himself, turn by turn, its coiffeur, its architect, etc., then, in the end, becomes a surgeon and suddenly suppresses its existence by what he calls '*the operation.*' "[29] Pierrot's performance is a continuous supersession of his existence in an endless making of himself.

---

[27] *OC* does not reproduce the two anterior versions, both of which offer significant variants. "Mimique" first appeared, without its title, as part of Mallarmé's "Notes sur le théâtre" in the *Revue Indépendante*, 3rd Series, I (November 1886), 42-43; a revised version was included in the chapter "Le Genre, ou des Modernes" in Mallarmé's *Pages* (Brussels: Deman, 1891); the essay was finally published in its definitive form, as "Mimique," in the *Crayonné au théâtre* section of *Divagations* (Paris: Fasquelle, 1897). Derrida conveniently prints all the variant paragraphs in *D*, pp. 196*n*-97*n*.

[28] Cf. A. R. Chisholm's note about capitals and small initials in *Igitur*: "The distinctions that Mallarmé makes are important. Thus *Nuit* is an absolute, different from *nuit*, which is a single night, a unit of measurement . . ." (*Mallarmé's "Grand Oeuvre"* [Manchester: The University Press, 1962], p. 131).

[29] Edmond Bonniot, "Préface" to *Igitur*, in *OC*, 427.

The "*moi intime*" is never a reality: it is only a "Dream" to which he makes "perpetual allusion," without ever "breaking the glass." Beyond the mirrors of memory and desire may lie a complete and stable self, but such a self is of course out of reach.

"At once page and quill," writes Derrida, "Pierrot is both passive and active, matter and form, the author, the means, and the raw material of his mimodrama. The histrion produces himself here" (*D*, 198). Produces and is produced. For although *Pierrot assassin de sa femme* is "*composé et rédigé*" by Margueritte, the mime is himself "composed" by his role. Such is the implication, as Derrida observes, of that ambiguous penultimate sentence: in this third (and definitive) version of "Mimique," the punctuation and syntax permit two meanings, encouraging us to read *qui* as both "which" and "whoever," *le* as "him" and "it," *comprend* as "embraces" and "understands."[30] By such ambiguity Mallarmé is suggesting that Pierrot is both made and making, "read and reading" (as Derrida would have it), "written and writing, between the two, in the suspense of the hymen [itself a paradox, both conjunction and partition], at once screen and mirror" (*D*, 224). Thus the suprarational "sacredness" of his "presence"; thus, also the "viciousness" of his indeterminate being: neither freedom nor determinism is an isolate reality, and so in neither may his being rest.

All of which suggests that his performance—indeed, his self—is a perpetual play of his texts. Leo Bersani has recently argued that all of the mature work of Mallarmé himself is informed by such a play, but he gives the argument a radical turn: the play is proliferate, at length uncentered, snapped free from a "self" altogether: "[. . .] the vibrating self-concentration which emerges as a major creative mood of Mallarmé's early years does not immobilize the 'thought'

---

[30] The anterior versions do not so easily permit such a reading: "This marvelous nothing, less than a thousand lines long, whoever reads it as I have just done will understand the eternal laws . . . [*Ce rien merveilleux, moins qu'un millier de lignes, qui le lira comme je viens de le faire, comprendra les règles éternelles . . .*]" (*Revue Indépendante*); "This role, less than a thousand lines long, whoever reads it will understand the laws . . . [*Ce rôle, moins qu'un millier de lignes, qui le lit comprendra les règles . . .*]" (*Pages*).

which it eroticizes. On the contrary: once a thought begins to vibrate, it also begins to be scattered or disseminated." The Mallarméan self, according to Bersani, "undergoes an ontological regression in poetry, it recedes into virtuality and becomes a play of fictions."[31] "*Un milieu, pur, de fiction,*" we recall, is what the mime "installs." But we should understand "fiction" in its late nineteenth-century sense—not as a free invention but rather as an expression of self-potentiality, at once directing its own narrative and directed from without. The self is a "play" of *certain* "fictions." We might do well to substitute "text" for "fiction," signifying a field of discourse, gestural or verbal, that reads its reader, even as it invites creative reading. The "scattering," "dissemination," of the Mallarméan *moi* among his objects of thought is, like the play of the mime between memory and desire, a rhapsody upon the texts of the self. It is in the self-conscious creativity with which their pages are read that the Pierrot—the poet—of Mallarmé differs from that of, say, Margueritte. In her stimulating essay, "La Poétique de l'érotisme mallarméen," Ann-Marie Amiot, like Bersani, notes Mallarmé's tendency towards an "*éparpillement du 'moi,'* " but for her it results in no death of the self: "The tendency towards the reduction [*démultiplication*] of the self in sensation does not engender [. . .] diffusion and the blissful explosion of being; it is constantly folding over upon itself in a reflexive consciousness, attentive to the acquisitions thereby obtained."[32] This certainly describes the author of "Mimique"—engaged intently in the act of understanding the mime's engagement, in uncovering the dynamisms of his texts.

The Pierrot that emerges from this reflection is radically different from his predecessors, even from Mallarmé's own. For the young poet of 1862, reviewing the *Poésies parisiennes* of his mentor, Des Essarts, Pierrot summed up "all the base instincts of man" (*OC*, 251). Such a formulation suggests, not a text "*toujours inédite,*" but a creature of stable "character," unchanged by his being in time. In his

[31] *The Death of Stéphane Mallarmé*, pp. 7, 42.

[32] *Europe: Revue Littéraire Mensuelle*, 54th Year, No. 564 (April-May 1976), 56.

formative years, Mallarmé himself seems to have vacillated between these two existential ideals. On the one hand he insisted to Eugène Lefébure that, "Before the page, the artist *makes himself.*"[33] Self-conscious as a child, subject to the disseminating self-divisions of irony, he rolled on the floor at the news of his mother's death, "at a loss to assume the proper countenance because of his lack of sorrow,"[34] and sprinkled false tears (*"moi, idiot saltimbanque"*) over a billet-doux meant for his future wife Marie (*C*, 41). "You know the gift of perversity?" he asked Henri Cazalis: "You know certain verses it's inspired in me?" (*C*, 53). He seems a young man of able (and willing) transformations: but during the famous crisis of the 1860s, he is all but paralyzed by an ideal of stasis. The implacably blank page then forbids the irruption of words; he is arrested in glacial attitudes of autonomous Thought; his goal, as for Igitur, whose death marks his "cure," is "a perfect Being, round like the 'lune au-dessus du temps' (*Ancienne Etude*)."[35] And yet the mature Mallarmé, as Judy Kravis has suggested in her valuable study of his prose, "separates himself [. . .] from the realm of rapture and miracle towards which the poet traditionally moves." Acceding to the impossibility of Being— we shall later return to this idea—he "installs himself at a point where such notions are only emergent, where the reader is still in a state of watching rather than a state of vision, and where he is fully aware, because of his own participation through reading, in the production of the 'imminent miracle.' "[36] Valéry has described the Picasso-like technique of the older poet, "throwing words here and there over the paper,"[37] violating its implacable whiteness in a

---

[33] Stéphane Mallarmé, *Correspondance, 1862-1871*, ed. Henri Mondor and Jean-Pierre Richard (Paris: Gallimard, 1959), p. 154. This volume will be cited throughout this chapter as *C*, with appropriate page numbers.

[34] Henri de Régnier, *Nos Rencontres* (Paris: Mercure de France, 1931), p. 192; cited in Henri Mondor, *Vie de Mallarmé* ([Paris]: Gallimard, 1941), p. 13.

[35] Robert Greer Cohn, *Mallarmé's Igitur* (Berkeley: University of California Press, 1981), p. 35.

[36] *The Prose of Mallarmé: The Evolution of a Literary Language* (Cambridge: Cambridge University Press, 1976), p. 214.

[37] Cited by Jacques Schérer, *Le "Livre" de Mallarmé: Premières Recherches*

courting of *le hasard*, allowing the chance of linguistic lines of force to initiate, dynamically, creation. As for his youthful ideal of the self-sufficient moon, Mallarmé dismissed it in a conversation with Coppée, in words of as much method as madness:

> The moon irritates him [Coppée confided to his journal]. He explains the symbolism of the stars, whose disorder in the firmament strikes him as the image of chance. But the moon, which he calls contemptuously "that cheese," seems useless to him. He seriously dreams of a more scientific age of humanity when it will be very easily dissolved by chemical means. A single point gives him pause: the cessation of the tides; and that rhythmical commotion of the sea is necessary to his theory of the symbolism of the human setting [*décor*].[38]

The movement of the tides, the "disorder" of the stars, the dynamism of art: such are the late Mallarmé's concerns. "*Je suis moi—fidèle au livre*" (*L*, 35[B]), he noted in the center of a blank sheet, preparatory, apparently, for the "Grand Oeuvre." Faithful, that is, not to the "*vide papier*" of "Brise marine," but to his ever-restless texts.

So, too, his Pierrot. "I could risk intermittent apparitions under this avatar," he remarked of Margueritte's creation, "and, for the pleasure of several connoisseurs [*délicats*], be 'the black-suited gentleman who, at an unexpected moment, draws this white sword from the scabbard.' "[39] An avatar of "intermittent apparitions": this is far from the stable symbol of all the base instincts of man. But Pierrot as the white sword of *le monsieur en habit noir* suggests that, however intermittent his being, he, like his creator, is faithful to "the book." "Pierrot is brother," as Derrida observes, "to all the Hamlets haunting the Mallarméan text" (*D*, 195). Both are "*latent*" figures of myth, unable to "*become*"—that

---

sur des documents inédits (Paris: Gallimard, 1957), p. 128. Schérer's study will be cited throughout this chapter as *L*, with appropriate page numbers.

[38] Manuscript cited in Mondor, *Vie de Mallarmé*, pp. 328-29; Coppée's entry was apparently made July 19, 1872.

[39] Margueritte, *Printemps tourmenté*, pp. 26-27.

is to say, to *be*.[40] Their "black presence" as "doubters" (like that of Igitur) seems to secrete the poison by which death gradually invades their stages. Both discover in the books of themselves—again, like Igitur—a thirst for purity that is inspired, at least in part, by an infantile sexual malaise. For even though "Mimique" makes no mention of Pierrot's puerile crimes, it is clear that for Mallarmé the pantomime was charged with regressive passion. On a sheet that Schérer publishes in *Le Livre*, Mallarmé sketched out the following relationships:

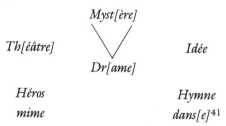

The "Mystery" (play) and the "Drama," he explained on another sheet, "are only the same thing turned inside out": "[In the] Dr[ama] the characters [are] outside and [in the] Myst[ery-play] inside" (*L*, 89[A]). The latter, as the spiritual expression of the community, has an impersonal, transcendent cast, unlike the secular (and author-centered) "Drama": such, at least, is the implication of another diagram of relationships:

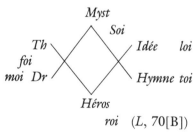

The "Mystery" mediates between the self ("*moi*") and the Other ("*toi*"); more specifically, perhaps, it encodes in the

<hr>

[40] Here and in the following two sentences I am alluding, of course, to Mallarmé's famous essay on *Hamlet* (*OC*, 299-302, 1564).

[41] *L*, 5(A). We should recall that only mime and dance seemed to Mallarmé "to necessitate a real space, or the stage" (*OC*, 315).

hypostatic imagery of mysticism their primitive, primordial bond. In the theater, the bond is disclosed by a decoding in space and time: "operation/—the Hero *extricates*—the Hymn/(maternal) that creates him, and restores/himself to the Th[eater] that it was—/from the Mystery where that hymn ["is" or "was" (the *ratures* suggest vacillation)] hidden" (*L*, 4[A]). In the course of giving voice to the song of himself, the Hero performs a double "operation": he both disengages himself from his originary texts (the "maternal" hymn that "creates him") and installs himself squarely in the "theater" originally constituted by those texts. The movement seems impossibly contradictory, until its reflexive nature is grasped. The operation "restores" the Hero to "Theater"—that is to say, to "fiction": it delivers him from his dancer-like identification with his "song" and impresses upon him its authority (and interpretability) as a text. In his self-conscious disengagement from the mystical aspirations of Mystery, he thus enters a relationship of perpetual potentiality with the erotic themes of himself.

Such is the import of Mallarmé's *ars pierrotica*, the second "Pitre châtié" (1887). In the first version of the poem (1864), the eroticism is explicit, but it shores up a conventional theme:

> *Pour ses yeux,—pour nager dans ces lacs, dont les quais*
> *Sont plantés de beaux cils qu'un matin bleu pénètre,*
> *J'ai, Muse,—moi, ton pitre,—enjambé la fenêtre*
> *Et fui notre baraque où fument tes quinquets.*
>
> *Et d'herbes enivré, j'ai plongé comme un traître*
> *Dans ces lacs défendus, et, quand tu m'appelais,*
> *Baigné mes membres nus dans l'onde aux blancs galets,*
> *Oubliant mon habit de pitre au tronc d'un hêtre.*
>
> *Le soleil du matin séchait mon corps nouveau*
> *Et je sentais fraîchir loin de ta tyrannie*
> *La neige des glaciers dans ma chair assainie,*
>
> *Ne sachant pas, hélas! quand s'en allait sur l'eau*
> *Le suif de mes cheveux et le fard de ma peau,*
> *Muse, que cette crasse était tout le génie!*
>
> (*OC*, 1416)

[For her eyes—to swim in those lakes, on whose embankments/Are planted beautiful lashes, penetrated by a blue morning light,/I, Muse—I, your clown—slipped through the window/And fled our booth where your Argand lamps smoke.//And inebriated by grasses, I plunged like a traitor/Into those forbidden lakes, and, when you were calling me,/Bathed my naked limbs in the white-shingled tide,/Forgetting my clown's costume on the trunk of a beech-tree.//The morning sun was drying my new body/And I was feeling, far from your tyranny, a freshening/Of my purified flesh by the snow of the glaciers,//Not knowing, alas! when over the water were disappearing/The grease of my hair and the rouge of my skin,/Muse, that this dross was the whole of genius!]

The poem establishes, in Bersani's words, "a rather clichéd tension between love and art":[42] he who abandons his craft for the sake of *jouissance* abdicates his powers as an artist; the "Muse" is an unnatural tyrant, but she confers genius upon her captive clowns. We are not far here from Banville's *sauteur du tremplin*, though Mallarmé has inverted the myth: Banville's clown leaps to freedom, propelled by his art; Mallarmé's flees art for "life."

The changes in the poem have—at least until recently—been regarded as primarily stylistic.[43] Informed by the hermetic "second style" and its aesthetic of extreme suggestiveness, the revised sonnet is simply, it is often argued, a more cryptic version of the first, a kind of rebus that its readers must "solve." L. J. Austin summarizes this position: the "second version deals with the same theme as the 1864 sonnet, but in a totally different style, compact and sugges-

[42] *The Death of Stéphane Mallarmé*, p. 21.

[43] Bersani's reading challenges this assumption, but he seems to bend the revised poem to the will of his thesis when he writes that its *pitre* "is motivated by nothing more definite than 'ma simple ivresse de renaître/Autre'" (ibid.). "Autre *que l'histrion*" is how the poem actually puts it. His interpretation, as a whole, seems to me to miss the point of the poem—and, in fact, to deradicalize it in the process of uncovering its radical posture. But he, like Wallace Fowlie—a solitary voice among the earlier critics (see his *Mallarmé* [Chicago: University of Chicago Press, 1953], p. 91)—makes a commendable case for the autonomy of the second version.

tive, where every word is charged with meaning and is completely functional, and no irrelevant details are retained. Although the first version is a most welcome aid to interpretation, the final version contains all the necessary hints for the patient and perceptive reader to work out the meaning for himself."[44] But surely there is more here than poetry as puzzle:

> *Yeux, lacs avec ma simple ivresse de renaître*
> *Autre que l'histrion qui du geste évoquais*
> *Comme plume la suie ignoble des quinquets,*
> *J'ai troué dans le mur de toile une fenêtre.*
>
> *De ma jambe et des bras limpide nageur traître,*
> *A bonds multipliés, reniant le mauvais*
> *Hamlet! c'est comme si dans l'onde j'innovais*
> *Mille sépulcres pour y vierge disparaître.*
>
> *Hilare or de cymbale à des poings irrité,*
> *Tout à coup le soleil frappe la nudité*
> *Qui pure s'exhala de ma fraîcheur de nacre,*
>
> *Rance nuit de la peau quand sur moi vous passiez,*
> *Ne sachant pas, ingrat! que c'était tout mon sacre,*
> *Ce fard noyé dans l'eau perfide des glaciers.*
>
> (*OC*, 31)

[Eyes, lakes [or "snares"] with my simple drunkenness of being reborn/Other than the poor actor who evoked, with a gesture/For feather [or "pen"], the ignoble soot of the Argand lamps,/I tore a window in the canvas wall.//With my leg and arms, a limpid traitorous swimmer,/In multiple leaps, denying the bad/Hamlet! it is as if I were innovating, amid the tide,/A thousand sepulchers in order to disappear, virgin, within them.//Joyous cymbal-gold excited by fists,/Suddenly the sun strikes the nakedness/Which, pure, was exhaled from my nacreous freshness,//Rancid night of the skin when you were passing over me,/Not knowing, ingrate! that

---

[44] Mallarmé's Reshaping of 'Le Pitre châtié,' " *Order and Adventure in Post-Romantic French Poetry: Essays Presented to C. A. Hackett*, ed. E. M. Beaumont, J. M. Cocking, and J. Cruickshank (Oxford: Blackwell, 1973), p. 59.

it was my whole consecration,/This makeup drowned
in the perfidious water of the glaciers.]

The eroticism is both less explicit and more disturbing: rather than climb through the window of his tent, the
clown tears a hole in the canvas wall, like a lover piercing
the hymen. His escape is not merely from his *habit de pitre*,
as in the earlier version, but from his role as poor Hamlet,
"*le seigneur latent qui ne peut devenir*" (*OC*, 300). "*L'eau
amoureuse*," in Richard's words, "delivers him from his paralysis."[45] But it delivers him up to death: "virgin," he disappears into the "sepulchers" of the waves. What we begin
to detect in an analysis of the revisions are the roots of his
erotic wish. Those "*Yeux, lacs*," as Will McLendon suggests, recall the imagery (and the blissful "oceanic feeling")
of Banville's "L'Attrait du Gouffre."[46] There the "chaste
and marvelous drunkenness" inspired by the lover's eyes
was the rapture of the narcissist who courted the fantasy of
a return to the maternal breast.

Mallarmé shared the fantasy, according to Henri Vermorel: the poet's lifelong project is a sustained act of
mourning, whereby a fantasmatic mother, lost in his early
youth, may be recovered in erotic reverie. Charles Mauron
has argued that his wishes are oedipal, the forbidden tenor
of which evokes fears of death: "Each depressive trough of
his [. . .] life is marked by a hostile threat of cold, shadow,
whiteness, inhibition, death, or madness."[47] But the glaciers and *blancheurs* of Mallarmé's poetry rarely suggest unambiguous hostility: his *pitre* bathes joyfully—to take an
immediate example—in "*l'eau perfide des glaciers*." The icy
peaks, like the immaculate page, are both inviting and perfidious because they lure the infant in the dreaming poet
to a profound and artless sleep. Mallarmé's mourning, like
his clown's tearing a hole in the hymen of life, awakens "an

[45] Jean-Pierre Richard, *L'Univers imaginaire de Mallarmé* (Paris: Editions du Seuil, 1961), p. 111.

[46] Will L. McLendon, "A New Reading of Mallarmé's *Pitre châtié*,"
Symposium, XXIV (spring 1970), 39.

[47] *Introduction to the Psychoanalysis of Mallarmé*, tr. Archibald Hender-
son, Jr., and Will L. McLendon (Berkeley: University of California Press,
1963), p. 15.

older nostalgia: the search for the lost paradise of which all poetry sings."

> It is the image [I quote Vermorel] of primary narcissism, the mythical epoch of the psyche that reconstructs retrospectively an ideal image of the *"vie antérieure"*: it is the reign of the One (and of the double), in which is born the oceanic feeling that a writer, Romain Rolland, suggested to Freud as the source of religious sentiment—but also, one might add, as the crucible of all artistic creation.[48]

And yet to insist upon this fantasy in the explication of Mallarmé's late verse would be, I think, a mistake. Unlike Baudelaire, Banville, or Verlaine, Mallarmé is not a naïve narcissist (he is naïve about little concerning himself); the dynamics of his poetry are but superficially served (despite Mauron's application to the task) by teasing out its "latent" themes. What is interesting, in fact, about "Le Pitre châtié" is Mallarmé's obvious awareness of the implications of his fantasy—of the necessity of its sublimation in a flirtatious dance of desire.

For the poem seems both to discover the fantasy (in the theatrical sense) and to displace it from the center of the text. Writing without apparent knowledge of the earlier version, Mauron seemed ignorant, in *Mallarmé l'obscur* (1941), of the erotic motives of the *pitre*: "If the 'eyes' [of the first line] are those of the clown, the sentence becomes 'my eyes like lakes, I tore . . .' (as one would say 'my arms before me, I tore . . .'). But the 'eyes' can be those of the public addressed by the clown: and the whole piece would acquire a complicated symbolism, but one which is by no means improbable, for all that—the artist plunging into the gaze of the Other, trying to lose his histrionic pose there."[49] Austin considers such speculation to be the result of "errors and confusions,"[50] commendably "corrected" by Mauron

[48] Henri Vermorel, "Les Chemins de la création dans l'oeuvre de Stéphane Mallarmé," *Revue Française de Psychanalyse*, XLIV (January-February 1980), 70.

[49] Charles Mauron, *Mallarmé l'obscur* (Paris: Corti, 1968), p. 71.

[50] "Mallarmé's Reshaping of 'Le Pitre châtié,' " *Order and Adventure*, p. 68n.

himself in his later studies of the poet. But the poem clearly invites the speculation: in the first detailed analysis of the sonnet, Emile Verhaeren identified the "*yeux*" as those of the spectators, and he claimed later that Mallarmé had found his reading "correct, save a remark about one incident."[51] The invitation, I think, is intentional. The poem asks to be read as Mauron first read it, to be disengaged from its naïve source. For the poem is itself a disengagement from the narcissism that it has flushed from its former self. The second version moves the drama out of the realm of sentimental wish—the infantilism of which is disguised—and onto a public stage: and it does so not by repressing the fantasy that motivates that drama but, as I have tried to show above, by subtly pursuing its dark implications. The *pitre* (like the *prêtre?*)[52] before the regard of his public is snared by the *lacs* of its attention: duped by the gaze (the "false appearance" of a present), he complicitously ("*lacs avec ma,*" etc.) exalts his performance to the *ekstasis* of Being. Not a poor player now but a Presence, he swims in the azure of the Absolute. Perhaps Mallarmé was inspired by a remark from a disciple of his *Mardis*: "[. . .] lifting for us," recalls Vielé-Griffin of a hieratic evening with *le Maître*, "the veil still covering the ideal bronze that his love is sculpting, in the feverish excitement about the Work to come and in the enthusiasm of his suave elocution, standing erect as if poised for flight, his right arm horizontally outstretched, his chest thrust forward, his head held high, with a look of proud serenity, he represented, on the stage of which he dreams, the plastic apparition of the mime."[53]

Plastic, motionless, *mort*. To slip into Being is to dive into the sepulchers of the self. It is to drown "*tout [son] sacre*" in the perfidious glaciers of a fantasmatic time out of

[51] *Impressions, troisième série*, 5th ed. (Paris: Mercure de France, 1928), p. 179. Verhaeren's explication appeared, unsigned, in an article of *L'Art Moderne*, November 20, 1887, entitled "Réponse mallarmiste."

[52] The pun is suggested by Walter Strauss: cited in Naomi Ritter, "The Anti-hero of the Commedia dell'Arte: From Pierrot to Petrushka," MS, p. 55.

[53] In *Les Ecrits pour l'art*, February 1887; cited in Mondor, *Vie de Mallarmé*, p. 505. "Le Pitre châtié" was first published in its revised form in Mallarmé's *Poésies* of October 1887.

time. And art—craft, performance, the poet's very identity—is thereby nullified in a stroke. Not so, apparently, for J.-P. Richard: in his reading of the sonnet, the clown emerges *"neuf et total,"* ready to assume the Mallarméan project—the "sure revelation of meaning."[54] But this seems a wishful conclusion: for to recover his "consecration" the *pitre* must reassume the mask-like *fard*; he must again refract meaning through the mountebank's poor *geste*. Reality, to repeat Derrida's observation, "indeed is death. It will prove to be inaccessible, otherwise than by simulacrum [. . .]." Metaphor, allusion, suggestion gesture towards it, but, as in the dance, the very incarnation of *l'idée*, the last veil is never lifted, a "banality" always persists between the Idea and the eye (*OC*, 306, 307, 308). That banality Derrida calls *la différance*; for Bersani it is "sublimation." Bersani's formulation seems at first impossible: "[. . .] desire, far from being disguised and disciplined by sublimation, is by nature an act of sublimation. Desire produces sublimation; to de-sublimate desire is to erase it."[55] But his conclusions are, in fact, inevitable. "Desire," as J. Gillibert remarks, "is always a mourning";[56] it is only by the relinquishment or recovery of our first Object that desire may be, in Bersani's words, "erased." For Mallarmé neither was possible other than by "simulacrum"—fortunately, we might hasten to add; for his poetry owes its richness (as it owes its life) to the play of his tropes around that transcendent, indescribable Center.

I think that the famous Book, the "Orphic explanation of the Earth" (*OC*, 663) envisaged by the poet, would have been a revelation of that mobility. In recalling Mallarmé's projects for *"l'Oeuvre rêvée,"* René Ghil described a strange scene introducing a character "who at a solemn moment was to appear on the stage":

A character would appear—hieratic, beardless, completely enveloped in preciously white fabrics, making no gesture: on his head, the papal tiara, dome-like and equally white, encircled with the three crowns set en-

---

[54] *L'Univers imaginaire de Mallarmé*, pp. 111, 546.

[55] *The Death of Stéphane Mallarmé*, p. 80.

[56] *Deuil, mort*, in *L'Oedipe maniaque* (Paris: Payot, 1979); cited in Vermorel, "Les Chemins de la création," p. 76.

tirely in precious stones: and this would be—this supreme Pontiff—a symbol of the Phallus, around which,
according to Mallarmé's conception, ritual dancers
would have doubtless performed evolutions.[57]

Phallus, priest, and Pierrot (with a hint of Hérodiade in
his jeweled tiara), the character is an icon of the articulation
of desire. He is Lacan's "transcendental signifier"—with this
important difference: he alludes to a transcendental signified. A Phallus that, in its chaste purity and motionlessness,
denies its own energies, he would erase himself to return
to the "real," to the sacred silence of *la vie antérieure*. It is
only by virtue of those dancers, defining ritualistically his
field of force, that he exists as a sexual presence. They are
the "banality" that comes between him and the public, the
veil that must not be lifted, the *différance* that makes revelation possible. The scenario recalls strongly a fragment from
Le Livre, a narrative that Schérer thinks part of the "content" of the Book. Itself tantalizingly fragmentary, ellipti-
cal, cryptic, it seems to describe an old man's descent into
the tomb, "like a priest deprived of everything," in order
to find *"le mystère cherché"* (*L*, 29[A], 30[A]). Once there,
he is joined by (or engenders) a young companion, who
has come "to know/[the] mystery before marrying": "for
one must die in order/to know the mystery" (*L*, 30[A],
32[A]). The latter is, apparently, *"le mystère d'amour"*; the
priest's is "this other need": the "priest must remain in ignorance, for the glory of humanity, of the mystery of
woman—from which (child between her legs) everything
will be resolved [. . .]" (*L*, 31[A], 29[A]). Doubtless the
priest's "need" is ("for the glory of humanity") revelation.
"Let us unite our two needs," one tells the other (*L*, 31[A]).
The young man, who now seems "cloistered in the/priest"
like an infant (*L*, 33[A]), emerges from the tomb, drawing
the old man with him—emerges "from [the] mystery that
one can know/only in accomplishing it—love—/proof—
child" (*L*, 33[A]).

The "child" engendered by the Mallarméan priest is the
Orphic revelation of desire; it originates in the primordial
maternal presence—"tomb," "glacier," "silence"—but it lives

[57] *Les Dates et les oeuvres: Symbolisme et poésie scientifique* (Paris: Crès et
Cie, 1923), pp. 236-37.

by turning away from its source in tireless gestures of sublimation. It lives to articulate the simulacra of that for which it mourns. But its gestures are not only tireless: they are often joyful and serene. Art for the mature Mallarmé was found in the pleasures of the simulacra—in the mobility rather than in the mourning. The *"loisirs du poste,"* the verses for fans and for Easter eggs, the delightful ventriloquy of *La Dernière Mode* all suggest the instinct uncovered by Bersani in Mallarmé's more "serious" art: that "appetitive, erotic curiosity," which "is a particularly civilized and an especially sociable sign of human desire."[58] It is a curiosity that all but dissolves the self as it darts about that self's fantasmatic center; as a consequence, his personae grow tenuous: Pierrot, as a "character," vanishes. Like the *prêtre*—or *pitre*, adrift in *l'idée*—he is ultimately a figure for the absence of desire—at which point, of course, he joins Igitur in the tomb. In life he must settle for the *ne-pas-devenir*, the almosting of Hamlet, the being of intermittent apparitions that Mallarmé saw in Margueritte's criminal clown. All the better for his interpreter: "Man is born curious and must remain so forever," Mallarmé once wrote to Cazalis: *"Learn and enjoy: therein lies everything"* (C, 27). The rest, for the poet, as well as for poetry itself, is silence.

[58] *The Death of Stéphane Mallarmé*, p. 73.

XI

∿

Epilogue: Eclipse

Pierrot
ta chandelle morte
que viens-tu faire ici?

Fée Electricité si bien se porte
Pierrot
ta chandelle est morte.

GEORGES ROUAULT
from "A feu Deburau," in *Funambules* (1926)

"This little book," wrote Margueritte of *Pierrot assassin de sa femme*, "[. . .] remained almost unknown: but I sent it to several writers. It made explicit, as early as 1882, what I hoped to draw from this moribund art, at a moment when, if anyone had hopes for it, no one thought that it could truly be revived."[1] One of those writers was probably Jean Richepin: in April of 1883 the Trocadéro produced his *Pierrot assassin*, a pantomime in which Pierrot murders for love of Colombine and then is disabused of his illusion. (The Pierrot was Sarah Bernhardt, who, "angular and spectral," according to Jean Lorrain, "and enshrouded, as it were, in the folds of the great white blouse," disturbed profoundly "the nervous system of her public.")[2] Its having received a professional production doubtless encouraged Margueritte. He now performed *Pierrot assassin de sa femme* wherever he could find an audience—in the salons, at a charity benefit, before a student gathering at the Café Procope, before another in the hall of the Société de Géogra-

[1] *Printemps tourmenté*, p. 77.
[2] "Laissez venir à nous tous les Petits Pierrots," unpublished article dated May 20, 1888, reproduced in Pierre Léon Gauthier, *Jean Lorrain: Un Second Oratoire: Chroniques retrouvées* (Dijon: Jobard, 1935), p. 104.

phie. In February of 1887, he presented *Pierrot* in its definitive form, with music by Paul Vidal, the young musical
director of the Opéra-Comique, at a soirée of Alphonse
Daudet's. Edmond de Goncourt had attended a rehearsal,
and had described its electric effect: "Truly curious, the
mobility of the author's mask, and the succession of figures
of grievous expression that he makes pass beneath his neurotic flesh, and the admirable impressions that he produces
of a gasping mouth full of terror."[3] At the performance was
the producer Antoine, long a friend and admirer of the
mime, and one year later, on March 23, 1888, Margueritte
appeared in the blouse of his Pierrot *satanique* on the stage
of the Théâtre-Libre. Zola had been indirectly responsible
for the production, having encouraged Antoine to stage
the work of his "opponents," the signatories of the famous
"Manifeste des Cinq," to which Margueritte—with callow
impetuosity, as he later admitted—had indignantly joined
his name. But the performance transcended literary politics.
Antoine had agreed to play the undertaker's mute, and when
he stumbled onstage—a streak of shadow beside the livid
Pierrot—a tremor ran through the *salle*: "I recall," wrote
Margueritte, "the stir in the house when, both of us stum-
bling with drunkenness and he holding me up, we surged
in—the door thrown open with a blow of the fist—under
a pallid ray of moonlight."[4]

The production, as Daniel Gerould has observed, was
Margueritte's "greatest public triumph" as Pierrot,[5] but for
the pantomime it merely announced a revival of which un-
imagined successes were still to come. Signs of the revival
had been visible since the *Pierrot sceptique* (1881) of Huysmans and Hennique. In 1882 the Chat Noir, a Montmartre
cabaret, had begun publishing a weekly review, and the
engaging Pierrots of Adolphe Willette, one of its most in-

[3] Edmond and Jules de Goncourt, *Journal*, III, 643. Goncourt also attended the performance proper, but his entry recording the event—and
repeating his praise for "*le talent le plus macabre*" of the mime—is primarily
an expression of his astonishment that "an intelligent man" like Margueritte should want "to pick up where Deburau left off" (III, 644).

[4] *Printemps tourmenté*, p. 179.

[5] "Paul Margueritte and *Pierrot Assassin of His Wife*" (*The Drama Review*), p. 109.

fluential cartoonists and illustrators, were soon synonymous with *la nouvelle bohème*. Arlequin had found a pros-
elyte in the mime and scenarist Raoul de Najac, whose *Petit
Traité de pantomime à l'usage des gens du monde* (1887) had
been written under the dictation of François Fredon, an
old *saltimbanque* who had performed as the Bergamask.[6]
The *Petit Traité* had extolled the pantomime as a salon rec-
reation and had called for the establishment of an "Acadé-
mie Funambulesque"—inspired, perhaps, by a notice in *Le
Matin* of the creation, a year earlier, of a Société des Amis
de la Pantomime.[7] And while Najac had been writing his
arlequinades and Margueritte performing *Pierrot assassin de
sa femme*, the novelist and journalist Félicien Champsaur
had begun to experiment with ballets and pantomimes that
abandoned Bergamo for the world of Ideas. In *Lulu* (1888),
first produced (with Agoust and Footit) in the ring of the
Nouveau Cirque, Schopenhauer appears on the scene: his
nose in a book, he trips over the heart that Lulu has lost
on the pavement, and until she reclaims it he puzzles over
its hermetic exterior, trying vainly to pry inside. *Lulu* was
lost in the depths of the circus hall; like the *monomimes* of
Margueritte and Najac, it called for an intimate stage—and
for an intellectually less republican audience. It found both
with the creation of the Cercle Funambulesque in the spring
of 1888.

The Cercle was the culmination of all this activity and
the happy issue of accident. Its moving force was Félix
Larcher, a ministry official, future theater manager, and
former collaborator on the *Revue d'Art Dramatique*. In 1886,
protesting to know nothing about the genre, Larcher was
asked to contribute a collection of pantomimes to the Librairie Théâtrale—a task for which he and his brother, Eugène, then stage-manager of the Renaissance, applied to
Paul Legrand. The material result was their edition of *Pantomimes de Paul Legrand* (1887); but the coincidental interests that their research had excited proved to be the more

[6] See Raoul de Najac, "Préface," *Les Exploits d'un Arlequin: Autobiogra-
phie d'un mime* (Paris: Hennuyer, 1888), p. vi.
[7] The Société apparently survived no longer than the announcement:
see the interview of Félix Larcher by Paul Hugounet, "Comment fut fondé
le Cercle Funambulesque," *La Plume*, IV (September 15, 1892), 406.

important fruits of their work. Eugène had discovered a taste and talent for pantomime: sometime during the winter of 1887-1888 he performed Legrand's *Le Papillon* before an audience that included Champsaur and Félicia Mallet, an aspirant to Pierrot's *casaque* and, later, the brightest star of the Cercle. His success was a revelation, both to Mallet and to his brother, Félix. The latter spent the following day in elaborating a plan for an association and in drawing up a list of its statutes. Eugène communicated the idea to Fernand Beissier, a colleague of Margueritte at the ministry who had written the preface for *Pierrot assassin de sa femme* and would later compose his own pantomimes. Beissier, in turn, introduced Margueritte and Najac to the Larchers; and not a week after Eugène's début in *Le Papillon* the Cercle Funambulesque was born. Félix recruited the support of his newspaper friends; Eugène brought in actors and musicians, including Coquelin *cadet* and Massenet; and Margueritte introduced Huysmans, Hennique, and Antoine to their ranks. By the time of the meeting of its constitutive assembly in February of 1888, the Cercle numbered seventy-five members; they included Champfleury, Richepin, Champsaur, Jacques Normand, Jules Chéret, Paul Legrand, Jules Lemaître, Auguste Vitu—an impressive gathering of writers, composers, artists, actors, and journalists who had ever expressed an interest in the pantomime. The first evening of performances, in May of 1888, took place at the Fantaisies-Parisiennes; the second and most subsequent soirées, until the demise of the Cercle in 1898, were held at the Théâtre d'Application, sometimes called the Bodinière.

The published aims of the Cercle were ambitious. To revive the "classical" pantomime of Deburau, the *parades* of the Boulevard, and the farces of the Foire; to present pieces from the *commedia dell'arte* and from the French Comédie-Italienne; to offer the composers and scenarists of the modern pantomime a theater, orchestra, and audience for their work; and to produce new playlets in prose or in verse inspired by the old Italian comedy of masks: these aims constituted the public program. But there was a private set of goals, both mercenary and high-minded, that had brooded over the Cercle's conception. Margueritte, Beissier, and Najac had wanted a close circle of associates, committed to the pantomime in a spirit of comradeship; the Larchers had had different ideas: "[. . .] a little older and so a little more experienced than our three collaborators," Félix later recalled, "we wanted—still while preserving the Cercle form, such as I had sketched out in the statutes—to approximate a theatrical organization, which, in our opinion, had the only chance of succeeding. Antoine and his Théâtre-Libre were to serve as models for us—with this difference: we resisted the intervention of amateur actors."[8] But even as they were taking steps to ensure financial solvency, they dreamed of a new Bayreuth at the Bodinière: "To suppress the conventional and unintelligible gestures of the old pantomime and, for that, to have recourse to actors," Félix mused, "to require a close and constant adaptation of the musical phrase to the situation on stage, to put the utterance of the gesture into the orchestra—that is to say, in the last analysis, to apply quite simply the best theories of Wagner to the pantomime: it seem[ed] to me that that should produce a most interesting spectacle for a small but select audience."[9] As these reflections suggest, the first two goals of the public program were soon forgotten. In the manifestoes issued by various members of the Cercle, the old pantomime was invoked with condescension, as an expression of *"l'époque primitive"* of the art.[10] Only one of Deburau's pantomimes was produced—as part of the second program, when the statutes were being conscientiously observed. Similarly, only one popular *parade, Léandre Ambassadeur,* was presented in the ten years of the Cercle's existence, and no scenes were performed from the rich repertoire of the Foire or of the Théâtre-Italien.[11]

[8] Ibid., p. 407.

[9] Ibid., p. 406.

[10] Félix Galipaux, "Comment on monte une pantomime," in Félix Larcher and Paul Hugounet, *Les Soirées Funambulesques: Notes et documents inédits pour servir à l'histoire de la pantomime* (Paris: Kolb, [1890-93]), p. 103. See also Jean Jullien, "La Pantomime et la comédie," and Félicien Champsaur, "Pantomime moderne," in *La Plume*, IV (September 15, 1892), 394-95, 402-403.

[11] A scene from Regnard's *théâtre-italien,* "Arlequin Barbier," was announced on the program for the first soirée, but the reviews make it clear that the piece was omitted (see Ro 11539 ["Rec. fac. d'art. de presse,

The Cercle was animated, like Champfleury in the 1840s, by the spirit of "reform," was intent upon "modernizing" the pantomime. For its most energetic publicist and chronicler, Paul Hugounet, this obviously meant infusing it with Wagnerian and Symbolist "poetry." When, for his book *La Musique et la pantomime* (1892), he interviewed the composers of the Cercle, he queried each on the use of the *leitmotiv*, of what he called "the Wagnerian tradition." (Most gave a tactful variant on Georges Pfeiffer's sensible reply: "*C'est bien grosse chose pour sujet menu.*")[12] The short articles interspersed among the synopses of *Les Soirées Funambulesques*, a compilation by Hugounet and Félix Larcher, conferred upon the pantomime the power to evoke "psychology" or, better, an *état d'âme*. "Today," wrote Félix Galipaux in "Comment on monte une pantomime," "[. . .] the study of character, of feelings—psychology, in a word—is the thing [. . .]. And the mime certain of pleasing the public is the one whose means are simple and varied, his gestures restrained, hardly perceptible, but extraordinarily suggestive!"[13] Hugounet's own pantomimes plunge into the Symbolists' destructive element, inducting Pierrot into the *au-delà* or confronting him with *la femme fatale*. In *La Fin de Pierrot* (1891), a Moreauvian Hermonthis offers Pierrot the elixir of oblivion, and in renouncing food, drink, love, and

---

progr., documents concernant le Cercle funambulesque, 1888-1895"], Bibliothèque de l'Arsenal, ff. 15-17). Titles of all the pantomimes given by the Cercle through the opening of its 1893 season, including a great number of detailed synopses, may be found in Larcher and Hugounet, *Les Soirées Funambulesques*; the *recueil* noted above in the Collection Rondel, Bibliothèque de l'Arsenal, permits a partial reconstruction of its programs from 1893 through the spring of 1895. Although its listing is clearly spotty and marred by errors of various sorts, the "Nomenclature chronologique des oeuvres mimées, créées à Paris de 1890 à 1908," in *L'Album Comique, Dramatique et Musical*, II (October 1908), 25-32, helps supplement the information offered by the documents in the Collection Rondel. For published *pantomimes funambulesques* produced by the Cercle both before and after the appearance of the synopses constituting *Les Soirées Funambulesques*, see my "Handlist of Pantomime Scenarios" following this chapter.
[12] Paul Hugounet, *La Musique et la pantomime* (Paris: Kolb, [1892]), p. 51.
[13] Page 104.

life, he wins the mystical *"trésor rêvé."*[14] ("In this work, at least, there is an idea," wrote a loyal reviewer of *La Plume*; "I must admit that I could not grasp it. But a friend assured me that it was very interesting.")[15] In the original version of *Doctoresse!* (1890), the curtain falls as physician Isabelle, who had earlier strangled a canary, prepares to dissect her bohemian husband, caught sleeping with Colombine.

But such pieces were apparently too avant-garde for the majority of the Cercle Funambulesque. And in having widened it beyond the confines of comradeship, the founders had entrusted it to majority rule. The ending of *Doctoresse!* as Félix Larcher recalled, "pleased some by its very boldness."

> But the majority of us thought it impossible on the stage. On one point everyone was in agreement: the murder of the bird, an act of coldblooded cruelty, rendered Isabelle utterly odious. The author yielded easily: he even admitted the possibility of another dénouement and, at the following meeting, he brought us the one that ends the play today.[16]

In the new ending, Isabelle animates the lovers (dead, now, in a suicide pact) by means of an electrical machine, and as they walk about like automatons she holds up a sketch of her new shingle: *Spécialité de résurrections.* The reforms of the Cercle were in fact very timid reforms. Pathos was permissible—was, indeed, encouraged—but rarely cruelty or irreverence. Pierrot, *artiste pauvre* and *pauvre artiste*, sometimes killed himself when robbed of his Colombine, as in Leclercq's *Noël triste* (1891), or when his playscript, like the *chef-d'oeuvre* of Lafrique's *Pierrot poète* (1892), seemed irrecoverably lost. But when he murdered a man (accidentally, of course) in Aubert's *Nuit de Carnaval* (1894), he set in motion the inevitable drama of Conscience from "Shakspeare aux Funambules," and when Colombine decapitated Arlequin in Najac's *Barbe-Bleuette* (1889), her blade

---

[14] Paul Hugounet, *La Fin de Pierrot, pantomime mystique en un acte* (Paris: Dentu, 1891), p. 32.

[15] Georges Roussel, "Critique dramatique," *La Plume*, III (May 1, 1891), 156.

[16] Hugounet and Larcher, *Les Soirées Funambulesques*, p. 20.

was simply the engine of a harmless fairy tale. What Hugounet called the "terrible representatives of the Censorship of the Cercle" were always on the *qui vive*: *Pierrot confesseur* (1892), by Galipaux and Pontsevrez, put a suspicious (and cassocked) Pierrot in the confessional—and set two of its auditors to making cuts to preserve the convictions of its audience from offense.[17]

The "reforms" were at once too radical and too tame for three of the first founders of the Cercle: Margueritte, Najac, and Beissier soon withdrew their names from its membership. There had been sharp ideological disagreement from the start. "Several painters and men of literature," Najac had written in his *Petit Traité de pantomime*, "have transformed Pierrot into a frightful scoundrel, into a phlegmatic criminal who can inspire only horror. Completely different is the Pierrot of my dreams." He is, as Najac had gone on to explain, a godchild of Molière's Pierrot, engagingly *bête* and naïve; never should he be accompanied by a character "evoking indecent or funereal ideas"—by an "apothecary armed with his . . . weapon," for example, or by a "*croque-mort*." The pantomime is an entertainment for the salon, and its scenarist must bow before the first social law: "One must [. . .] not forget that one is in good company."[18] Najac had no patience with a "symbolic" Pierrot, and he was understandably shocked and dismayed when his anodyne comedy *Barbe-Bleuette* was turned by the Cercle—by the actors and composer, Francis Thomé—into an "old melodrama rejuvenated by indecent innuendoes."[19] *Barbe-Bleuette* was a great success—one of the greatest in the history of the association—but in his *Souvenirs* Najac renounces all claims to it, at least in the version produced by the Cercle. Their appropriation of it was apparently the motive for his rupture with the group; his later pantomimes were presented under different auspices—in the salons, at the circus, and on stages outside the Bodinière.[20]

[17] Ibid., pp. 113-14.
[18] Raoul de Najac, *Petit Traité de pantomime à l'usage des gens du monde* (Paris: Hennuyer, 1887), pp. 23, 27.
[19] Raoul de Najac, *Souvenirs d'un mime* (Paris: Emile-Paul, 1909), p. 38.
[20] For his activities outside the Cercle, see his *Souvenirs*, cited in the previous note.

Epilogue

It was for quite different reasons, one suspects, that Margueritte broke with his associates. He was perhaps closer than any other author to the spirit of Deburau's stage. The two mimes could hardly be confused, of course: Baptiste had been neither literary nor "tragic"; he had never performed in a *monomime*; but when he had harrassed Colombine it had been for sex, not, winsomely, for "love," and his frustrations had always inspired sublime (and ingenious) cruelties. It was the savagery as much as the "poetry" of Pierrot that attracted Margueritte—and that estranged him from the sympathies of those associates charmed by the vapidity of Legrand. "If you could come back to us, Pierrot," Margueritte wrote in 1891, "in some way other than a journey, and in some place other than the fantasies of artists and writers, where I should wish to see you is at the Théâtre-Impossible."

> On the elastic boards of a house with scenery painted by the most fervid colorists and pervaded by strains of the "enervating and caressing" music of the most suave musicians, it would charm me if, for the amusement of a few simple—or very complicated—souls, there could be presented the prodigious and tragicomic farces of life, love, and death, written exclusively by authors who had no connection whatsoever with the Society of Men of Letters.[21]

The Men of Letters of the Cercle seemed uneasy with the farce of death: at least when it was informed—as it was often in Margueritte's pantomimes—by a nakedly cruel intent.[22]

What they favored, apparently, were the frustrations and *fourberies* of the familiar Legrandian Pierrot. The Cercle was, despite its intentions, the very triumph of banality. Pierrot loses his fiancée when his "art"—of thievery—inspires him

---

[21] "Eloge de Pierrot," *La Lecture*, February 25, 1891: Ro 11367, Bibliothèque de l'Arsenal, pp. 428-29.

[22] It is not clear what prompted Beissier's severance with the group: perhaps it was his friendship with Margueritte. His own pantomimes— whether cleverly didactic, as in the early pieces (*La Lune* [1889]), or tearfully sentimental, as in the late (*Noël de Pierrot* [1900])—accord perfectly with the tastes of the Cercle.

Epilogue

to reckless heights (Najac's *L'Amour de l'art* [1888]); he botches his own suicide and then, stuffing the noose in his pocket for luck, is emboldened to court Colombine (Boussenot's *La Corde de pendu* [1892]); he plays out a dream of heroic exploit that leads *alla gloria militar* (Ferdal's *La Rêve du conscrit* [1892]); he is educated by Feeling *après ses noces* on the etiquette of bedding his Agnès (Carré and Colias's *L'Ecole des vierges* [1892]); he retains as lovers both his wife and his servant by a bit of photographic illusion (Boussenot and Beissier's *Instantanées* [1894]). Sometimes his drama has a hackneyed lesson to teach: Woman is fickle (Camille de Saint-Croix's *Blanc et noir* [1888]); Earth's the right place for love (Beissier's *La Lune* [1889]); Art is born of Suffering (Arbel's *Le Coeur brisé* [1890]). Sometimes it is tearful, in the manner of the old-fashioned *comédie-larmoyante*: it was in such plays that the Cercle in fact found its most bankable pantomimic form.

The most durable of them was Carré's *L'Enfant prodigue*, first produced in 1890, with Félicia Mallet as the prodigal Pierrot. Its success carried it into the commercial theaters and onto the stages of London and New York; it was revived well into the 1920s, and was the first stage-play to be filmed.[23] A manuscript of the pantomime, now in the Bibliothèque de l'Arsenal, preserves the tone of its first production. At rise, we are introduced *chez* Monsieur Pierrot, a good bourgeois who loves his wife as he did "*au premier jour.*" Both dote on their son, young Petit Pierrot—until the night he steals their hard-won savings and tiptoes stealthily from the house. At first pretending to be asleep, they sit up at the sound of the falling latch, the eyes of both "full of tears": they "look at the door through which their son has left, their eyes meet, and they fall, sobbing, into each other's arms." In the next act little Pierrot is presumably in Paris, where he has become "*tout-à-fait mo-*

[23] It was premièred in London, at the Prince of Wale's Theatre, in April of 1891, and in New York, at the Booth Theatre, in September of 1916. The film was made in 1906, with Georges Wague as Pierrot *père* (see Tristan Rémy, *Georges Wague: Le Mime de la Belle Epoque* [Paris: Girard, 1964], pp. 122-23). In Paris there were numerous *reprises* of the pantomime, in various theaters, through 1928, in which year it was produced at the Théâtre-Femina to a cool reception in the press.

derne": he now wears the black suit of Willette's wickedly decadent Pierrot. While his Phrynette sleeps late, the concierge brings him bill after bill to pay: his mistress has endearingly extravagant tastes. Finally stirring, she sends him out to raise money, declares willfully that she *will be* rich, and then runs off with a wealthy baron, who has opportunely come to call. Pierrot staggers in, bowed under sacks full of stolen jewelry, and reads Phrynette's letter in an agony of despair. Two policemen lead him out. The third-act curtain rises on the household of M. and Mme Pierrot: the former "has no longer his jovial expression of the old days. Mme Pierrot's hair has turned white." After denouncing his son in mute gestures of outrage, M. Pierrot leaves the room—and Pierrot *fils* comes through the door. The mother knows her child in a glance: "And there they stand, both sobbing in each other's arms." When Pierrot *père* returns, he at first will have nothing to do with his son; he declares he will not even see him. But Mme Pierrot has the boy get down on his knees, his head bowed in profound repentence. The father is softened and, raising Pierrotin to his feet, holds out his arms to the prodigal: "In tears, little Pierrot throws himself into the embrace." Tableau, swell of music, and curtain.[24]

To paint *l'état d'âme* of these characters: so the composer, André Wormser, described his collaborative goal.[25] The rather damp souls of these Pierrots are of course closer to the spirit of the melo than to the moods of the dramas—*symbolistes, wagnériens*—that are immediately evoked by that phrase. The piece was clearly conceived without irony; in production, the "sincere" sensitivity of Pierrot *fils* was doubtless heightened by Mallet's "feminine" grace.[26] As drama, it all seems hopelessly *démodé*, even for its own day.

[24] Michel Carré *fils*, *L'Enfant prodigue, pantomime en 3 tableaux*: uncoded and unpaginated MS in the Collection Rondel. My quotations are from the following scenes: I.1.7; II.1; III.1.2.3. For the "Phrinette" of the MS, I have adopted the spelling that one encounters consistently in all the synopses and reviews.

[25] In Hugounet, *La Musique et la pantomime*, p. 70.

[26] Although that grace may have been restricted to her form and attitudes: more than one spectator made note of a cruel cast to Mallet's mask (see, e.g., Séverin, *L'Homme blanc*, pp. 166-67).

And yet it held the stage fitfully for nearly forty years. Where, then, lay its power to please? Not in its "truth," quite obviously, but in the presence of its three Pierrots. Without them the pathos would have soon seemed ludicrous; with them it is charming, being the issue of an ideal (though patently fictional) innocence and naïveté. But what seems obvious to a twentieth-century audience was not so to the enthusiasts of the late nineteenth: such naïveté was no fiction for most children of Wagner (like Wormser and his librettist, Carré), and it was not solely the province of Pierrots. In fact, for Charles Aubert, a mime and theorist of pantomime, Pierrot had no place in mute revelations of unironized *états d'âme*: "*L'Enfant prodigue*," he wrote in *L'Art mimique* (1901), "is a realistic play in the most bourgeois mold, which could only gain in conserving the appearance of the strictest truth in all its details." It then follows that "Pierrot is useless and even inadmissible": he should be banished—not only from *L'Enfant prodigue*, but from every "modern" pantomime. "Has the face of a mime," Aubert asks with rhetorical assurance, "a greater power of expression when it is white?"[27]

The question assumes that the mime is a transparent medium for emotion; more importantly, it assumes that emotions (and countenances) are, like *la famille Pierrot*, pure and simple things.[28] (For Deburau, oscillating between fear and ferocity, neither the mask nor the emotion had been simple.) Indeed, a fiction, like Pierrot's chalky face, may attain to idealized simplicity, but such simplicity misrepresents (as Mallarmé understood) the mobility of the *moi intime*. The real reason for the success of *L'Enfant prodigue* was lost on the authors of the Cercle, as it would later be

[27] *L'Art mimique, suivi d'un traité de la pantomime et du ballet* (Paris: Meuriot, 1901), p. 203.

[28] The axiom that usually preceded these assumptions—and that still precedes them today—is that gesture, unlike speech, is a "direct" expression of emotion. Thus Jean Jullien writes in "La Pantomime et la comédie": "[. . .] the gesture is governed directly by the brain, it is the natural and universal language *par excellence*; mime is thus an art anterior to speech, more sincere, and superior to the latter" (*La Plume*, IV [September 15, 1892], 394). In conceding that mime is an "art" and a "language," Jullien of course seriously undermines his argument, but in 1892 he was in no position to be enlightened by, say, the *lanterne sourde* of Derrida.

lost on Aubert. And in confusing Pierrot's fiction with
"reality"—the ultimate injury incurred by Champfleury's
Realist reforms—they misvalued and, consequently, denied
his importance to the pantomime as a whole. If Pierrot can
express a sublime *état d'âme*, why cannot any character?
And would his expressiveness not gain in nobility and power
by being severed from the familiarity of the type? Would it
not, moreover, acquire "symbolic" intensity in being freed
from the comic mode? Almost all of the discussions of the
pantomime by the Cercle seem to resolve themselves into
these questions. Often the assertions are contradictory, as
if acknowledging on the one hand Pierrot's "expressive"
eloquence and denying on the other his right to it.

In a series of articles, dating from even before the founding of the Cercle, Jules Lemaître had established these poles
of argument. In the ideal pantomimic theater, he wrote,
"these silent spectacles would work their magic by awakening in us a crowd of memories, impressions, and dreams."

> For example, a scene of jealousy followed by reconcil-
> iation between Colombine and Arlequin, by the very
> fact that it would unfold completely in signs and atti-
> tudes, would evoke and sum up for us all of the anal-
> ogous scenes written by Molière, Racine, or Shake-
> speare. The smallest gesture of Pierrot would be
> suddenly glossed, in our memory, by some six or seven
> great poets.[29]

Indeed, in *Pierrot assassin de sa femme*, Pierrot's livid features had already seemed to acquire the dignity of the classical mask:

> [. . .] this simplified, artificial, hairless head, its features
> without relief: this oblong moon on which one sees,
> against the flat whiteness of the background, only the
> holes of the eyes and nostrils, and the line of the eye-
> brows and mouth: this head is quite truly tragic . . .
> In fact, it is tragic in precisely the same way as those
> other artificial heads, those masks with which the ac-
> tors would cover themselves to perform the dramas of

[29] May 23, 1887: *Impressions de théâtre, deuxième série*, 8th ed. (Paris:
Société Française d'Imprimerie & de Librairie, 1897), p. 354.

Aeschylus and Sophocles, and which surely gave to the
ingenuous Greeks no desire whatsoever to laugh.[30]

But for Lemaître this mask is as restrictive in its suggestiveness as it is artfully eloquent, for Pierrot is a member
(as Gautier had observed) of a family of invariable types:
"*Arlequin, c'est l'Amoureux; Léandre, c'est l'Imbécile; Cassandre, c'est le Bourgeois* [. . .]."[31] Consequently, "a certain
monotony" always attends upon the spectacles of his stage:

> At bottom, there is only one subject for tragic panto-
> mime. Yesterday Pierrot murdered Colombine by tick-
> ling the soles of her feet; today [in Margueritte's *Co-
> lombine pardonnée*] he stabs her with a knife. So it will
> always be Pierrot killing Colombine or her love Ar-
> lequin—unless it is Pierrot killed by Arlequin or Co-
> lombine . . . And there is also only one subject for
> comic pantomime: Arlequin marrying Colombine in
> spite of the police-commissioner and in spite of Pierrot
> or Polichinelle. . . .

The "crowd of memories, impressions, and dreams" is, in
other words, a fairly thin crowd: to invoke one of richness
and complexity, we must look to the dramatic stage. And
yet "one must love the pantomime," Lemaître concludes,
"but only as a philosophical interlude that relaxes us after
the more learned and discursive genres, and that suggests
to us—after we have thought, 'How complicated is the human heart!'—this equally legitimate reflection: '*Mon Dieu!*
how simple it is!' "[32]

His error, like Aubert's, is the Realist's error: identifying
the idealized passions (and impoverishing coherence) of *fin-
de-siècle* pantomime with the "simplicity" of the human heart.
But it was an error that the Cercle Funambulesque seemed
lamentably eager to embrace. In a lecture given at a soirée
of the Cercle in April of 1892, Maurice Lefèvre spoke of
the pantomime as a "symbolic" drama that permits us, the
spectators, "to express everything, to see everything, to understand everything, without interrupting the dream that

---

[30] May 28, 1888: *Impressions de théâtre, troisième série*, 4th ed. (Paris:
Lecène et Oudin, 1889), p. 351.

[31] *Impressions, deuxième série*, p. 353.

[32] *Impressions, troisième série*, pp. 355-56, 357.

lulls our reason." He went on to pronounce the demise of
the old *commedia* masks: "What had killed these symbolic
characters," he declared, "was the absence of symbol [in
their pantomime]." *L'Enfant prodigue* was "a great victory
for the friends of this charming art"—not for the fictive
intensity of its Pierrots, apparently, but for the "symbolic"
truth of their "expressiveness."[33] Of course the Cercle had
always welcomed pantomimes conceived in the "modern"
mode: as early as 1889, *Lysic*, a *monomime* by Eugène
Larcher, in which a young maid from the country makes
comic acquaintance with her new Parisian quarters, had
shared the stage with Legrand's *Le Papillon*. The last pantomime in *Les Soirées Funambulesques* is *L'Hôte* (1893), a
three-act melo by Carré and Hugounet, in which no *commedia* characters appear. In a note to the concluding article
of the collection, "Le Mimodrame," by Henry Maret, Hugounet congratulates himself upon the play's success, interpreting it as one of the signs of the public's "disaffection"
with *"la véritable pantomime italienne."*[34] But *L'Hôte* survives only in the yellowing pages of *Les Soirées Funambulesques*: Pierrot's life was hardly over, and neither was the
life of his pantomime—even after the death of the Cercle
itself in 1898.

For the Symbolists working outside its orbit, he lived of
course only to die: or to be etherealized into an ideal "soul"
refined of animal appetite. Usually careless of theory and
sometimes indifferent to the practicalities of the stage, they
seized as instinctively upon Pierrot for their occasional pantomimes as for their lily-strewn, swan-whitened verse.[35]

[33] "La Pantomime, conférence faite au Théâtre d'Application, le 29 avril
1892," *Revue d'Art Dramatique*, June 1892: Ro 10099, Bibliothèque de
l'Arsenal, pp. 260, 263, 264.

[34] Hugounet and Larcher, *Les Soirées Funambulesques*, p. 218.

[35] That the Pierrot of Symbolist poetry was wont to etiolate into pure
spectrality is suggested by a few titles of the late 1880s: Louis Gaillard's
"Berceuse funèbre pour Pierrot défunt" (1888), Rémy Saint-Maurice's
"Ballade des Pierrots morts" (1888), Albert Dupuy's "La Mort de Pierrot"
(1889), Rémy Broustaille's "La Mort de Pierrot" (1889). All these pieces
appear in Adolphe Willette's *Le Pierrot*, which was published at the height
of *la mêlée symboliste*: for readers interested in versified Pierrots of the *fin-
de-siècle*, this review offers a representative anthology—of both the moon-
mad and insouciant types.

Banville had already celebrated his purity; Verlaine had set him twisting pathetically in a lightning-rent cosmic wind; Margueritte had made him "tragic." He had become a locus of intense fascination, of what the century was wont to call "poetry": not least because of his chaste (though always ardent) courtship of Notre-Dame la Lune. In a sensitive and suggestive meditation on the figure, Paul Guigou's "Le Mythe de Pierrot" (1893), the little ballad attributed to Lulli is given a crucial role in his "myth":

> Through it is finally recognized and proclaimed the secret harmony that will one day join so closely in mystical betrothal the droll scourer of nocturnal streets and the ever-compassionate Planet [*Astre*], the light of which, shed from heaven, seems to me the gently flowing river that Shakespeare called the milk of human kindness. Over the cradle of Pierrot leaned the white moon.[36]

Guigou's metaphors betray the secret source of Pierrot's "poetry": the oral fantasies of Verlaine and Banville are now indistinguishable from public conceits, and when the moon leans over the Pierrot of the Symbolists, she will offer the same sweet lacteous oblivion.

But few pantomimes acknowledge the narcissistic wish that draws Pierrot to moonlit lucarnes: in them it is translated into Idealist terms—into an uncompromising quest for Purity, for Fidelity, for True Love, for Dream. The enemy is always the flesh, or those spurs of the flesh, the instincts. So, in Hughes Delorme's *Pierrot amoureux* (1888), after Pierrot loses Colombine to his black-masked rival, he wins her back when she lifts Arlequin's *loup* and shrinks before his "ignoble head"—his "low forehead, squinting eye, sensual lips."[37] When Pierrot (quite literally) gives up his heart in *Pierrot coeur d'or* (1893), by Cressonnois and Mercklein, he turns suddenly brutish, devouring food and drink and bawling out an obscene lyric. *Pierrotin* (1892), by Charles Chincholle, suggests the danger of such degra-

[36] *La Revue Hebdomadaire*, November 4, 1893: Ro 11553, Bibliothèque de l'Arsenal, p. 134.

[37] *Pierrot amoureux, pantomime-ballet en 1 acte* (Rouen: Deshays et Cie, 1888), p. 7.

dation: here Pierrot initiates Pierrotin (whom he has found in an egg in the park) into the escalating pleasures of the senses—first eating and drinking, walking and dancing; then, smoking, tippling, and ogling women. The shocks are too much for the boy: he dies and his soul flies away as a sparrow (*un moineau*: that is to say, *un pierrot*), its neck encircled with white ribbons. Better to stay aloof, obviously, and die into a private vision, like that of the hero of *Pierrot inconstant* (1893), who abandons Colombine for the moon: "*Il veut des amours étherées*," writes his creator, Jean Philippe, "*d'idéales amours avec elle, la grande enchanteresse, son éternelle amante, l'adorable berceuse de ses rêves imprécis.*"[38]

The most memorable of the Symbolist experiments is *Le Ventre et le coeur de Pierrot* (1888), a pantomime by Léo Rouanet. Unfolding in a succession of expressionist landscapes—of blueish distances glimpsed through forest trees, of red clouds on winter horizons, of glacial moons in steelgray skies—it propels Pierrot through a drama rich with the oppositions (and regressive fantasy) of *fin-de-siècle* idealism. Having been teased into love by Colombine, a fairy, as he lay drunken in the woods, Pierrot now pursues her everywhere: but she, coquette, flees before him, admonishing him for his appetites, instructing him to drink no more and to eat "delicately, like a bird." He tries, and fails ("*son naturel prend le dessus*"), then doggedly tries again. Finally, he appears "transfigured by love; his face has nobler features, his eyes a less bestial gaze." But still Colombine will not be won. Faithful in his fashion, he once more takes to drink—and to the embraces of the servingmaid, Nérine, of the inn at the forest's edge. When at last he falls, defeated and senseless, into the last deep snows of the wood, Colombine appears to express her perplexity at his suffering. Her instincts are not a lover's, obviously, but a mother's for her child. "I'll warm you up," she tells him: "You'll be warm in my arms, and I know some kisses that will take the chill off your poor frozen hands." Pierrot stops crying and rubbing his fists in his eyes ("*à la manière des tout petits*"); he "lets himself be rocked, and plays childishly with

[38] *Pierrot inconstant, pantomime en un acte* (Niort: Imprimerie Lemercier et Alliot, 1893), p. 14.

the frills on the Fairy's bodice." She kisses him, and then they kiss as one. In a sublime transformation, spring suddenly comes to the forest, and it showers the couple—this *maman* and *moutard*—with the blossoms that cling to the wedding-veil (or that are traditionally strewn on tombs).[39]

Perhaps it was this narcissistic wish for a *liebestod* that also motivated Pierrot *décadent*. *L'Ame de Pierrot*, by Jean Richepin, explicitly suggests this was so. The pantomime is the creation of one Marchal, called "Tombre," a mime in Richepin's novel *Braves Gens* (1886) who incarnates "*un fantôme réel*." He describes the character to his friend Yves de Kergouët:

> "[. . .] Pierrot in a suit, without a hint of linen, and his face and hands completely white: but not of a gay whiteness, no. A pallid whiteness. An American alcoholic whiteness, a lugubrious whiteness. [. . .] No longer a Pierrot exciting laughter. A Pierrot exciting shudders, and thought. Thought especially. In a word, the Pierrot-Ombre."
>
> He strongly pronounced the *t* of the liaison.[40]

In *L'Ame de Pierrot*, this phantom consigns his soul to the devil (he gives Colombine, that is, to Arlequin) and steeps himself deliciously in crime. But without a soul, he is without remorse, and soon even "crime itself seemed to him insipid." He decides to win back his spirit and, to that end, renounces his vices: but his pursuit of Colombine comes to resemble the dreamlike flight of Rouanet's Pierrot after *la fée*:

> In the measure that he atoned for his crime and merited the repossession of his soul, that soul grew purer, assuming forms that were more and more noble and beautiful. Colombine finally became a kind of personification of Death itself, of that Death which he desired so much, and which was the supreme object of all his love.[41]

[39] *Le Ventre et le coeur de Pierrot, pantomime en 2 actes et 6 tableaux* (Paris: Parvillez, 1888), pp. 21, 22, 25, 34, 35.

[40] *Braves Gens, roman parisien*, nouv. éd. (Paris: Charpentier-Fasquelle, 1913), p. 61.

[41] Ibid., pp. 177, 178.

In Hannon and Hansen's *Pierrot macabre* (1886), the balletic action traces the same sort of curve. Pierrot *cynique* stands reluctant watch over Colombine's freshly dug grave; he is prevented from joining his friends in the tavern only by a conscientious crowd of spooks. At the funeral, however, he is offended by the mourners' rude snoring—and, alone, he swallows, grieved and remorseful, the contents of a bottle labeled "OUBLI." When Colombine's kiss brings down the curtain, it does so presumably upon Pierrot's own happy death.

Crime, remorse, death: the path was well-trodden—perhaps because it gave a *raison d'être* for Pierrot's self-destructive love. It was that moon-madness, apparently, that thirst for the Ideal, that was intended to resonate through Jean de Villethiou's *Illusion-baiser* (1895) and *La Dernière de Pierrot* (1895). Odd little pieces, in a realistic style, in which Pierrot skillfully seduces two women in nearly identical ways, they betray a cynicism that is both perverse and innocent in its respect for the sexual act. Pierrot shows no remorse here, and he does not die—unless he may be thought to expire (as a type) with the idealism that he besmirches. But his conscience is elsewhere unrelenting. In Paul Lheureux's *Le Testament* (1891), or in his *Crime et châtiment* (1891), or in *Mimes rouges* (1896), a "*mimodrame fantastique*" by Champdeuil and Moret, crime leads to the punishment of remorse and terror, sometimes in a "decadently" reckless prose. Gilles kills the Marquis in *Mimes rouges*, jealous of his own Gillette, and, with his bloody blouse hidden beneath the Marquis's cape, he drinks himself into oblivion:

[The murder] is a very old piece of business, already, something he has almost forgotten—thanks to the clear golden wine, thanks to the red mouth of Gillette that he kisses, that he nibbles. And Gillette gives him back his kisses: and Gilles loosens her bodice, pushes back the fabric, tears off the lace, and her breast is bare (how Gilles' fingers play over that breast!) for one other than Gilles, who is Gilles. But she no longer thinks of Gilles. What does Gilles matter, since Gilles is not here and someone is touching her breast, and she is drunk, and a mouth is kissing her, biting her, furiously, deliciously![42]

Decadent rapture can go no farther, at least upon a pantomime stage.

Until the mid-1890s, such rapture was generally confined to one's *théâtre à fauteuil* or to occasional experimental performances: the popular *cafés-concerts* that offered pantomime to the public eschewed the higher literary sublimities. The Moulin-Rouge and Folies-Bergère had a vested interest in appetite, of course, and their directors were chary of crime, unless it was the senseless and apparently harmless knockabout of the popular Hanlon-Lees. Consequently, when a *"pierrot fin de siècle"* appeared on one of their stages, as in *Pierrot et Pierrot!* (1890) by Courtès and Pougaud, he was paired with an engaging "Ancien Pierrot," naïve and sentimental, endearingly gauche in his linen beside that black-suited, monocled, cane-bearing gentleman *"d'une allure très-décidée."*[43] While the latter reads *Le Chat Noir* over a bottle of champagne and makes bald propositions to Colombine, the old Pierrot unfolds *Le Constitutionnel*, sipping cheap wine, and drafts a lyrical declaration of love. (Colombine picks the man with the money, but all three exit arm in arm.) It is clearly not thought (or idealism) that these Pierrots are meant to excite, but the laughter of health and pleasure. "J'aime la gaieté, la jeunesse et les éclatantes couleurs," declares the Colombine of *L'Arc-en-ciel* (1893), a ballet-pantomime by Amédée Moreau produced at the Folies-Bergère. "Le Blanc, c'est fade": thus she dismisses the artist Pierrot.[44] And only when her suitor, "a poor ragged Shepherd," is clothed by the handmaidens of the Rainbow Fairy and finally stands before her as Arlequin, does she give up her light heart.

Bright spectacle, sharp ankles, and a fairy-tale homily: such were the ingredients of these pantomimes. René

[42] René Champdeuil and Gabriel Moret, *Mimes rouges, mimodrame fantastique mêlé de danses, en 3 tableaux* (Paris: Bibliothèque des Modernes, 1896), pp. 12-13.

[43] V. Courtès and D. Pougaud, *Pierrot et Pierrot! pantomime en un acte* (Paris: Benoît, [1890]), p. 4.

[44] *L'Arc-en-ciel, ballet-pantomime en 3 tableaux* (Paris: Dupont, 1893), pp. 11, 12.

Epilogue

Maizeroy's *Le Miroir* (1892) is typical in all these respects. When poor shepherdess Nivette is reunited with her father, from whom she has been separated for seventeen years, she must part from her lover, Pierrot. But she is ever true to her attachment: so Pierrot discovers when he arrives at her palace and, in his presence, she makes up in a little mirror, his own last gift to her. In such banality Jules Bois found an answer, pure and simple, to the tortured reflexivity of the Symbolists:

> From Stéphane Mallarmé to the latest disciples of Henri de Régnier, inspired youth has delighted in masks and mirrors, the principal props of juvenile reveries. The ever-deepening falsehood of reflecting glasses, the artificial falsehood of fabrics or pasteboards, grimacing on faces or walls, has possessed a generation too disgusted, perhaps, by Naturalism to look upon reality with anything but horror.
>
> [. . .]
>
> In M. Maizeroy's pantomime, the mirror is an instrument of truth and justice in coquetry and grace, and I like it but all the more for that.[45]

Pierrot's candor and *clarté* were weapons that could be used skillfully against his own *rêves imprécis*, and not only reviewers but also authors of pantomimes were often eager to make him see reason. Like the writers of verse, whose *comédies funambulesques* proliferated in the 'eighties and 'nineties,[46] they conceived him as frequently as a *simple enfant* as an adept of Symbolist mysteries.

---

[45] "Folies-Bergère," article in unidentified newspaper, dated—by hand—1892: Ro 11361 ("Rec. fac. de progr. et d'art. de presse, concernant 'le Miroir,' pantomime en 2 tableaux, par René Maizeroy, 1892"), Bibliothèque de l'Arsenal, f. 5.

[46] Much of what I have said about the pantomime may be extended to the vaudevilles and comedies in verse of these years; the reader wishing an acquaintance with these pieces may consult the following names: Anon. (*Cassandre, fils & Cie* [1895]), Paul Arène (*Le Secret de Polichinelle* [1897]), Gaston Arman de Caillavet (*Colombine* [1891]), Théodore de Banville (*Le Baiser* [1888]), Ernest Benjamin (*Le Montreur de marionnettes* [1893]), Joanny Bonichon (*Arlequin chez Pierrot* [1893]), Hippolyte Bonnardot (*Le Souper de Arlequin* [1892]), Theódore Botrel (*Pierrot-Papa* [1892]), Arthur Cantillon (*Pierrot devant les sept portes*), Coustans-Milleret (*Pierrot*

Epilogue

But at the end of the decade, towards the turn of the century, his images were consolidated into a single figure, the naïve and "tragic" artist. The association had never been very far from Pierrot, but the professional mimes of *la Belle Epoque*, particularly Séverin and Georges Wague, refined the association into myth. In doing so, they completed a process that had been advanced by the authors of *L'Enfant prodigue* and sustained by the grim *mimodrames* of the Decadents: they inspired him with sublime and impossible passions, often in the name of expressive truth, and so put an end to his life in the old infantile world of wish.

For the mimes of the "School"—that is, of the traditions passed from Baptiste to Legrand and to Deburau *fils*, and thence to the Marseille Pierrot, Louis Rouffe—Paris in the 1880s must have seemed ungenerous towards classical pantomime. Before Legrand had been summoned before the "small but select" public of the Cercle Funambulesque, he had performed for two years at the Théâtre-Vivienne. Its "Prologue d'ouverture" (1886) suggests the degradations that his art suffered there. Announcing that "it is for them, for the wee ones," that the theater had been constructed, a

---

riche, *Pierrot pendu* [1896]), Hughes Delorme (*Pierrot financier* [1891]), Jérôme Doucet (*La Damnation de Pierrot* [1893]), Armand Ephraïm and Colias (*Polichinelle* [1894]), Paul Eudel and Evariste Mangin (*Polichinelle et la Mort* [1893]), Albert Fox (*Pierrot infidèle* [1891]), Albert Giraud (*Pierrot Narcisse* [1887]), Jules Guillemot (*Le Mariage de Colombine* [1889]), Fernand Hauser (*Pierrot* [1891]), Henry Kist (*Pierrot amoureux* [1891]), A.-F. La Pérelle (*Pierrot Ministre* [1896]), Stephen de La Tour (*La Tentation de Pierrot* [1891]), Marc Legrand (*Pierrot et la Lune* [1888]), André Léneka and Gandrey (*Le Divorce de Pierrot* [1892]), Georges Lorin (*Pierrot voleur!* [1896]), Jacques Madeleine (*Pierrot divin* [1887]), Jules de Marthold (*Pierrot municipal* [1896]), Alexis Martin and Robert de la Villehervé (*Pierrot magnétiseur* [1882]), Bertrand Millanvoye (*Le Dîner de Pierrot* [1881], *Les Ruses de Truffaldin* [1892]), André Maurevert (*Pierrot divorce* [1900]), J. Noury (*Arlequin Ministre* [1894]), Maurice Ordonneau and Emile André (*La Princesse Colombine* [1887]), Henri Remond (*Pedrolino* [1890]), Léon Riffard (*Pierrot Baron* [1892], *Pierrot Herboriste* [1892], *Pierrot Politicien* [1892]), Edmond Rostand (*Pierrot qui pleure et Pierrot qui rit* [1899]), Rémy Saint-Maurice (*Pierrot sceptique* [1892], *Madame Polichinelle* [1892]), Albert Semiane (*Pierrot mordu* [1890], *Pierrot puni* [1888]), Paul Sonniès (*Arlequin séducteur* [1889]), Léon Supersac (*M. et Mme Polichinelle* [1881]). The best of these playlets are by Giraud, Legrand, and Madeleine; the most tedious by Riffard.

304

"*valet de comédie*," addressing the house, congratulates the management for attending to their interests:

> *Mais quoi! le grand Paris n'avait pas une scène*
> *Où devant une farce au gros sel, vive et saine,*
> *Pussent rire d'accord le père avec l'enfant.*

[But what's this? the great Paris did not have a stage/ Where, before a broad farce, wholesome and lively,/ The father and child could laugh together.]

"*Eh bien! consolez-vous!*" he cries: "*car Pierrot est vivant.*"

> *Moi, j'apporte en cadeau la grosse comédie,*
> *Courte et bonne, morale, et jamais trop hardie:*
> *Mais gaie! Ah! mes enfants! . . . Un trésor de plaisir.*[47]

[I'm bringing the gift of crude comedy,/Short and good, moral, and never too bold:/But gay! Ah, my children! . . . A treasure-house of pleasure.]

The only pantomime to survive from its repertoire, *Pierrot patriote* (1886), is dispiritingly "*morale*" and "*gaie*": Pierrot shudders with fear when a military-school student upbraids him for thieving food, and then he is "transfigured" by a sense of duty when the student unfurls the flag.

Rouffe, who had received instruction from Charles Deburau in the last years of the latter's career, refused to play in Paris, enjoying great success before his Marseille public, elaborating an art that was very personal, almost eccentric. An eyewitness reported that he was never the same for two nights in a row and that, "if he happened to fall into vulgarity, in the next instant he astonished [his spectators] with some incomparable lucky find."[48] He was intent upon establishing a "grammar" for his art, matching words with gestures, composing "sentences" out of a series of movements. His own student, Séverin, noted that he rarely performed in Pierrot's *souquenille*, preferring character costume, merely whitening his face, inspiring his public's affectionate epithet "*l'Homme Blanc.*"[49] Arlequin, Cas-

---

[47] AN document F[18] 1344[2], unnumbered, undated, and unpaginated MS.

[48] Guigou, "Le Mythe de Pierrot," p. 139.

[49] *L'Homme blanc*, pp. 47, 60.

sandre, and Colombine were no longer familiars of his pantomime: he abandoned them often for more prosaic *com-
pères*.

Séverin, an intelligent and articulate mime, regarded these
innovations with restraint. He told Barrett Clark that, although he had studied with Rouffe, he felt "close to the
original line" of the School, having been fascinated, as a
boy, by a performance of Deburau *fils*.[50] Like his master,
he regarded Pierrot as a "symbol of all mankind," but he
chose to retain the white blouse and to ignore Rouffe's
"grammar" of mime. Instinctively respectful of the power
of the mask, he argued the necessity of convention in the
pantomime, ridiculing the efforts of the Cercle Funambulesque to cultivate a "natural" expressiveness (*"toutes les lan-
gues sont des conventions"*) but decrying Rouffe's experiments as arcane and provincial.[51] He apparently found his
way slowly: after Rouffe's death in 1885, when Séverin was
twenty-two, he was often complimented for reviving onstage the image of Rouffe *lui-même*. "That annoyed me,"
he recalled in his *Souvenirs*: "It was, perhaps, quite vain on
my part, but I wanted to be *me*. I began to write [my own]
plays."[52] In 1890 he was drawn to Paris by the success of
L'Enfant prodigue, and in the following year he performed
there *Pauvre Pierrot*, a piece conceived in collaboration with
Thalès, also a mime and student of Rouffe. Then, largely
through the agency of Paul Arène, he was introduced to
Catulle Mendès, the poet and novelist who seems to have
kept *au courant* of every tremor on the artistic scene.
Mendès's secretary, Paul Franck, was himself an aspiring
mime: and in recalling to his *maître* Gautier's "Shakspeare
aux Funambules," he encouraged Mendès to compose the
masterwork of *fin-de-siècle* pantomime: *Chand d'habits!* premièred by Séverin at the Théâtre-Salon in 1896.

Mendès announced the performance with a long article
in the press, and the acuity of its reflections on the enfee-
blement of Pierrot merits the quoting of a paragraph here:

[50] Barrett H. Clark, "The Last of the Pierrots," *The Drama*, XIII (August 1923), 352.
[51] Séverin, *L'Homme blanc*, pp. 215, 218.
[52] Ibid., p. 160.

Because Pierrot is white like Leda's swan, because
Pierrot is white like the melancholy wanness of the
moon, we have, little by little, turned him into an elegiac guitarist who sends aubades to the closed windows of a beloved, a poet in love with reverie, the
likeness of dreamers leaning at the sills of garret lucarnes to see passing, in the flight of clouds, exquisite
likenesses of the Ideal. We are mistaken: deceived by
the same lunar snow, we have transformed into the
poetic, subtle, and even perverse Gille of Wateau [sic],
the popular Pierrot, the true Pierrot, the former mil-
lerboy who regards rhymes with nothing but ridicule
and who, ingenuously and brutally, being an embodiment of childish instinct served by virile strength,
having no knowledge of the complexities of the over-
subtle soul, flings himself without premeditation and
without remorse, without cleverness or conscience [*sans
science et sans conscience*], towards all the satisfactions,
even should they lead him through crime, and, jingling in his hands, which are perhaps red with blood,
the purse that he has stolen, rejoices in his good luck
with the droll expression of a cat that has just been
lapping at the milk. Or else he will lie down after the
murder in the bed of the woman he has widowed—
because he had to do it, to make his way—and will
caress her with the murdering hands of a child, no
more disturbed than if those hands had been crushing
strawberries. For he is desiring—and uncomprehending—Instinct.[53]

There is a *fin-de-siècle* flavor about the details in those final
sentences, evoking the "Jacobean" *zanni* of *Le Roman d'une
nuit* (1861), one of Mendès's youthful verse plays. But, on
the whole, the passage is an admirable summary of Pierrot's
fallen fortunes, from the Funambules to Laforgue. "We poets
have been wrong," he concludes: Pierrot should be restored to the popular theater. *Chand d'habits!* will be a step
in that direction, for in Séverin, he avers, the old type lives,
the type "far from the Pierrot that has been applauded for

[53] *L'Art au théâtre, deuxième année (1896)* (Paris: Charpentier-Fasquelle, 1897), pp. 240-41.

some time in the theaters and esteemed in the Cercles [Funambulesques]."[54]

But the *zeitgeist* was against such restoration, and neither Mendès nor Séverin was hardly the embodiment of unreflecting and insouciant Instinct. Séverin's *Pauvre Pierrot* had disconcerted his Marseille audience by its spectacle of a doomed Pierrot: and yet the applause that followed had given him the confidence to persist in his experiments: "Henceforth Pierrot could suffer and even die, like every human being."[55] The *rêve pierrotique* of Mendès was invariably of a romantic outlaw, driven by fate (and absinthe) to bloody crime in the melodramatic mode. In 1893 he had conceived for Peppa Invernizzi, a Milanese mime in the Opéra, the role of Pierrot in *Le Docteur blanc*, in which the charlatan murders his wife. Mendès's talent was cleverly synthetic, fusing "Decadent" themes with conventional sentiments: in, for example, *Le Collier de saphirs* (1891), in which Invernizzi also performed, Gilles is imparadised in the dénouement: for his crime—again a murder, to gain a necklace for his Gillette—was committed, forgiveably, "for love." Despite his encomium to the popular Pierrot, Mendès's talent was hopelessly "literary." And that *felix culpa* of Théophile Gautier, "Shakspeare aux Funambules," was precisely the vehicle for his (and Séverin's) Parisian theatrical *coup*.

For if it exploited a fashionable literary taste for the perverse, it assured its audiences that Conscience brooks no transgression. And it immediately won their sympathies for the criminal by portraying him as a pathetic victim: at rise, we encounter not a Pierrot calculating an entrée *chez* the duchess, as we do in "Shakspeare aux Funambules," but a flour-faced wraith, starved of food and love, dangling by his neck from a lamppost. It is a dancer, Musidora (Gautier's "duchess"), who cuts him down, and in this way Mendès establishes a sentimental—and "artistic"—bond that Gautier's characters had not enjoyed. And when the ghost of the peddler comes to haunt Pierrot, the murder and theft once accomplished, he seems less an infernal specter than

[54] Ibid., pp. 240, 241.
[55] Séverin, *L'Homme blanc*, p. 179.

the balm of easeful death: "Embrace me, Pierrot," he tells his assassin, "my lips await your kiss of peace."⁵⁶ In every instance, Mendès's alteration of detail heightened the pathos of the pantomime, endowing Pierrot with artistic sensitivity and his conscience with euthanasiac compassion. In this way, the drama acquired "sublimity" and "grandeur"— and an audience, in the same year, at the Folies-Bergère.

The confusing of conscience, the stern social voice, with the instincts of the "tragic" artist proved an immensely successful formula, and, although Séverin's repertoire included comedy, he came to be identified by the public at large with dramas of crime and remorse. In 1897, he revived a shortened version of Mendès's *Docteur blanc* with great success at the Folies-Bergère; at his own Funambules (which survived for one season, during 1898-1899), he performed, among other pieces, *La Conscience*, a *drame* by Mélandri and Hawkins; he wrote later, with Durel, director of the Kursaal in Geneva, a pantomime of the same title, drawn from an earlier piece called *Remords*. His final creations offered no new departures in theme. In *Plaisirs d'amour* (1907), his last collaboration with Mendès, his Pierrot commits suicide with one Lira Liron after murdering the latter's rich lover. In *Mains et masques* (1920), his "artistic testament," according to Tristan Rémy,⁵⁷ only Pierrot's face and hands play over the stage, ominous symbols of ghostly remorse, orchestrating the anguish of a criminal Arlequin.

With its severe restrictions of corporeal play, *Mains et masques*, writes Rémy, suggests the triumph of the technique of Georges Wague, "who had long taught that the hands and face should be the essential, if not absolute, sources of expressive means of the mime."⁵⁸ Wague, largely a self-taught artist, had developed his technique, throughout the

⁵⁶ From a detailed description of the pantomime by Nozière, reviewing a revival at the Olympia in 1920: unidentified newspaper, dated—by hand—February 15, 1920: Ro 11382 ("Rec. de programme et art. de presse concernant la représentation à l'Olympia de 'Chand d'habits!' pantomime en 1 acte et 3 tableaux, tirée du feuilleton de Théophile Gautier par Catulle Mendès, musique de J. Bouval, fèv. 1920"), Bibliothèque de l'Arsenal, f. 9.

⁵⁷ *Georges Wague*, p. 154.

⁵⁸ Ibid., p. 153.

1890s, in the cabarets of the Latin Quarter. Making his début at the soirées of *La Plume* with recitations of verse in 1892, he was soon interpreting the songs of Xavier Privas by miming the fortunes of a lyrical Pierrot. Called *cantomimes*, these performances featured Wague in gestural accompaniment to a piano and voice in the wings. A poor Pierrot serenades Colombine, promising his heart as a New Year's gift (*Noël de Pierrot* [1894]); dying, he bequeathes his debts to his creditors and his irony to wayfaring poets (*Le Testament de Pierrot* [1895]); he sings passionately to Tanit, the moon, his coy, departed Muse (*Pierrot chante!* [1899]); he drinks, this *"chevalier de la Fantaisie,/Ce frère des lys et des cygnes blancs,"*[59] to forget his vain quest after happiness (*Sommeil blanc* [1899]). Wague's Pierrot was the apotheosis of Pierrot *artiste*. And of Pierrot *tragique*, as well. Outside the *cantomimes*, his first pantomime, *Le Voeu de Musette* (1895), was performed at the Théâtre-Montparnasse as part of a program organized by a group of artists: its Pierrot sings over the tomb of his beloved until she rises to claim him for death. In his next important première (in a piece uninflected by Privas's music), the curtain falls on an all but lifeless Pierrot: finding Pierrette in a swoon, he assumes she is dead, and so prepares a brazier for his suicide; Arlequin (the secret source of the lady's prostration) drowns out all of the coals, but before Pierrot recovers, Pierrette, in her weakness, has consented to be drawn out the door. Thus the grim consequences of Hey Niger's title, *La Première Faute de Pierrette* (1899).

Wague, who became a teacher and director of mime, developed gradually a minimalist aesthetic, seeking in immobility and subtlety of facial expression a way of exteriorizing the unspoken—"movements of thought, bouts of conscience, secret sensations." "THE MINIMUM OF GESTURES," read a sign in his rehearsal-hall, "CORRESPONDS TO THE MAXIMUM OF EXPRESSION." He regarded Deburau's art, the *pantomime classique*, as merely puerile and embryonic, averring (erroneously) that, whereas "modern" pantomime expressed feelings, the so-called

[59] Xavier Privas, *Sommeil blanc, pantomime en 1 acte* (Paris: Imprimerie de E. Marcilly, 1899), n.p.

"classical" mime simply translated words by movement. Like the theorists of the Cercle, he sought "expressiveness" in "natural" gesture—apparently finding it in the stylized grandiloquence that raises smiles in the beholder of his photographs today. Not surprisingly—again like those theorists—he saw "progress" in Pierrot's demise, in his effacement from pantomime by "the heroes of present-day life, of different countries, now fictional, now real—characters less conventional, more human."[60] Although he never completely abandoned the mask, he found his calling in the pantomime *dramatique* and, later, in the silent film. "If the *Chansons de Pierrot*," writes Tristan Rémy, "allowed him to take his first steps, they [were] only anecdotes, brief communiqués."

> Pierrot was the only figure in whom it was still possible to translate scenically the contradictions of life and dream, since Cassandre, Arlequin, and Polichinelle had lost their original characters. But the white costume of Pierrot had something ridiculous about it, in conformance with his role as an unfortunate, a "lunatic," in the English sense of the word.
>
> Wague had to send what he had loved up in smoke in order to mount higher.[61]

In doing so, he may have shortened the life of the pantomime itself, since it was Pierrot's mobile irony—his vacillation *à la* Baptiste between life and dream—that had sustained its small claim to truth. But, as with Séverin, the lure of sublimity, of "expressive" power, proved to be too potent an attraction for Wague. The Pierrot of the *cantomimes*, as Rémy observes, had been not an end but a means:[62] and once the depths of "tragic" expression had been fathomed, the lunatic mask could be laid aside.

To close up our account of Pierrot's pantomimic decline, we might turn to an interpreter for whom the mask seemed

---

[60] Georges Wague, *La Pantomime moderne, conférence prononcé le 19 janvier 1913, dans la salle de l'Université Populaire* (Paris: Editions de l'Université Populaire, [1913]), pp. 8, 9, 10, 11, 17; and Rémy, *Georges Wague*, p. 27.

[61] *Georges Wague*, p. 48.

[62] Ibid., p. 186.

unremovable, who would live and die a *lunatique blafard*. That man was, of course, Adolphe Willette, cartoonist for *Le Chat Noir*, editor of a review called (inevitably) *Le Pierrot* (1888-1889, 1891), illustrator, *affichiste*, and, finally, writer of pantomimes. He had early dreamed of seeing his Pierrots on the stage (to the accompaniment of an orchestra of harps), but it was apparently not until the first decade of the new century that he began converting his cartoons into scenarios. In 1907, at the Palais des Beaux-Arts de Monte Carlo, Georges Wague appeared in his *L'Age d'or*, a pantomimic disquisition on the eternal cupidity of Woman. *Illusions!!!* (1910) then followed (in which Wague mimed the same torment) at the Théâtre-Michel in Paris. After several other pieces—*Pierrot jardinier* in 1911, *La Lettre* in 1912—Willette wrote his most ambitious pantomimic "*fantaisie*," *Montmartre* (1913). Produced at the Folies-Bergère, with dances by Mariquita and music by Bosc, it was a celebration of *la vie de bohème* that had nurtured his irresistibly charming art. La Butte de Montmartre is its magical setting; its hero is Pierrot, "of pagan times," a miller fought over by muses and bacchantes, a poor tenant whose black cats devour his mean landlord, a painter who fends off *la Vache enragée* by offering his palette to be licked. For the reviewer of *Oui*, the pantomime was less a celebration than a threnody, reviving ghosts of a vanished past:

> In following the adventures of his Pierrot and his Colombine, one cannot escape a vague feeling of sadness. It seems—and this is not the least part of the enchantment of this little entertainment—that one is in the presence of phantoms. These characters seem like specters—amiable and smiling specters. The battle of the artist against the landlord, who looks like old Monsieur Vautour, the betrayal of Colombine, who is not insensible to Arlequin's gold, the putting to death of the *vache enragée*—everything has an antiquated charm. The black cats that prowl about in the atelier evoke the days of Rodolphe Salis—a time that has completely disappeared. We are conscious that the setting itself, the old Montmartre, no longer exists, and that

the last vestiges of it are going to vanish. What remains around the basilica, itself rather too new? The old church, the cemetery, where the millers of old repose, the Place du Tertre, the Place du Calvaire, the Rue des Saules, the Rue Saint-Vincent. . . . Everywhere tenements are being erected. The gardens have been pulled up. The old walls are being torn down. The characters of Willette are revenants flitting about on the ruins.[63]

Paris had changed; its myths were passing. And the next year would mark the commencement of the pantomimic agony: "*c'était la guerre*," writes Rémy, and the "traditional, classical pantomime [. . .] was not to survive that cataclysm."[64] As for Pierrot, he was to lose his power as a dramatic fiction, receding into the planes of Georges Braque's cubism, or held in the envelope of nostalgic reverie by the thick black outlines of Rouault, or bound to the randy Arlequins of Picasso as a talisman of innocence and restraint. And he was to survive always as a figure from the past: as a surface to be cut up and reassembled, as an image inviting and frustrating repossession, as an emblem of the guilelessness of the child. In other respects, he was to be now nothing *but* a fiction, a *fantoche* invoked for his artificiality, part of the bric-à-brac of fashionable affectation, summoned up and dismissed at will. Pierrot *poète*, Pierrot *artiste*, expressing the passions of a generous soul, was an embarrassment for the twentieth century. And the change had set in well before *Montmartre*. In the famous photograph of Stravinsky with his Petrouchka, the urbane composer, impeccably dressed, capable of nothing that would compromise a well-bred gentleman, seems bored—though

[63] By an unidentified reviewer in an article dated—by hand—September 9, 1913: Ro 11498 ("Rec. fac. d'art. de presse sur 'Montmartre,' fantaisie dansée du peintre Ad. Willette et de Mme Mariquita, mus. d'Augustin Bosc, 1 sept. 1913"), Bibliothèque de l'Arsenal, f. 4. *La Vache enragée* (literally, "the enraged cow") is most familiar in the slang expression *manger de la vache enragée* ("to rough it," "to have a hard time of it"): hence Willette's visual pun. Rodolphe Salis was the proprietor of the Chat Noir and editor of its review.
[64] *Georges Wague*, p. 113.

patient, forbearing, polite—at having been posed with a fool.

If the new sensibility had altered irrevocably the artist's relationship to Pierrot, it had also altered the public's perceptions of pantomime. When, after the war, Séverin revived *Chand d'habits!* at the Théâtre des Champs-Elysées, a reviewer spoke of it as *"la fameuse oeuvre romantique"*—and others were less euphemistic: any well-made film, remarked Pierre Scize, was "a hundred times less puerile than *Chands d'habits!*"; "really a bit elementary in its melodramatic naïveté," wrote Raoul Brunel in *L'Oeuvre*.[65] It was the emotional falsity, so apparent in *Chand d'habits!* that at last estranged the mime from his public. Every reason but this one was offered: the success of the silent film, the poor technique of amateur mimes, the incomprehension of audiences before a now unfamiliar art, the lack of students to follow Séverin. Young mimes struggled to keep the art alive—Farina, especially, who, in 1926, again opened a Funambules. But it was never to regain its vanished power, for it was never to relinquish the sentimental idealism of the mimes of *la Belle Epoque*. Today one watches it with misgiving, charmed by the technique, amused by the farces of trivial life, but exasperated by the "serious" pieces. Baptiste's Satan-*bouffe* has become a dying Icarus, his wings drooping in pathetic failure; the rich routs of Pierrot and Arlequin have turned into political allegories, in which Good (when it is not Downtrodden by Evil) unseats a paper-thin tyrant. It is an art that is animated by simple ideas, not the dynamics of the psychic life. Such simplicity was alien to Gaspard Deburau of the Théâtre des Funambules: "He is closed up in the majesty of his role," George Sand once wrote, "and he seems to ponder all its profundity."[66] He inspired a century of artists to ponder it with him; now, the pantomime inspires indifference. In watching Bip skate through the park, one longs for the surprise of a playful

[65] All these remarks are quoted from Ro 11383 ("Rec. fac. de programme et art. de presse concernant la reprise au Théâtre des Champs-Elysées de 'Chand d'habits!' pantomime en 3 tableaux de Catulle Mendès, musique de Jules Bouval, mars 1921"), Bibliothèque de l'Arsenal, ff. 9, 12, 17.
[66] "Deburau" (*Le Constitutionnel*).

transformation, the pleasure of a Pierrot juggling with the *commissaire*'s head, the glee of a Colombine, accomplice to the dunking of papa Cassandre in the depths of a cardboard latrine.

Vain dreams of a *pierrotiste*.

Handlist of Pantomime Scenarios

ARCHIVES NATIONALES DE FRANCE

Censure dramatique: Manuscrits de pièces [...] représentées à Paris et dans la banlieue: Classement par théâtres [numbers in parentheses are dates of registration]:

Théâtre des Funambules (1835-1879):

F^{18} 1083: MS 56, *Le Souterrain, pantomime à spectacle en 3 tableaux, avec dialogue explicatif* (9.26.35); MS 112, *Les Epreuves, grande pantomime-arlequinade-féerie en 13 tableaux, mêlée de danses, travestissements, etc., précédée de: Le Cheveu du Diable, prologue en un acte et en 2 tableaux, en vers libres, mêlé de chants, danses, etc.* (10.22.35); MS 252, *Les Dupes, ou les Deux Georgettes, pantomime comique mêlée de danses en 3 tableaux* (1.9.36); MS 542, *Jack l'orang-outang, pantomime à grand spectacle, en trois actes, mêlée de paroles et de couplets* (6.26.36); MS 750, *Pierrot et ses créanciers, pantomime en sept tableaux* (12.5.36); MS 797, *Le Diable boiteux, pantomime dialoguée en 7 tableaux* (12.24.36)

F^{18} 1084: MS 1324, *Le Rempailleur de chaises, pantomime grivoise en 2 tableaux* (12.1.37); MS 1451, *Roberta, chef de brigands, pantomime en cinq tableaux* (2.9.38); MS 1485, *La Chatte amoureuse, grande pantomime arlequinade en onze tableaux précédée d'un prologue* (2.23.38); MS 1640, *Le Voile rouge, pantomime à spectacle en 4 tableaux* (4.23.38); MS 1685, *En v'là des bamboches, pantomime comique en deux tableaux* (6.18.38); MS 1735, *L'Eau et le feu, pantomime féerie en 13 tableaux mêlée de paroles* (7.19.38); MS 1778, *L'Espiègle, ou la Leçon d'amour, pantomime en quatre tableaux* (8.10.38); MS 1868, *Un Secret, pantomime-dialoguée en trois tableaux, mêlée de chant et de danse* (10.10.38); MS 1957, *La Sorcière, ou le Démon protecteur, pantomime* (11.15.38); MS 1987, *Pierrot errant, pantomime féerie, dialoguée, en neuf tableaux et à grand spectacle, mêlée de chants et de danses avec transformations, trans-vestissements* [sic], *etc. précédée de: La Fée du désert, prologue-vaudeville-féerie en un tableaux* (11.24.38); MS 2049, *Le Ton-nelier et le somnambule, pantomime comique en trois tableaux* (12.19.38)

F¹⁸ 1085: MS 2232, *Le Rêve d'un conscrit, ou la Suite du Billet de 1000 francs, pantomime en neuf tableaux* (4.4.39); MS 2448, *Les Recruteurs écossais, pantomime, en 3 tableaux* (8.2.39); MS 2692 [C. Charton?], *Pierrot partout, arlequinade-féerie, en 9 tableaux* (11.30.39); MS 2853, *Souffre-douleur, pantomime-arlequinade dans le genre anglais à grand spectacle & en 12 tableaux, précédée de* [sic] *un prologue, pantomime dialoguée, mêlée de couplets, etc., etc.* (2.21.40); MS 2904, *L'Amour et la Folie, ou le Grelot mystificateur, pantomime arlequinade en 6 tableaux* (3.18.40); MS 3035, *Les Cosaques, ou la Ferme in-cendiée, pantomime villageoise à spectacle en 4 tableaux* (5.15.40); MS 3357, *Pierrot et Croquemitaine, ou les Ogres et les mou-tards, enfantillage-féerie, mêlée de pantomime, de dialogue & de chant, en 6 tableaux* (11.10.40)

F¹⁸ 1086: MS 3493, *M. de Boissec et Mlle de Boisflotté, pan-tomime en 6 tableaux* (1.22.41); MS 3584, *Biribi, grande pan-tomime féerie en 9 tableaux, précédée de: Aux enfers, prologue en un acte* (3.13.41); MS 3639, *Satan Ermite, pantomime arle-quinade en 9 tableaux* (4.10.41); MS 3685, *Les Naufragés, pantomime comique en 3 tableaux* (5.10.41); MS 3924, *Pierrot et l'aveugle, pantomime comique en 5 tableaux* (11.25.41)

F¹⁸ 1087: MS 4087, *Les Trois Bossus, pantomime arlequi-nade en 6 tableaux* (3.7.42); MS 4297, *Pierrot en Afrique, pantomime comique* (6.27.42); MS 4319, *Les 3 Godiches, pan-tomime-arlequinade-féerie en 11 tableaux* (8.17.42); MS 4426, *Le Marrrchand d'habits! pantomime comique en 5 tableaux* (10.17.42); MS 4440, *Hurluberlu, pantomime comique en 4 tableaux* (10.31.42); MS 4523 [C. Charton?], *Le Mandarin Chi-han-li, ou les Chinois de paravent, pantomime-dialoguée en 5 tableaux* (12.1.42); MS 4598, *Les Jolis Soldats, pantomime comique en 5 tableaux* (1.14.43); MS 4844 [Varez], *La Nais-sance de Pierrot, pantomime en 9 tableaux précédée d'un prologue* (5.27.43); MS 4917, *Pierre-le-Rouge, ou les Faux-Monnayeurs, pantomime en cinq tableaux* (6.24.43); MS 5437, *Pierrot chez les Mohicans, pantomime comique en 5 tableaux* (12.27.43)

F¹⁸ 1088: MS 5642, *L'Ile des Marmitons, pantomime en 5*

tableaux (2.13.44); MS 5850 [C. Charton?], *Les Trois Quenouilles, pantomime dialoguée, en huit tableaux, précédée d'un
prologue* (4.18.44); MS 6013, *Mistigris, ou les Tribulations de
Pierrot, pantomime-arlequinade-féerie en dix tableaux* (6.22.44);
MS 6115, *Fra-Diavolo, ou les Brigands de la Calabre, pantomime en quatre tableaux* (8.17.44); unnum. MS, *Bamboches
& taloches, pantomime-arlequinade-féerie à grand spectacle, en 9
tableaux* (n.d.); MS 6589, *Les Sorcières de Macbeth, pantomime
en 6 tableaux* (3.6.45); MS 6612, *Harlequin Snowball, or the
Majic* [sic] *Talisman (Arlequin boule de neige), pantomime-arlequinade anglaise en 10 tableaux* (3.17.45); MS 6650, *Les
Noces de Pierrot, pantomime villageoise en 5 changements*
(4.17.45); MS 6844, *Les Deux Mousquetaires, pantomime villageoise en 3 changements* (7.30.45); MS 6974, *La Pagode enchantée, pantomime chinoise en 7 changements à vue* (10.22.45);
MS 7016, *Les Deux Pendus, ou Lequel des deux, pantomime en
un acte* (11.23.45); MS 7032, *Le Corsaire algérien, ou l'Héroïne de Malte, pantomime en 7 changements, mêlée de combats*
(11.25.45)
   F[18] 1089: MS 7214, *La Roche du Diable, ou le Rêve de
Pierrot, pantomime féerie en sept tableaux* (3.19.46); MS 7398,
Pierrot et Polichinel [sic], *ou les Quatre Rivaux, pantomime arlequinade en 8 changements* (8.12.46); MS 7437 [C. Char-
ton], *L'Oeuf rouge et l'oeuf blanc, ou le Pouvoir des génies, grande
pantomime-arlequinade-féerie en 16 changements, mêlée de chants,
danses, combats, etc.* (9.16.46); MS 7441 [Champfleury], *Pierrot, valet de la Mort, pantomime en 7 tableaux* (9.19.46); MS
7444 [Champfleury], *Pierrot, valet de la Mort, pantomime en
7 tableaux* (9.19.46); MS 7553, *Pierrot et les Bohémiens, ou le
Revenant, pièce mimée, dialoguée, mêlée de chant, de danses, de
combats et d'évolutions, tragi-comi-burlesque, en* quatorze
changemens à vue; *ornée de costumes analogues, soutenue par
un pierrot à gros bec; enjolivée d'une nourrice sans caractère; far-
cie de plusieurs traîtres; bourée d'un enfant mal élevé; lardée de
Bohémiens bons vivants; egayée par un fantôme maladroit et ré-
chauffée par un torrent* (12.7.46); MS 7585 [Champfleury],
Pierrot pendu, pantomime avec douze changements (n.d.)
   F[18] 1090: MS 7652 [C. Charton and Ambroise], *Une Vie
de Polichinelle, pantomime arlequinade féerie en 11 changements*
(2.10.47); MS 7667 [Horebourg], *Pierrot récompensé, féerie
en 12 tableaux, mêlée de couplets, danses, travestissements à grand
spectacle* (2.29.47); MS 7701, *Pygmalion, ou la Statue vivante,
scène de pantomime comique et burlesque en deux changements,
mêlée de danses grotesques* (3.13.47); MS 7778 [E. Martin],

Handlist

Pierrot Pacha, pantomime avec neuf changemens à vue (4.15.47);
MS 7863 [J. Viard], *Pierrot marié* [struck by censor: *et Polichinelle célibataire*], *pantomime en 17 changements, de Mr Jules*
(5.25.47); MS 8010 [J.-G. Deburau?], *Pierrot en Espagne,
pantomime militaire en 9 changemens, mêlée de combats et d'é-
volutions* (8.24.47); MS 8061 [E. Grangé?], *Les Trois Planètes, ou la Vie d'une rose, grande pantomime arlequinade féerie,
dialoguée dans le genre anglais, en trois parties et douze changemens à vue, mêlée de danses, transformations et travestissemens*
(9.20.47); unnum. MS [Champfleury], *Pierrot Marquis, pantomime en 10 tableaux* (n.d.); MS 8179 ["Père Jean"], *Les
Pérégrinations de Pierrot et de Polichinelle, ou L'on n'a rien sans
peine* (12.2.47); MS 8279 [Champfleury], *Madame Polichinelle, ou les Souffrances d'une âme en peine, pantomime en 10
tableaux, par Mr Champfleuri* [sic] (1.28.48); unnum. MS, *La
Fiancée de Pierrot, pantomime comique en 4 tableaux* (n.d.)

F¹⁸ 1091: unnum. MS [A. Jouhaud], *Les Trois Pierrots, ou
Pierrot le rusé, Pierrot le naïf et Pierrot le dévoué, pantomime
arlequinade en 12 tableaux, précédé* [sic] *de Le Baptême des
Pierrots, prologue, précédé de Le Directeur et l'auteur, préface*
(n.d.); MS 94, *Pierrot a deux faces, pantomime en 8 tableaux*
(9.16.50); MS 437, *Les Deux Cuisiniers, pantomime comique
en quatre tableaux* (n.d.); MS 559, *Les Amours de pierrots,
ballet pantomime en 3 tableaux* (n.d.); unnum. MS [C. Char-
ton], *L'Etoile de Pierrot, grande pantomime arlequinade en douze
tableaux, précédé* [sic] *de Le Ciel, le feu et l'eau* (n.d.); MS
3175 [C. Charton], *Les Prisonniers de la Tchernaïa, pantomime
comique en huit tableaux* (10.23.55); unnum. MS [C. Char-
ton], *Le Soldat Belle Rose, pantomime comique en sept tableaux*
(n.d.); MS 5119, *Pierrot étudiant, pantomime en 8 tableaux*
(10.15.59); MS 5616, *Le Sergent Lambert, ou la Fille soldat,
pantomime à spectacle en 4 tableaux* (11.6.60)

F¹⁸ 1092: unnum. MS, *Le Valet du Diable, ballet pantomime en 1 acte, avec trucs, changements à vue, etc.* (n.d.); MS
5812, *Le Loup garou, pantomime villageoise, mêlée de danses, en
3 tableaux* (4.17.61); MS 6130 [C. Nodier?], *Le Songe d'or,
ou Arlequin et l'avare, pantomime anglaise en 11 tableaux*
(1.7.62); MS 6162 [C. Charton], *Le Crocodile de Java, pantomime à grand spectacle en 12 tableaux, avec combats, incendie,
démolition, jeux, danses, etc.* (1.31.62); MS 6181 [A. Guyon
and Duché], *Le Rameau d'or, féerie arlequinade mêlée de chants
et de danses, en 19 tableaux* (2.15.62); MS 8969, *Pierrot mitron, pantomime féerie en un acte* (10.18.67); MS 9012, *Une
Journée d'accidents, ou Rococo, le bon diable, arlequinade féerie*

en un acte avec danses, cascades, évolutions de calottes, coups de pieds et coups de battes (11.9.67); MS 9079, *La Statue vivante, ou les Tribulations de Pierrot, pantomime en un acte* (12.21.67); MS 9112, *La Tante Grognon, ou Lubin et Louisette, pantomime en 3 tableaux* (1.18.68); MS 9165, *Pierrot, ou les Racolleurs* [sic], *pantomime en deux tableaux* (2.20.68); MS 9205, *Pierrot Nouricier* [sic], *pantomime en deux tableaux* (3.17.68); MS 9268, *Pierrot Tonnelier, pantomime villageoise en 3 tableaux* (4.21.68); MS 9311, *La Fée aux roses, ou le Triomphe d'Arlequin, pantomime en 3 tableaux* (5.23.68); MS 9346, *Les Deux Nanettes, ou les 3 Dupes, pantomime* (6.17.68); MS 9442, *Les Moissonneurs, pantomime villageoise en 4 tableaux avec danses* (8.20.68); MS 9480, *Pierrot et le brigand, pantomime en deux tableaux* (9.15.68); MS 9574, *Pierrot Bûcheron, ou la Forêt enchantée, pantomime, arlequinade, féerie en quatre tableaux, avec travestissements, transformations, trucs* (10.23.68)

F¹⁸ 1093: MS 9860, *Le Puits et le trésor, ou les Deux Statues, pantomime en un acte* (3.12.69); MS 9917, *La Maison isolée, ou les Brigands de la Forêt Noire, pantomime en trois tableaux à grand spectacle, mêlée de danses, combats, évolutions et cascades* (4.10.69); MS 10,053, *Pierrot parle, féerie-vaudeville en 1 acte* (7.12.69); MS 10,061, *Pierrot Sorcier, ou les Pilules de Lucifer, pantomime en trois tableaux* (7.23.69); MS 10,129, *Les Fourberies de Nichette, ou Cassandre amoureux, vaudeville en un acte mêlé de pantomime* (8.27.69); MS 10,140, *Un Pierrot sur la branche, vaudeville pantomime en un acte, mêlé de chant* (9.4.69); MS 10,645, *Pierrot chez les Mohicans, pantomime mimodrame en 3 tableaux avec danses, balets* [sic], *combats, évolutions* (8.9.70)

Théâtre des Folies-Nouvelles (1854-1859):

F¹⁸ 1023: MS 2575 [T. de Banville], *Les Nouvelles Folies* [sic], *prologue d'ouverture* (9.30.54); MS 2576 [E. Durandeau], *L'Hôtellerie de Gautier-Garguille, pantomime en 5 tableaux* (9.30.54); MS 2692 [C. Bridault and P. Legrand], *Pierrot Dandin, pantomime* (11.25.54); MS 2741 [M. Altaroche], *Le Possédé, pantomime-ballet en 1 acte* (12.27.54); MS 2760 [P. Mercier], *Biribi le sapajou* (1.13.55); MS 2877 [P. Mercier and P. Legrand], *La Soeur de Pierrot, pantomime en cinq tableaux* (3.29.55); MS 2908 [C. Bridault], *Quand les chats n'y sont pas, pantomime en un acte* (4.17.55); MS 2981 [J. Dantan *jeune* and P. Legrand], *Pierrot indélicat, charge-pantomime en 5 tableaux* (5.31.55); MS 3418, *Les Vendanges de Bourgogne* [produced as *En vendanges*], *pantomime en 1 acte de P. Legrand et Doyen* (9.12.55); MS 3224 [P. Legrand and

Blondelet], *Le Médecin des moutards, parodie pantomime en trois tableaux* (11.28.55); MS 3326 [F. Desnoyers], *Le Bras noir, pantomime en 4 tableaux* (2.1.56); MS 3408 [P. Mercier and P. Legrand], *Pierrot bureaucrate, pantomime en un tableau* (3.31.56); MS 3450 [Laurent], *Le Nabab* [produced as *Un Oncle d'Amérique*], *pantomime en un tableau* (4.28.56); MS 3546 [Julian], *Vertigo, pantomime en quatre tableaux* (7.7.56); MS 3604 [P. Mercier and P. Legrand], *Les Deux Noces, pantomime en cinq tableaux* (9.10.56); MS 3646 [P. Mercier and P. Legrand], *Les Carabins, pantomime en un tableau* (10.13.56); MS 3743 [C. Bridault and P. Legrand], *Les Jeux innocents, ballet-pantomime en un acte* (12.16.56); MS 3744 [J. Perraud], *Gribouille, pantomime en 3 tableaux* (12.17.56); MS 3847, *La Comète de 1858, ou la Fin du Monde, pantomime en cinq tableaux* (3.12.57); MS 3924 [C. Plantade], *Polichinelle notaire, pantomime en quatre tableaux* (4.30.57); MS 4106 [H. Ballue], *Les Brigands pour rire, pantomime en 4 tableaux* (10.1.57); MS 4182 [C. Bridault and P. Legrand], *Une Razia galante, ballet-pantomime en un acte* (11.7.57); MS 4203 [Champfleury], *Pierrot Millionnaire, pantomime* (11.30.57); MS 4224 [C. Bridault and P. Legrand], *Un Drame à Venise* [produced as *A Venise, ou Poignard, potence et mort-aux-rats*], *pantomime en cinq tableaux* (12.30.57)

F[18] 1024: unnum. MS [C. Bridault], *Les Folies Nouvelles, peintes par elles-mêmes, prologue de réouverture* (n.d.); unnum. MS [M. Altaroche], *La Femme qui trompe, pantomime en un acte* (n.d.); unnum. MS [J. Dantan *jeune* and P. Legrand], *Pierrot épicier, folie épicée en un tableau* (n.d.); unnum. MS [Lubize], *Un Drôle de monde, pantomime en 4 tableaux* (n.d.); MS 4255 [J. Dantan *jeune* and P. Legrand], *Pierrot Robinson, pantomime en 3 tableaux* (1.30.58); MS 4379 [C. Bridault and P. Legrand], *Ni hommes ni femmes: tous auvergnats* (4.14.58); MS 4350 [P. Mercier and P. Legrand], *Le Rêve de Pierrot* [produced as *Pierrot qui rêve*], *pantomime en cinq tableaux* (3.30.58); MS 4661 [P. Legrand and Baric], *Le Grand Poucet, pantomime en quatre tableaux* (10.8.58); unnum. MS, *Quick-Silver, or the Dancing Schotman* [sic], *pantomime* (n.d.); unnum. MS [P. Legrand], *Les Bamboches de Pierrot* (n.d.); unnum. MS [C. Bridault and P. Legrand], *Le Petit Cendrillon, pantomime* (n.d.)

Théâtre des Fantaisies-Parisiennes (1865):

F[18] 1214: MS 7832 [Champfleury], *La Pantomime de l'avocat* (11.8.65); MS 7888 [C. Deburau and Vautier], *Double blanc, pantomime en un acte* (12.22.65)

Handlist

Théâtre-Vivienne (1886):
F[18] 1344[2]: unnum. MS [P. Legrand and Bouvret], *Pierrot Patriote, pantomime en un acte* (12.4.86)

Collection Rondel:
Boussenot, Fernand, and Fernand Beissier. *Instantanée* [sic], *pantomime en deux tableaux.* [uncoded MS of pantomime first produced by the Cercle Funambulesque, February 8, 1894]

Carré *fils*, Michel. *L'Enfant prodigue, pantomime en 3 tableaux.* [uncoded MS of pantomime first produced by the Cercle Funambulesque, June 10, 1890]

Rec. des pantomimes jouées au Théâtre des Funambules et copiées par Henry Lecomte. [one uncoded volume containing the following pantomimes: *L'Amour Forgeron, ou les Deux Arlequins rivaux, pantomime-féerie et comi-arlequinade en 3 actes, mêlée de danses, changements à vue, etc.* (1818); *Arlequin, chef de brigands, pantomime-arlequinade en 3 actions et à grand spectacle* (n.d.); *Arlequin séducteur, ou le Chien victime de sa fidélité, pantomime historique en 3 actes, ornée de tout son spectacle, changements à vue, transformations, etc.* (n.d.); *Arlequin sorcier, ou la Fête du Seigneur, pantomime-féerie en 3 actions, ornée de tous* [sic] *son spectacle* (n.d.); *Le Génie protecteur, ou la Vengeance d'Arlequin, pantomime en 3 actes, à grand spectacle, ornée de combats, ballet, évolutions, incendies, etc., etc.* (n.d.); *La Pauvre Mère, ou Arlequin bon fils, pantomime à grand spectacle, changements à vue, transformations, etc.* (n.d.); *Le Petit Poucet, ou Arlequin écuyer de l'ogre des montagnes, pantomime en 6 changements et à spectacle* (n.d.); *Saphir l'enchanteur, pantomime en 3 parties* (n.d.)]

Rec. fac. de pantomimes d'Hippolyte Demanet, jouées aux Funambules. [two uncoded volumes containing the following pantomimes: *Pierrot pêcheur, ou les Bords du Gange, opérette-ballet-pantomime en un acte* (1871) [two copies]; *La Fille du bandit, ou l'Auberge de Céprano, pantomime dialoguée en un acte mêlée de chants, danses, etc.* (1872); *Le Petit Poucet, conte-pantomime en un acte mêlée de dialogue, chants, danses . . .* (1872); *Cendrillon, conte-pantomime en un acte mêlée de dialogues, chants, danses, etc.* (1873) [two copies]; *La Petite Poule aux oeufs d'or, pantomime-féerie en un acte mêlée de dialogues, chants, danses, cascades* (1873); *Pierrot bûcheron, ou la Corne enchantée, pantomime-féerie en un acte mêlée de dialogues, chants, danses, transformations* (1873); *Le Savetier de Seville, panto-*

mime dialoguée en un acte (1873); *La Mère Angot, pantomime en un acte* (1873); *Pierrot portier* (n.d.)]

Rec. fac. des pantomimes jouées au Théâtre des Funambules et copiées par Henry Lecomte, classies par ordre alphabétique d'auteurs. [one uncoded volume containing the following pantomimes: *Le Frère tyran, ou l'Orpheline indienne, pantomime dialoguée et féerie, avec travestissements, changements à vue, transformations, par Delachassaigne* (1817); *Arlequin libérateur du Génie Blanc, pantomime en 3 actes, à grand spectacle, par M. Martial* (1816); *Le Spectre vengée* [sic], *ou le Crime dévoilée* [sic] *par Arlequin, pantomime anecdotique en 3 actes, ornée de danses, combats, évolutions, aparitions* [sic], *etc., à grand spectacle, par Monsieur Martial* (n.d.)]

Les Trois Godiches, pantomime-arlequinade-féerie en 10 tableaux. [heavily emended uncoded MS of pantomime first produced at the Théâtre des Funambules, 1842]

BIBLIOTHÈQUE NATIONALE

Flaubert, Gustave [and Louis Bouihet]. *Pierrot au sérail.* MSS n.a.fr. 14153. [two autograph scenarios, both bearing additions and cancellations, and a one-page synopsis, all bound in one volume]

BIBLIOTHÈQUE SPOELBERCH DE LOVENJOUL

Manuscrits trouvés dans les papiers de Th. Gautier: C515, ff. 26-39:

Habits-Galons, pantomime en cinq tableaux (ff. 26-39)

Untitled scenario bound with preceding item (ff. 22-25)

II. PUBLISHED SCENARIOS

[Date and place of first production, when known, follow entry in brackets.]

Anon. *Le Diable d'or.* Paris: Dechaume, n.d. [Funambules, 1860]

———. *La Fée Carabosse, grande pantomime en 12 tableaux* [after Cot d'Ordan]. Paris: Dechaume, n.d. [Funambules, 1861]

Arène, Paul. *Pantomime de la Statue.* Paris: Supplement Littéraire, Musical et Artistique de *Paris-Noël*, 1889.

——— and Gustave Goetchy. *La Fleur de coca, pantomime.* Paris: Silvestre, [1892]. [Théâtre Angelo Mariani, June 29, 1892]

Aubert, Charles. *Pantomimes modernes.* Paris: Flammarion, [1895?]. [contains the following scenarios by Aubert: *La Puce* (Casino de Paris, 1894), *Le Réveil d'une Parisienne* (Folies-Bergère,

1894), *Le Suicide de Pierrot* (Cercle Funambulesque, [1894]), *A la belle étoile* (Casino de Cabourg, n.d.), *Le Rideau* (Cercle Funambulesque, [1894]), *Les Deux Spadassins* (Casino de Cabourg, n.d.), *Le Portrait* (Concert Parisiana, n.d.), *Eve* (n.p., n.d.), *Le Cigare* (n.p., n.d), *Têtu* (n.p., n.d.), *La Statue amoureuse* (n.p., n.d.), *Procès en adultère* (n.p., n.d.), *Chez la danseuse* (Concert de La Cigale, [1894]), *Pierrot domestique* (n.p., n.d.), *La Reine s'ennuie* (n.p., n.d.), *Pierrot savetier* (n.p., n.d.), *Nuit de Noce* (n.p., n.d.), *Nuit de Carnaval* (Cercle Funambulesque, 1894), *Paris-Sport* (Comédie-Parisienne, 1895), *Peaux de lapins* (n.p., n.d.)]

Beissier, Fernand. *Histoire d'un Pierrot, pantomime en trois actes.* Paris: Choudens, n.d. [Théâtre Déjazet, January 4, 1893]

———. *La Lune, fantaisie-pantomime en 3 tableaux.* Paris: Choudens, [1890]. [Cercle Funambulesque, March 11, 1889]

———. *Noël de Pierrot, mimodrame en trois actes.* Paris: Ricordi & Cie, 1900. [Bodinière, March 26, 1900]

Bridault, Charles, and Paul Legrand. *La Fausse Douairière, pantomime en deux tableaux.* [Paris]: Maulde et Renore, n.d. [Folies-Concertantes, February 8, 1954]

———. *Pierrot Dandin, pantomime en cinq tableaux.* Paris: Typographie de Jules-Juteau, n.d. [Folies-Nouvelles, December 6, 1854]

Byl, Arthur, and Louis Marsolleau. *La Folie de Pierrot, mimodrame créé par Mévisto.* 2nd ed. Paris: Ondet, 1900. [La Scala, 1891]

Carré *fils*, Michel. *L'Enfant prodigue: Argument de la pantomime.* Rouen: Cagniard, 1892. [Cercle Funambulesque, June 10, 1890]

Champdeuil, René, and Gabriel Moret. *Mimes rouges, mimodrame fantastique mêlé de danses, en 3 tableaux.* Paris: Bibliothèque des Modernes, 1896.

Champfleury [Jules-François-Félix Husson, known as Fleury, known as]. *Les bons contes font les bons amis.* Paris: Truchy, n.d. [contains *Polichinelle et le chat, pantomime*]

———. *La Pantomime de l'avocat, en 1 tableau.* Paris: Librairie Centrale, 1866. [Fantaisies-Parisiennes, December 2, 1865]

———. *Pierrot, valet de la Mort, pantomime en sept tableaux.* [Paris]: n.p., [1846]. [contains, besides other matter, scene titles of the pantomime produced at the Funambules, September 28, 1846]

———. *Les Trois Filles à Cassandre, pantomime bourgeoise, en huit tableaux.* Paris: Dechaume, 1850. [Funambules, 1849]

——— and Albert Monnier. *La Reine des carottes, grande pantomime fantastique, en douze tableaux.* Paris: Dechaume, [1848]. [Funambules, September 23, 1848]

Champsaur, Félicien. *Les Bohémiens, ballet lyrique en 4 actes et 9 tableaux*. Paris: Dentu, 1887.

————. *Les Ereintés de la vie, pantomime en un acte*. Paris: Dentu, 1888. [Cirque Molier, June 6, 1888]

————. *Lulu, pantomime en un acte, préface par Arsène Houssaye*. Paris: Dentu, 1888. [Nouveau Cirque, October 1, 1888]

[Charton], Charles. *Arcadius, ou Pierrot chez les Indiens, pantomime en onze tableaux*. [Paris]: Dechaume, n.d. [Funambules, May 6, 1852]

[————]. *Les Epreuves, grande pantomime en 13 tableaux dans le genre anglais, de feu Deburau et de M. Charles*. Paris: Dechaume, 1849. [Funambules, 1833]

[————]. *L'Etoile de Pierrot, grande pantomime-arlequinade en douze tableaux, précédée de Le Ciel, le feu et l'eau, prologue en deux tableaux*. [Paris]: Dechaume, n.d. [Funambules, January 18, 1854]

[————?]. *Le Génie des eaux, pantomime dialoguée en 11 tableaux*. Paris: Dechaume, n.d. [Funambules, August 10, 1855]

[————]. *Les Mille et une tribulations de Pierrot, grande pantomime féerie en quinze tableaux, précédé* [sic] *de Le Pacte infernal, prologue en deux tableaux*. Paris: Dechaume, 1851. [Funambules, December 8, 1851]

[————]. *Les Pêcheurs napolitains, pantomime dialoguée en dix tableaux*. Paris: Dechaume, 1851. [Funambules, April 22, 1851]

[————]. *Pierrot et les bandits espagnols, pantomime à spectacle, en neuf tableaux*. Paris: Dechaume, n.d. [Funambules, after 1850]

[————]. *Pierrot le possédé, ou les Deux Génies, pantomime-arlequinade en 10 tableaux*. Paris: Dechaume, n.d. [Funambules, October 1848]

[————]. *Pierrot maçon, pantomime comique en cinq tableaux*. Paris: Dechaume, n.d. [Funambules, January 25, 1851]

[————]. *Pierrot sorcier, pantomime comique en dix tableaux*. [Paris]: Dechaume, n.d. [Funambules, November 27, 1852]

[————] and Ambroise. *Les Naufrageurs de la Bretagne, pièce dramatique et comique, à grand spectacle, mêlée de pantomime, de combats au sabre, à la hache et au poignard, en treize tableaux*. Paris: Dechaume, n.d. [Funambules, May 4, 1849]

[————] and Ambroise. *Une Vie de Polichinelle, pantomime-arlequinade, féerie en onze tableaux*. [Paris]: Imprimerie de Bureau, n.d. [Funambules, February 27, 1847]

[————] and [J.-G.] Deburau. *L'Oeuf rouge et l'oeuf blanc, ou le Pouvoir des génies, grande pantomime-arlequinade-féerie, dans le genre anglais*. Paris: Marchant, 1846. [Funambules, October 20, 1846]

[———] and Vautier. *Polichinelle Vampire, grande pantomime dans le genre italien, à grand spectacle, en 15 tableaux, mêlée de dialogues, de métamorphoses, de travestissements et de danses.* [Paris]: Dechaume, n.d. [Funambules, May 25, 1850]

Chincholle, Charles. *Pierrotin, pantomime en quatre scènes.* Paris: Librairie de l'Estampe, 1895. [Jardin des Tuileries, August 19, 1892]

Courtès, V., and D. Pougaud. *Pierrot et Pierrot! pantomime en un acte.* Paris: Benoît, [1890]. [Moulin-Rouge, November 8, 1890]

Cressonnois, Lucien, and Abel Mercklein. *Pierrot coeur d'or, pantomime en un acte.* Paris: Imprimerie de P. Dupont, 1893. [Divan-Japonais, February 7, 1893]

D. *Le Génie rose et le génie bleu, ou les Vieilles Femmes rajeunies, pantomime féerie en deux actes, à grand spectacle.* Paris: Morisset, 1817. [Funambules, February 13, 1817]

Deburau [Charles]. *Le Songe d'or, pantomime fantastique, genre anglais, en 18 tableaux.* Bordeaux: Bord, 1864.

[Deburau, Jean-Gaspard (?)]. *Pierrot en Espagne, pantomime militaire en neuf changements à vue.* [Paris]: Gallet, n.d. [Funambules, 1847]

——— and Charles Deburau. *Pantomimes de Gaspard et Ch. Deburau,* comp. Emile Goby. Paris: Dentu, 1889. [contains the following undated pantomimes, most of which seem to be C. Deburau's adaptations of pieces first performed by his father at the Funambules between 1826 and 1845: *Pierrot coiffeur, Pierrot mitron, La Baleine, Le Duel de Pierrot, ou les 20 Infortunes, Pierrot en Afrique, Les Deux Jocrisses, L'Abbé-Capitaine, ou les Sept Péchés capitaux, Les Noces de Pierrot, Les Dupes, Les Jolis Soldats,* [J.-G. Deburau?] *Les Français en Espagne, La Perle de Savoie, Le Loup-garou, Le Joueur, Le Berger suisse, Pierrot dans le sac, Le Billet de 1,000 francs,* [Champfleury] *La Pantomime de l'avocat*]

Delor, Maxime. *Analyse burlesque de la Mère Gigogne, pantomime-arlequinade en deux actes et vingt tableaux, tirée du conte de M. Albert Monnier.* Paris: Dechaume, 1859. [Funambules, March 24, 1859]

Delorme, Hughes [Georges Thiébost, known as]. *Pierrot amoureux, pantomime-ballet en 1 acte.* Rouen: Deshays et Cie, 1888. [Rouen, Folies-Bergère, 1888]

Demanet, Hippolyte. *Pantomimes comiques pour jeunes garçons.* Nouv. éd. Paris: Le Bailly, n.d. [contains the following undated pantomimes: *Pierrot photographe, La Journée aux aventures, Une Auberge tranquille, Le Seigneur Pierrot, Le Petit Poucet,*

Pierrot portier, L'Argent du Diable, Pierrot spirite, Les Bords du Gange]

Desnoyers, Fernand. *Le Bras noir, pantomime en vers*. Paris: Librairie Théâtrale, 1856. [Folies-Nouvelles, February 8, 1856]

Doucet, Jérôme. *Notre Ami Pierrot, une douzaine de pantomimes*. Paris: Ollendorff, [1900]. [contains a dozen pieces evidently intended to be read rather than performed]

Dufresnau. *Pierrot et le revenant, pantomime fantastique en quinze tableaux*. [Paris]: Dechaume, n.d. [Funambules, September 21, 1855]

Eudel, Paul. *Théâtre, avec une préface par Jules Claretie*. Paris: Librairie Molière, 1903. [contains the following pantomimes by Eudel, most written with a collaborator: *La Statue du Commandeur* (Cercle Funambulesque, 1892), *Retour de bal* (Salle d'Harcourt, 1893), *L'Orage* (Cercle Funambulesque, 1893), *La Geisha* (Salle de la Rue de Lancry, 1893), *Nuit blanche* (Théâtre-Vivienne, 1894), *Le Trottin* (Théâtre de la République, 1895), *Ruy Blas* (Cercle Funambulesque, 1898), *Lucette* (n.p., n.d.)]

——— and Evariste Mangin. *La Statue du Commandeur, pantomime en 3 actes (d'après Champfleury)*. Paris: Heugel, 1892. [Cercle Funambulesque, January 14, 1892]

Flaubert, Gustave [and Louis Bouilhet]. *Pierrot au sérail, pantomime en six actes, suivie de l'apothéose de Pierrot dans le paradis de Mahomet*, in *Oeuvres complètes*, VII. Paris: Club de l'Honnête Homme, 1972.

Gayda, Joseph. *Pierrot volage, pantomime-ballet*. Paris: Ollendorff, 1886. [Folies-Bergère, September 25, 1886]

[Grangé (?)], Eugène. *Les 3 Planètes, ou la Vie d'une rose, grande pantomime, arlequinade, féerie dialoguée à grand spectacle dans le genre anglais*. Paris: Gallet, 1847. [Funambules, November 5, 1847]

Hanlon-Lees, Frères. *Mémoires et pantomimes des frères Hanlon Lees, avec une préface de Théodore de Banville*, [ed. Richard Lesclide]. Paris: Reverchon et Vollet, [1880]. [contains detailed synopses of the following undated pantomimes, first performed in Paris between 1872 and 1878: *Le Frater de village, Pierrot menuisier, Pierrot terrible, Do mi sol do, Les Cascades du Diable, Le Dentiste, Le Duel, Singes et baigneuses, Une Soirée en habit noir, Les Quatre Pipelettes*]

Hannon, Théodore, and J. Hansen. *Pierrot macabre, ballet-pantomime en un acte et deux tableaux*. Brussels: Cranz, [1886?].

Hennique, Léon. " 'Pierrot à Stamboul,' pantomime inédite de Léon Hennique," ed. James B. Sanders. *Revue de la Société d'Histoire du Théâtre*, I (July-September 1980), 232-47.

————. *La Rédemption de Pierrot, pantomime*. Paris: Ferroud, 1903.

————. *Le Songe d'une nuit d'hiver, pantomime inédite*. Paris: Ferroud, 1903.

Hugounet, Paul. *La Fin de Pierrot, pantomime mystique en un acte*. Paris: Dentu, 1891. [Cercle Funambulesque, March 25, 1891]

————. *Mimes et Pierrots: Notes et documents inédits pour servir à l'histoire de la pantomime*. Paris: Fischbacher, 1889. [contains slightly abbreviated scenarios of the following pantomimes: Laurent *père*, *Le Boeuf enragé* (Funambules, 1827); A. Jouhaud, *Les Trois Pierrots* (Funambules, 1850); J. Richepin, *Pierrot assassin* (Trocadéro, 1883) and *L'Ame de Pierrot* from his novel *Braves Gens* (1886); Camille de Saint-Croix, *Blanc et noir* (Cercle Funambulesque, 1888)]

———— and Félix Larcher. *Les Soirées Funambulesques: Notes et documents inédits pour servir à l'histoire de la pantomime*. Paris: Kolb, [1890-93]. [contains detailed synopses of the following pantomimes, all first produced at the Cercle Funambulesque in indicated years: M. Le Corbeiller, *La Révérence* (1890); P. Hugounet and G. Villeneuve, *Doctoresse!* (1890); Arbel, *Le Coeur brisé* (1890); P. Leclercq, *Noël triste* (1891); J. Jullien, *Illusions perdues* (1891); P. Hugounet, *La Fin de Pierrot* (1891); P. Eudel and E. Mangin, *La Statue du Commandeur* (1892); F. Boussenot, *La Corde de pendu* (1892); F. Galipaux and Pontsevrez, *Pierrot confesseur* (1892); H. Dreyfus, *Monsieur est en retard* (1892); M. Carré *fils* and Colias, *L'Ecole des vierges* (1892); A. Lafrique, *Pierrot poète* (1892); M. Lefèvre and F. Régamey, *Conte de printemps* (1892); Ferdal, *Le Rêve du conscrit* (1892); Berrier, *Fin d'amour* (1892); E. Larcher and A. Mélandri, *Le Bahut* (1892); M. Carré *fils* and P. Hugounet, *L'Hôte* (1893)]

———— and G. Villeneuve. *Doctoresse! pantomime en 1 acte*. Paris: Dreyfus, n.d. [Cercle Funambulesque, December 17, 1890]

Huysmans, J.-K., and Léon Hennique. *Pierrot sceptique*, in *Oeuvres complètes de J.-K. Huysmans*, V. Paris: Crès et Cie, 1928.

Janin, Jules. *Deburau, histoire du Théâtre à Quatre Sous pour faire suite à l'histoire du Théâtre-Français*. Paris: Librairie des Bibliophiles, 1881. [contains *Ma Mère l'Oie*, less its prologue (Funambules, 1830)]

Jouhaud, Aug[uste]. *Les Deux Pierrots, pantomime-arlequinade, en quatorze tableaux*. [Paris]: Dechaume, n.d. [Funambules, October 18, 1849]

————. *Les Trois Pierrots, ou Pierrot-le-rusé, Pierrot-le-naïf, Pierrot-le-dévoué, grande pantomime en douze tableaux, précédée de Le Directeur et l'auteur, préface, et de Le Baptême des Pierrots, pro-*

logue. [Paris]: Dechaume, n.d. [Funambules, November 7, 1850]

Larcher, Eugène. *Lysic, pantomime en trois scènes*. Paris: Librairie Théâtrale, 1890. [Cercle Funambulesque, February 2, 1889]

Laurent *père*. *Le Boeuf enragé, pantomime-arlequinade en 12 tableaux, dans le genre anglais*. Paris: Dechaume, n.d. [Funambules, May 15, 1827]

Lefèvre, Maurice. *Scaramouche, conte, suivi de l'argument du ballet*. Paris: Ollendorff, 1891. [Nouveau-Théâtre, October 17, 1891]

Legrand, Paul. *Pantomimes de Paul Legrand*, comp. Félix and Eugène Larcher. Paris: Librairie Théâtrale, 1887. [contains the following pantomimes, first performed by Legrand between 1854 and 1887: *Les Fourberies de Pierrot, Le Duel de Pierrot, Le Rêve de Pierrot*, [P. Mercier and Legrand] *Pierrot bureaucrate, Pierrot rosière, Pierrot amoureux, La Statue, Un Ténor dans l'embarras, La Fiancée de carton, Le Villageois et le serpent, Le Diable s'en mêle, Le Papillon, Les Tribulations d'un patissier, Pierrot en ménage, Le Mannequin, Satan dupé*]

Lheureux, Paul. *Pantomimes*. Paris: Ferreyrol, 1891. [contains the following undated pantomimes: *La Veuve Pierrot, pantomime . . . rimée; Une Piqûre; Trois Heures du matin; Taylor* [sic] *pour Messieurs; Déjeuner bouffé; Sans douleur!; La Corde de pendu; Le Testament; Crime et châtiment*]

Maisonneuve, Thomas. *Pierrot surpris, ballet-pantomime en un acte*. Paris: Heugel & Cie, 1894. [Eden-Théâtre, February 21, 1891]

Maizeroy, René [René-Jean, Baron Toussaint, known as Mora, known as]. *Le Miroir, pantomime en 2 tableaux*. Paris: Ollendorff, 1892. [Folies-Bergère, February 6, 1892]

Margueritte, Paul. *The Death of Pierrot*, in *Pastels in Prose*, tr. Stuart Merrill. New York: Harper & Brothers, 1890.

———. *Pierrot assassin de sa femme*. Paris: Schmidt, 1882. [Théâtre de Valvins, 1881]

———. *Pierrot assassin de sa femme*. 2nd ed. Paris: Calmann-Lévy, 1886. [Théâtre de Valvins, 1881]

——— and Victor Margueritte. *Nos Tréteaux: Charades de Victor Margueritte, pantomimes de Paul Margueritte*. Paris: Les Bibliophiles Fantaisistes, 1910. [contains the following undated pantomimes, first performed and/or published between 1881 and 1910: *Pierrot assassin de sa femme* [perf. 1881, pub. 1882], *Amoureux de la lune*, [F. Beissier and Margueritte] *Colombine pardonnée* [perf. 1888], *Au cou du chat, Pierrot mort et vivant, Pierrot Mormon*, [Victor and Paul Margueritte] *La Peur*]

Mendès, Catulle. *Le Collier de saphirs, pantomime*. Paris: Dentu, 1891. [Bouffes-Parisiens, December 10, 1891]

———. *Le Cygne, ballet-pantomime en un acte*. Paris: Heugel & Cie, 1899. [Opéra-Comique, April 18, 1899]

———. *Le Docteur blanc, mimodrame fantastique en 12 tableaux*. Paris: Choudens, 1893. [Menus-Plaisirs, April 2, 1893]

———. *La Fête chez Thérèse, ballet-pantomime en deux actes*. Paris: Heugel et Cie, 1910. [Académie Nationale de Musique, n.d.]

Mérante, Louis, and Nuitter [Charles-Louis-Etienne Truinet, known as]. *Les Jumeaux de Bergame, ballet-arlequinade en un acte [. . .] (d'après Florian)*. Paris: Tresse and Stock, 1886. [Opéra, January 26, 1886]

Mercier, Pol, [and Paul Legrand]. *Biribi, pantomime*. Paris: Typographie de Jules-Juteau, 1855. [Folies-Nouvelles, January 28, 1855]

——— [———]. *Le Chevrier blanc, conte-pantomime à grand spectacle, en cinq tableaux*. Paris: Raçon, 1856. [Folies-Nouvelles, December 27, 1855]

——— [———]. *La Soeur de Pierrot, mimodrame à spectacle en 5 tableaux*. Paris: Dondey-Dupré, 1855. [Folies-Nouvelles, April 7, 1855]

Moreau, Amédée. *L'Arc-en-ciel, ballet-pantomime en 3 tableaux*. Paris: Dupont, 1893. [Folies-Bergère, September 14, 1893]

[Nadar (Félix Tournachon, known as)]. *Pierrot Ministre, pantomime républicaine en huit tableaux par un pair de France sans ouvrage*. [Paris]: Gallet, n.d. [Funambules, June 8, 1848]

Najac, Raoul de. *Barbe-Bleuette, pantomime en un acte*. Paris: Hennuyer, 1890. [Nouveau-Théâtre, November 25, 1891]

———. *J'attends Colombine, pantomime en un acte*. Paris: Hennuyer, 1890. [Théâtre-Najac, May 27, 1907]

———. *La Leçon de danse, pantomime en un acte*. Paris: Hennuyer, 1890.

———. *Le Retour d'Arlequin, pantomime en 1 acte et à seul personnage*. Nouv. éd. Paris: Hennuyer, 1899. ["in the salons," 1887]

———. *Les Sept Péchés capitaux, ou l'Origine du masque d'Arlequin, pantomime en un acte*. Paris: Heymann, 1888. [Salon of Mme P.-L. B***, May 31, 1888]

———. *Souvenirs d'un mime*. Paris: Emile-Paul, 1909. [contains scenarios or detailed synopses of the following pantomimes by Najac: *Le Retour d'Arlequin* (1887), *L'Amour de l'art* (1888), *Barbe-Bleuette* (1889), *Rose et noir* (1893), *Pierrot décoré* (1893), *Pierrot huisier* (1894), *Un Drame sur une table* (1897), *Le Poète, ou l'Inconstance des femmes* (1904), *Le Coeur sur la main* (1904), *La Fille tambourinée* (1905), *Loin des yeux . . .* (1905), *Pierrot bigame* (1905), *Peau d'âne* (1906), *Faust marié* (1907)]

Najac, Raoul de. *Le Succube, pantomime en trois actes, mêlée de dialogue.* Sabbatville: Librairie Cabalistique, [1912?]. [Théâtre-Najac, January 12, 1912]

Nerval, G., and A. Lamy. *Brelan de pierrots, ballet-pantomime en un acte.* Bordeaux: Imprimerie de G. Canizieux, 1892. [Bordeaux, Grand-Théâtre, April 26, 1892]

Niger, Hey. *Pierrot déménage, monocantomime en 1 acte.* Paris: Coutarel, n.d. [Fêtes du Casino d'Enghien, January 21, 1900]
————. *La Première Faute de Pierrette, pantomime en 1 acte.* Paris: Coutarel, n.d. [Bodinière, June 17, 1899]

Normand, Jacques. *Le Réveil, prologue joué à la représentation d'ouverture du Cercle Funambulesque à Paris le 15 mai 1888.* Paris: Lévy, 1888.

Octave [Octave, Baron de Cès-Carepenne, known as]. *La Clef des songes, pantomime en treize tableaux.* Paris: Dechaume, n.d. [Funambules (?), after 1846]

Péricaud, Louis. *Le Théâtre des Funambules, ses mimes, ses acteurs et ses pantomimes depuis sa fondation, jusqu'à sa démolition.* Paris: Sapin, 1897. [contains complete scenarios of the following pantomimes: C. D., *Le Faux Ermite, ou les Faux Monnayeurs* (1816); *Poulailler, ou Prenez garde à vous!* (1827); Laurent père, *Le Boeuf enragé* (1827); [Charles Nodier (?)] *Le Songe d'or, ou Arlequin et l'avare* (1828); *Pérette, ou les Deux Braconniers* (1829); *Pierrot en Afrique* (1842); [Charles Charton (?)] *Le Génie des eaux* (1855); [Emile Durandeau] *Les Quatre Intrigants, ou Suites funestes des amours occultes d'une princesse désordonée, ou le Fâcheux Etat de la péninsule avant Christophe Colomb, et ses découvertes* (1860)]

Philippe, Jean. *Pierrot inconstant, pantomime en un acte.* Niort: Imprimerie Lemercier et Alliot, 1893. [Niort, Théâtre du Manège, January 22, 1893]

Privas, Xavier [Antoine Taravel, known as]. *Pierrot chante!* Paris: Joubert, [1898].
————. *Sommeil blanc, pantomime en un acte.* Paris: Imprimerie de E. Marcilly, 1899. [Bodinière, February 20, 1899]
————. *Une Heure de musique avec Xavier Privas.* Paris: Editions Cosmopolites, [1930]. [contains the following *cantomimes: Noël de Pierrot* (1894), *Le Testament de Pierrot* (1895), *Noël de Pierrette* (1901)]

Privat d'Anglemont, Alexandre. *Pierrot, suppôt du Diable, pantomime.* Paris: Imprimerie de J. Frey, 1847.

Remi, Jules. *Arlequin mort et vivant, pantomime en deux tableaux.* [Paris]: Imprimerie de Benard, [1847]. [Spectacle-Concert, July 6, 1847]

Handlist

Richepin, Jean. *Théâtre chimérique*. Paris: Charpentier-Fasquelle, 1896. [contains *La Gloire du geste, conférencemime en manière d'épilogue*]

Rimbert de Neuville, Vincent. *Les Joujoux de Bric-à-brac, pantomime en 15 tableaux et à grand spectacle*. Paris: Dechaume, n.d. [Funambules, September 10, 1852]

Rouanet, Léo. *Le Ventre et le coeur de Pierrot, pantomime en 2 actes et 6 tableaux*. Paris: Parvillez, 1888.

Vautier. *L'Homme des bois, ou Pierrot chez les Caffres, pantomime en trois tableaux*. Paris: Dechaume, n.d. [Funambules, after 1850 (?)]

Verlaine, Paul. *Motif de pantomime: Pierrot gamin*, in *Oeuvres en prose complètes*. Paris: Gallimard [Bibliothèque de la Pléiade], 1972.

Verrier, J. *Pierrot chez les indiens coup'choux, pantomime bouffe en 1 acte et 2 tableaux pour jeunes gens*. Nouv. éd. Orléans: Moutier, n.d.

Viard, Jules. *Pierrot marié et Polichinelle célibataire, épopée-pantomime féerique en 3 parties et 19 tableaux*. Paris: Gallet, 1847. [Funambules, June 8, 1847]

Villethiou, Jean de. *Illusion-baiser (petite scène mimée en 2 tableaux). La Dernière de Pierrot (pantomime en 1 acte et 2 tableaux)*. Paris: Imprimerie Moderne, [1895].

N.B.: More accessible than many of the above items, the following volumes may be consulted for a number of brief but useful synopses of pantomimes produced at the Funambules, the Folies-Nouvelles, and the various cabarets and theaters where Georges Wague performed: Champfleury, *Souvenirs des Funambules* (Paris: Lévy Frères, 1859); Théophile Gautier, *Histoire de l'art dramatique en France, depuis vingt-cinq ans* (Paris: Magnin, Blanchard et Cie, 1858-59), 6 vols.; L.-Henry Lecomte, *Histoire des théâtres de Paris: Les Folies-Nouvelles: 1854-1859, 1871-1872, 1880* (Paris: Daragon, 1909); and Tristan Rémy, *Georges Wague: Le Mime de la Belle Epoque* (Paris: Girard, 1964). In the Theatre Collection of the New York Public Library, Lincoln Center, and the Collection Rondel of the Bibliothèque de l'Arsenal, Paris, are newspaper clip-files, theater programs, extracts from journals, etc., that provide invaluable documentation for the study of pantomime.

333

Index

Index

Index

Index

Index

Index

Index

Index

Index

351

Library of Congress Cataloging in Publication Data

Storey, Robert F., 1945-
Pierrots on the stage of desire.

Bibliography: p.   Includes index.
1. Pantomime—France. 2. French literature—
19th century—History and criticism. 3. Psycho-
analysis and literature. I. Title.
PN1948.F7S8   1985   792.3′0944   84-42904
ISBN 0-691-06628-0